MORAL
CLARITY

MORAL CLARITY

· · · · · · · ·

A GUIDE FOR
GROWN-UP IDEALISTS

· · · · · · ·

Revised Edition

SUSAN NEIMAN

Princeton University Press
Princeton and Oxford

Published in the United States and Canada in 2009 by
Princeton University Press, 41 William Street, Princeton, New Jersey 08540
press.princeton.edu

First published in Great Britain in 2009 by
The Bodley Head
Random House, 20 Vauxhall Bridge Road,
London SW1V 2SA

Library of Congress Control Number 2009927370
ISBN 978-0-691-14389-7

This book has been composed in Granjon

Printed on acid-free paper

Printed in the United States of America

2 4 6 8 10 9 7 5 3 1

To my mother,
Judith Chayes Neiman

CONTENTS

· · · · · · ·

Introduction   *1*

PART ONE   *Ideal and Real*
1. Hard Facts   *29*
2. Ideals and Ideology   *60*
3. Facing Gallows   *93*

PART TWO   *Enlightenment Values*
4. Myths or Monsters   *121*
5. Heaven and Earth   *138*
6. Happiness   *163*
7. Reason   *189*
8. Reverence   *226*
9. Hope   *253*

PART THREE   *Good and Evil*
10. *The Odyssey:* An Excursion   *299*
11. What about Evil?   *334*
12. Enlightenment Heroes   *381*
13. Moral Clarity   *422*

Acknowledgments   *438*
Bibliographical Notes   *440*
Bibliography   *447*
Permissions Acknowledgments   *456*
Index   *457*

MORAL CLARITY

INTRODUCTION

. . . .

S odom and Gomorrah are places good as any to reflect on goodness and evil, but the reasons may surprise you. They usually
stand for simple cases of crime and punishment: The Sodomites sin
and God destroys them, turning a thriving town into a pile of rubble
and a woman into a pillar of salt for a wistful backward glance.
For fundamentalists, the sin is sexual license in general, homosexuality in particular, making both into abominations that threaten
community survival. For gay people, the towns' destruction is an
example of the injustice of traditional religion. For the Marquis de
Sade, the story was an invitation to imagine the kind of violence
that stands law on its head. Sade knew the Bible better than most
contemporary readers.

The story may be clear, but it's marvelously complex. To begin
with, you needn't be a fundamentalist to abhor the sin that does in
the Sodomites: It isn't fornication or homosexuality, but the local
demand to drag out and gang rape two strangers whom the good-
hearted Lot had offered to shelter. Ancient Mediterranean convictions
about what hosts and guests owe each other formed the basis of
traditional morality, and violations threatened social bonds at their
core. The Greeks thought such violations reason enough to start
the Trojan War. Lot takes his duties as host so seriously that he
offers the raging mob his virgin daughters if they'll leave his guests
alone. The guests turn out to be angels, who blind the Sodomites

storming the door and prove their undoing. But whether or not you believe in angels or ancient rules of hospitality, you're likely to find the Sodomites' transgressions beyond every pale.

Some versions expand on the account in Genesis, as if gang raping your guests were not quite enough to merit annihilation: They suggest that the Sodomites were not simply immoral, but deliberately antimoral. According to one Jewish tale, gang rape of strangers wasn't an accidental occurrence, but prescribed by Sodom's laws. According to another, helping strangers was punishable by death – a fate suffered by one of Lot's daughters, who was burned on a pyre for giving bread to a poor man, and by another nameless maiden who was smeared with honey and left on a bee-swarmed rooftop for doing the same. Even its taxes were perversely regressive: Owners of two oxen were liable for one day's civic service, while those with one ox were assessed for two. Sodom's crimes were all the worse for being thankless, for the city was showered with wealth. Gardeners rinsing greens in its water could shake down gold flakes from the soil that clung to their roots, sapphires lined its streets in place of stones, and each of its paths was shaded by seven trees – grape, fig, pomegranate, walnut, almond, apple, and peach. Yet blessed with such abundance, the Sodomites only dread that they might have to share it. One source says Sodom killed all its birds lest they take even a peck at the grain. Where kindness to strangers forms the framework of civilization, what the Sodomites do is a double outrage. Many places ignore moral law; Sodom turns it upside down.

The most important part of the story, however, is what happens before the cities' destruction. Having called Abraham into His confidence and promised to make him mighty, God reveals His plan to destroy the cities. Abraham's reaction is awesome. Until then, he received God's word without question; now he pauses and speaks up. *What if there are fifty innocent people among the sinners? The judge of all the earth cannot be so unjust as to let innocent and guilty suffer alike!* The judge of all the earth agrees; if there are fifty righteous people in Sodom He will leave the city alone. *But surely the Lord is not a pedant. What if the number turns out to be smaller? Would He destroy the whole city for lack of a mere five?* The answer is readily forthcoming: The Lord will save Sodom if forty-five righteous people can be found there. *But the Lord cannot be arbitrary! What if there are only forty good people in the city?* Abraham bargains God all the way down to ten, and the number isn't an accident. It's easy enough for a handful to flee a burning city, which is just what turns out to happen. Though Lot tries to warn them, even some of his family refuse to listen, so he gathers the others and runs.

Three things about Abraham's action stir hearts like mine. One is his resolute universalism. Abraham's concern for the innocents of Sodom is not concern for his friends or his neighbors, it's concern for innocents everywhere. The people of Sodom are abstract and nameless and still worth the risk of his life. Another is his resoluteness, period. In his concern for innocent life he endangers his own. This is not, after all, a democracy, but a world in which kings are ill inclined to let subjects rebuke them. Abraham dares to remind the King of Kings that He's about to trespass on moral law. The text makes plain that Abraham is scared. His words are neither proud nor wheedling, but the plea of a servant to a master who could extinguish him with a glance. 'Here I venture to speak to my Lord, I who am but dust and ashes' is what he says to get the negotiation going. 'Let not the Lord be angry if I go on' is what precedes the line that bargains God down to thirty. The third striking point to this story is its attention to detail. Moral judgment is not a matter of decisions made once and for all, but of keeping your eye on distinctions. Numbers matter. Gradations matter. Abraham's tone may be that of a merchant, but his mind is the mind of a moralist. If he can make God stop and think about small differences, none of us is ever exempt. Moral judgments are slow, specific, and seldom absolute. Yet two things in the biblical story emerge perfectly clear: Rape is a criminal action – and so is collateral damage.

We have moral needs, needs so strong they can override our

instincts for self-protection, as the story of Abraham shows. It also shows those needs are not based in religion, or any form of divine command. They include the need to express reverence and the need to express outrage, the need to reject euphemism and cant and to call things by their proper names. They include the need to see our own lives as stories with meaning – meanings we impose on the world, a crucial source of human dignity – without which we hold our lives to be worthless. Most basically and surprisingly, we need to see the world in moral terms. These needs are grounded in a structure of reason. While they may be furthered by religion, or emotion, that is not what keeps them alive. As I will argue, they are based in the principle of sufficient reason that we use as a compass. Moral inquiry and political activism start where reasons are missing. When righteous people suffer and wicked people flourish, we begin to ask why. Demands for moral clarity ring long, loud bells because it is something we are right to seek. Those who cannot find it are likely to settle for the far more dangerous simplicity, or purity, instead.

This book began in response to needs expressed by readers of my last book, *Evil in Modern Thought.* Conceived as a history of philosophy, it stirred readers beyond academia who were hungry for serious discussion of ethics and value. More people than I'd ever expected said it was the sort of thing they'd always hoped for from philosophy, and asked me to go one step further. I had reinterpreted the history of modern Western philosophy to show that its major thinkers were driven not by epistemological puzzles, but by the search for the meaning of evil and suffering as seen in the events of their day. Was I prepared, readers asked, to give an account of my own views in relation to contemporary events?

I was not. The task was daunting, and it seemed presumptuous even to try. Perhaps nothing but the 2004 U.S. election would have persuaded me to do so. Like many who were dismayed on that third of November, I was stunned by the claim that voters chose George W. Bush because they cared about moral values. Either they had been utterly bamboozled, or the opposition had dramatically failed. The election was probably a result of both, but that's now for historians to settle. The most useful thing I could do as an American philosopher was to examine philosophical underpinnings of contemporary political discourse, and offer a framework for alternatives. The phrase *moral clarity* wasn't a conservative invention – journalist William Safire traced it back to a 1934 speech at the American Philosophical Association – but by 2001 it was firmly in conservative hands. In America, the phrase is so deeply associated with Bush that only his defenders were inclined to use it. This book is committed to taking it back.

For it was never enough to argue that if Republicans had captured the field of individual virtues, Democrats still cornered the market on social ones; or to point out that many people go to church not in search of spiritual solace, but to get simple services now missing elsewhere. In *Conservatives Without Conscience*, Nixon's former legal counsel John Dean even argued that the culture wars were constructed to give the right a platform as its traditional targets collapsed with the Cold War. All these claims may be true, but they overlook a gnawing gap. Western secular culture has no clear place for moral language, and its use makes many profoundly uncomfortable.

The 2004 election made some things crystal clear. All over the world, people argued about what caused its outcome, but this much was certain: Everyone, everywhere, was running on moral passion. Whether voters were moved by their views about terrorism, or the war in Iraq, or abortion, what did *not* decide that significant election was the bottom line. Bush supporters were likelier to be those his economic policies had hurt, while many of his fiercest opponents stood a chance of benefiting from his tax cuts. Cynics, and old-fashioned Marxists, must return to the drawing board. 'Erst kommt das Fressen, dann kommt die Moral,' Bertolt Brecht's famous claim that grub comes first, and ethics later, turns out to be just a matter of chronology. As soon as our bellies stop rumbling, we begin to moralize.

Barack Obama's ability to address moral needs was the key to his improbable 2008 victory. When the first edition of this book went to press that January, I had already done a bit of canvassing – much to the amusement of my savvier friends, who insisted that only an intellectual who'd lost touch with America could give Obama a fighting chance. Reading his book *Dreams* had refired my own: that a man of deep intelligence, palpable integrity and quiet passion might actually become president of the U.S.A. Almost superfluous to mention the fact that it would fulfil aspirations of the civil rights movement, which had formed my own political consciousness. Born in the South half a century earlier, I'd heard men and women of nearly superhuman patience sing lines like 'I'm gonna be a registered voter one of these days.' However high our hopes may have run in the sixties, no one imagined *any* African-American coming so far. Nor need one rely on childhood memories: I hadn't begun to envision, one short year earlier, that someone running for the American presidency could regularly end campaign rallies with lines like: 'OK, Pennsylvania, let's go change the world.' It's a line he delivered with the hint of coolness that undercut possible pathos, while running the best campaign organization in recorded history. Talk about grown-up idealism!

But not twenty-four hours after the election, there was ready analysis: it was the economy, stupid. Critics who pride themselves on their ability to cut through cant insisted that the fall's financial crisis left voters so desperate they were willing to ignore their other hopes and fears. Those inclined to providential explanations called the Wall Street meltdown an act of God. (I heard this argued by a black Southern Baptist nurse as well as by a Jewish fair-trade entrepreneur.) Within a month such claims began to harden into conventional wisdom: Obama's unlikely victory was the result of an even less likely event, the worst economic crisis since the Great Depression. Indeed, some said, the crisis was so deep that Republicans didn't *want* to inherit it – and were thus willing to forego some of the dirtier tricks that had brought them victory in the past.

A small flurry of cartoons suggested Obama was just another black man hired to clean up the mess white folk leave behind.

Hard on the heels of the economic explanations were the demographic ones that stalked the election. Graphs and charts gave them the air of hard science. It was inevitable, some said, that the Republicans lost the election, because their position on immigration undercut the Hispanic vote. Long analyses that broke down the American population by category felt no need to defend their most basic assumption: when all is said and done, what counts is tribal loyalty.

Perhaps from a distance such analyses looked sensible, but they made no sense of the facts on the ground. Millions of Americans across races and classes and generations spent time and money they didn't have to participate in the process with everything they did; the wit and creativity that studded the campaign were at least as impressive as the numbers. What tribal impulse moved the 45,000 lawyers who stood at the polls from dawn to dusk to make sure no votes were stolen this time? Like the steel workers and housewives and doctors who registered voters and knocked on doors across America, they were seeking the common good – the Roman *res publica* that formed the basis of the word *republic*. They were too different on every matrix to reduce to statistics; perversely persistent cynics would conclude they had drunk an invisible potion.

It's always easier to reach for familiar explanations than to acknowledge a truth that challenges them. You could see such truth in the faces gathered in Chicago on the night of November 4 to celebrate what everyone knew would be a moment of history. Call it what it was: nobility. When the Wall fell in 1989, Berliners watered their gray streets with champagne. Obama's election, by contrast, streamed sheer sombre joy. These were the faces of those inspired as we should be – by ideals that, in the person of Barack Obama, have a chance of coming closer to realization than we had long dared hope. No doubt the state of the economy played a role; economic changes often produce political ones. But what got people onto the streets in the right kind of way – instead of simple mob rage, or crowds demanding fascism – was not economic anxiety, but the right kind of ideal. If we do not understand why this election was won, we will have little chance to realize its promise.

This is even clearer in view of the international reaction to Obama's victory, which cannot be reduced to any particular interests at all. Wave after wave swept in with a force that wasn't explained by simple relief: that the most powerful country in the world would no longer be run by men nobody trusted. In Germany, the newsweekly that had spent the year making jaded references to the candidate's supposed messianic pretensions suddenly proclaimed Obama's victory to be nothing less than a second American revolution. From Kuala Lumpur to Cape Town, leaders joyfully demanded that America resume its title as leader of the free world. Israel's lowbrow daily ran a two-word headline: *HaTikvah*, which was stunning for those who know that the words, which mean *The Hope*, are also the title of the haunting Israeli national anthem that serves as a secular hymn. Nobody was surprised when Kenya declared the day after Obama's election a national holiday. But who could predict that an Irish group would write a song with the chorus 'O'Leary, O'Reilly, O'Hare and O'Hara/There's no one as Irish as Barack Obama'? Or a Beduin tribe in the Galilee hurry to claim him as member? The Israeli paper *Ha'aretz* concluded 'The day of his election wrought a change in the entire world, and will grant those living there a reason to look forward to the future with hope.' The headline of the national paper *The Scotsman* put the same thought more bluntly: ALL THINGS ARE POSSIBLE.

These words are all risky. As I write them, Barack Obama hasn't had much time to disappoint. Even his own victory speech warned that disappointment is inevitable, given the height of the hopes that were raised. Yet we are still living in a long moment to be savoured, whatever turns out to follow. To be sure, good news is hard to savour. Like many things, from airplanes to the enfranchisement of women, Obama's election went from seeming impossible to ordinary in very short time. International elation was succeeded by a general rush to worry, for counting the ways it might go wrong felt familiar. Lingering in the moment was disorienting: outside of the movies, we've come to expect that the good guys lose the fight, or lose their souls.

Two centuries ago, Immanuel Kant sought signs of progress in human history. As this book will show, neither he nor any serious Enlightenment philosopher thought progress inevitable. Kant saw so many reasons to doubt it that he was willing to settle for very little: the hope people felt, all over the world, when they learned of the French Revolution was sign enough that the human race could be moved by a vision of a better world – and hence had the chance to progress towards it. He was writing in 1794, when the French Revolution already displayed clear marks of moral rot. Yet the collective hope and joy that attended its onset was enough to sustain Kant's faith in humankind's future.

The 'Yes, We Can' T-shirts printed in Korean and Hindi and Russian suggest that Obama's election was another such moment, which will have meaning whatever happens next. If it is to be more than one brief shining moment we must understand how it came about. Untangling the ideas of the previous decades will enable us to do so. Far more importantly, it will prepare us to take up new and active positions in a deeply connected world. Understanding the ideas that lead to action is especially important where memories are as short as the temptation to revisionism is strong: partly, no doubt, to forestall prosecution, the Bush years are already being rewritten as a failure of excessive idealism. How this came to pass – and how to avoid such revisions in the future – is one of the questions this book will answer.

Of all the forces that contributed to the rightward turn in American culture, none is more surprising than the philosophical exertions behind contemporary conservatism. In the sixties, conservatives used the very word *intellectual* as a term of abuse – remember Spiro Agnew? But when the left turned its sights on matters more pragmatic, the right went off to build think tanks. Under the influence of writers like Leo Strauss and Ayn Rand, young conservatives were reading Plato and Aristotle. Through organizations like the Liberty Fund and the Olin Foundation, midwestern businessmen who made their fortunes producing chemicals and telephones were sponsoring seminars in the mountains of Hungary on the nature of evil, or flying scholars to Chicago to discuss law and virtue. Meanwhile, in the interest of being effective, the left decided to forsake utopian visions for the more solid ground of interest-based politics. It was a fatal mistake, for it meant jettisoning the moral compass that had guided the best efforts of the sixties – the civil rights movement, the opposition to the war in Vietnam, the demands for women's equality. While many left-wing activists were taken up with identity politics, many left-wing academics were caught up in arguments about postcolonial concepts. The arguments that not only right and justice, but the self and the world are constructed by interest and power, were too abstruse to bother many people outside the academy, but they took up no end of the energy of those within. As the right was completing its study of the classics, the left was facing conceptual collapse. The end of the Cold War gave the East access to goods its citizens wanted, and the West information it did not: that the dreams of socialism had transmuted into nightmare. The crisis that was growing through the seventies as the new left failed to produce a better revolution than the old left came to a head with the revelations of how awful the old one had really been. The end of the Soviet Union revealed an empire that only the most stubborn could deny had been just what Ronald Reagan had called it. What else could the arbitrary, cold-blooded murder of millions of men and women be, if not evil? Even those inclined to cling to the old saw that you can't make an omelet without breaking eggs had to acknowledge that the results were revolting. From Berlin to Beijing, millions of people who had lived under a system subscribing to principles meant to liberate them were now rejecting decades of slavery.

Arbitrary imprisonment, famine, and murder were not new, though the scale seen in the twentieth century was. What was devastating about Soviet crimes was that they were committed in the name of principles most of us hold dear. The rebuttal to this is easy enough: Theoretically speaking, Stalin's gulags no more undermined the legitimacy of socialist ideals than the Inquisition undermined Christian ones. But after all was said and argued, what was left at the end of the century was less the inclination to discard particular principles than the very idea of acting on principle itself. Stalinist terror killed off its bravest citizens; what survived in the East was a bleak, bitter culture wracked with cynicism and envy. If *that* was the outcome of struggle for the ideals of freedom and justice, wouldn't the world be better off if we sat on our hands? Though never stated explicitly, this was the only reasonable conclusion to draw after reading popular political authors whose proud pessimism left little room for movement in any direction.

Those whose business it is to think about morality have been remiss in other ways. Philosophers certainly examine moral concepts, but their language is often inscrutable, cut off from daily concerns. Recent philosophy has produced superb work in ethics, none better than that of John Rawls, who was not only a brilliant theorist, but a man whose personal integrity was renowned. He fiercely condemned, for example, American use of atomic weapons, without ever mentioning that as a member of the U.S. Infantry slated to invade Japan before Hiroshima, his was probably one American life the bomb saved. Yet his own work remained abstract enough to stand for all the ages, nearly devoid of historical specificity. Though he knew – and cared – an immense amount about the concrete moral cataclysms of the twentieth century, he kept them out of his texts and his classrooms. Years after I had the good fortune to be his student, I ventured to ask why he'd never spoken directly about matters like the Holocaust. 'Oh,' said Rawls, in the warm southern drawl the Ivy League never dented, 'I don't understand them well enough to do that.'

This sounds like the stance that Irish poet W. B. Yeats described long ago: 'The best lack all conviction / while the worst are full of passionate intensity.' Now Rawls, like others, had deep convictions about many things, but he was trapped by his own humility. Faced with dauntingly urgent moral problems the everyday world presents, what many honest philosophers feel is not lack of interest but inadequacy. But behind admirable attempts to avoid sanctimony and self-righteousness, there often lurks a fear of expressing moral judgments in particular cases. The noninterference pact that leads philosophers to refrain from talking about history, and historians from talking about morality, pretty much insures that few people with professional competence will jump into the fray – except in discussions too qualified to interest anyone but other specialists.

Qualifications reflect scruples, and awareness of how complex moral judgments can be. But complexity can paralyze. Sometimes, as Wittgenstein warned, scruples are misunderstandings. What arose in humility and moral refinement led to attitudes that make moral judgments themselves look misguided – a hypocritical attempt to assert arbitrary power over those with whom you disagree. The relativism that holds all moral values to be created equal is a short step from the nihilism that holds all talk of values to be superfluous. Truly equal values cancel each other out. And the vistas thereby opened are so bleak that many shut the door on moral reflection altogether, and turn to the simplest moral messages in their neighborhood. William Bennett, and even Bill O'Reilly, reach millions of readers desperate for some talk of values, for nobody else is making an offer. Not the positions their books defend, but the fact that questions of goodness and justice and character are being discussed with apparent seriousness, without jargon, sends most readers to these books – and thereafter to the polls. Not everyone in Kansas may be reading Plato, but lots of them are reading writers who have, and are not ashamed to embrace ideas that sound like his.

Words like *realistic* and *idealistic* are thrown around so glibly in current political discussions that philosophers are likelier to wince and groan than to take them seriously. But the fact that a use is careless doesn't make it insignificant. The casual use of ideas with which philosophers have wrestled for millennia affects our political landscape. Examining them is not a question of political philosophy, but of a metaphysics strong enough to support a moral standpoint – in particular, the fact that we act, and want to see ourselves as acting, on moral grounds.

Is morality driven by faith? Many people, religious and secular, assume that it is. The belief is so common that Abraham's stand at Sodom attracts very little attention. His plea for the unknown Sodomites is far less familiar than his silence before the Lord's command to kill his own son. The binding of Isaac sustains orthodoxies of every kind. When a voice calls you to take your son, your only son whom you love, and journey to a distant height that will be indicated later, you saddle up your ass and do it, secure in the faith that the Lord will solve whatever problems arise on the way. For Christians, Abraham's willingness to sacrifice his son foreshadows God's willingness to sacrifice His. For Muslims, that willingness is so fundamental that Ishmael, the forebear of Islam, rather than Isaac, is portrayed as the intended victim. Medieval Jews facing murderous crusaders took courage from the story and slaughtered themselves and their children to escape forced conversion. However long Jewish, Christian, and Muslim theologians struggle to find multiple meanings in the text, the dominant one is this: Abraham's unquestioning readiness to heed God's command to sacrifice the thing he loves most is the act that qualifies him to father what are still called the Abrahamic faiths.

Pagans practiced human sacrifice from Mesopotamia to Mexico, and as Greek tragedy reminds us, even slaughtering one's child wasn't out of the question. For the ancient world, the most striking part of the story was God's commandment to stop the sacrifice. For our purposes, what's important is that the command comes from on high. The same man who just challenged God to spare the lives of innocent strangers waits quietly for an order to save his own son.

This makes the story central for most of tradition. For orthodox religious thinkers, faith is authoritarian. As some Christians put it, real faith is willing to crucify the intellect, to believe in a view just because it's absurd. For such believers, the Abraham of Mount Moriah is an icon. If he trusted in his heavenly father on a matter of such moment, the rest of us should be able to take lesser leaps of faith.

Now I have no qualms about being partisan. The Abraham who risked God's wrath to argue for the lives of unknown innocents is the kind of man who would face down injustice anywhere. He is deeply human in the best of all senses, afraid and imperfect, but neither his fear nor his frailty stand in the way of his own reason. He is reverent but not deferential, for his faith is based on his moral backbone, not the other way around. He is, in short, what I'll call an Enlightenment hero. As Kierkegaard taught us, the Abraham who takes his son to Mount Moriah has left ethics and enlightenment behind. Kant's comment on that passage was no less unequivocal: Abraham should have reflected, and concluded that anyone who asked him to do *that* could not be God. You can tell which side he's on.

Still, I'd be cheating if I tried to argue that the Abraham of Sodom and Gomorrah is the most genuine one. The Old Testament itself is magnificently equivocal. And though religious thinkers will fight fiercely to show their standpoint to be the one that religion really sanctions, each religion has signposts pointing both ways. One insists on faith as submission, underscoring the need to obey laws whose reasons we need not understand. Fundamentalists like to claim that the moral code that flows from their faith needs no intellect to follow. What the Lord wants you to do is easy to read in the Good Book. But while they may preach that the word of God is transparent, fundamentalists need interpretation as much as anyone else. Their interpretations focus on passages and practices that emphasize obedience and external authority, whether the authority of the Lord Himself, or that of His deputies in the clergy. Common study of the Bible or the Koran is often part of fundamentalist culture, but the zeal there is for individual witness, not individual analysis. In the end, fundamentalist authorities deny that unadorned human reason can decide questions of right or justice or truth.

But instructions are rarely self-evident, and holy books are written in codes that must be deciphered like any others. This is not a matter of applying ancient principles that once were obvious to modern situations that are not. No law applies itself, ever. Much of ancient scholarship itself began in the need to work out which moral judgments followed from which moral claims. Thus each of the three Western religious traditions has a rationalist strain, opposed to a fundamentalist one, stretching back to the ancient religious academies where the modern notion of scholarship was shaped. The dialectical thinking practiced in the yeshivot of Babylon and Jerusalem after the Temple's destruction was the basis for the Talmud, but it influenced legal reasoning in every tradition. The fine distinctions teased out under the gothic vaults of the Sorbonne were attempts to work out church doctrines of salvation; they affected not only our concepts of essence and accident, but of philo-sophical thinking to the present day. The koranic studies still prac-ticed in the archways of the al-Azhar University in Cairo recall the early medieval times when the Moors brought science to southern Europe. All these houses of learning arose in devotion, from those engaged in the task of making daily sense of what followed from the texts they held sacred.

Far from viewing our capacity to reason as threatening our capacity to obey God, this tradition sees thinking as its very fulfill-ment. (Some Jewish parables show God laughing with pleasure when His children defeat Him with a particularly good argument.) If reason is God's gift, He meant us to use it, and on this tradition our ability to make sense of the world is just one more proof of God's goodness, and hence of His glory. Remembering these facts should stop us from dividing the world along religious and secular lines. For many rationalist religious thinkers have more in common with secular Social Democrats than with fellow believers; many a fundamentalist is closer to postmodern nihilism than he knows. Belief in a worldview *because* it's absurd makes equal sense for both. Far less important than your belief that God exists, or that He doesn't, is what you think your belief entails. Does it direct your behavior by rules and commandments that are set out before you, or does it require you to think them through yourself? Does it require you to try to make sense of the world, or does it give up on sense itself?

The difference between the two moral paradigms is far more important than whether you call yourself religious or secular. Those paradigms could be described in drier terms, without mentioning Abraham, or God, at all. But the greatness of the Bible – even if you're not sure what it means to call it divine – is that it sets out the choices so starkly that nothing since has come close to being as clear. So let's call the first paradigm that of Abraham at Sodom, who refuses to rest in the humility of resignation and demands that his world make sense. Those who subscribe to this paradigm hold fast to the principle that there must be reasons for everything that happens, and that those reasons are up to us to find. This is the fundamental law to which everyone, including God, must answer, and it leads us to seek not only justice but transparent justice. The second paradigm is that of Abraham at Mount Moriah, who doesn't ask anything at all. To do so, he thinks, would be an act of superstition, even violence. Does trust mean asking no questions? Does love mean never having to say you're sorry? This man of faith is certain: The demand to find reason after reason is at odds with a grateful acceptance of creation, and arrogant at that.

The two Abraham stories are pages apart in the Bible, and worlds apart in their message. One urges us to submit to God's orders; however outrageous they appear to be, they'll lead us right in the end. The other urges us to question, for even a message that comes in God's voice may need to be reconsidered. (Those who insist that God is never wrong argue that He was just testing

Abraham's compassion at Sodom. On this reading the pupil is not God, of course, but Abraham, who passed the test with flying colors. But whoever is the teacher, the idea that ethics must be learned through reflection remains the central point.) Both stories are deeply part of our repertoire, anchored firmly in the very first book of the Bible on which so many others depend. More than one contemporary Jewish theologian has claimed that the two Abrahams are compatible parts of a single soul, but their arguments show that even those who believe in biblical authority won't find it decisive here. They have to decide how the book should be read.

Any serious reading of it will raise the question: Are things good because God loves them, or does God love them because they're good? As readers of Plato will remember, this question isn't confined to monotheism. Socrates was executed for alleged impiety. His crime wasn't atheism – he really did worship the local gods – but insisting that reason be put before them. Goodness isn't arbitrary. Things must be good in themselves, which is what makes the gods love them; the gods' choice cannot make something good that is evil just because they are gods.

For fundamentalists this sort of view is not just an expression of pride. It's the first step down a path in which God Himself, if subject to any limits, including the limits of reason, is no longer really God. It's an interesting argument, but I don't want to get stuck in theological debates, since I don't think they are really responsible for the tenacity of the assumption that we need religion to maintain ethics. It's the assumption behind the old adage that if God didn't exist we would have to invent Him, and many believers and unbelievers still think that it's true. Traditional religion paints a nightmare of anarchy and violence that erupts whenever divine authority is missing, and there are people who claim that they would up and kill their neighbors without religious prohibitions on murder.

We know they do not. Virtuous atheists have been around, and been noticed, for centuries, but most of them now suspect the language of virtue. Though they don't accept the idea that moral values are empty without religious ones, they accept no alternative framework. Worse than that: They've seen too many frameworks abused. Rules conceived as universal values have too often been used as sugarcoated ways of forcing one people's will on another. As a result, the rebuke *Don't be judgmental* is now firmly embedded in secular, liberal jargon. Though it began in good conscience – to express the discovery that many of our judgments were based on assumptions the whole world does not share – it has ended by stifling conscience altogether. The resolve not to impose your moral world-view by force often ends with the resolve to make no judgments at all. For those who live without divine sanctions, judgments of good, and especially of evil, are off-limits.

Both Abraham and Socrates offer another perspective. Whether the tradition is monotheist or pagan, it has central sources for denying that we need religious authority to maintain morality. The Abraham of Sodom and Gomorrah certainly didn't; it was he who risked his life to give God lessons in ethics – and this story comes at the start of monotheistic tradition. This gives lie to the claim that religion obviates the need for thinking, a claim often held by fundamentalists and atheists alike. For the fundamentalists Abraham's message is clear: however close you may be to the Lord's word, you are responsible for thinking it through on your own. For their opponents, the lesson is just as important, since hostility to religion often begins with the assumption that religion insists on moral immaturity, making secularism grown-up in a way no religion can ever be. The story of Sodom shows us that real ethics and real religion demand moral maturity. This is true because religion is an expression of morality – not, as so often assumed, the other way around. Any ethics that depends on religious commandment is bad ethics; any religion that claims we can't behave without it is bad religion. Of course there are plenty of both around, a practical question that must be dealt with practically. But first we must see that neither genuine religious nor genuine moral impulses are ever expressed in standpoints that tie the two essentially together.

Those who view religion as necessary for morality reduce us to the moral level of four-year-olds. *If you follow these commandments you'll go to heaven, and if you don't you'll burn in hell* is just a spectacular version of the carrots and sticks with which we raise our children: *If you clean up your room you'll get the cookie, and if you don't you'll stay inside.* Those of us who have raised them, however, know that even if we rely on bribes and threats in the short term, the moral behavior we seek to instill requires us to get beyond them. We want to prepare our kids to be responsible and generous and straightforward even when rewards are not forthcoming, as they often are not in the parts of the world we don't control. Serious believers, on the other hand, despise the sort of faith that springs up in foxholes. The religious feeling they cherish is not about a being who can be bribed: *I'll do whatever you say if only you'll save me.* They hold this attitude to be no better than that of a pagan who thinks the gods will protect him if only he serves up a particularly tasty bit of entrail. True faith, they think, is not a matter of bargaining, but of gratitude – certainly for creation, and possibly for salvation as well.

If you acknowledge that serious religion and serious ethics are thus separate matters, you must believe things are good or evil independent of divine authority. At this point in the argument many people turn to self-interest. Moderation, argued the Greek philosopher Epicurus, is a virtue because gluttony and drunkenness are bad for your health. Enlightened self-interest, therefore, is all you need to be temperate. Keeping promises, said the Prussian philosopher Kant, is an expression of honesty, but even he knew that it also builds strong communities. Or would you choose to live in a world where you could not take people at their word? Today evolutionary biologists argue that altruism has adaptive advantage; generous behavior will be selected because it increases the species' chances of survival. Richard Dawkins argues that you needn't focus on the survival of the fittest species; altruistic behavior is already rewarded at the level of the gene pool. But he concedes that biological self-interest cannot account for the kinds of sacrifice we hold central to moral experience. At such points, many secular thinkers retreat to the view that the basis of morality is political, a system of law constructed – more or less nefariously – to maintain civil order.

All such arguments depend on the view that if religion doesn't tell us to be moral, something else has to do so; self-interest and order look like the sort of hard-nosed bases to which unsentimental souls can appeal. And it is certainly true that much – perhaps most – moral behavior is to our own and our communities' advantage. Honesty is often the best policy, kindness is often reciprocated; even observing traffic rules creates a measure of order and safety that benefits us all. Hence a great many rules that are both ethical and useful have been shared, and internalized, throughout different times and cultures, so that we are socialized – perhaps hardwired – to do the right thing with astonishing frequency.

Yet sometimes morality and self-interest part company, and when they do, such arguments leave us helpless. For though they seemed sober and scientific, they implicitly rely on a notion of preestablished harmony that is both ancient and suspect. What a marvelous system that keeps our needs and the world so finely calibrated that self-interest and morality run on parallel tracks! Bishop Joseph Butler, the eighteenth-century founder of Natural Theology in England, didn't know from gene pools, but he considered it self-evident that *it is in our constitution* to condemn falsehood, violence, and injustice. In his day it was called providence: the assumption that virtue and happiness are perfectly balanced by an invisible guiding hand. Even Job knew enough to question that.

If morality is settled neither by the claims of religion nor the claims of self-interest, must we believe there's an otherworldly standard of goodness, fixed and eternal in a transcendent world? Plato seemed to think so, and his metaphysics provided centuries of fuel for postmodernist fires. (Not all postmodernist claims are recent.) What was attacked was more fairy tale than Plato's own views; it's unlikely that he pictured ideas as ghostly objects in the heavens beaming down at the shadows below. Still, he did believe that things are good, or true, or beautiful because they participate in ideas far above and beyond them. What all these views have in common is the thought that morality must be commanded – if not by God then by nature; if not by nature then by a supernatural metaphysics with the features of both. This will pose problems for anyone who rejects a particular source of commandment. Perhaps even more important: What about those who believe that being moral is not a matter of following orders, whether natural or super-natural, but about the dignity of freely choosing to do right?

With consequences too unhappy to be ironic, most of the voices willing to speak in universal moral terms at all now consider them-selves conservative. And this is what's true in the claim that the left has trouble with values, a claim that can, understandably, make its targets' blood boil. What's at issue here is not private goodness: Corrupt, decent, or generous people can be found on any political scale. When revelations of corruption underscore that those who preach about moral values may be furthest from practicing them, some people are tempted to dismiss talk of values altogether – under-standably enough, in the wake of the mind-boggling corruption of the Bush administration, or the way its discussion of moral values was restricted to matters like who gets married rather than who gets tortured. But to dismiss the right wing's appeal to values as phony is to forget what it offers. However shabbily its partisans may behave in private, they offer a public conception of goodness the left no longer knows how to defend. Right-wing talk of moral clarity and honor and heroism is often empty, but that is not the same as being meaningless. Empty concepts remain concepts, in search of an application. The left, by contrast, has deflated the concepts themselves. What the left lacks isn't values, but a stand-point from which all those values make sense – and a language with which to defend them. Several decades of conservative work in that direction has made possible the situation the American political theorist Michael Walzer has described so well: 'No one on the left has succeeded in telling a story that brings together the different values to which we are committed and connects them to some general picture of what the modern world is like and what our country should be like. The right, by contrast, has a general picture.'

They also lack something that may be even more important than what they have. They lack embarrassment. They may abuse words like *evil* and *hero*, but they aren't ashamed to take them in their mouths. Wary of simplification, and even more afraid of sounding sappy, the left tends to reject not only words like *true* and *noble*, but even words like *legitimate* and *progress*, which were meant to replace them. If used at all, such words are subject to quotation marks – sometimes called scare quotes – that express the speaker's discomfort in the ultimate postmodern gesture, fingers wiggling beside ears in a little dance that says: *I can use it, but I don't go so far as to mean it, and it all matters so little anyway I can make myself look silly to boot.* What matters is putting distance between you and your beliefs.

This book aims to reclaim moral concepts that the left no longer uses with full voice. Reclaiming them from the right isn't a matter of packaging but of the conviction that without them we will lose our souls – whatever we take our souls to be. We will also lose our footing, and our young. The language of the left has been called the language of suspicion, but it's also one of disappointment, the determination not to get fooled again, having seen through sham before. Such language will never win hearts, nor very good minds, either.

Re: very good minds: The sources I use to assemble the framework that's needed are resolutely eclectic, and often old. If the following pages turn from Genesis to Plato, from *The Critique of Pure Reason* to modern songwriters, it's because we need all the help we can get. (Undoubtedly we in the West need help from non-Western sources as well, and my scant use of them is just the result of my own scant knowledge.) It should go without saying, but I'll say it anyway: The authors I cite deserve, and have elsewhere been given, a more exhaustive discussion than will be offered here. My goal is not to provide definitive readings or criticisms of any one of them, but to draw on the voices of many to construct a view we can use. Turning to great classic texts will reveal unexpected agreement. The voices struggling with one another in the books I'll discuss suggest a universalism of uncertainty in wrestling with similar questions. The same author gave us both Abrahams – perhaps. The same author created Achilles and Odysseus – perhaps. Where dissonant voices grapple with basic decisions, readers are often inclined to solve the problem by positing different authors for different standpoints. There may have been no Homer who wrote both our first novels; the Bible's contradictions may be explained by the sort of committee bickering that produces incoherent texts. These are matters for scholars to explore. It's just as likely that the greatest authors remained inconclusive, for the questions at issue are not the kind to resolve once and for all.

Looking back at traditional uses of moral concepts is not a search for foundations. I believe most of the interesting things philosophy can say about that search were already said by Immanuel Kant, who argued that the validity of our concepts cannot possibly be proved from outside experience, since they shape the possibility of experience itself. Not even this much can be said of moral concepts, since Kant held they were not about truth at all: Truth tells us how the world is; morality tells us how it ought to be. Those who were dissatisfied with his answer spawned a small but tenacious industry devoted to proving our concepts are legitimate, the dominant business of twentieth-century philosophy. It may be possible to continue examining the problems with foundationalism or the nature of relativism forever. But for anyone more likely to be moved by Dylan than Descartes, the hour is getting late.

This book will question your sense of the inevitable. It will not offer proposals for changing policies, or specific political platforms, though it will often use contemporary situations to illustrate general claims about good and evil. And though it is critical of positions in every political tradition, it is certainly committed to some. How best to describe them, when we know that traditional political categories are hopelessly out of date? While the end of the Cold War made terms like *right* and *left* seem outmoded, the intervening years rendered them almost useless. Traditionally, for example, the right has underlined the notion of responsibility, while the left has stressed the importance of rights. To say we have both rights and responsibilities sounds bland and banal. Is that enough reason to suppose they conflict? Here both make claims to values I cherish, but real existing conservatives and real existing leftists have failed so often in recent decades that their very language is depleted. Refusing to recycle the words *right* and *left* need not, however, conclude in soulless centrism. For in the end neither word is a position, but an accident. (In the Paris parliament, clergy and nobility were seated on the right, while the commoners took their place on the left.) Two centuries after the French Revolution it seems pointless to base our political discourse on the seating arrangements at the Estates-General.

What are the alternatives? In part that depends on where you are: *Left* and *right* are different in London and Vienna, different again in Chicago and Shanghai. Despite occasional attempts to revive it, the very word *liberal* is insipid and confusing; what is characterized as slightly left of center in the U.S. is nothing but the commitment to free markets in most of Europe. For years, *progressive* has been used more from caution than conviction, a timid search for a cost-free way of avoiding the controversy words like *left* (or in the U.S., even *liberal*) can provoke. Perhaps even worse, it's a word often used by those whose beliefs imply that progress itself is impossible. Unlike *left* or *right*, however, *progressive* implies a view: that the world as it is can be moved closer to what it should be through the concerted actions of men and women working together. One way of putting power behind the word *progressive* was shown by Abraham at Sodom. For all those who take risks by challenging power to seek justice for innocents they do not know, he stands as a model.

As legal scholar Kingman Brewster put it, 'The presumption of innocence is not just a legal concept. In common sense terms, it depends on that generosity of spirit which sees the best, not the worst, in every stranger.' Such generosity is demanded in a world that connects millions of strangers by mouseclick every microsecond of the day. *Progressive* retains this residual commitment to universalism. It's also a word that expresses impatience at the way the world falls short of what it could be – and determination to decrease that gap wherever it's possible.

Yet all the available labels carry historical baggage I'd like to jettison. None of them seems likely to contribute to moral clarity, and any of them can prove a hindrance to it. Rather than ponder which political terms best fit them, let us turn to the moral positions themselves. This book will offer a twenty-first-century framework for an Enlightenment standpoint that no twentieth-century political direction succeeded in making its own.

I've divided the book into three parts. 'Ideal and Real' lays out the broadest philosophical questions that shadow contemporary political debates. I discuss the roots of concepts like idealism and realism, and show that neither the right nor the left has a coherent picture of either. Without a clear picture, we have few resources to understand terrorism or jingoism or most major problems that face us. 'Enlightenment Values' argues that the eighteenth century is the best place to look for those resources. Why turn to the much-maligned Enlightenment? It's no accident that rejections of the Enlightenment result in premodern nostalgia or postmodern suspicion; where Enlightenment is at issue, modernity is at stake. A defense of the Enlightenment is a defense of the modern world, along with all its possibilities for self-criticism and transformation. If you think such a defense is a cause long lost, you're invited to look again – at an Enlightenment whose values are not just the pale outspent ones of tolerance and fairness, but the unflagging demands for happiness, reason, reverence, and hope. 'Good and Evil' examines those virtues in action. What kinds of heroes are modern heroes? How do we talk about evil without slinging curses and mud? Learn to make moral judgments without clear instructions? Where does optimism end, and hope begin? Part One is focused on the present, providing the philosophical background that's needed to make sense of current policy debates. Part Two moves from contemporary questions to timeless ones, while Part Three returns to show how classic moral concepts can be used to meet the challenges we face now.

The inevitability of cynicism often looks like the twentieth-century legacy, but one goal of philosophy is to enlarge our ideas of what is possible. This is philosophy's practical force, for you will not oppose what you think is absolutely necessary, nor try something you are certain is bound to fail. Totalitarian governments may have been the first to exploit these facts, but democratic ones have been quick to seize on them, too. How many elections were won because the media projected a particular victory as inescapable? You may hum the tune on Broadway, but dreaming impossible dreams is the sort of thing you're likely to leave to Don Quixote – who was created as an object of gentle mockery five hundred years ago.

The possibility of principle will take us back to concepts that have been abandoned to the right: *good* and *evil, hero* and *dignity* and *nobility.* These concepts are part of an ethical vocabulary we need to use if we are to reclaim the ground we've lost. To express the hope that their usefulness can be manifest is not to subscribe to a pragmatist theory of truth, but to refuse to enter that debate. No set of arguments or stories will convince all its readers; ideas are not proofs. Convincing every would-be fanatic is not a reasonable goal. This doesn't mean our choices are blind: We can describe the virtues sustained by each position, the lives led by those who choose one path rather than another. It would be enough to offer a set of ideas we can defend – and pass on to our uncertain children, in ways that could make them proud.

PART ONE

IDEAL AND REAL

CHAPTER ONE

HARD FACTS

O f all the things in the world that need changing, metaphysics may not be high on your list of priorities. But to understand how metaphysics circumscribes your life, consider what you mean when you tell someone: *Be realistic*. A good translation would be: *Decrease your expectations*. It's a sentence you use on someone who is younger than you are, or someone you want to feel that way. He still has dreams and goals you've given up, or never had in the first place, and they are a standing challenge to the limits on life you have long since accepted. He wants more of the world than the world tends to give. Realizing his plans would require changing pieces of reality you believe to be fixed. And so you meet him with a palette of platitudes about human and other sorts of nature, the most harmless of which seems to be the well-meant advice to be realistic. These are matters we usually refer to individual psychology. Do you treat the world cynically, or can you meet it with a measure of hope? Whatever combination of nature and nurture gave rise to your stance toward the world, there is a metaphysics that grounds it. Whether or not you acknowledge it is immaterial; indeed, the tendency to overlook metaphysical dependencies only makes them deeper. For they determine, among other things, what you hold to be self-evident and what you hold to be possible; what you think has substance and what you can afford to ignore. People who resist cynicism are called idealists because they don't believe the world as it's given to us exhausts reality as a whole; they are convinced that ideas, too, have force and consequences. Hope is based on, or undermined by, a metaphysical standpoint.

Observers of contemporary American conservatism have spent much time speculating on the beliefs of particular conservatives: Was Cheney ever dedicated to anything but the greater glory of Halliburton, or Bush really captured by his own visions of redemption? These are questions about individual sincerity, and they are less important than they seem. Cynicism and fanaticism can be equally ruthless. Understanding the two completely distinct metaphysical strands that underpin conservative positions, on the other hand, is simpler and more important.

One strand rests on the conservative worldview that goes back to the English philosopher Hobbes, and probably even further. On this view, reality is fixed in a rather grim frame. What moves people, and the nations they compose, is an unending struggle for power, goods, and glory. People who believe this call themselves realists, and they're careful not to call this a belief but a fact. Anything else is just the rhetoric we produce to disguise our real ends. Appeals to justice and dignity and duty are smokescreens sent up to blind weaker people to the motives of the strong. (Occasionally the weak turn the tables when the strong are napping, and use the same rhetoric to manipulate those they couldn't beat in fair fights.) It might be nice to live in a world where justice and honor had substance, but growing up requires us to accept the realities of this one. Good sense, even honor if you seek it, demands that you see through the bombast with which morality and religion obscure the motors that drive the world. Anyone who takes it seriously is at best naive, and at worst . . . Well, didn't Stalinism show us what happens to those who think the world can be run on ideals?

'The only world we have ever lived in is one where those with power, believing they have right on their side, impose their sense of justice on others.' It's easy enough to find claims like this in the editorial section of most any newspaper. Made by Robert Kagan, it is worth examining because the opinions of this influential neoconservative provide good general clues to the changing views of the Republican party. He is also the only contemporary conservative writer to be explicit about the philosophical questions at issue in international affairs. While his treatment of these questions is confused enough to leave him defending opposite views with each successive book, he deserves thanks for showing that metaphysical issues resound in the contemporary political world. His 2003 *Of Paradise and Power* defended the U.S. attack on Iraq. It became an international bestseller – the *Washington Post* called Kagan 'the rock star of international affairs' – because it went beyond immediate foreign policy questions to offer a worldview that seemed to explain the state of the West as a whole. His description of the growing distance between Europe and the U.S. was memorably captured by the claim that Europeans are from Venus, Americans from Mars. The two continents were separated not by any old difference, but one that divided the ancient heavens: one continent is enthralled by the seductive charms of the goddess of love and other luxuries, while the other stirs to the manly claims of the god of war.

Why not? We may be from another galaxy entirely, for all we know or care. Far more important was Kagan's less catchy assertion, 'One of the things that most clearly divides Europeans and Americans today is a philosophical, even metaphysical disagreement over where exactly mankind stands on the continuum between the laws of the jungle and the laws of reason.' Americans, he concluded, are Hobbesians, while Europeans are Kantians; Europeans have withdrawn into a cocoon that is shielded from the harsh circumstances of conflict only because the U.S. remains in the anarchic and unstable center of history, acknowledging how bad things really are and using military power to prevent them from falling apart entirely. Europeans think we have reached the Kantian dream, in which ideas of peaceful negotiation, international courts, and common concern for sharing global wealth make things work. But though we, too, would like to live in a dream world, Americans recognize the hard facts of this one, and are resolute enough to respond to them – thereby taking on the burdens that allow Europeans to dream on.

So what were Hobbes's realities? 'Fear and I were born twins,' the philosopher wrote of his premature birth in England in 1588, when his mother went into labor on hearing of the approach of the Spanish Armada. His long life continued to be dramatic, and frightening. In addition to his studies at Oxford, several journeys to the Continent may have made him more aware than most that England was on the brink of civil war. In his urge to find a theory that might prevent it, Hobbes wrote books controversial enough to put him in danger. Escaping to Paris in 1640, he prided himself on being 'the first of all who fled,' returning to England only after Charles I's execution, which put him in the middle of the civil war he had dreaded. Despite the provocative elements of his writings – in particular his denial that kings rule by divine right – Hobbes had to fear for his life once again only. After the Great Fire of London followed the Great Plague of 1665, a parliamentary committee investigated the grounds for the punishments with which England had been visited. Hobbes's *Leviathan* was briefly accused of fomenting the atheism that must have provoked such heavenly wrath. But the charges were dropped, and though Hobbes was prevented from publishing, he was left alone to play tennis and translate Homer into a ripe old age.

Taking the framework of one's own life for granted is a common sort of shortsight; regarding your own conditions as natural is one of the things that's natural. Hobbes was no exception. One whose birth was heralded by invasion and whose life was plagued by civil war will find it hard to imagine anything else as the norm. Stripped of the fragile safeguards law had provided, the civil society he knew was truly wretched, and he couldn't envision another. But Hobbes moved from what might have been a simple description of life in its natural state as, memorably, 'solitary, poor, nasty, brutish and short,' to positing such conditions as a state of nature. It's only a linguistic shift, but the move elevated description to a blend of metaphysics, transcendental anthropology, and negative theology all at once. There is no argument for the claim that humankind's natural state is the bloody and frightening chaos of early seventeenth-century Britain – nor could there be one. Rather, Hobbes draws a picture of a state of nature that reflected the state he knew. In the move from descriptive analysis of the reality he experienced to suprahistorical claims about reality in general, Hobbes took a step that would have enormous consequences for political theory, and politics itself.

It would be silly to dismiss Hobbes's theory solely on the grounds that it was influenced by the circumstances of his life. Whose theory is not? Hobbes's bleak description of humankind's struggle for power might reflect seventeenth-century England and nevertheless be accurate for the rest of us. Perhaps he would have drawn similar conclusions about human nature had he lived in ninth-century Polynesia, or fin-de-siècle Paris. The point is that *none* of those perspectives can serve as a base for pronouncing on the natural state of humankind. To read current conditions back into a prehistoric state to which we have no access, further argument would be needed, and Hobbes cannot provide it. In place of the missing argument, contemporary conservatives tend to hammer out phrases like 'Hobbesian realities,' as if repetition were enough to suggest that anyone who views the world differently is blinded by wishful thinking. John Gray's little essay 'Back to Hobbes' is one typical example, quickly dismissing 'the make-believe world of liberal philosophers' before concluding, 'As Hobbes knew, what human beings want most from the state is not freedom but protection. This may be regrettable, but building a political philosophy on the denial of human nature is foolish. It is better to face facts.'

It is no less a fact that some men risk their lives to save strangers in a city subway as it is a fact that others run amok to push strangers before an oncoming train. And facts that seem immutable can turn

on a dime; the expansion of ever-more predatory forms of capitalism looked inevitable until the Wall Street meltdown forced even
neoliberals to ask why the invisible hand was so lame. Hobbesians
pick the facts they want us to face with care. If life were all that
Hobbes thought it's cracked up to be, it's hard to know why anyone
would complain about its duration. But consistency is said to be for
little minds, and Hobbes's was a great one. His most important
work, *Leviathan*, argued that surrendering all our power to an
absolute sovereign is the only way to prevent the war of all against
all that occurs when nature is unrestrained by human law. For
Hobbes thought the words *good* and *evil* meant nothing apart from
the wishes of those who use them. It isn't the longing for goodness
that moves us, but the longing for power and glory. Since we are
all roughly equal in body and mind, the wishes of millions of glory
seekers can only end in chaos, anarchy, and death. Fear of death,
however, is the lever that can be used to move us, for even the
simplest of us knows that life is the basis of everything else we may
ever want. Hobbes thus imagines a state of nature whose wild hordes
are just rational enough to stop their rush toward doomsday by
agreeing to obey any sovereign who will prevent further war. The
ruler must be absolute, with the power to punish disobedience with
death, for only fear of death is strong enough to overcome the
struggle for power that otherwise drives us.

This view led some to charge Hobbes with atheism. Rulers had
had absolute power before, at least in theory, but they'd based their
claims to it on divine right and religious tradition. In denying that
right Hobbes argued that pure reason, and empirical observation
of the bloody chaos around us, should lead to one conclusion: Any
restriction of freedom is better than being hostage to constant terror.
The state of *Leviathan* brings peace, not justice. Indeed Hobbes's
world is even starker. Unlike Plato or Aristotle, he neither begins
nor ends with the question: *What kind of state is good, or just?* Hobbes
thinks only one question matters: *What kind of state will impose order
on bloody madness?*

Now for Hobbes, as for Kant two centuries later, the rule of law was paramount. Civilization begins when individuals agree to put their conflicting wills into a framework that sets limits for all of them. But the differences between the two philosophers are much greater than the similarities. For Hobbes, any framework is better than the chasm that opens where we have none – with the possible exception of a framework that threatens your life directly. Kant, by contrast, thinks the framework has to be right, grounded in ideas of justice prior to any rules that try to track them. For Hobbesians, law comes first; the rule of the absolute sovereign is the basis for all other rules of any kind, and allegiance owed to him is absolute. (Though Hobbes does suggest you can resist anyone prepared to take your life. On that view, presumably, Abraham may be silent before God on Mt. Moriah, but Isaac has the right to resist.) For Kant, by contrast, ethics is primary. God must obey laws of reason that are prior to everything, and if Abraham happens to see them better than the Lord does before the gates of Sodom, it's his obligation to point them out. For Hobbes, without the framework the sovereign provides, there is nothing to see but the abyss.

Hobbes's greatest contribution to modern political theory was his insistence that state power has a secular basis, but religion was nonetheless a presence throughout his work. Leviathan and Behemoth are the monsters the Lord mentions in the book of Job. While Hobbes rejected the traditional idea that a king's right to rule is sanctioned by divine authority, he titled his books to invoke the absolute claims of the King of Kings Himself. Before the Enlightenment, Job was viewed as a lesson that *almighty* might makes right: God can do whatever He pleases, and need give no reasons for doing so. For Hobbes, the book of Job was a 'moral treatise' unique in all of scripture, and he was the first to highlight the Leviathan, or to use the beast as a metaphor for commonwealth. Using the Bible itself to undermine religious bases of political authority is an interesting strategy, but why pick one of its most brutal passages, in which God seems to mock Job's misery by emphasizing his powerlessness? Why would Hobbes name his books after the monsters God uses to taunt Job for questioning His justice? One reason is this: If God Himself holds power – not justice – to be the thing that matters, Hobbes has divine sanction for rejecting claims of justice after all.

Job can be read very differently, as I'll do at the close of this book. But let's return to ask how far Hobbes's views describe our own world. The interminable cycle of fear and submission he believed to govern reality does capture one impulse in recent U.S. foreign policy, where an endless unpredictable war on terror could make life nasty, brutish, and short for the foreseeable future. Only a ruler with unlimited power has a chance of containing it. Just which nation neoconservatives find most suited to take up the role of international absolute sovereign should come as no surprise.

Kagan's transatlantic analyses were widely criticized on historical grounds. European historian Tony Judt, for example, reminded readers that the international structures like the UN that Kagan excoriates were, in fact, the work of strong powers – notably the U.S. – as Europe lay in ruins. 'The norms that Washington currently violates are its own,' Judt concluded. 'There is nothing uniquely European, much less postmodern, about the rule of law or the desirability of peace over war.' And former German foreign minister Joschka Fischer remarked that far from being Venusians, today's Europeans are children of Mars: not the illusions of comfort, but the memories of two world wars lie behind European insistence on peaceful solutions. Kagan's brushstrokes were as broad when talking about European history as when talking about philosophy; both were really ornaments to the political claim that being able to run the world gives you the right to cut moral corners. Yet for a time, Kagan's views stuck – not only as the subject of discussion in foreign-policy circles all over the globe, but as a basis for policy formulations. So a March 2005 National Defense Strategy document concluded, 'Our strength as a nation state will continue to be challenged by those who employ a *strategy of the weak, using international fora, judicial processes, and terrorism*' (italics added).

The Defense Department had no trouble drawing implications. What's real is (military and economic) power. Those who have it can afford to be honest about what drives them; those who lack it resort to a series of ruses designed to cripple their stronger neighbors just as surely as the Lilliputians tied Gulliver's hands. If you can win wars, you will consider war a viable part of international relations. If you cannot, you will praise the virtues of negotiation. For contemporary conservatives the message was clear: The U.S. is the most powerful nation not only on earth but in history, and having won the competition for domination it can take off the gloves. Europeans, by contrast, can no longer undertake major military actions. Their objection to American unilateralism is therefore not based on commitment to principles of world order but on the fear that the U.S. will do what they cannot do themselves. Here Kagan himself was initially consistent. He acknowledged that the early U.S. was attracted to views that emphasized things like rights and treaties. What else would you expect from a fledgling republic struggling to its feet in the midst of European colonial scrambles? If the world-views have been reversed since 1776, it's because the balance of power was reversed as well.

My concern is less with historical description than with the shape of the metaphysics proposed: What's real are the military and economic relations guaranteed by U.S. power, and everything else is self-serving fluff. Let's agree to call this view Hobbesian, though the real Hobbes was subtler and richer than most views that appeal to his name. It's a view that fit much of the U.S. foreign policy statements made shortly after the attacks of September 11, and throughout the first term of George W. Bush. The satirical paper *The Onion* was only mildly exaggerating when it summarized Bush's speech before the UN General Assembly with the headline *Bush Unveils his U.S.-Does-Whatever-it-Wants Doctrine*. Certainly many actions of the Bush administration brought us closer to Hobbesian realities than anyone could have imagined. The disasters following Hurricane Katrina allowed many a glimpse of the breakdown of civil society that mars the lives of Americans at home. And while American foreign policy – like that of other nations – has always been willing to overlook the flaws of its allies, only recently did the willingness to serve American interests become the sole criterion for being an ally. As one former CIA agent told American journalist Jane Mayer, 'We told them we'd help them join NATO if they helped us torture people.' The United States' treatment of the International Criminal Court is alone enough to reveal a policy that is Hobbesian to the core. The court, after all, was established in an attempt to promote a universal standard of right that is independent of might. When the administration demanded immunity for American soldiers accused of war crimes, it implied that you need not worry about right if you're mighty enough. It's hard to get more brazen, but the government has tried. When it cut foreign aid to bitterly poor countries, like Niger, who did not support the U.S. bid for immunity, it showed a ruthlessness in the pursuit of power that few can match.

But practices are one thing, and premises another. The main trouble with calling Americans Hobbesians had little to do with the history of political theory, but much to do with American self-understanding. Americans have seldom seen the world as an endless jungle, or politics as a matter of controlling humankind's unlimited will to power. On the contrary, complained Henry Kissinger in 2005, the U.S. is probably the only country in the world in which *realist* can be used as a term of abuse. Americans uphold the ideal, not the accidental; our patriotism demands allegiance to ideas along with blood and soil. Whatever power we may have, or want, is thus the power of reason: not to cave in to reality, or to accept the conditions that our parents' parents left us, but to create different ones. Unlike Napoleon's army, we don't even need bayonets to carry our revolution forward. The poor, the tired, and the hungry will come on their own because we offer an opportunity history never did: to make your own world anew. America's state of nature was not Hobbes's, but Locke's: a place where people were often moved by the prospect of gathering wealth, but never by the presence of fear. 'Give me liberty or give me death' was an American slogan because, even more than fearing death, Americans feared tyranny. As a result, rather than seeking an absolute power to protect them, Americans established a balance of three. Avoiding absolute claims to power was so important to the framers of the U.S. Constitution that they followed French philosopher Montesquieu's insistence that sovereign power should be divided between executive, legislative and judicial branches of government.

Earlier conservatism came from, and was suited to, the Old World. It begins with the premise that things cannot possibly get better, so the task of political culture is to keep them from getting worse. From this standpoint, ideas are the products of intellectuals, who use them to create things like Jacobin and Stalinist terrors. Better to stay with the tried and trusty customs and habits that have preserved whatever order can be imposed on the chaos within and without. That view was adopted by traditional American conservatives, and plays well in some military quarters. But it could not appeal to a majority of Americans, whose images of themselves and their histories are diametrically opposed. Only when conservatives began to provide a framework for those images did they really gain ground. Few Americans will accept a worldview that, in the end, promotes resignation to a grim and fixed reality. Hobbesian convictions could no more sustain the American right than Marxism sustained the American left, and the reasons are the same. Whatever their political convictions, Americans incline toward a metaphysics that underpins their belief that ideas of right and justice can transform just about any old world.

From its very beginning, the United States was held to be Enlightenment made tangible. Europe may have invented the Enlightenment, but America was in a position to realize it. European thinkers speculated about whether men were created equal; American thinkers wrote it into law. Indeed, historian Henry Steele Commager argued that America's founding vindicated Plato: For the first time in history all its statesmen were philosophers, and all its philosophers statesmen. It's a claim that will sound strange to those who regard thinkers, by definition, as people who never act. Such assumptions may lead us to regard Franklin and Jefferson as politicians whose dabblings in theory deserve the same good-natured amusement as Rousseau's drafts of constitutions for emerging states.

But in the eighteenth century, on both sides of the Atlantic, theory and practice were part of a package. The difference was that in America, the Enlightenment seemed to work. By the mid-eighteenth century, the plans drawn by European philosophers looked doomed to oblivion. Frederick the Great flattered Voltaire endlessly, but drove him out of Potsdam; Catherine the Great asked Diderot to revamp the Russian educational system, but thoroughly ignored his proposals. Neither the Poles nor the Corsicans showed real interest in the constitutions Rousseau had drawn up for them. Europe seemed mired in the networks of hierarchy and bureaucracy, where no fresh idea could flourish. The sense of suffocation was present in the metaphors used for the very earth itself: Europe's exhausted soil had no chance against the virgin lands of the young continent. And the colonials declared independence from their monarch thirteen years before their French colleagues declared theirs; the Bill of Rights penned in Philadelphia inspired the Parisian Declaration of the Rights of Man. 'The French Revolution,' says historian Simon Schama, 'began in America.'

'We can no longer say there is nothing new under the sun,' wrote Thomas Jefferson, 'for this whole chapter in the history of man is new.' Jefferson's biblical allusions are as striking as Hobbes's: *America has trounced the world-weary wisdom of King Solomon.* From his day to ours, it all may have been more or less the same cycle of boredom and vanity, but now, said Tom Paine, 'we have it in our power to begin the world over again.' Dramatic expression was by no means confined to Americans. French philosophers, in particular, waxed positively purple. Raynal expected that 'a new Olympia, a new Arcady, a new Greece will perhaps give birth on the continent to new Homers, new Theocrites, and new Anacreons.' Turgot wrote that 'this people is the hope of the human race. It may become the model.' Condorcet thought America, as the highest stage yet reached by civilization, proved the reality of progress. Fragonard's painting of Ben Franklin, commanding both lightning and justice in a cloud of biblical and Roman references, left no doubt about where the power of the future lay.

The picture of America as powered by the Enlightenment is the sort drawn in Gertrude Himmelfarb's recent *The Roads to Modernity*. Himmelfarb is a conservative historian specializing in the Victorian period, whose virtues she has expounded in a prodigious number of books and essays. When prominent neoconservatives invoke the Enlightenment, it's a sign that something important has changed. Himmelfarb's turn to the eighteenth century in her revisionist essay was thus as interesting a barometer of conservative shifts as Kagan's second contribution to political history, *Dangerous Nation*. In that account of American foreign policy, Hobbes entirely disappeared. The book began instead with a quote from Lincoln, evoked to lend a blessing to the thesis that America has always been guided by an indissoluble blend of interests and ideals. This is much stronger than the reasonable claim that most actions reflect a mixture of motives. In Kagan's second viewpoint, every aspect of American policy, foreign and domestic, reflects the preestablished harmony of the material and the moral. Suddenly, American actions, from trading policy to invasions, were driven by ideals that happened to advance American interests but were always driven by universal ones: power and paradise perfectly converged. A typical sample describes U.S. policy in 1890s Asia: 'All this involvement in the Far East resulted primarily not from American commercial ambitions or from narrow national security interests but from moral and humanitarian concerns and a sense of obligation stemming from an offer of "good offices" more than a decade before.'

On this view, Europeans who cast doubt on the decency of American motives in, for example, the 1898 war with Spain, were driven by anti-American prejudice. While Himmelfarb's effort to wrest the Enlightenment from French hands echoed the attempt to turn *pommes frites* into freedom fries, Kagan ably gathered old quotes that mirror international reaction to the war in Iraq. Of McKinley's decision to invade Cuba he writes:

> While most Americans believed they had gone to war out of the highest of motives, that is not how they were perceived throughout most of Europe . . . European commentators of all ideological stripes took the occasion of the war to revive long-standing images of American materialism, greed, vulgarity, selfishness and barbarism . . . They perceived the intervention 'as a betrayal of American tradition and universal values.' The war 'brought a sense of loss, of innocence irremediably sullied, as the American myth was shattered before their eyes . . .' There was a good deal of concern in liberal internationalist circles and among peace advocates that the United States, by intervening in the internal affairs of its neighbor, had done severe damage to the international legal order.

Sound familiar? Change the locus, Kagan argues, still the conflict is the same: America's national identity, founded on a commitment to universal rights, requires a foreign policy committed to spreading justice that is often resented by weaker nations.

What's odd about this view is not just the unacknowledged – yet total – reversal of the earlier one; in place of a constant opposition between Hobbes and Kant was a union so happy it was never in doubt. Universalism replaced unilateralism without pausing for breath. Even more problematic was the author's refusal to raise any questions about authenticity. To assume that every American appeal to moral ideals is genuine is just as dogmatic as the assumption that none of them are. To call something ideal is to praise it. Not everything that calls itself an ideal is genuinely praiseworthy, however, and Kagan's willingness to take at face value every claim that commerce is a moral imperative is flat indeed – particularly in view of his earlier devotion to Hobbes.

The recent right-wing discovery of the language of universal ideals has not been confined to America. As writer Ian Buruma explains,

> There is a long and frequently poisonous history in European politics of left-wing internationalism and conservative defense of traditional values. The Left was on the side of universalism, scientific socialism and the like, while the Right believed in culture, in the sense of 'our culture,' 'our traditions.' During the multicultural age of the 1970s and 1980s, this debate began to shift. It was now the Left that stood for culture and tradition, especially 'their' cultures and traditions, that is, those of the immigrants, while the Right argued for the universal values of the Enlightenment. The problem in this debate was the fuzzy border between what was in fact universal and what was merely 'ours.'

Far more problematic than fuzzy borders was suspicious timing: Christian Democratic leaders across Europe displayed a sudden concern for the ideas of the French Revolution their forefathers abhorred in the moment when Turkey looked set to join the European Union. And just as the Christian Democrats' discovery of feminism happened to be timed to keep Muslims out of the EU, Enlightenment language was amplified in America as it became clear that the Iraq war was propelled not by ideals but a stinking mess of interests: in regional supremacy, oil, and distracting attention from what was already emerging as the worst presidency in U.S. history. As former neoconservative Francis Fukuyama noted, Republicans revved up the rhetoric about democracy to justify the Iraq war only after no weapons of mass destruction could be found to do so. One canister of sarin might have spared us hours of oratory.

Was American journalist Joe Klein right to define neoconservative foreign policy as 'unilateral bellicosity cloaked in the utopian rhetoric of freedom and democracy'? Or, in British author Dan Hind's sharp-sighted analysis, was the unexpected emergence of fundamentalist terror an opportunity that allowed established forces to find legitimacy in a heritage they would bend to suit most any political purpose? In *The Threat to Reason*, Hind writes,

> The terrorist attacks on New York and Washington did much to obscure the history of the preceding decade. The idea that the enlightened inheritance was under attack from irrational enemies had received sudden, spectacular confirmation; the defenders of the established order could once again consider themselves enlightened. There was an air of relief among advocates of neoliberal, corporate-friendly globalization that the accumulating evidence of intellectual bankruptcy suddenly belonged to a previous era, to the years before everything changed.

Taking Hind's suggestion seriously doesn't require that we view the recent conservative embrace of the Enlightenment as a deliberate ruse. Self-deception is always an option; many conservative policy makers' use of Enlightenment rhetoric was doubtless sincere. Indeed, abandoning the steely tones of the war's beginning must have been a relief: the cognitive dissonance between being American and being Hobbesian is just too great. But in politics, subjective states count for little; whatever ideals the neocons *meant* to be pursuing, their efforts trampled on most of what the Enlightenment managed to achieve. Your belief that you are saving the world for democracy may be perfectly genuine, but if you legalize torture, suspend the right to *habeas corpus*, withdraw the limits on surveillance of your citizens, and undermine the balance of state power, you have recreated the world that Diderot and Voltaire fought to extinguish.

Good theory was as absent in neoconservative circles as good practice: apart from claiming that Enlightenment values are universal ones, very little was said about the nature of those values themselves. Closer looks at their views of humankind reveal why their Enlightenment rhetoric rang hollow: the Hobbesian assumptions about how people work undercut the possibility that the rhetoric could be realized. As we'll see in chapter 9, being committed to

Enlightenment doesn't require you to believe that progress is necessary, but you must believe that it's possible. Otherwise you are left with what Hind called a piece of enchantment:

> In current circumstances, the language of Enlightenment itself, the language of universal human rights and modernity, has been successfully reduced to the stuff of world-historical kitsch, on a par with the apocalyptic fantasies of America's benighted and confused Evangelicals. In this way, Enlightenment provides cover, and perhaps comfort, for a ruling class that no longer feels able to function in conditions of peacetime democracy and requires instead the resources of an ongoing emergency.

Yet conservative invocations of the Enlightenment, however deficient, resonate far more with *American* realities than their earlier attempts to adopt Hobbes. Indeed, one can go further. National ideals of universal right were constitutive of the U.S. from its inception. America was always the country of the ideal – a place where people went for a reason, rather than a piece of turf on which hordes of wanderers happened to land. Being American meant being part of an idea, not part of a tribe, and it's telling that while the millions of slaves who were dragged to its shores hardly chose the idea of America, the vast majority of their descendants did. Rather than rejecting the ideal, African-Americans worked long and hard to force America itself to live up to it. Facts like these distinguish the American experience from its European counterparts: Europeans may have told themselves they were beneficently carrying a heavy burden, but their empires were built on principled beliefs about their own biological superiority. America's progress towards realizing itself is far from complete, or even steady. But its founding conception as a nation held together by common principle rather than common ancestry had influence far beyond its borders, and was crucial in reducing racism in international affairs. Seen from afar, liberty, equality, and fraternity are things that come naturally to Americans, and they needn't be bought with the bloodshed that accompanied European attempts to establish the same notions. Americans were neither a chosen people nor one thrown together by happenstance; being American was itself a choice. All that was what made it a new world.

Europeans' admiration for America is often accompanied by a touch of condescension. Sometimes this erupts into outright hostility, but on the whole they approach Americans with the ambivalence adults often feel toward children: full of a mixture of admiration and envy for the energy with which they rise and approach the morning's tasks, full of a mixture of sadness and self-satisfaction in the knowledge that more will likely go wrong than they realize. Americans assume that good will and hard work can remake the world for the better. Europeans often regard that conviction with bemused detachment, and occasional downright contempt. But even when they find our belief that the world could be improved on the wings of ideas to be naive and childish, they tend to find it wistfully appealing nonetheless. Europeans approach the world with caution built on centuries of watching how many things go wrong. Americans have less experience over which hope need triumph. Ideals are the stuff of which Americans were made – and if our fearlessness has often been a figure of fun, it has often been an object of admiration as well. So in 2008 the philosopher Bernard-Henri Lévy could describe French anti-Americanism as the fruit of a narcissistic wound, born of resentment over the fact that:

> Far, far away, in the New World, a real place, not a dreamland or a paper construction – where, we're told, people have come from every end of the earth, people with different skin colors, different languages, different histories and traditions, different gods, different heroes, have decided to come together, to agree on a contract and to gather in a nation – there is a country, America, where Jean-Jacques Rousseau's project, that almost unthinkable doctrine that all people needed to do was make up their minds, then say it and swear to it in order to create a political body.

Descriptions of American dreams used to ignore the millions of captured and murdered Africans and slaughtered Native Americans on whose blood and bones the Europeans' search for a better life was built. Today, national crimes are duly remembered in American classrooms, which now recall that the Pilgrims arrived to defend not principles of religious freedom, but their own intolerant sect; or that if some immigrants were escaping from pogroms and violence, the primary vision guiding the Polish peddlers or Irish farmers who braved the long journey was that of a full stomach. But despite all the corrections that recent historians have made to the mythologized version of America's origins, the idea of America as a refuge from realpolitik persists both at home and abroad. (In a language shy of foreign imports, *realpolitik* is one of the few words that has no English translation.) Even for those who no longer believe they can be realized, America remains the home of ideals. It's the appeal of a world not determined by the traditions you draw from the past, but the visions you have for the future. It's a world in which hierarchies are at most natural ones of intelligence and energy – all you need to change the realities into which you were born. It's a world that wasn't given, but made. Even when they do it with more than a touch of skepticism, millions still look to the United States as the place where liberty, equality, and possibly even fraternity are matters of deep instinct, not institutions.

Significantly, contemporary European institutions reflect Enlightenment aspirations far more than American institutions do. Measured in hard terms, Europeans live in as Kantian a set of structures as the world has yet devised. The most conservative European government will not demolish the social democratic frameworks that keep gaps between rich and poor within limits, and consider housing, healthcare and education to be not benefits but rights. This is not just a matter of protecting equality but democracy itself. Anyone who needs more than one job to guarantee her family's basic needs, or regards two weeks' vacation as a prize to be cherished after years of service, is unlikely to have much energy to ponder her society's political arrangements. By sponsoring culture, and the time to appreciate it, European governments support not just rest and pleasure – worthy enough things to support – but the groundwork for active citizenship. Even Britain, whose social system suffered far more under Thatcher than that of its continental neighbors, offers healthcare for which most Americans would be grateful. Across the ocean, the mess of malnutrition and homelessness, of children with guns and without healthcare, of rising rates of imprisonment and sinking standards of living does indeed make large pockets of the U.S. look like Hobbes's state of nature.

Kant, and many since him, were convinced that democratic powers don't start wars. Even if the connections between domestic and international policies are less direct than he hoped, they influence each other powerfully. If you live under warlike conditions you will come to believe they are normal. When a Baltimore lawyer casually asks if the streets of Europe are as safe as they were twenty years ago he betrays an unstated assumption: things naturally deteriorate, and get scarier every day. Those kinds of assumptions prevent Americans from asking questions about social relations or gun laws that could be fixed or changed or varied. And once you believe the only thing that can be altered is the tempo of decline, you have accepted a world in which perpetual war is part of the framework, to be kept – at best – perpetually at bay. The lawyer who posed this question is no neoconservative, but his query revealed a worldview which concedes Hobbesian premises from the start. No wonder: if you live in a place where economic differences divide the world into the blocks that are safe for your children to play in and the blocks that are not, it's hard to imagine another one. As this example shows, Americans themselves are divided: after decades of watching the gap between their ideals and their realities continue to expand, it's no surprise that many began to assume the sort of pessimism they mean to deplore. American domestic violence thus prepares the road for American violence abroad, making both look like unfortunate but unavoidable pieces of a world where Hobbes's principles hold sway.

Since the Second World War, the institutional realities of the two continents have indeed grown very different. Remarkably, the ideas driving each remain quite stable. Americans believe in most dreams of the Enlightenment and their own ability to realize them; Europeans believe in the glum calculations of *realpolitik*. Americans may seem bent on creating a Hobbesian jungle, but they see themselves as serving ideals of justice and rights. Europeans may have constructed a Kantian garden, but they take pride in underselling their own achievement.

Doubtless some Europeans refuse to describe their world in idealistic terms in pursuit of self-criticism. They know their commitment to social justice remains only partially fulfilled at home, and barely begun abroad. It takes no more than a cheap vacation in India to see that the European paradise depends on international purgatory, and the recent photos of Africans braving Sahara and submachine guns to scramble into the gated community on the Mediterranean affected nothing but the occasional conscience. Thus if a European tells you that she lives in a world that is as far from Kantian ideals as Mars is, she may be affirming them: keeping faith with an ideal means being honest about how little your world contains it.

Should we conclude that each continent simply suffers from an absence of self-knowledge? It's true that many American expressions of idealism are self-deluded, and much European self-deprecation is a matter of honesty. But a different suggestion may illuminate more: in Europe, democratic institutions are far ahead of the instincts; in America it's just the reverse. Americans are democrats in their sinews and nerves, while Europeans are singing a song they have studied. Nothing to be said against studies; but if they start too late they may not go deep, as anyone who ever watched a European socialist beam and bow the moment he spots a government minister will know. (Or a minister's deputy. The level of floating obsequiousness in European capitals is very high.) Americans live under conditions Europeans may consider nearly feudal, but they do it with a poise that can put Europeans to shame. A true progressive vision would combine the best of each, embracing the European institutions which provide the infrastructure for democracy and equality, while igniting the American civic culture that keeps them alive.

Earlier American politicians routinely gave voice to those civic instincts, and they were generally held to be credible. These are some of Grover Cleveland's remarks to Congress, in 1893, on the gunboat diplomacy used by American corporations set on annexing Hawaii:

> It has been the boast of our government that it seeks to do justice in all things without regard to the strength or weakness of those with whom it deals. I mistake the American people if they favor the odious doctrine that there is no such thing as international morality, that there is one law for a strong nation and another for a weak one, and that even by indirection a strong power may with impunity despoil a weak one of its territory. By an act of war, committed with the participation of a diplomatic representative and without authority of Congress, the government of a feeble but friendly and confiding people has been overthrown. A substantial wrong has thus been done which a due regard for our national character as well as the rights of the injured people requires we should endeavor to repair.

As it happened, the sugar companies were able to bide their time until Cleveland's term of office expired and a president less attached to universal interests was elected. Today many Americans fear that their democratic customs are only a matter of fashion. The American habit of calling perfect strangers Bill or George masks one of the greater gaps between rich and poor on the planet. The persistence of Americans' belief that they will make the leap from dishwasher to millionaire is matched by the probability that two shifts as a dishwasher won't earn enough to cover the healthcare, and is barely enough for the rent. And recent American refusals to practice what it preaches can easily make American ideals look like so much sham. When celebration of the free press is undercut by the buying of friendly journalists and the bombing of unfriendly ones; when separation of church and state is effaced by the insistence on personal piety as a political qualification; when commitments to human rights are scuttled by the legalization of torture, many Americans worry that the commitment to those ideals is merely self-deceptive.

Yet to dismiss America's commitment to ideals is to accept a reductionist worldview that accepts as real only material conditions, and treats everything else as humbug. You may have suffered vapid schoolteachers or dishonest politicians, and find the very sound of the Declaration of Independence seems hollow. But seen from the world of Hobbesian contracts and Machiavellian negotiations, the American Revolution was nothing short of miraculous. 'We hold these truths to be self-evident, that all men are created equal' was, metaphysically speaking, an astounding move. In the eighteenth century the idea that even all white men were created equal was anything but obvious; most of the world thought it patently false. In 1776 a band of colonials had the audacity to declare the idea self-evident – and thereby began to make it come true.

Thus it was very much in American tradition that a senior Bush advisor told a *New York Times Magazine* reporter that

> guys like me [i.e., reporters and commentators] were 'in what we call the reality-based community,' which he defined as people who 'believe that solutions emerge from your judicious study of discernible reality.' I nodded and murmured something about enlightenment principles and empiricism. He cut me off. 'That's not the way the world really works anymore,' he continued. 'We're an empire now, and when we act, we create our own reality. And while you're studying that reality – judiciously, as you will – we'll act again, creating other new realities, which

you can study too, and that's how things will sort out. We're history's actors ... and you, all of you, will be left to just study what we do.'

People on all sides of the political spectrum found this widely quoted statement appalling. To be sure, it's impossible to know what the Bush administration really believed about truth; all that's certain is how faithless it was in expressing it. Combined with the refusal to acknowledge the disastrous facts on the Iraqi ground, these remarks confirmed many people's sense that the administration was ignoring reality in ways that verged on madness – or worse. (Grimly enough, the administration *did* create its own realities – such as terrorist organizations that did not exist in Iraq before it invaded the country on the pretense of fighting them.) In George Orwell's *1984*, the government is most terrifying not when it tortures or annihilates its opponents, but when it insists on determining their reality. Remember O'Brien, the party boss who forces the hero into submission? Before he breaks his spirit with the threat of the rats, he insists on destroying his mind. 'You are no metaphysician, Winston,' he says ... 'You believe that reality is something objective, external, existing in its own right ... But I tell you, Winston, that reality is not external ... Whatever the party holds to be truth, is truth.' No wonder so many people rushed to distance themselves from standpoints that sounded eerily like this one. Conservatives like Francis Fukuyama and William Kristol criticized the eerily crusading stance of their fellows; others recalled that many had begun their careers as Trotskyites; and even liberals found themselves yearning ruefully for the solid ground of old-style power politics represented by the first Bush administration

But the jibe at reality-based communities is far deeper than any particular government, and goes to the heart of American dreams. *When we act, we create our own reality.* This is, in fact, what Americans have consistently done. It's idealism, pure and simple, and it fits the American framework far better than any appeal to *realpolitik,* a word whose very meaning urges the acquiescence to someone else's reality. Here the neoconservatives mirrored American self-understanding far better than the self-described realists on the left or the right. Americans are unlikely recruits for a Hobbesian war, which fits neither their understanding of the world nor their place in it. So in the *New York Times Magazine,* Canadian author and politician Michael Ignatieff wrote:

> A relativist America is properly inconceivable. Leave relativism, complexity and realism to other nations. America is the last nation left whose citizens don't laugh out loud when their leader asks God to bless the country and further its mighty work of freedom. It is the last country with a mission, a mandate and a dream, as old as its founders. All of this may be dangerous, even delusional, but it is also unavoidable. It is impossible to think of America without these properties of self-belief.

Ignatieff argued that the 2004 election showed the American impulse to choose 'the gambler over the realist. In 2004, the Jeffersonian dream won decisively over American prudence.' This conclusion was hasty. For one thing, it didn't distinguish between what the public wants to believe about its government, and what the government believes about itself. How much idealism was really embodied in the government's rhetoric is very much open to question. It would be comfort, however cold, to think that the Republicans won the 2004 election because they appealed to America's best instincts and dreams. In fact the appeal to fear – whether of terrorism or homosexuality – was at least as decisive, and we will probably never know if the voting machines worked. Perhaps no single cause was, by itself, enough to determine the outcome.

Yet Ignatieff is absolutely right to emphasize that conservatism has flourished by tapping into Americans' belief that ideas can be practical. *Ideas Have Consequences,* the title of a conservative classic, is a phrase that's become a right-wing mantra, from Rush Limbaugh's talk shows to the University of Chicago. For the story the Bush administration told about its actions – however you judge them – is closer to Americans' understanding of themselves than what most of the left was able to say. Indeed, even foreign observers find a Hobbesian reading of American foreign policy disconcerting. Millions of non-Americans have been drawn to Kennedy and Clinton and Obama for their particularly American idea that foreign policy should be driven by a vision of a better world, just as their ancestors thrilled to Franklin and Paine. It's a vision with consequences even when Americans choose to ignore them. So the 1998 Rome Statute that established the International Criminal Court invoked the Declaration of Independence as a source for the ideals to which it owed its existence. And even after eight years of watching American dreams turn rancid, European papers clamored for their return. In 2008, Germany's weekly *Die Zeit* insisted that Obama 'should lead the world', because 'the new powers of Asia have more power than ideas. The world needs America.' Going even further, Matthew Parris argued in *The Times* that how the world sees America matters to the world, for:

> . . . the element of nobility has always been a strong strand in the legend of America . . . But whether legend or fact, few would deny that the idea of nobility has been important to the way the United States sees itself, and the way we outsiders have seen the United States. I don't think the Statue of Liberty represents an entirely hollow idea, or that the words 'Give me your poor, your tired, your huddled masses . . .' are without resonance. Or that they and the exalted spirit animating them could easily be attached to the name of any other nation on Earth.

Words like these explain the strange consensus that began to emerge during the Bush administration's second term. For most European as well as American commentators, an excess of idealism was the source of what went wrong. In other parts of the world, the claim that the invasion was driven by idealism raised little but eyebrows and laughter; but within the transatlantic alliance, the Hobbesian tones that dominated the earlier Bush years were charitably forgotten. In their place was the later appeal to universal values said to drive not only the war in Iraq, but conservative foreign policy in general. Reluctance to sanction the use of military force became known as realism, while the willingness to wage war was suddenly idealistic. Pages were filled with analyses debating the genesis of the former trend from neoconservative tutors like Leo Strauss, as even those public intellectuals who hadn't supported the Iraq war itself rushed to give it a noble pedigree by defending, at the least, the intentions they said were behind it.

The connections between intentions and evils will be examined in chapter 11. I don't believe that intentions are the key to actions. If good intentions can lead to infernos, they are never enough to excuse. Nor do they provide legal defense against most forms of prosecution – a point that should be remembered by those whose emphasis on the good intentions of the war's architects is meant to forestall charges of war crimes. What you do in the world matters more than the reasons why you do it. Still what you say about your actions reflects them profoundly. As I'll argue, men who joke about bombing countries or finding mass weapons cannot be idealistic, merely grotesque. Since the publication of the Downing Street memo at the latest, we know that Bush's government was determined to go to war whether or not connections between Iraq and Al Qaeda, or weapons of mass destruction, were ever found – the first two justifications that were offered for bombing Baghdad. The spectacle of a government publicly groping for some reason or other to wage war should have led the world to suspect the one reason they finally lit on that was impossible to challenge directly. Instead, any number of writers and critics politely overlooked the growing signs that, as American journalist Mark Danner summarized, '. . . serving as it has as a handy and near-inexhaustible rationale for accruing centralized power, the War on Terror has approached as close as we have yet come to Orwell's imagined perpetual war, accruing to those in control the increased power that comes with war but without the endless costs.'

In the face of so much evidence that a Hobbesian worldview – at best – was the one animating the war's architects, what led writers as different as Christopher Hitchens, Nick Cohen, André Glucksmann, Adam Michnik, and Paul Berman to argue that the war was waged in pursuit of the highest ideals? A skeptic might tell you that it wasn't the first time intellectuals used their skills to buttress power, an art Rousseau described as 'weaving garlands of flowers around the chains that bind us.' But here was no sign of venality. Having shown so little interest in public opinion when it went against them, neither Bush nor Blair gave reason to imagine they would reward it when it went in their favor.

Sometimes banal explanations are the best ones. Memories are short and wistful, and one reason the idealist account of the war grew increasingly popular is because it was offered last. But neither bad morals nor bad memory is enough to explain the alacrity with which the idealist account was accepted. More importantly: most of us would rather be gullible than cynical. It's nicer to believe we were led into a deadly disastrous war by simple-minded men of good intentions than by sinister unprincipled rogues. Psychologically speaking, this trait is appealing, even if it requires a series of intellectual contortions. Acknowledging that so much devastation occurred with so little cause means confronting a world that's very much worse than it should be. For Britons, it would mean the final shattering of all the hopes that attended the rise of New Labour. For the French, it would mean consigning the nation that liberated them at Normandy to the lower reaches of purgatory. For Germans, it would mean the corrosion of the nation that served as the model of democracy while they dug themselves out of the ruins of the Second World War, hence a reason to doubt what those principles guaranteed. For Americans, it would mean confronting a heart of darkness deeper than anything Vietnam had revealed. Rather than facing the consequences the more squalid reading of the war entailed, many preferred to lay the blame on an overdose of idealism – even at the cost of discrediting idealism itself.

John Gray's book *Black Mass* displays this trend perfectly. Rather than challenge the Bush government's claim to be driven by an idealistic desire to remake the world, he observes the devastation it wrought and concludes that all such desires are dangerous. Dismissing ideals allows him to dismiss liberals who believe in constitutional guarantees of freedom, for '*they have failed to grasp the Hobbesian truth,* which Leo Strauss applied to the Weimar Republic, *that constitutions change with regimes*. A regime shift has occurred in the U.S., which now stands somewhere between the law-governed state it was during most of its history and a species of illiberal democracy' (italics added). This is tantamount to saying that because some people break laws, the laws are whatever people make of them, but what other position is open to this sort of realist? If you believe ideals are nothing but dangerous humbug, you have nothing against which reality can be measured – and nothing to conclude but whatever's real, is right.

Conservatives play with two metaphysical strands they can pluck at will: When what they call realism becomes too grim, they can always reach for idealism. (The claim that we create our own reality is actually better captured by Hegel's Absolute Idealism, a far more uncompromising kind of idealism than anything Kant offered, but the history of philosophy is not our subject here.) American conservatives now inhabit two distinct frameworks: the world according to Hobbes's nightmare, and a world moved by American dreams. No conservative thinker has acknowledged the gap between them, much less offered an account of how they might be compatible.

Even those who made their name as intellectual analysts show scant interest in thinking things through. After defending first one strand, then the other, in two successive books, Robert Kagan offered a cloudy mixture of both in a third. Its title, *The Return of History and the End of Dreams*, was vaguely ominous, but its author seemed relieved to proclaim that 'the world has returned to normal'. The twenty-first-century, it argued, will see a return to the struggles between great powers vying for regional dominance. Thus future foreign policy should be designed to manage and win the fight between clashing national ambitions that differed only in the cast of national characters. If Russia and China would do for the twenty-first-century what Germany and France did for the nineteenth, the endless struggle for power and prestige that constitutes the history of nations would be just the same. Meanwhile, Machiavelli replaced Hobbes and Lincoln in Kagan's own pantheon, leaving readers one more reason for gratitude that John McCain – in whose service the book was written – did not get far enough to follow its recommendations. *The Observer* concluded that the book 'makes clear that "democracy" is a realist concern – a word trotted out by clever states and statesmen to smooth over the play of their own interests. The new old neoconservatism: with Henry Kissinger at the wheel.' A suspicious reader might wonder if the whole exercise was a ruse: did the neocons take up the mantel of idealism in order to discredit it forever – and thereafter return, unencumbered, to the old world of power politics?

Neoconservative views and White House rhetoric changed in harmony. Before 2004, U.S. foreign policy was defended with Hobbesian rhetoric; as the world's most powerful nation, declaring something to be self-defense was all the justification required to do anything at all. After 2004 this form of bravado was replaced with talk of remaking the world according to American ideals. In the *Washington Post*, E. J. Dionne called Bush's second inaugural address 'the Freedom Shuffle – he's an idealist on Thursday and a realist on Friday.' Most conservative politicians slide between the two standpoints as easily as their intellectual shock troops, using the grander view to appeal to a broader public while saving the grimmer one for a selected few. Sometimes the positions are simply used as battering rams. This makes it easy, for example, to dismiss those who press for humanitarian intervention in Darfur with remarks about the hard facts of alliance in the real world that utopian dreamers forget. If Hobbes can be invoked to support one course of action, Hegel can be put to service for another: Why were war critics too timid to join the world-historical project of remaking the Middle East in our own image?

But neither sincerity nor consistency matters much here. Conservatives have two distinct metaphysics – one in which the only reality is material reality, and another in which ideas move mountains, or anything else that gets in the way. It's a double strategy that allows the right to claim both hardheaded intellectual supremacy *and* moral high ground. Who cares how they fit together? Sometimes you need a hammer, sometimes you need a wrench: The right uses each standpoint as a tool to be wielded when needed to mobilize their own forces or undermine their opposition's. The left, by comparison, is empty-handed. Stuck between traditional conservative appeals to the hard facts of reality and the absolute idealism of a government prepared to ignore the empirical world, it has no metaphysics to offer at all.

CHAPTER TWO

IDEALS AND IDEOLOGY

Sincerity, of course, isn't everything. You may be willing to kill and die in genuine commitment to the worst of causes. But just because sincerity isn't a sufficient condition for an idea to be acceptable doesn't mean it isn't necessary. Minimal harmony between your words and your deeds is the first thing you need to establish if you want me to take either of them (or you, for that matter) seriously. The more right-wing rhetoric appealed to ideals that its actions undercut, the more left-wing suspicion about ideals in general seems confirmed. Passionate speeches about the need to fight tyranny, wherever it occurred, had once driven George Orwell, or the members of the Abraham Lincoln Brigade, to fight the Spanish Civil War. Perhaps Saddam was as seemly a target as Franco. But seventy years later, it was disconcerting to hear the same words used by parties who had dismissed those volunteers as 'prematurely anti-fascist' – as the FBI called those Americans who enlisted to support Republican Spain when the U.S. was still neutral toward the growing fascist powers. Nor was it clear why those who had dismissed attention to human rights as 'moralistic' when it came from Sunday-schoolteacher Jimmy Carter suddenly found it bold and visionary. With its traditional language assumed by the right, and without a coherent alternative of their own, those leaning to the left had little to demand but a return to realism. The left could accept the idealistic declarations of those who supported the war at face value, or they could retreat to what was called realism; few were inclined to articulate an alternative course of action that was based on universal values. *Realism* replaced what once was called *pragmatism*, in a move that had less to do with reflection than with the rhetoric of upping the ante. Pragmatism, after all, isn't always a virtue. You may willingly choose to be unpragmatic – when you fall in love, for example, or give in a moment of spontaneous generosity. Choose to be unrealistic, by contrast, and you've opted out of action.

The call for realism is not, of course, a search for metaphysics, but for a political common denominator: Whatever moral and political positions they took before the U.S. invaded Iraq, few observers could deny that the war was damaging Western interests. Desperate for an argument that would appeal to all sides of the political spectrum, scores of writers called for realism as the route to consensus. The more conditions in Iraq deteriorated, the nobler the justifications for the occupation grew. The gap between what was happening and what the government said left everyone hungering, to begin with, for plain truth. The *New York Times* called *realism* the hottest word of 2006. 'We are all realists now,' wrote liberal author George Packer in a much-quoted *New Yorker* column.

He might have said: We've returned to pre-Socratic culture. For while the right may balance blithely between Hobbes and Hegel, the left strove to complete its retreat to a tone that hasn't measurably improved in two-and-a-half millennia. Consider the beginning of Plato's *Republic*, the first great book of philosophy ever written, and arguably the most important. While the Socrates we meet there may have been a hero, he certainly wasn't a saint. His repertoire includes a fair amount of bullying, humiliation, and the sort of fast-talking trickery he disdained in the Sophists; still his virtues more than compensate for it. Above all he reminds us that philosophy began not in the university, but in the marketplace. The subjects it sought to analyze are not technical terms, but concepts that run through all our lives.

Like *justice* and *right*. *The Republic* begins in a rich man's house that radiates the easy confidence that inherited money turns into tradition. Socrates and his friends have gathered there to pass the time with the pleasures of good talk before a night festival begins. *By the way,* says Socrates softly, *this thing called justice – do we really know what it means?* The room begins to burble with hesitant replies. Telling the truth and giving back what you've received? *Sounds alright till you wonder whether you should return a weapon to the friend who appears at your doorstep looking drunk or crazy. Should you return it? Are you required to tell him the truth about where it's stashed?* The first attempt at defining justice is too specific, demolished by a single counterexample. But the second is so general as to be almost entirely empty. Giving all people what's due them may sound like a fine concept of justice, but how do you know what is due? *Is the same thing due to your enemies and your friends?* Of course not, comes the answer, for you owe your friends good and your enemies evil. This definition cannot survive a few minutes of Socratic challenge. *Should we help our apparent friends or only the true ones? Do we always know the difference? What to do when our true friends are up to no good? And speaking of goodness: Can it be good to do harm? Every horse and every hound gets worse when you hurt them. Can it ever be right to make our enemies worse, even if – or just because – they are enemies?*

After a few rounds of this kind, Socrates' audience is left helpless. The principle *help your friends, hurt your foes* leads to conclusions so foolish that the young heir who tried to defend it is positively embarrassed. For short, we'll call it Xerxes' view, since Socrates suggests it can only come from him or some other 'rich and mighty man who had a great opinion of his own power.' It can survive as a default position because it describes what people actually do, but they are all at a loss to defend in moral terms.

Their helplessness is the backdrop for Thrasymachus, who bursts onto the scene, Plato tells us, like a wild beast. He is young and rude and impatient, and his real fury is directed at Socrates. For, he claims, either Socrates is fooling his audience or he's just a fool himself. Virtue? Justice? All smoke and mirrors, with no meaning at all. What we call justice is always victors' justice, ideas used by people in power to maintain their power. Most often this leads to injustice, and why shouldn't it do so? We are all of us out for our own interests, and injustice is usually what suits our interests best. Good hearts may seek justice, but good judgment seeks injustice. Powerful interests may invent moral rhetoric to convince others that their own interests are general ones, but anyone who takes them seriously is just another sucker. Perhaps Socrates needs a nurse, taunts Thrasymachus, since he can't tell the difference between a sheep and a shepherd. If he's so naive as to think the shepherd's efforts are really devoted to the sheep's welfare, he needs someone to wipe his face clean.

Contrary to his usual inclination, Socrates reacts to Thrasymachus without much in the way of irony: He says the young man makes him afraid. The ten books of *The Republic* form a sustained attempt to answer him by offering an alternative to those two positions: that justice is always provincial, and that it's anyway nothing but hype. These positions can support each other, or even merge, in more than one way. Most obviously, a clearsighted Xerxes is likely to give up the standpoint that justice is a matter of helping your friends and hurting your enemies as an unstable stop on the road to nihilism: Those who see nothing but tribal justice will eventually despair of the existence of justice at all. If it's based on unprincipled friend- ship, it's no more than the wobbly justice practiced by most thieves. Conversely, those who deny the reality of moral concepts altogether may find themselves supporting the sorts of tribal loyalties that hold people together – not only because such loyalties are practical, but because loyalty is something, other things being equal, that most people want. Even Thrasymachus, presumably, will occasionally find it useful. As Socrates showed, it's a contingent virtue. Unconditional loyalty has nothing to do with justice, and may even lead you to oppose it. If loyalty to your friends leads you to cover up their crimes, your commitment to justice is frayed.

These are views about the nature of justice, but also about the nature of ideas in general. Are any of them real, or is the very idea of something above and beyond particular and partial perceptions bound to be illusion? Contrast ideas with particulars. Your idea of a dog is your idea of what's common to pugs and collies and terriers; your idea of a tree must embrace whatever pines have in common with palms. Empirical concepts like these provide puzzles enough, in Socrates' day as in our own; but next to disputed concepts like beauty or justice, they look easy to define. Socrates shows that all these ideas are connected. If justice can make no general claims, but only rests on tradition and habit, then no other idea – not even the idea of a dog – has a chance. If Thrasymachus is right, and appeals to justice are just smokescreens for duels about power relations, then all appeals to ideas are either for fools or for those who want to dupe them. *The Republic* offered concrete proposals for how an ideal state should be governed. Its more important task was to show that ideas themselves are real.

Plato went overboard on so many matters that his doctrines have been largely discarded. Not even the wildest cultural commissar in Soviet-occupied Europe followed his proposal to ban most of Homer, or to permit no music but military marches. Plato's defense of radical polygamy was formidable – you will feel responsible for all the community's children if you never know which ones are yours – but no major society ever adopted it. And in his passion for the ideal he went so far as to argue that ideas are not only just as real as anything else, but significantly more so. You believe that material things are more substantial only because your experience of ideas is indirect, like the experience of bodies that you get from watching their shadows. Could you but perceive an idea in all its immediacy, you would take objects no more seriously than you take shadows now. Even later philosophers who called themselves idealists thought Plato had constructed a metaphysical fairy tale.

Plato continues to hold our attention less for the answers he offered than the tenacity with which he wrestled with questions that plague us today. For the problems he faced are dismally familiar.

Challenges to Plato's idealism came of age in the works of Machiavelli, and in the norms of high-court maneuvering. Hobbes's insistence that what we all strive for is power after power clearly stands in a similar tradition. The political theorist who stepped most clearly into Xerxes' shoes was probably the German legal philosopher Carl Schmitt. Schmitt argued that the only genuine political distinction is that between friend and foe. Morality is concerned with goodness, politics with power; and if war is a continuation of politics by other means, it's because both are fundamentally a matter of 'the most intense and extreme antagonism.' You may not actually have to kill your opponent, but you should never forget the need to vanquish him. Liberals seek a neutral framework to settle opposing claims, not by strength, but by justice. But they are, Schmitt believed, either hypocrites or fools, for any supposedly neutral framework represents nothing but the triumph of a stronger faction over a weaker one. True politics makes no claims to neutrality, or indeed morality, at all. Political and social justice, therefore, are nothing but a matter of cultivating alliances. This is the sort of argument that the British philosopher Bernard Williams called an ancient form of deflationary rhetoric. 'It consists in taking some respected distinctions between the "higher" and the "lower" such as those between reason and persuasion, argument and force, truthfulness and manipulation, and denying the higher element while affirming the lower: everything, including argument or truthfulness, is force, persuasion and manipulation (really). This trope has its uses . . . But besides the fact that it soon becomes immensely boring, it has the disadvantage that it does not help one to understand those idealizations.' Still less, Williams continues, does it help explain the differences between listening to someone and being hit by him.

Though Schmitt offered his services to the Nazis, they rarely appealed to his views, preferring to rely on more traditional virtues.

Calls for moral straightforwardness and clarity, sacrifice and loyalty, sustained far more Germans on the battlefield than the stark amoralism of Carl Schmitt. This point is important. The crimes of the Third Reich were among the worst ever committed, but they were preceded by years of instruction which prepared ordinary citizens to be accomplices to murder with talk of a common good. Socrates held that no one looks evil in the eye, and wants it. His view may seem optimistic, but the Nazis' care to drape the most immoral actions in moral terms suggests they believed him: most of us need to think what we're doing is good – even when it's not.

Thus the same political system could make separate but equal use of views that praise traditional ideals, and views that dismiss them as humbug. While Schmitt may have been the Third Reich's leading legal theorist, he was not its leading propagandist. In Nazi Germany as elsewhere, this kind of argument was best kept under wraps. Machiavelli himself wrote that the prince who best heeds his advice will be most circumspect about doing so. As Voltaire commented when Frederick the Great wrote the treatise *Anti Machiavel*, the Italian philosopher himself would have applauded: A ruler who wants to gain power over his people could do no better than begin by writing a refutation of Machiavelli.

While it was counterproductive for the right to appeal to Thrasymachus or Xerxes explicitly, the right seemed the appropriate home for appeals to power it called necessary, and to privilege it called natural. For according to Schmitt, liberals' view of human nature tends to be sanguine, whereas 'all genuine political theories presuppose humankind to be evil.' The picture of opponents locked in antagonism that only pauses when one is defeated is a picture of human nature that has no room for ideals. Like Thrasymachus, Schmitt was full of scorn for any political position that tried to rest its claims on them. Ideals? What were they? Where were they? How do we perceive them? Agree on them? Act on them? Surely there are simpler ways to explain what we do. We help our friends and hurt our foes because we are led to do so – whether by tradition or biology is unimportant. Any claims to right or justice beyond that are attempts to bamboozle. As Thrasymachus already told us, anyone who believes them is as silly as a sheep who believes its shepherd's attempts to fatten him are all for the sheep's own good.

The saddest of ironies is that Schmitt's kind of view has increasingly come to dominate discourse on the left. As Bernard-Henri Lévy commented, 'A whole segment of the European – and notably French – intelligentsia is marching as a single man behind the strange and, the more one thinks about it, hallucinatory idea that we need a Nazi thinker to help the Left out of its gridlock.' The turn to Schmitt's diagnosis of liberal ideals was not without cause: postwar crumbling of colonial empires laid bare the ways in which simple greed, dosed with racism, underlay much universalist rhetoric. Why not embrace anyone who exposed the hypocrisy that had accompanied so many liberal ideals? These days those who emphasize that hypocrisy are more likely to cite the Italian philosopher Giorgio Agamben than the Russian revolutionary Trotsky. But the claim that moral concepts are (at best) self-deluding or (at worst) hype devised by the powerful is a claim that goes back to ancient Athens. Few contemporary thinkers put the matter so starkly; clarity is one Socratic aspiration that's gone out of fashion. But though such assumptions are rarely stated, they fuel cultural and political discourse from the center to the left.

If you ask for an argument, you are likely to get history: So many claims to universal virtues have proved to be justifications for particular violence and injustice that any such claim must be contaminated. Better to correct, if you can, some small local injustice, than to lose yourself in false hope and bombast about universal values. Or you may hear something more hard-bitten: If so many claims to justice have proved rotten, why retain claims to justice at all? The language of power is ugly, but it's honest – perhaps the last remaining virtue in a world rank with deceit.

The belief that justice can only be local found expression in the attack on universalism that characterized left-wing thought from the early 1970s. The unity of purpose that made the civil rights movement an American beacon was lost in a struggle for the interests of each group. This didn't, and needn't, slide into a *war* of all against all, but it did make the common cause of fulfilling universal visions seem as outdated as op-art or bouffant hairdos. The civil rights movement began as a demand to realize the Socratic principles the Enlightenment maintained: All men have equal rights to justice if all men are created equal. The women's movement began by extending the same argument, pointing out that women had been effectively excluded from the universal rights proclaimed by men. Both these movements are part of a struggle for human rights, in the service of ideals that had been proclaimed, but imperfectly realized, centuries earlier. Later, however, demands for justice become little more than scrambles to insure that my tribe gets no less than yours. This has nothing to do with justice, but with the pre-Socratic idea that justice means no more than helping your friends and hurting your foes.

If left-leaning activists turned to the particular in political struggles, left-leaning academics saw themselves as fighting the same battle on another front. When they turned their attention to intellectual canons, they stumbled over the gaps left in the West's understanding of the world. Until recent decades, history was written by the victors, and the victors left out a great deal: Europeans without the skills to write their stories, non-Europeans whose narratives had been ignored, women whose work had been forgotten. Any history that was ignorant of them could not be all the history that counted, those scholars insisted. The turn to cultural studies that they launched sought to bestow dignity on those whose stories were untold. Such a turn could easily be seen as a consequence of the Enlightenment, whose zeal to understand the rest of the world produced the first criticisms of Eurocentrism. But rather than understanding its own turn to other cultural traditions as something inspired by the Enlightenment, the contemporary left saw only antagonism between them. What should have been a triumph of the Enlightenment was viewed as a sign of its failure.

That failure is described with bits and pieces of both positions Socrates opposed: that virtue is helping your friends and hurting your foes, and that any talk of virtue is simply bombast. More often, virtue is left out of the discussion entirely. Robert Bellah's classic study *Habits of the Heart* examined the moral assumptions of middle-class Americans through a series of complex interviews in 1985. Its most striking finding was the gap between behavior and self-description. Even people whose lives were clearly guided by deep commitments to moral values were reluctant to speak in moral terms. From a Catholic community organizer in California to a dedicated Southern psychotherapist, those who were interviewed acted consistently better than they said they did. Their language made their lives sound more arbitrary than they actually were. This might speak for their humility, were it not for the fact that, as Bellah concluded, 'The primary American language of self-understanding limits the ways in which people think' – and eventually act. Those who describe their lives as determined by economic self-interest may sometimes act independently of it. We are more likely to agree on particular virtues than on a general understanding of virtue itself. But without a moral vocabulary, we cannot act out of conviction, merely out of habit – and habits rarely take us as far as we need to go.

Moral vocabularies have been shrinking since Bellah's study. Contemporary sociologist Alan Wolfe extended many of Bellah's findings, and calls *Don't be judgmental* the eleventh commandment. William Bennett suggests that Americans mistake the reluctance to judge for democratic virtue, as if not just all men but all ideas must be created equal, too. But Americans are far more comfortable with moral language than their European counterparts. As one theorist told me, 'I grew up in fascist Spain, where the appeal to traditional values was hammered in to cover up the death and torture that went into the Civil War. For me the language of morality is dishonest; I don't trust it. The language of economic interest and class just feels cleaner.' Though the Communist Party is partly responsible for the death of Republican Spain, its materialist vocabulary survives in those who mourn. In Western Europe, the language of value was most often used by the same church that had failed when confronted with fascism. This made all such language feel contaminated, while reinforcing the assumption that moral concepts are ineluctably tied to religious ones. In Eastern Europe, by contrast, any reference to notions of the common good, or heroic self-sacrifice, seemed inevitably debased by communist appropriations. As exiled Soviet writer Sergei Dovlatov noted, dissidents lacked an original vocabulary; all the good and noble words had already been used by the communists. Thus even the project of emancipation, so long the goal of idealistic endeavors however differently understood by the right and the left, was declared to be 'always situated beyond good and evil ... Morality is a residue of the old world,' concluded French philosopher Alain Badiou.

Comparing national attitudes to moral language, and understanding all the factors that have undercut our taste for it, would fill another book. Here I wish merely to note two sources of disappointment that contributed to them. The roots of the first lie in the contradictions of classical Marxism. For though its emotional appeal was a passion for truth and justice as strong as Socrates', its intellectual premises were a medley of exactly the targets that Socrates attacked: Justice is doing good to your (class) comrades and evil to your (class) enemies, and everything else is just bourgeois ideology. This view collapses into Thrasymachus' in the end. Efforts to construct a Marxist moral theory out of the writings of the young Marx and the practical commitments of many socialists foundered, not, in the first instance, on the collapse of real existing socialism, but on the hard tack of historical materialism. The practice may have been brutal, but the theory was incoherent.

Marxism's main attraction was its moral fervor, its commitment to slash through liberal hypocrisy and defend the hitherto defenseless with something more than mere words. Marx drew followers with claims of realizing the moral ideals of justice that the Enlightenment had formulated but had left dangerously unsupported, and hence unfulfillable. Perhaps the Enlightenment guaranteed freedom of speech, but the freedom of those who could buy a printing press was clearly not equal to that of those who stood on a soapbox – or those who had no leisure to do either. It was a powerful, progressive critique. Yet the ideals that fueled the movement were undercut by its allegiance to a view of reality that was at bottom too close to Thrasymachus. For Marxists, all ideas are ideology – rationalizations of real bases. Whether through philosophy, art, or religion, all are produced in order to obscure the real (that is, economic) relations that determine our lives. The bourgeois philosopher who claims to be serving ideals of universal justice does no more than forestall possible objections to the capitalism that built his ware- and townhouses. If sheep could rebel, then the shepherd would have to croon while he fed them. The bourgeois philosopher does no more.

It didn't take long for many to notice the paradox: a philosopher propounding new ideas with brilliance and passion, while maintaining a very old view about the flimsiness of ideas in general. Marx himself, and any number of his admirers, struggled to resolve the paradox by trying to understand relations between ideas and the world in more adequate terms. After all, when the young Marx wrote that life determines consciousness, he wasn't talking about dead matter. In his early years, Marx believed that the path between ideas and objects was far more of a two-way street than Thrasymachus suggests: Ideas and matter influence each other, a metaphysics that current neuroscience seems to confirm. But the version of dialectical materialism that triumphed encouraged the picture that, in the process of cosmic production, ideals were like foam: the froth (or the scum) that bubbled up from the real stuff you need to quench your thirst. It's the sort of picture that emerges from Trotsky's tortured tract *Their Morals and Ours*:

> The clerks of the ruling classes call the organizers of [com-munism] 'amoralists.' In the eyes of conscious workers this accusation carries a complimentary character. It signifies: Lenin

refused to recognize moral norms established by slave-owners for their slaves and never observed by the slave-owners themselves; he called upon the proletariat to extend the class struggle into the moral sphere too. Whoever fawns before the precepts established by the enemy will never vanquish that enemy!

As long as such pictures persisted, the hard-edged critique of bourgeois failings could not inspire the steady engagement that a sturdy moral framework provides. Faced with the problem, one German socialist leader called for the Enlightenmnent against his more dogmatic colleagues. 'More Kant!' cried Edouard Bernstein. 'Kautsky don't turn pale.' That was at the Second International, just before the most idealistic wave of socialism foundered so horribly on the First World War. Later Marxists like Adorno and Marcuse reached for Freud rather than Kant, but no ingredient yielded a theoretically digestible mix. It's daunting to think how many minds spent their best years, and intentions, trying to make the view work. Squaring circles might have been more fruitful. Change the details as you wish: A commitment to justice cannot be coherently maintained so long as you even suspect that Thrasymachus was right about justice after all.

Suspicion is what's left over after reading Michel Foucault. I use the word precisely. Foucault was the greatest modern theorist of power, but in this, as in other questions, he resisted clear conclusions. Like many, I share his refusal to fit all truths into one system, not only because the attempt to do so has become intellectually fruitless, but because its political consequences have been so dangerous. The damage that resulted from utter reliance on the invisible hand of the market is different from that of the more intrusive appendages of the state, but both have given us plenty of reason to distrust final solutions. Eclecticism seems both smarter and saner than any alternative. Thus few people today will insist that Foucault (or anyone else) adhere to a strict system, or refrain from changing his mind. Yet anyone turning from his extraordinary analyses of power in places like prisons and madhouses, to his general views about what power is, will be repeatedly, perhaps systematically, frustrated.

Foucault is far more interesting than Thrasymachus; that's why he was influential. Rather than simply declaring that justice is power, he showed how power works. His questions were brilliant, his eye for eloquent examples astute, and his particular observations often so good that they lead you to trust his general ones. Foucault's exploration of examples is more absorbing than most contemporary philosophy. By delving into history he showed what philosophy at its best can achieve: expanding our sense of the possible by showing how particular concepts and practices evolved – one way of showing they could have evolved otherwise. Yet for all his elusions he did write that justice is power, and power is justice, in enough times and places for the claim to stick. Here's one way he described his project, which may convey the excitement it generated: 'The way power was exercised – concretely and in detail – with its specificity, its techniques and tactics, was something that no one attempted to ascertain; they contented themselves with denouncing it in a polemical and global fashion as it existed among the "others" in the adversary camp. Where Soviet socialist power was in question, its opponents called it totalitarianism; power in Western capitalism was denounced by the Marxists as class domination; but the mechanics of power themselves were never analysed.' Foucault insisted that power is not merely repressive: If it never did anything but say no, why would anyone ever obey it? Power produces, among other things, pleasure and knowledge. This is fine until you try to move from particular truths to abstract ones. Either power becomes so abstract that it could mean almost anything, or it's pulled back into the frame of violence and obstruction we knew from Schmitt and Hobbes and Thrasymachus.

One example must suffice here. Through its shrewd discussion of ways in which punishment became more repressive while becoming more gentle, Foucault's best-known book, *Discipline and Punish*, influenced movements for prison reform. Foucault himself was active in some campaigns, but insisted that his goal was nothing so trivial as to improve prison conditions, but 'to question the social and moral distinction between the innocent and the guilty.' As Michael Walzer has argued, this isn't a distinction prisoners themselves would deny. They may point out that innocent people are wrongly convicted, and that criminal justice systems are racist and arbitrary. They may point out that unjust social structures encourage crimes that wouldn't be committed under different circumstances. But all such demands rest on the distinction between guilt and innocence, which is basic to any conception of justice, a conception Foucault – sometimes – longed to undermine. In a televised discussion with Noam Chomsky he made this explicit: 'If justice is at stake in a struggle, then it is as an instrument of power; it is not in the hope that finally one day, in this or another society, people will be rewarded according to their merits or punished according to their faults.' Nor did he flinch from implications: When the proletariat takes power, as he expected in 1971, it may exert violent, dictatorial, and bloody power toward the classes over which it has triumphed. 'I can't see what objection one could make to this,' he told Chomsky, who described him afterward as the most amoral man he ever met. To be sure, Foucault wasn't a Maoist forever; nor did he always use the declarative form. Suspicion, after all, is better transmitted by particular kinds of questions:

> Isn't power simply a form of warlike domination? Shouldn't one therefore conceive all problems of power in terms of relations of war? Isn't power a sort of generalized war which assumes at particular moments the forms of peace and the state? Peace would then be a form of war, and the state a means of waging it.

Where is Orwell when we need him?

The end of real existing socialism, and the failure of so many Marxist predictions, might naturally have led to a turn toward idealism. Historical materialism had reached a dead end. Anyone who still doubts that human beings – or what passes for them –

can turn the course of history need only imagine what the twentieth century would have looked like had Stalin or Hitler been replaced by other leaders. Even more recently, anyone contemplating the impact that 535 Florida ballots had on world history must allow that history is made by individuals. Anyone who still wonders if ideas have force need only consider the power of nationalism at midcentury, or religion at its close. But few on the left took such directions. They seemed rather to assume that French philosopher Merleau-Ponty had been right when he wrote that 'to renounce Marxism is to dig the grave of reason in history. After that there can be only dreams and adventures.' More exactly: Even if you post them later on YouTube, dreams and adventures became something you have in private.

If Marxist politics had undermined the reality of justice in the act of trying to realize it, post-Marxist politics were even bleaker. Reasonably enough, the left was radically unsettled. The hopes of the sixties had blossomed, not into an adult progressive movement, but into a choice between cultural reaction and consumer excess. Eastern Europe didn't morph into democratic socialism, but threatened to crumble into bitter nationalistic ruins. And where major changes occurred, they seemed to combine the worst features of capitalism and communism, nourishing wildly unequal economies while mowing down students in Tiananmen Square. All these produced deepest disappointment, and self-doubt on the left made good sense. Minimal honesty (and the ever-dimming hope of getting it right next time around) meant asking where things went wrong. But distress made many easy prey for the view that what went wrong was not in the theory, but in the very appeal to theory at all. Perhaps it was the sense that too many late nights in smoky rooms arguing about differences between Lukács and Gramsci had been simply wasted; no adjustments to the theory were going to get it back on the road. Perhaps there was a longing for sobriety after too many raucous tangles with postmodernist epistemology: We might no longer be sure what truth is, but we know how to recognize lies. What was at stake was not the revision or rejection of particular principles, but the commitment to any principles at all. Suddenly the failure of Marxism seemed easily explained: Politics that appeals to theory instead of reality will always go wrong. It's a claim that Kant found trite and stale in 1792, but two centuries later most were too weary to argue. In abandoning historical materialism, they kept the culture of suspicion and discarded the hope of radical change. This meant retaining some very grimy bathwater indeed.

Most important, it retained the equation of ideals and ideology. Like most metaphysical assumptions, this isn't an equation that's often explicitly stated, although it's explicitly attacked by the right, not only in theoretical tracts, but in aggressively lowbrow rants like Rush Limbaugh's *The Way Things Ought to Be*. 'I believe in specific ideas, and I believe that those ideas have consequences,' wrote the powerful talk-show host. No one on today's left actually says they do not. Yet it repeatedly if implicitly suggested that ideas, especially moral ideas, are what used to be called superstructure. You no longer have to be Marxist to believe they're superfluous, and to think that what really moves us is the drive for power. You may no longer call it false consciousness, and still accept an even stronger claim: that ideas aren't merely superfluous, they're also deceptive. If ideas are ideologies, they are stories made up to convince us that humankind is a finer species, and the world a better place, than any clear-eyed view can warrant.

Foucault was a master of this kind of equivocation. While criticizing positivist tendencies in Marxism, he called Marxism itself inescapable, and seemed to support the commitments to liberation that were always Marxism's strength. But while the feeling he generated by reconsidering possibilities is genuinely liberating, the liberated reader is left without any sense of direction – partly because Foucault's analysis of power leaves us all so enmeshed in it that we cannot even see it properly. As the philosopher Richard Rorty concluded, 'The Foucauldian academic left in contemporary

America is exactly the sort of left that the oligarchy dreams of, a left whose members are so busy unmasking the present that they have no time to discuss what laws need to be passed in order to create a better future.' Nothing promotes inertia like cynicism. In a courageous critique of Foucauldian trends in feminist theory, the philosopher Martha Nussbaum maintains that the rudderlessness of Foucault's readers is even more sinister. His views, she argues, could support an attack on democratic institutions by right-wing militias just as easily as anything else. The position 'looks liberating, because the reader fills it implicitly with a normative theory of human equality or dignity. But let there be no mistake: . . . for Foucault, subversion is subversion and it can in principle go in any direction.'

In the interview published as 'Truth and Power,' Foucault said he was skeptical of the term *ideology* since 'like it or not, it always stands in virtual opposition to something else which is supposed to count as truth.' It's a formulation meant to cast doubt on the concepts of ideology and truth at once, and Foucault peppers the work with rejections of reductionism in every direction. Yet the same interview concludes with the claim that 'the problem is not changing people's conciousnesses – or what's in their heads – but the political, economic, institutional regime of the production of truth.' This kind of writing undermines the reader's impatience by making her feel that simple formulations are simply tacky. But saying that your view is deeper than crude forms of Marxism doesn't make it so, any more than saying that reductionism is mistaken means that you've avoided it. Foucault may not sound like Thrasymachus – though both were clearly drawn to the aura of transgression that led Plato to call the young man a wild beast. But though Foucault's views bore more fruit in cultural studies, it is hard to find a stable political difference between him and the pre-Socratic youth.

Nowhere is the absentminded equation of ideas and ideologies more evident than in contemporary historical practice, which, far more than any theories of history, has profound implications for our political self-understanding. Dismissing the history of ideas as elitist, those historians who wanted to remain progressive focused on the social conditions of other eras, rather than the terms in which those eras understood themselves. This made good Marxist sense: If every idea is an ideology – a story told to distract us from the real forces at work in history – why waste time studying matters that were at best superficial, and at worst simply lies? Which side are you on, boys? 'Social historians assume that writing about the working class is somehow acting politically in their behalf,' observes historian Anthony Grafton, 'an assumption which would have had my parents, both union members, rolling on the floor with laughter. Anyone knows the assumption is absurd as soon as it's stated, but it animates historical practice.' It's a practice that not only ignores the gap between understanding and action, but fails to do justice to understanding – unless you subscribe to the historical materialism most thinkers have long since discarded.

This practice is especially self-defeating when applied to historical events whose contemporary observers were certain could only be explained by reference to principle. Both the Enlightenment and the Counterenlightenment were united in believing that it was philosophy – *l'esprit philosophique* – that had undermined the institutions of authority and tradition. So Jonathan Israel's *Enlightenment Contested* argues:

> In recent decades it has become deeply, and more and more unfashionable among historians, to explain the French Revolution, the greatest event on the threshold of modernity, as a consequence of ideas. Marxist dogma with its stress on economic reality and cultural superstructure helped generate this near-universal conviction. But another major justification for this distinctly peculiar article of the modern historian's creed is the growing democratization of history itself: students especially, but professors too, readily take to the argument that most people, then as now, do things for exclusively 'practical' reasons and have no interest in matters intellectual.

As Israel points out, ideas can have consequences even for people who don't understand them. The number of those who have been influenced by the Bible, for example, is hardly the same as the number who read it carefully, and eighteenth-century people were no more inclined than we are to wait to express their opinions until they knew what they were talking about.

But if few of us actually think ideals are equivalent to ideologies, even fewer stop to think about the relationship between them. What remains is a matter of tone: The one sounds hard-nosed and the other smarmy – enough to keep people who want to talk tough using a Marxist vocabulary long after the theory has been scrapped.

The constant slide between ideals and ideologies allows everyone to sit on the fence without noticing how precarious their position really is. (It's a slide that's especially insidious, for language is more powerful when its presuppositions are left unstated.) You can propound any systematic worldview you like and strike whichever note is needed: When you want to project sincerity, you can call it an ideal; when you're worried about kitsch, it was just ideology. What's left is a metaphysical murkiness that insures no one ever knows how seriously things are taken, and thus allows them to be taken just as seriously as you like.

This tack takes many toward views their good sense saves them from stating out loud – which makes much contemporary theory the literary equivalent of mumbling. Some theorists are vague from a deep sense of scruple. Uneasy about unwarranted claims of authority, they evade any claim to authority at all. If you don't sound resounding, you cannot be accused of arrogance, or trying to foist your perspective on me. Avoiding straight prose is a form of misplaced modesty: Who am I, after all, to use the declarative? But not every obscurity is a backfired scruple; giving up on clarity can bolster authority as well as renounce it. Orwell spoke of writing that anesthetizes the brain, but no one described it better than Nietzsche: 'They muddy the waters to make them seem deep.' Deliberate obscurity lasts no longer than the king's new clothes do, but while it lasts it looks regal. Though shame may be less evident than it used to be in moral questions, embarrassment is still a prime mover in intellectual ones. Implying that your opponent can't assess your claims till he's mastered the later Heidegger can silence him faster than argument.

Such murkiness enshrines a sense of permanent distrust. While abandoning Marxist claims about progress in history, the left was united in its determination to believe in nothing else. Liberals, by contrast, recoil from the complete rejection of moral language just as surely as they recoiled from the unilateralism of the early George W. Bush. Hoping to temper the tone of that administration, whose scorn for international opinion was inflaming hostility in friend and foe alike, many political observers urged the importance of *soft power* – a term that undermines itself by conceding all the important ground from the start. The arguments themselves were hardly controversial: U.S. strength is not just a matter of military threats, but of a web of institutions from the movies to the Marshall Plan. You needn't even send the Peace Corps; we won more allies by deploying Elvis than any number of troop divisions. Political scientist Joseph Nye reminded American governments to use the mechanisms of persuasion as well as of intimidation. Nye wrote, 'Hard and soft power are related because they are both aspects of the ability to achieve one's purpose by affecting the behavior of others. The distinction between them is a matter of degree.' The big stick, in short, was plainly in view; couldn't the Bush administration speak a little softer?

Talk of soft power was meant to turn down the volume on the Hobbesians by trying to mix goodness and self-interest. The message was one the neocons' grandmothers might have told them: You catch more flies with honey than with vinegar, so why bully your allies when you can beguile them instead? The message to the liberals seemed just as sweet: If you can assure world domination through the nets that Hollywood and globalized capital have used to capture domestic hearts, you can have your cake and eat it, too.

This fusion of goodness and self-interest was, like most such attempts, neither very good nor really in anyone's interest. It wasn't very good – intellectually or morally – because it took for granted the assumption that power, and only power, makes the world go round. Nothing else matters, and nothing else moves us; but it acknowledged that most of the world is more steadily moved by carrots than by sticks. Our interests are easier to advance when they're muted, so why not veil the edges, muffle the tones? Put this way, talk of soft power is talk of disguises, which is concerned with presenting not a better worldview than the Hobbesians, but simply a more effective one. 'Command power,' Nye continued, 'is the ability to change what others do. Co-optive power is the ability to change what others want.' Foucault would have had a field day; it's hard to find a better statement of his view that modern institutions abolished torture and terror only to develop slicker forms of coercion. Advocates of soft power never question Hobbes's picture of a world fundamentally at war; they just think the war is best won with a Trojan horse.

But the appeal to soft power is not, in the end, really in our interest, and its use is just an illustration of liberal failure. For metaphors matter. Language matters. The term itself expresses a touch of Machiavellian cynicism, for soft power is just as poor a substitute for real power as role models are for heroes. *Soft* is a qualification of *power*, but what counts is the thing being qualified. Think of soft versus hard science, soft versus hard sell, soft versus hard data, soft . . . Well, the erotic undertones are undeniable. We value softness in things like blankets and kittens, but in more important matters, real men and women want the hard stuff.

No wonder we were told that Europeans were from Venus and Americans from Mars. Conservatives would never have won so much of this country's faith if they hadn't understood its psyche. Some people may be consoled by the more palatable picture of a world in which jungle instincts can be tamed. Not the hard tools of war, but the soft ones of advertising (whether the vulgar advertising of commerce or the refined advertising of culture) may secure us a place on top of the heap that emerges from the war of all against all.

For most Americans, ideals are too embedded in tradition to abandon. This fact goes a very long way toward explaining why Marxism never had the resonance in the U.S. that it found elsewhere. Americans cannot accept worldviews that deny the constitutive premises of their history; long before Stalin's crimes were visible, American progressives rejected the view of reality that relegates the ideal to a spin-off. Like Hobbes's world, Marx's was too materialist: for both, real power was in the gold that fills coffers and the iron that defends them. In neither world is it clear how ideas could possibly count. When I argued this in a recent discussion, an historian rushed to disagree: Not ideological preferences, but the early and violent suppression of American labor unions had destroyed Marxism's chances in the U.S. The problem with her rebuke is that it doesn't explain enough. It's important to recall the brutality with which U.S. government and industry combined to attack labor, but smashed movements can be rebuilt – if their ideas have sufficient resonance. The thought that the life of a principle counts more, in the end, than the life of a person who upholds it is as American as 'The Battle Hymn of the Republic.'

The deep connection between American individualism and American universalism is only an apparent paradox. Americans want to choose their identities and choose their commitments, not have them determined by accidents of birth. Identity politics does no more justice to our needs for universalism than to our needs for individualism. They leave no place for universalism because they have no space for justice in general, no room for asking whether a principle is valid in every case; here the special case is all there is. Xerxes' principle rules: Identity politics may not commit you to hurting your enemies, but it commits you to no more than helping your friends.

American sociologist Todd Gitlin's superb critique of identity politics in his *Letters to a Young Activist* acknowledges its power: 'Your starting point is that your identity has been singled out for victimhood. You didn't choose it, but you refuse to walk away from it.' But the primordial passion that fuels identity politics proves to be its weakness: 'However often it makes the blood race, [identity politics] often enough glosses over a profound impotence.' For, he argues, identity politics tends to stop thought; it confuses grand passions with minor irritations; and it mocks broader goals as mere rhetoric. 'On this view, the goal of politics is to make sure your category is represented in power, and the proper critique of other people's politics is that they represent a category that is not yours ... Even when it takes on a radical temper, identity politics is interest-group politics. It aims to change the distribution of benefits, not the rules under which distribution takes place.' Ultimately, Gitlin concludes, identity politics point backward, anchoring us in the past.

Still, it's a form of reasoning that has persisted, in part because it was mistakenly perceived to grow naturally from the civil rights movement that, from Selma to Johannesburg, represented the clearest progress the second half of the twentieth-century had to offer. Hence African-American intellectuals have been particularly important in questioning its credibility. From every point on the political spectrum, many have attacked the assumption that your political commitments are determined by what collection of people can claim you as their own – rather than what you believe in. Philosopher and theologian Cornel West argued that racial reasoning discourages moral reasoning. Law professor Stephen Carter complained that American commitments to individual choice are violated by the attempt to determine our political preferences from our group identities. Efforts like theirs prepared ground for Barack Obama's standpoint, which has been described as post-racial. It is not. It's a simple return to the demand that character, not color, is decisive – the guiding demand of the early civil rights movement. 'When I'm trying to get a cab outside your building, nobody thinks "There's that mixed-race guy",' Obama told one interviewer. Still his far-flung family must have made a rejection of racial reasoning natural; with so many tribes to choose from, identifying with one is improbable. But Obama's ability to win the 2008 election, and the international excitement surrounding it, was a measure of how many people of every background long to return to a universalist worldview.

Given the long decades in which progressives preferred the language of particular identities, it's no surprise that conservatives took up the language of human rights. But this more recent development, in turn, makes progressives' tasks harder. However genuine some supporters' commitments to human rights may have been, they were clearly used as empty rhetoric by those whose vision went no further than power and profit, and whose willingness to treat international law as a discardable fig leaf revealed a minimal commitment to ideals of justice. They might sound disconcertingly like Socrates, but their actions are no better than those of his most primitive adversaries. Helping your friends and hurting your foes is the maxim that guided U.S. foreign policy for decades; while from Chile to Saudi Arabia, the notion of friendship seems more suitable for gangsters (or at very best, playgrounds) than for anything else. Had conservatives studied Nye's discussion of soft power and simply changed their public-relations strategy? And if their behavior was as pre-Socratic as their rhetoric was idealistic, wasn't it time to discard our remaining illusions about idealism, period?

These sorts of questions led *realism* to become the buzzword of the present, in the growing consensus that foreign policy should return to it – with a dose of decency on the side. The best example of the view that idealism was the cause of failed foreign policies is *Ethical Realism*, coauthored by Anatol Lieven and John Hulsman, senior political scientists working in think tanks on the left and the right, respectively. They are convinced that what went wrong following 9/11 was that 'a messianic commitment to spread democratism has become the keystone of America's political strategy in the war on terror.' Their goal, therefore, is to 'bring morality down from the absolutist heights to which it has been carried, and return it to the everyday world.' They propose to do so, however, not by returning to classical realism in the style of Henry Kissinger and Zbigniew Brzezinski, which they criticize 'not only for its lack of a sense of ethics but also for its lack of any sense of the long-term goals of that policy, beyond a short-term defense of the national interest and a temporary status quo that favors that interest.' In a dig at Kagan, they cited Eisenhower as a source for the view that '"moral authority" is not just a phrase for the weak.' But since the behavior of all states 'is determined chiefly by interests,' all such behavior is chiefly gray. If it eschews the sort of black-and-white terminology used in the infamous Axis of Evil speech, and follows the principles laid down by Niebuhr, Morgenthau, and Kennan, America can find a policy that furthers its interests without sacrificing too many of its principles. Present policy, they believe, has sacrificed America's interests for the sake of principle.

Generosity is a great virtue, but there's good reason to think Lieven and Hulsman's reading of current U.S. policy is overly charitable. For however decent any individual soldier or public servant might have been in carrying out that policy, what went wrong is precisely that our principles were *not* maintained. The rhetoric about spreading democracy that followed the U.S. invasion of Iraq was undermined by U.S. scorn for international democratic procedure at every stage of the war. Many of Lieven and Hulsman's concrete proposals were welcome; gathering detailed information about the countries you invade, or trade or form alliances with, is surely better than proceeding in ignorance. They were also right to insist on 'a capacity to distinguish clearly between different grades of evil, and to choose firmly between them.' We must pick our battles, and cannot do everything at once. It's hard to quarrel with maxims that encourage prudence, humility, study, and responsibility. These virtues loom especially large where they have been absent. Nor will anyone deny that small-scale prevention of damage is better than the catastrophic promotion of large-scale ideas. But the reader is left thinking that this notion of ethical realism comes to little more than the homilies that advise us to avoid fruitless confrontation and 'let the magic of capitalism do its work.' Few would disagree that the second Bush administration was far more damaging than the first – or than the Truman and Eisenhower administrations, the authors' favorite examples. But is nostalgia for a president who never regretted using the world's first nuclear weapon, or refused to pass a law against lynching, the best we can hope for under a policy that calls itself ethical?

Lieven and Hulsman's examples are as troubling as their virtues are uninspiring, and the reasons are not hard to find. We are told just as little about the ethical as we are told about the real. Sometimes *realism* seems to mean no more than the advice to plan ahead before you start a war. Sometimes *realism* means the recognition that the world cannot be divided as neatly into good and evil as George W. Bush's more notorious speeches would suggest. Sometimes *realism* means nothing more than *cynical* or even *bad*, which leaves *ultrarealist* to mean simply *very bad*. So *ultrarealist methods* include 'torture, kidnapping, aggressive war, indifference to civilian casualties, and contempt for democratically expressed international opinion.' Ultrarealism? What assumptions have you made about reality?

This is more than a matter of careless writing. *Ethical Realism*'s inability to be clear about what realism is betrays the same weaknesses seen in Nye's phrase *soft power*. Both are proposing a kinder, gentler form of materialism, but the bottom line is still drawn by Thrasymachus. The warning to look before you leap is as unobjectionable as the reminder that honey is good for catching flies. But these are prudential maxims, not ethical ones. There's every reason to celebrate the moments when the two come together, but when they diverge, these theories cannot help us any more than their language can rouse or tempt us. This realism is about as ethical as power is soft.

Appeals to the magic of capitalism notwithstanding, what underpins these views are the residues of that Marxism that sees no difference between idealism and ideology. To understand what has gone wrong in recent years, and provide a basis for doing better in the future, we must be clear about the difference between them. Let's define ideology as any comprehensive system of beliefs about the world. I follow philosopher David Gauthier in understanding ideology as part of the deep structure of self-consciousness. This means that ideologies concern our capacity to understand ourselves in relation to other people, and that they function at a very fundamental, often preconscious level. This definition is deliberately neutral, without implications that such a system is derived from or reducible to something else. While it is therefore not opposed to idealism, it is very clearly distinct from it. For idealism is not neutral at all: Let's define it, for the moment, as the belief that the world can be improved by means of ideals expressing states of reality that are better than the ones we currently experience. *Ideology* is thus a much broader notion than *idealism*; ideologies can be made up of most anything ever believed long enough to be taken seriously.

Current conceptual confusion was nowhere better illustrated than in an interview that former national security advisor Brent Scowcroft gave to CNN. Arguing that the neocons still remain in control of the Republican party, Scowcroft said, 'I think we developed in the Republican Party a – well, you know, the buzzword for it is "neoconism". But I think what it is, it's an ideology – it's really an idealistic approach to things. But it's a combination of idealism and, if you will, brute force.' But as I've argued, *idealism* and *ideology* have no more in common than three initial letters. Carl Schmitt's claim that true politics means dividing the world into friends and foes may (just barely) be an ideology; idealism it is not. Take another example: one *might* refuse to negotiate with Iran on idealistic grounds – if one has a moral commitment to negotiate only with those governments that fulfill certain commitments to human rights or democracy. But this would require formulating principles that would apply generally, and thus rule out negotiations with, say, Saudi Arabia, Egypt, or Pakistan. Refusing to negotiate without any principles but Schmitt's division of the world into friend and foe may be maintaining an idée fixe, but it has nothing to do with idealism. The lesson of the war in Iraq is not that realism is better than idealism, for neither of them was ever really tried.

Can't we do good without theory? Thousands of political activists are working today to renew a progressive vision without paying much attention to defining it. They are busy teaching abandoned children, rebuilding crumbling neighborhoods, lobbying against war, building businesses committed to global fair trade. Does it matter that their theoretical bases are scant? Richard Rorty was one philosopher who thought it did not; we could still, he argued, uphold commitments to progressive politics without clear commitments to principle. In an essay called 'The Continuity between the Enlightenment and Postmodernism' he wrote, 'I sometimes find myself being called a "postmodern" because of my pragmatist views about truth and rationality. But I am nervous about being thus labeled, since in many contexts the term "postmodern" is used to refer to an attitude of political helplessness.' To show that where you stand on metaphysics makes little difference to where you stand politically, he says that if they lived in the same country, he and philosophers as different as Jürgen Habermas and Slavoj Žižek and John Gray and Jacques Derrida would vote for the same candidates and reforms. This may be true, and Rorty's rejection of what he called Enlightenment rationalism did not undercut his commitment to what he called Enlightenment liberalism. No American philosopher of his generation spoke so clearly or openly about contemporary politics, and his book *Achieving Our Country* remains a powerful analysis of the strengths and weaknesses of old and new lefts. To do this, *he* needed no clearcut commitments to any principles at all; as he wrote, he came from a thoughtful, politically active family, in which critical engagement was a matter of habit. Perhaps for that reason, and perhaps out of professional humility, he thought metaphysical questions much less significant than many nonphilosophers do. But in many fields with practical bearing on how lives are led – like law, and psychoanalysis, and the arts – the metaphysical questions Rorty dismissed are of great concern. For habits are just habits, and those that require any effort tend to succumb to inertia in the absence of principle. Neither Rorty nor his ironist colleagues sufficiently appreciated the effects of those styles of thought he summarized perfectly: 'This distinction between the theoretical and practical point of view is often drawn by Derrida, another writer who enjoys demonstrating that something very important – meaning, for example, or justice, or friendship – is both necessary and impossible. When asked about the implications of this paradoxical fact, Derrida usually replies that the paradox does not matter when it comes to practice.'

Here Rorty and Derrida were wrong, for this kind of writing often leads to disillusionment with the process of thinking itself. If it comes to nothing but contradictions its leading lights say have no practical consequences, why not spend your time elsewhere? Lots of things are more fun to play with than paradoxes. Wouldn't you rather read Toni Morrison than Derrida – or for that matter, listen to music, watch a movie, or take a nap? Absurdity breeds hopelessness without content or passion. Where outrage itself is exhausted, even despair is impossible. The resulting inertia is not the result of an ideology, postmodern or otherwise. But anyone who wants to oppose it must oppose an ideology that makes inertia the most rational response.

This isn't the time to revive Plato's metaphysics, or Socrates' bravado. But it is time to recognize that we have forgotten their basic moral advances. Socrates was the first to insist that we should rise above whatever particular mire happens to grip us, in order to seek something better and truer. He was thereby the first to introduce moral concepts backed by no authority but our own ability to reason. This is why his enemies put him on trial for undermining religion. If religion is fundamentalist, demanding absolute obedience on no other basis than the revelation of a divinity, then Socrates was guilty as charged. His brand of piety meant putting ethics before religion, not the other way around. By insisting on this distinction, Socrates insisted that moral authority is different from religious as well as political authority. Abraham knew that at Sodom, but it was philosophy's task to work out ways in which our concepts should be backed with arguments rather than authority.

There is more than one reason why the left has failed to win contemporary hearts. Many thoughtful writers are working to understand them. Here I have emphasized the role metaphysics has played in that failure: our views of what is real, what is possible, and how humankind can mediate between them. For we are indeed torn. We want a worldview that doesn't blink when confronted with reality, that doesn't wish away what it doesn't wish to see. This is not just pragmatics but pride: Grown-up men and women look the world in its face. At the same time, we want a view that allows us not merely to resign ourselves to the reality that's shaping us, but to play a role in shaping it. And most of us want to do so neither with weapons nor with soft power, but with the real power that the ideas of the Enlightenment once possessed.

'The true strength of our nation comes not from the might of our arms or the scale of our wealth, but from the power of our ideals,' said Barack Obama in his victory speech on November 4, 2008. Nothing soft about that. It came at the end of an empirical proof that idealism can work wonders, for nobody listening that night had reason to expect, twelve months earlier, that this candidate would win. It would not have happened without his ability to reawaken the idealism of millions of Americans. Those who had supported him were not calculating that the average donation of $93 in 2008 would bring them a tax reduction in 2009. Identity politics might have motivated the African-Americans shouting tearstained prayers of thanks that they had lived to see the day (though one dreadlocked young man in Grant Park that night assured me, stamping his foot in joy, that his tears were '*not* because he's black!'). But why were so many white people crying? We wept because the ideals we were taught as children, and had grown to view as hollow, had suddenly been realized. It was bigger than getting rid of the Bush gang, or electing a black man to the world's highest office – wonderful as those things are. It was about virtues like intelligence and integrity, hard work and decency actually doing what they're supposed to: triumphing over their opposites.

Obama's positions, it's often noted, are not traditionally left. But this is not a matter of pragmatic centrism, the recognition of compromise as a necessary part of political bargaining, but a genuine belief that more ground is common than we think. Philosophically, this means giving up the notion of class struggle central to Marx and returning to the notion of community central to Rousseau. Rather than attacking wealthy people as malevolent and exploitative, Rousseau wrote with depth and feeling about the ways in which great extremes of inequality make all of us wretched: the rich man who is forced to barricade himself against robbery and kidnapping lest his property or his life be taken just as much as the poor man who is forced to grovel in the struggle for basic needs. Neither is living with the dignity he deserves – and which could be ours if we structured our societies to serve both of them. That's a thought expressed in a poignant civil rights song which maintained 'All men are slaves till our brothers are free.' A restructured society could be the expression of what Rousseau called the general will – so long as it was produced not through fiat, but the efforts of good grassroots organizing. Obama's own metaphysical commitments were displayed, among other places, in his criticism of influential community organizer Saul Alinsky. 'Alinsky understated the degree to which people's hopes and dreams and their ideals and values were just as important in organizing as people's self-interest,' Obama told one reporter. 'Sometimes the tendency in community organizing was to downplay the power of words and of ideas when in fact ideas and words are pretty powerful. "We hold these truths to be self-evident, all men are created equal." Just words. "I have a dream." Just words. But they help move things. And I think it was partly that understanding that probably led me to try to do something similar in different areas.'

This is a long step away from both Hobbes and Thrasymachus.

While the right has tended to lean toward one, and the left toward the other, their metaphysical bases are not very different. Both are missing something crucial: a philosophical basis for understanding the difference between the actual and the possible, and a framework for getting from one to the other. Although it's a distinction he insists on, Obama, like any politician in office, will fall short of what progressives must hold to be possible. It is up to all of us, internationally, to limit how far is the fall. What is certain, for now, is that language shapes our beliefs about possibility, and Obama's use of language has already been important in shaking up international political assumptions. This opens up ways to think about twenty-first-century political categories that would take us further than left and right. The rest of this book is devoted to getting there.

CHAPTER THREE

FACING GALLOWS

Imagine a man who says temptation overwhelms him whenever he passes what Immanuel Kant called 'a certain house.' (Unlike our own, the eighteenth century was discreet.) No matter what he tells himself beforehand, when he reaches the whorehouse he has to go in. He'd like to be prudent, he'd like to be faithful; perhaps he thinks sex is one thing that doesn't belong on the market. But no tie of love, no fear of disease or shame is stronger than the claims of the flesh. Can we understand him? Easily, says Kant. But what if he knew he would be hanged immediately upon emerging from its sin-sating depths – and a gallows were installed before the brothel to remind him? Suddenly he discovers he can withstand temptation very nicely, thank you. For however bright ordinary desires may be – for sex or wealth or any other form of mortal pleasure – all of them pale before the desire for life itself. This is almost a matter of logic: Without life, no consumption. All the sweets of the world put together cannot weigh against that.

Let the same man be summoned before an unjust ruler, and given a choice. The ruler intends to execute an innocent subject fallen afoul of his regime, but there is still a semblance of law in the land, and it demands the appearance of just procedures. Someone must write a letter denouncing the innocent, bearing false witness to a capital crime. Our roué is asked to do it. Should he refuse, the ruler will make sure he is executed himself.

As in the first case, Kant thinks it's easy to imagine being in this fellow's shoes. But unlike the first case, we suddenly waver: *We do not know what we would do*. Kant always emphasized the limits of knowledge, and one thing we never know for certain is the inside of our souls. None of us is so righteous as to be sure not to crumble in the face of death or torture. Most of us probably would. But all of us know what we *should* do: Refuse to write the letter though it cost our own lives. And all of us know that we *could* do just that – whether or not we would totter in the end. In this moment, says Kant, we know our own freedom, in a breath of awe and wonder. Not pleasure, but justice can move human beings to deeds that overcome the strongest of animal desires, the love of life itself. And contemplating this is as dizzying as contemplating the heavens above us: With this kind of power, we are as infinite as they are.

Kant says this sort of example is simple enough to be grasped by 'businessmen, women, and ten-year-old schoolboys.' Change the terms as you want to: He seems to be right. It's a thought experiment nearly anyone can make, and the answers are surprisingly similar. You may want to vary the example. Writing letters is easy – so easy, in fact, that *desk murderer* became the German word for Nazi bureaucrats like Adolf Eichmann. Putting marks on paper is so far removed from the violence that takes life that many people could swallow their qualms about doing so even though they could not execute the violent act itself. When I taught this example in a Yale ethics course, one student insisted he knew perfectly well what he'd do. He was a coward, he wanted to live, and he would sign any number of unjust letters to do so. Indeed, he claimed he would do anything. We fenced for a while until I upped the ante: Was he certain he could kill children, if ordered, to save his own life? With machine guns? Machetes? He wavered. We know it has happened: Perhaps the most awful reports from contemporary Third World wars are those describing children who were given the choice to hack up other children, or be destroyed themselves. Some of them didn't do it.

What's the point of this example? It's the only answer the leading modern philosopher ever gave to the leading moral question philosophers are routinely asked. Is anything absolutely right, or absolutely wrong – and if so, how would I know it? Kant offers the example at a crucial juncture in the *Critique of Practical Reason*, just when readers hope he's about to give them a proof that the moral law is true. Those hopes are bound to be disappointed. For moral principles are never true. Truth is a matter of the way the world is; morality is a matter of the way the world ought to be. To know whether a claim is true, you must find out if it corresponds to a reality that is fixed independently of anyone's dreams and nightmares. Sometimes you need only look out the window to see whether my claim that 'snow is white' is correct. In harder cases, the process may be so long and complex that some theorists prefer to give up talk of correspondence altogether. But however hard it may be to find out whether a statement corresponds to the world, the processes used in deciding claims like 'snow is white' are different from the ones used to decide that 'slavery is wrong.' Strictly speaking, *right* cannot be a matter of knowledge, though it's often the thing we want to know most of all. Yet it's wrong to conclude with Thrasymachus that ideas of right are therefore unreal. For ideals – ideas of what is right – can be practical: When we use them as orientation, we can use them to change reality itself.

I will argue that the distinction between *is* and *ought* is the most important one we ever draw. If morality is never a matter of fact, trying to convince moral skeptics with objective proofs is senseless. Nor should we be urged to live rightly because it's in our self-interest to do so. Such arguments leave us helpless whenever morality and self-interest part company; in the times when they don't, we don't need morality to move us.

Then how do you answer the skeptic who asks why he should be moral? Kant says you do it by talking about heroes: those who risk their lives rather than resign themselves to injustice. The Abraham who challenged God at Sodom and Gomorrah is the sort of hero Kant had in mind. He had nothing to gain, and everything to lose, and he did not let injustice go unchallenged. 'Here virtue is worth so much because it costs so much.' Anyone can think of false heroes: people who did the right thing for the wrong reasons, or the wrong thing for the right reasons, and died with an air of unearned glory. We cannot be certain that any person in particular, in history or fiction, really acted from pure love of justice, and deflating other people's heroes is easy enough. But when we engage in such discussions, each of us will imagine one person, at least, who we believe defied death to do what was right: Your hero's motives may have been vain or petty, but my hero's were beyond reproach. Holding on to the image of one such person is a way of preserving an image of humanity, for such examples provide a glimpse of human dignity nothing else can replace – and lift us out of the world of sense into realms more exalted.

This kind of rhetoric might make you nervous. At the very least, a plea for intoxication from the most sober of philosophers may seem hopelessly dated, a relic of the time when children were raised on tales from Plutarch's *Lives*. For the record, Kant's discussion of heroes was obsolete in 1786, and he knew it. Even Stoic circles thought they'd make less headway by emphasizing the sublimity of virtue than by underlining its advantages. But Kant's kind of example does what theirs cannot: It shows beyond doubt that morality is possible. For most ordinary questions that confront us mix ethics with self-interest. Do you pay your taxes because cheating on them is wrong, or because the revelation that you hadn't could compromise your career? Paying up looks the same in both cases, and motives are the sort of things we never know for sure. Fortunately many things that are right will also make us happy. The satisfied mind that Stoics thought so important that it outweighed all others is only one of the advantages that being virtuous usually brings. Self-interest and virtue coincide very often

– just not often enough to call them identical, and to collapse virtue into self-interest. Most empirically and secularly minded people still persist in trying to equate them anyway. The more they find examples where acting rightly furthers (their own and other people's) interests, the more they feel they have succeeded in pushing back the realm of the transcendental. In fact, it's a realm they depend on. For any good empiricist can count cases in which acting rightly does *not* further your interest. To insure it all comes right in the end you must believe in a deus ex machina, patiently weaving the threads of history so that the right action that got you into trouble somehow gets rewarded in the end. Reducing virtuous behavior to self-interested behavior requires so many extra metaphysical assumptions that it's easier to assume that it doesn't, and simply be grateful when it does.

Kant is usually portrayed as a dour and puritanical defender of virtue so pure that it shouldn't be enjoyed. In fact, Kant *wants* virtue to lead to happiness just as much as anyone else does. He simply tells the truth: that it often does not. Just because they are tragic, such cases give us something no others can. In a chilling 1945 essay about German guilt, Hannah Arendt wrote:

> Whether any person in Germany is a Nazi or an anti-Nazi can be determined only by the One who knows the secrets of the human heart, which no human eye can penetrate. At any rate, those who actively organized an anti-Nazi underground movement today would meet a speedy death if they failed to act and talk precisely like Nazis ... The most extreme slogan which this war has evoked among the Allies, that the only 'good German' is a 'dead German,' has this much basis in fact: the only way in which we can identify an anti-Nazi is when the Nazis have hanged him. There is no other reliable token.

Only life-and-death examples can show us that action for moral reasons is possible: When we consider a hero we have to stop short. To be sure, you can go to the scaffold with mixed motives, too, but at some point doubt will end. 'What's absolute,' says Cornel West, 'is what I'm willing to die for.'

The gallows example yields one thought experiment anybody can perform; ergo, the moral law. It's the universality of the experiment that carries its weight. For it's an answer to conservative critics, today as in the past, who believe the mass of humanity is driven by crude desires. Perhaps, they argue, a few great souls act on moral principles. (Thrasymachus would deny even that.) But most of us have nothing more noble in view than bread and circuses. Our appetites for variety of gluttony and entertainment remain nearly insatiable, and nothing else really moves us. If our lives revolve around consuming the objects of these simple passions, a benevolent despotism that manages those passions is the best form of government. We care about getting stuff, and distraction from pain; they care about getting it to us. Who could possibly complain?

This argument has been used to defend despotism in the past, and then as now it depended on the premise that people don't want to be free, but happy. If Kant's thought experiment works, the consequences are great. As part of the good life we want all kinds of pleasure, but we want something more: a sense of our own dignity that allows us to deny pleasure itself if it violates something we hold higher. Of course wanting dignity isn't the same as having it; many a sweet, lazy dream of something grander remains just that. But if most of us can imagine wanting to be Kant's hero, even for a moment, then a government that appeals to our best instincts can't be dismissed out of hand. If each of us envisions a moment in which we want to show our freedom by standing on the side of justice, each of us should work toward a world in which freedom and justice are paramount. The bread and the circuses would take care of themselves.

Each of us? Kant never traveled forty miles from his native Königsberg, and got his information about other places from books and seamen's tales. Our sense of universality is stronger. We can imagine this thought experiment producing similar results in the most dissimilar people: antiapartheid activists in Soweto, for example, and antiabortion activists in Texas; orange-draped revolutionaries in the Ukraine, and firefighters in New York; mujahideen, and members of Pakistan's parliament.

Pakistan isn't entirely accidental. I chose it because of all the images of Islamic fundamentalism broadcast in the West since 9/11, one from Pakistan struck me hardest. It's a photo my local paper showed of two women veiled in white cloth with holes just large enough to reveal their very thoughtful eyes. Even this is enough to reveal quite different expressions. One looks down with something like sadness; her muted gaze suggests awareness of how hard her road will be. A sympathetic observer would call her wise, at least; a little imagination would call it the glance of a madonna. Her companion's gaze is another entirely. The eyes are fixed forward, up and unwavering, determined to endure whatever it takes to reach the end she sees as clearly as you see this page. Depending on your perspective, you will find her glance frighteningly fanatic – or a picture of courage. Both women wear glasses, and the newspaper caption identifies them as members of parliament, come to power as part of a coalition of radical Islamists who in 2003 won the greatest victory in the history of Pakistan.

We know it isn't the downtrodden who have swelled the ranks of Islamic fundamentalists. The bitterest opponents of Western civilization are not largely those who have been shut out of its fruits; most new recruits are well educated and well off. Empirical studies of radical fundamentalism undermine strict materialist explanations. Those who turn to fundamentalism are not the earth's most wretched, or those who have nothing else to turn to. As anthropologist Scott Atran summarizes, 'In fact, study after study finds suicide terrorists and supporters to be more educated and economically well-off than surrounding populations. They also tend to be well-adjusted in their families, liked by their peers, and – according to interrogators – sincerely compassionate to those they see themselves as helping.' In the process of creating a global jihadi database under a Defense Department contract, Atran interviewed hundreds of supporters of jihadism. He concludes that the jihadi story is far more likely to appeal to 'bright and idealist Muslim youth than the marginalized and dispossessed.' His conclusions are echoed by most other researchers. Saad Eddin Ibrahim, sociologist at the American University in Cairo, described Islamic recruits of the 1970s as 'model young Egyptians. If they were not typical, it was because they were significantly above the average in their generation.' Lawrence Wright's Pulitzer Prize-winning *The Looming Tower* states that besides their urbanity, cosmopolitan backgrounds, and computer skills, Al Qaeda recruits share a fondness for Arnold Schwarzenegger films.

The men who came to train in Afghanistan in the 1990s were not impoverished social failures. As a group, they mirrored the 'model young Egyptians' who formed the terrorist groups that Saad Eddin Ibraham had studied in the early eighties. Most of the prospective Al Qaeda recruits were from the middle or upper class, nearly all of them from intact families. They were largely college-educated, with a strong bias toward the natural sciences and engineering. Few of them were products of the religious schools; indeed many had trained in Europe or the U.S. and spoke as many as five or six languages. They did not show signs of mental disorders. Many were not even very religious when they joined the jihad.

Such conclusions haunted me as I contemplated the picture of the two women, while imagining the logistical challenge of negotiating burka and glasses. I still don't know how the glasses stay on, but there's no more radical way to enslave one's head from the outside than the way these women have chosen. One look at what can be seen of their faces leaves no doubt this was a choice made with open eyes.

What does it give them? Not easy answers to the problems of life in a complex world, or some other such condescending description. Here and there a bumpkin may be consoled for any amount of misery by visions of seventy-two dark-eyed virgins in paradise, or whatever the equivalent reward for female mujahideen would be. But neither the ability to endure, nor the ability to kill and die, is normally born from such crude calculations. For his recent film *Suicide Killers*, French filmmaker Pierre Rehov interviewed would-be terrorists whose bombs had failed to explode. 'Every single one of them,' he relates, 'tried to convince me that it was the right thing to do for moralistic reasons. These are kids who want to do good.' Atran writes that 'all leaders of jihadi groups that I have interviewed tell me that if anyone ever came to them seeking martyrdom to gain virgins in paradise, the door would be slammed in their face.' Rather, some forms of life serve as their own reward, for they meet deep desires not fulfilled by anything else. Forced to choose between cynicism and madness, many people will reject cynicism.

You might call Pakistan a special case, since Islamist victories there were fed by anger at Musharraf's unpopular government. But every case is special, one way or another, and there's no reason for opposition to corrupt military regimes to take the form of taking the veil. The truth is that despite increasing and sometimes excellent research on the subject, we are still a long way from understanding the rise of radical religious movements in recent years.

The language of sacrifice seemed on its way to anachronism; in the 1990s, risk was something you took on the stock market. Kant's gallows example looked obsolete. Post-Cold War consensus was that ideologies were over, and if people had acted according to ideals in the past, they weren't going to do so in the future. Now it turns out that many of them still do. Perhaps you would sign the letter and let an innocent man go to the gallows. You might not be willing to die for an idea, but you could easily be blown up by someone who is.

Predictably, most reactions to this revelation have been focused along political lines. Much of the right reacted to Islamic fundamentalism by claiming, 'They hate us for our freedoms.' A little later, Islamic fundamentalists were described as fascist, which had the double advantage of sounding vaguely scientific while beating the drums for the last war of which Americans and their allies can be unequivocally proud. Anybody in the business of fighting fascism can do no wrong. The left was not much better. Its residual Marxism pointed to the material conditions in which fundamentalisms grow – an appeal considerably weakened by the fact that those most oppressed and exploited were not the ones who have got (much) religion. At this point many liberals tend to throw up their hands and conclude that fundamentalists simply belong to the forces of darkness that were never overcome. Some radical secularists think those drawn to fundamentalism just haven't heard the message, and devote books and conferences to shouting the secularist creed a little louder. For others, the rise of radical fundamentalism, whether in Afghanistan or in Texas, is just one more nail in the coffin of the Enlightenment. Concluding that its light was too feeble to perform the task of rooting out religion, they cannot imagine anything else more effective. Thoughts like these easily lead to the darker views of writers like Hans Magnus Enzensberger, who in 1993 predicted the growth of terrorism driven by no vision of another world, but by sheer lust for the destruction of the present one. He believes the past decade only confirms his view: Suicide terrorists are nihilists who make Russian youths of a bygone era seem like models of moral principle. Contemporary terrorists, by contrast, want to destroy for no other reason than the fact that they cannot create. In Britain, novelist Martin Amis echoed these sentiments when calling Islamism '. . . illusion upon illusion. It is not merely violent in tendency. Violence is all there is.'

These standpoints reduce the possibilities for understanding funda-mentalism to few alternatives. There's the clash-of-civilizations model, which sees fundamentalists as relentlessly driven by a resent-ment toward our values that nothing can alter. In addition to offering no possibilities for resolution besides military ones, this model requires that we overlook any similarities between our fundamentalists and their fundamentalists. Testifying before Congress, Rand Corporation terrorism expert Brian M. Jenkins's analogy underscored this:

'Unless we can impede radicalization and recruitment, then we are condemned to a strategy of stepping on cockroaches one at a time.' Every comparative study of terrorism insists, on the contrary, that we belong to the same species. Louise Richardson, author of *What Terrorists Want*, argues that terrorists are highly rational actors with considered goals and calculations. 'The viewpoint of the terrorist is rational, he sacrifices himself for something higher. Here there is no great difference to soldiers who have been sacrificing themselves for their fatherlands for centuries.' Scholars such as Jessica Stern and Hans Juergensmayer have confirmed this by interviewing terrorists whose commitments range from global jihad to outlawing abortion to establishing a Greater Israel on the West Bank.

The materialist model often used to explain these similarities depends on false consciousness. It views fundamentalists as focused on the pie in the sky the next world may offer to compensate for their hunger in this one, although nowadays religious fundamentalists are sure to provide snacks to keep the faithful sustained on the journey as well. Barbara Ehrenreich describes how religious institutions have developed to fulfill material and social needs that secular cultures have neither met nor extinguished. In one giant Virginia church that is full every night of the week, 'dozens of families and teenagers enjoy a low-priced dinner in the cafeteria; a hundred unemployed people meet for prayer and job tips at the "Career Ministry"; divorced and abused women gather in support groups. Among its many services, MBC distributes free clothing to 10,000 poor people a year, helped start an inner-city ministry for at-risk youth in DC and operates a special-needs ministry for disabled children.' Ehrenreich rightly compares the network of social services – and the resulting political power – such churches provide with the miniature welfare state Hamas offered needy Palestinians before it was voted into power. She finds it particularly insidious that the Christian right advances by offering its own welfare state while attacking the scant public one that remains, and she urges the left to provide alternative services, as it did on smaller scale in the 1960s.

I share her concerns and admire many of her analyses. If soup kitchens and homeless shelters were no longer needed, if genuinely equal opportunities offered vistas to inner-city youth instead of despair, if medical care was not considered a benefit but a right, we would have gone a long way toward meeting the fundamental human needs that most Western cultures now leave to chance. There's no doubt that working toward these goals should be a matter of national priority. Still, there's no reason to think that meeting them would remove the motivation for fundamentalism. The fact that nationally as well as internationally, fundamentalist revivals are rarely fueled by the most disadvantaged leaves such explanations in doubt.

Against all we expected, the past decade has seen one part of the world after another reject a worldview based on the bottom line: the idea that material needs are what moves us, and everything else is expendable froth. Part of what's being rejected is just hypocrisy: an international finance system that forces poor countries to open their doors to the free market while allowing rich ones to close theirs; a superpower whose commitments to democracy evaporate when dictators better suit its interests. But even where standard principles of free-market capitalism and liberal democracy are actually followed, many people feel they're not enough.

Conservative author Dinesh D'Souza was justly criticized for his recent book *The Enemy at Home*, but he was honest enough to acknowledge that the similarities between Islamic and Christian fundamentalism were not just an invention of left-wing critics. Rather, 'The right-wing Christian movement has the courage to pursue the logic of Bush-era conservativism all the way to the end.' The deepest contemporary political divide is not on matters of economics, but between the polar values of authority and autonomy. D'Souza's stupendous claim that the American left was responsible for 9/11 obscured what he called his central point, that 'the culture war and the war on terror are not separate and distinct but one and the same.' D'Souza believes that the left 'wants America to be a shining beacon of depravity, a kind of Gomorrah on the Hill,' and argues that the right should give up on finding common ground with Western liberals. Instead, he thinks they should make alliances with traditional Islamists who share their critique of American society as 'a collection of casinos, supermarkets and whorehouses linked together by endless highways passing through nowhere.' In the words of his most quoted sentence, 'Yes, I would rather go to a baseball game or have a drink with Michael Moore than with the grand mufti of Egypt. But when it comes to core beliefs, I'd have to confess that I'm closer to the dignified fellow in the long robe and prayer beads than to the slovenly fellow in the baseball cap.' One of the many problems with D'Souza's argument is its neglect of the fact that traditional religious cultures are based on revelation and authority. Islamic, Christian, and Jewish fundamentalists have indeed deep tendencies in common: None will challenge Abraham's silent submission at Mount Moriah. None is likely to concede much further truth in the sacred texts of the other, but D'Souza is right to argue that many who turn to traditional religion as a rejection of contemporary consumer culture are seeking something similar. I have argued, in addition, that they are seeking something noble that the left often ignores. According to Orwell, the problem is long-standing. In his 1937 book *The Road to Wigan Pier*, he wrote:

> Socialists have, so to speak, presented their case wrong side foremost. They have never made it sufficiently clear that the essential aims of Socialism are justice and liberty. With their eyes glued to economic facts, they have proceeded on the assumption that man has no soul, and explicitly or implicitly they have set up the goal of a materialistic Utopia. As a result Fascism has been able to play upon every instinct that revolts against hedonism and a cheap conception of 'progress.'

Where materialist explanations come to an end, contemporary liberals are left with nothing but gloom. Here again the left retains the materialism of Marxism without its visions of transformation.

The right, by contrast, has views. They may be simplistic in their understanding and violent in their consequences, but they are views. Some of them even resemble explanations. The left has little to provide but the grim and condescending suggestion that most people have always been duped. Not long ago, anyone who concluded that the majority of humankind was naturally doomed to stupidity and blindness would gravitate to a conservative movement. Today it's more likely to be the left that, dismayed by the rise of religious fervor, has nothing to offer but one or another echo of a sideshow con man. If a sucker is really born every minute, efforts to enlighten them at the rate we are going are hopeless.

I believe that many people are drawn to fundamentalism in search of a vision of human nature far closer to the Enlightenment imagination than what's offered in postmodern culture. Is the Enlightenment too weak to provide an alternative to fundamentalism? We will not know without a better understanding of both. At the moment we do not even know all the needs fundamentalism fulfills. To understand why the Enlightenment did not lead to the abolition of religion, we need to bring to evangelical revivals at least the respect for meaning that, say, the great anthropologist Clifford Geertz brought to Balinese cockfights. At present, most secularists' comments on the revival of religious traditions treat it with a contempt they would be ashamed to show toward other cultures.

The most common explanation for the turn to religion is that it fulfills new needs for certainty: In a complex and confusing world, where every point in a person's identity is up for grabs, people grasp at old straws to keep, for a moment, from drowning. This can be put in the sophisticated prose of the social sciences, but it's no more than a version of the sort of claim found sprinkled in George W. Bush's addresses: 'What every terrorist fears most is human freedom.' What both the left and the right imagine here is a golden Middle Ages, in which religion formed the rock on which all else stood fast. Like a symmetrical pyramid, the truths of religion ordained and implied the general truths of morality, from which, in turn, everything else could be inferred: how you should be born and how you should die and every part of your public and private worlds in between. But we need only describe this fantasy to discard it: Nobody ever believed in a structure of knowledge that stable and secure. The seventeenth-century German philosopher Leibniz formulated something like it as a goal precisely because he thought it would lead to the end of the religious wars tearing through the principalities that made up his Europe. He never got far with the project, nor found anyone willing to follow him. Indeed, he was ridiculed by Voltaire, and anyone else who appreciated how uncertain religion had made the world.

Some parts of pre-modern life were usually clear: where people would live, for example, and how they would make a living. Barring the intrusion of disaster, most people's choices were the same as their parents' had been. But besides place and profession, not much else was fixed. God may have reigned supreme (though atheists challenged His existence very early), but His nature was the subject of debate more complex and passionate than anything we now entertain. Was He benevolent, and if so, how to explain the suffering in His Creation? Was He all-powerful, and if so, how to explain all its flaws? Was He one, or two, or several beings, and how were their natures related? Was He perhaps indifferent, or even malevolent? On the threshold of the Enlightenment, God was variously compared to a vain and heartless mother, a cruelly narcissistic father, a hapless infant, a doddering old fool, and an ostrich – for starters. It's enough to make Nietzsche's claim that He was merely dead sound almost timid. Most important, it shows us how very unstable the rock-solid foundation really was. Armies of men, and any number of individuals, slaughtered one another regularly to prove one position or another. Some absolute certainty.

If religious truths were hardly stable, neither were any of the other truths thought to follow from them. In particular, moral truths were neither inevitable nor obvious. Nihilists who want to give up values because they think the bottom has fallen out of them have a phantom vision of what bottoms do. Even if it were good theory, foundationalism was never much use in practice. Western religious strife may have been muted since the Peace of Westphalia, but the violence of recent conflicts between Shi'ia and Sunni reminds us that bedrock conviction in the truth of your religion may cause more political problems than it solves.

If not peace, did foundations provide meaning? It's often said that the revival of religion meets human needs for meaning: fixing our place in the world and telling a story that gives sense to what are often brief and painful lives. Fundamentalist religion does lend meaning, but this is too broad and general a service to explain much of anything, or to give any cues about what else might do so as well. Nor is it enough to say that religious communities provide the sense of connectedness largely absent in the contemporary Western world. These claims are true enough, but the one I'm proposing is more controversial. Secular observers view fundamentalism as a way of making believers' lives both easier and more passive. It's a view that's both condescending and dangerous, for it doesn't grasp the fundamentalist appeal. Its religions offer rules that make some decisions easier, and no doubt that's one reason why many people are drawn to them. But there are deeper reasons that must be faced head-on. It turns out that part of what people often want is responsibility for their lives. Religion doesn't only make people passive, by shouldering some of the burdens of decision; it makes them feel more active as well. The window of transcendence it opens onto the everyday is an injection of spirit into a world of sluggish torpor.

Metaphors have long lives, and Marx's description of religion as the opium of the people helped mislead us all. In fact, though Marx was the first thinker to show how deeply our worldviews may be shaped by material needs, his views of religion are more complex, and less condescending, than those of most critics who followed. Far from reducing religious needs to economic ones, Marx called the criticism of religion the first premise of all other criticism because he understood religion's power. Here's what he actually says in the passage leading up to the famous one-liner:

> Religion is the general theory of the world, its encyclopedia, its logic in popular form, its spiritualistic *point d'honneur*, its enthusiasm, its moral sanction, its solemn complement, and the general ground for the consummation and justification of this world . . . Religious suffering is at once the expression of real suffering and the protest against real suffering. Religion is the sigh of the oppressed creature, the heart of a heartless world, just as it is the spirit of spiritless conditions. It is the *opium* of the people.

Sitting in the local library, Marx may have got his drugs wrong. In his account, religion is anything but a sedative; it sounds more like cocaine. In Marx's description, religion is the force that keeps the world awake. *Heart of a heartless world* calls up love as well as courage; hearts are also sometimes seats of purity, another quality one longs for when one longs for faith. But saccharin allegories aside, anatomically speaking, the heart is an organ that keeps us alive.

Marx's judgment of the forces arrayed against religion was just as savvy as his judgment of its power. His description of what capitalism did to the world it found might, with few changes, have been written by religious believers in Afghanistan – or Arkansas:

> The bourgeois . . . drowned the most heavenly ecstasies of religious fervor . . . in the icy water of egotistical calculation. It has resolved personal worth into exchange value, and in place of the numberless indefeasible chartered freedoms, has set up that single, unconscionable freedom – Free Trade . . . All that is solid melts into air, all that is holy is profaned.

Of course this is irony, and verbal acrobatics, but it's also ambivalence. Marx's attitude toward the religious standpoint is not really one of scorn. Something fateful was lost when bourgeois calculation replaced religious devotion, and we are right to feel bereaved. Marx's ambivalence toward the holy is echoed in contemporary critics of globalization from the left as well as from fundamentalist forces on the right. As the freedom to buy cell phones or sneakers expands from Boston to Beijing, something within us contracts; the price of this world is an absence of soul. You don't need to have a political direction to view the process with disgust, and yearning. Whether out of disgust for principles preached but not practiced, or for principles one would rather not practice at all, the cry for a heart in this heartless world grows louder every day.

It's at this point that religion and morality meet and join hands. Theirs need not be a cynical alliance. Some crude critics suggest that religion handles morality like a prod or a whip, producing the behavior it seeks through a series of bribes and threats. But this is the abuse of morality, not its essence. However often priests of one sort or another may have mobilized their flocks with promises about heaven and warnings about hell, such manipulation is political, and therefore incidental to the realms of both religion and morality. Nor does religion make moral choice transparent. Whatever pictures may be colored by nostalgia and longing, religion makes life neither safe nor easy.

It does make it meaningful in the way only dignity can, and this is one point where religion has deep moral roots. Looked at from the outside, religious fundamentalists deliver themselves into the hands of authority: Faith offers them freedom from decisions and leaves their lives determined by someone else. The vision of a Being commanding obedience *no matter what* seems a vision of relief. Looked at from the inside, faith itself is a choice, and it means rejecting a life determined by the rules of buying and selling that frame consumer culture. Even those of us who are aware of those rules find them hard to escape. Suppose you get your news from America's most serious daily newspaper. Be perfectly honest. Paging through the *New York Times*, which really feels more urgent: the genocide in Darfur, or the next Macy's sale? Try as I may to alter it, I know what gets my attention.

The Cold War was fought on common ground, as if capitalism

had said to Marxism: We'll beat you on your own turf. *You want materialism? We'll show you materialism!* Flooding the markets with better stuff for the masses to yearn for was an ironic bow to the worst features of Marxist metaphysics, but though both systems can numb our spirits, neither can quite satisfy or kill them. In Marx's time it made more sense to connect religion with quietism: When cultural and political frameworks were structured in religious terms, it required considerably more effort to chart a course without them. Today the balance is almost reversed: In cultures where the status quo is secular, it's religious life that demands constant choice. For those who decide to risk or take their lives, that choice becomes the highest proof of freedom. Kant's gallows show that this choice is neither esoteric nor irrational. The sense being sought is entirely comprehensible: We want to determine the world, not merely be determined by it; we want to stand above the things we may want to consume. You can call this the urge for transcendence, so long as you don't call it mystical. We are born and we die as part of nature, but we feel most alive when we go beyond it. And we go beyond it often – every time, as we'll see, we explore the world instead of simply taking it in. As I will argue, even your ability to ask why something happened one way rather than another depends on principles that are never known from experience, but demand that you go beyond it. To emphasize our need for a dignity that cannot be bought or sold is not to say we cannot live without it. We can. As history all too dismally reminds us, dignity is a need of human nature we may choose to disregard. But human life gains meaning in opposition to experience: To be human is to refuse to accept the given as given.

Genuine religion and morality unite in the determination to hold out for something better than the world we know – or possibly can even imagine. This is the messianic impulse, but it's an impulse that insists on a messiah who never comes. Kant called one moment in Jewish thought sublime: its prohibition on images of God. It thereby tries to imagine the sacred without lingering on anything tangible. Similarly, Kant rejected attempts to embellish morality with material advantages. Instead of making morality attractive, advantage weighs it down – when what we wanted morality to do was to make us fly.

To be human is to have needs for transcendence over the brute and shiny objects of experience, needs that both religion and morality at their best fulfill. Skeptical readers will see those needs as ways we've been duped. But the idea that religion lulls us into enduring a miserable present for the sake of a make-believe future depends too much on the opium metaphor to stand. Rather, the urge for transcendence expresses two drives. One is to criticize the present in the name of the future, to keep longing alive for ideas the world has yet to see. The other is to prove our freedom, and dignity, by having a hand in bringing those ideals about through some form of human creativity. Far from being soporific or sheeplike, this is an urge to be so active that it comes dangerously close to challenging the Creator Himself.

This means there are deep connections between Kant's hero, who is willing to die for an ideal of justice, and contemporary suicide terrorists. Of course the latter are determined to kill others in pursuit of their ideals. Starting from the same willingness to sacrifice their own interests for the sake of something greater, they go on to sacrifice others. They may believe they are acting in God's service; in fact they are acting in His stead. And unlike the God of Abraham, the one they worship has no qualms about collateral damage. From the perspective of the victims and those who love them, this will be all the difference in the world. But while focusing on the fundamentalist terrorists' willingness to kill for ideals, we have paid too little attention to their willingness to die for them.

To be sure, some have always viewed the present life as the gateway to a future one, and look to a martyr's death as the quickest way of passing from one to another. This has driven Shiites to bomb markets in Baghdad just as surely as it has driven Christians to bomb abortion clinics in Florida. If this is indeed your worldview, there's nothing nobler about your willingness to blow yourself up than my willingness to undergo a root canal; both are brief and painful trials that have to be endured to get to an enduring, better state. But for many of the faithful, the willingness to die for an idea is much less instrumental. Where everything else can be explained away by interest, the willingness to give up your life may seem your only chance to live it in dignity. In her book *Terror in the Name of God*, political scientist Jessica Stern writes:

> It is part of human nature to desire transcendence – the kind of peak experience that most of us encounter all too rarely through contemplation of beauty, love or prayer. As odd as it sounds, a sense of transcendence is one of many attractions of religious violence for terrorists, beyond the appeal of achieving their goals. More broadly, it is not just the accomplishment of their goals that terrorists seek; it is also the act of pursuing them.

The most acute discussions of Islamic terrorism have focused on wounded dignity. Muslim cultures have been the object of particular humiliation. Once far superior to Europe in any measure of science or civilization, the Islamic world has fallen steadily behind. To what extent this humiliation is the product of prejudice is a matter of much debate, but the experience itself is clear: The rage-soaked language of young Muslim men, in particular, is the demand to reclaim lost dignity. (The demands and the language are twisted and bitter, but that's what losing dignity means.) If Muslim history has a particular experience of humiliation, the needs for dignity are those we all share. In studying the common ground between religious terrorists in fundamentalist Jewish, Christian, and Muslim communities, Stern and others emphasize the centrality of the experience of humiliation. What's missing is the sense that they, as individuals, can transcend the framework they were given. Where every other action can be explained by reference to factors that are determined and given outside you, only the willingness to sacrifice your life can prove that your freedom is real. The French writer

Stendhal wrote that nothing confers honor like a death sentence, for it's the only thing that cannot be bought. This impulse is not unique to cultures with monotheistic religions. Until the war in Iraq, the greatest number of suicide terrorists were found in the Tamil Tigers, whose ideology of liberation is as fiercely secular as it is proudly nationalist. And the starkest statement of this impulse was offered by Japanese psychoanalyst Takeo Doi: 'For the Japanese, freedom in practice existed only in death.'

I have argued that the impulse behind much religious terrorism is neither instrumental (martyrdom as the quickest trip to paradise) nor nihilistic (a general urge to maximum destruction in a world where creation seems futile). Rather, it is often rooted in the same impulse that has always fueled the desire for heroism: the desire for transcendence, or the refusal to stay mired in a world where everything is negotiable. This is neither irrational nor mystical but simply the desire to experience the sort of freedom that makes us feel most alive. What looks like a longing for death is less a crude desire to enter another world than a desire to overcome the constraints of this one.

But this is precisely the sort of conclusion that makes some people's hair stand on end. If suicide terrorists can be seen as acting on impulses we view as heroic, shouldn't we abandon the heroic itself? Instead of transcendental values, shouldn't we appeal to material ones? While they may provide only the lowest common denominator, it's a denominator on which all can agree. Better to be vulgar and innocuous than sublime and deadly. Few things command more consensus these days than the idea that the path to global peace lies in abandoning strongly held beliefs, whether moral or religious, in favor of increasing consumption. Even if you've never been inside a Middle East marketplace, all it takes is a picture of fused-together scrap iron and body parts in the wake of a suicide bombing to begin to believe that anything that prevents moral passion this destructive has got to be preferable to it. Let those whose lives are untouched by mutilation and murder worry about life without soul.

If consumerism really were successful, it might indeed be preferable. But increasingly, people in many parts of the world refuse to be treated like children who can be distracted from quarrels by dangling trinkets. Shimon Peres's vision of a Middle East in which people were too busy trading to fight was proposed during the negotiations for the Oslo Accords, but we are further from it today than ever. In a presentation to the National Security Council, Scott Atran reported that controlled experiments from Israel to Indonesia showed political and economic proposals for resolving conflict to be not only insufficient, but counterproductive. In those experiments, people respond to the suggestion that they trade moral for material values with outrage, and even disgust. (Suppose you were coolly asked to relieve your financial pressures by selling your child into slavery?) Atran shows that in contrast, apologies for past injustice – even more than reparations – can be more significant than any material compensation for making peace.

Perhaps you think this natural in traditional societies, where notions of honor have not yet been entirely replaced by the dull but calculable hand of capitalist achievement. All the more reason to speed up the process of globalization, in which all other values will be replaced by market ones. (In recent years China has adopted Christmas lights, Santa statues, and gift buying as a measure of what's considered being modern. Apparently they have yet to be informed that no modern Western Christmas is complete without a televised discussion of whether Christmas has lost its meaning.) But despite all efforts to the contrary, we have seen this approach fail as thoroughly in midwestern suburbs as in Middle Eastern slums. Thomas Frank's bestselling *What's the Matter with Kansas?* described how one part of the nation was slowly transformed from left-wing vanguard to a centerpiece of red-state populism. Time after time, Kansans voted for Republican candidates whose policies undermined their own economic well-being – all for the sake of the vague set of issues they called 'values.'

A number of social scientists have raised empirical challenges to Frank's account, but these are not my present concern. As elsewhere in this book, my interest is in the unexamined philosophical assumptions that animate our views. It's clear that cheap electoral politics, disinformation, and distraction often play a role. Particularly when government officials fail to display the virtues they use to beat electoral drums, the results can be maddening. But to suppose that Kansans and their cohorts were merely manipulated is as condescending as it is dogmatic. Though Frank never states it, his discussion rests on a concept of economic rationality that takes us back to historical materialism. His book begins with a friend's question: 'How can anyone who has ever worked for anyone else vote Republican?' Her question, Frank writes, 'is apt; it is, in many ways, the preeminent question of our times. People getting their fundamental interests wrong is what American political life is all about. This species of derangement is the bedrock of our civic order; it is the foundation on which all else rests.' Frank's descriptions can make his fellow midwesterners sound positively unhinged:

> Strip today's Kansans of their job security and they head out and become registered Republicans. Push them off the land and the next thing you know they're protesting in front of abortion clinics. Squander their life savings and there's good chance they'll join the John Birch Society.

On this view, Kansans – and Oklahomans, and the like – are suffering from what used to be called false consciousness: Instead of acting on their real (that is, economic) interests, they were fooled into supporting an ideology (that is, a lie) that actually works against them. The assumption behind that, once again, is metaphysical: Ideas are illusions, and only the stuff of which things are made is real. If you pursue the latter, you are hardheaded, realistic, and rational. If you ever give the former priority, you are weak minded, or even deranged: at worst a fanatic, and at best a fool.

This is not to deny that material well-being is crucial, and perhaps Brecht was right about timing: Largely because it provides certain forms of independence, the grub should come first. A measure of economic security is part of what John Rawls called the basis of self-respect. The Nobel Prize given to India's Grameen Bank for its microlending enterprises focused recent attention on the ways in which even very small economic independence provides poor people with a measure of dignity. But just this example shows that what's at issue is not full bellies, but upright heads. Aid programs that offer only handouts have very different results from development programs that offer a chance at autonomy. Those who ignore their economic interests to vote on matters of individual conscience may often be misguided, but that doesn't mean they are deluded. For many people *insist* on voting for ideals that are larger than their own individual interests. They ignore bread-and-butter questions because they do not want to live on bread alone.

So are they choosing opium? Sometimes. Turning attention from earthly to heavenly matters is one form of distraction from the facts on the ground, and there have always been politicians willing to exploit religion for cynical ends. There's no doubt we should improve the economic options of young people tempted by fundamentalism, whether in Kansas or Khartoum. But none of this will matter if we cannot repopulate their dreams.

Being an ideal is no guarantee for being good. You needn't think about jihad, or the Chinese Cultural Revolution, to confirm this; even the ordinary-looking fellow running amok at the local mall was likely triggered by a concept of honor. But the fact that ideals can be perverted doesn't mean we can do without them; if our need for transcendence isn't satisfied by the right kind of ideals, we may turn to the wrong ones. Count all the ways that love can be perverted; still, the urge to forswear it in favor of the brothel only comes when your heart has been broken.

The desire for transcendence can be met with a variety of cynical responses. Traditionally, elites encouraged one or another form of fundamentalist religion as a way to fulfill the needs of ordinary people, while reserving polite skepticism (along with profane pleasure) for themselves. This approach will not work if we allow that the longing for transcendence is a longing for freedom at least as much as it is a longing for certainty. The present-day right can meet both needs, albeit in different moments; the present-day left can meet neither. Is there a metaphysics that meets both at once?

I believe Kant's work can be used to provide a metaphysics capable of meeting our needs both for truth and for freedom. Understanding it is vital for establishing an alternative to fundamentalism that doesn't oblige us to accept the current Western order as final, much less right. Defending what the Enlightenment has achieved doesn't require us to ignore what it hasn't. On the contrary Enlightenment is not a fixed state of mind but a demand, and maintaining it requires vigilance. And that vigilance requires the kind of self-examination that squarely faces the ways in which human needs for truth and freedom remain unsatisfied in Western culture. If we seek an Enlightenment whose values are robust enough to provide an alternative to fundamentalism, this examination must begin now.

PART TWO

. . . .

ENLIGHTENMENT
VALUES

CHAPTER FOUR

MYTHS OR MONSTERS

A few days after Hurricane Katrina destroyed much of the Gulf Coast, the German newsweekly *Die Zeit* published an interview with British novelist J. G. Ballard. Ballard said the catastrophe in New Orleans revealed the collapse of the Enlightenment. Not only was it payback for global warming, itself a result of Enlightenment technology; human reactions to the hurricane showed that we are irrational creatures who don't always act for the best, and who, like bored chimpanzees in a zoo, often seek senseless violence. Humankind, in short, can only partly be civilized; the Enlightenment is dead.

Katrina?

There are more distinguished sources for the litany of charges made against the Enlightenment, but none that take it as far. Ballard's complaints are wholly unoriginal, but his example, to my knowledge, is not. The Enlightenment has been called the source of fascism, imperialism, communism, colonialism, and a host of lesser crimes. Once it's responsible for Katrina, it's really to blame for everything.

As a matter of fact, the Enlightenment had its own Katrina. Though they had nothing to rely on for information but words and woodcuts, distant observers of the 1755 Lisbon earthquake were as moved by it as the people who sat in their living rooms 250 years later watching CNN coverage of black Americans trying not to drown. The earthquake that destroyed the great port of Lisbon and some ten thousand of its inhabitants on All Saints' Day could be called the first global catastrophe. Prayers were offered from Paris, boats of donated supplies were sent from England, and four months after the disaster, several German states canceled carnival celebrations out of respect for the victims. (Frederick the Great thought this was overdone.) Voltaire wrote a long poem, as well as a chapter of *Candide*, to come to terms with it; Kant published three little essays in the local paper to reassure readers that earthquakes can be understood scientifically, and don't happen in East Prussia anyway; Goethe recalled the disaster decades later as the intellectually formative event of his childhood.

Goethe was not alone there. The Lisbon earthquake had profound implications. It catalyzed a set of questions about the relationship between reason and reality that was already in motion; after Lisbon, the old rationalist idea that creation is bound and permeated by order became largely an object of scorn. The Enlightenment was reconsidered; it certainly matured. But only the most conservative of Jesuits thought it should be rejected, and they landed, literally, on the ash heap of history.

For the differences between the Lisbon earthquake and Hurricane Katrina are far more profound than their similarities. Catastrophes feed superstitions, and plenty of priests saw the earthquake as God's punishment for religious deviations of one sort or another. Portugal's prime minister, the Marquis de Pombal, a master of the moderate Enlightenment, insisted that the earthquake could be naturally explained. He immediately commandeered stores of grain to prevent famine, organized the disposal of corpses to prevent plague, and ordered up the militia to prevent looting within the city and attacks by pirates from without. The marquis knew information was crucial, and he was so efficient that he was able to insure that Lisbon's weekly paper continued without missing an edition. He also knew that the more the priests urged fasting and repentance, the harder it would be to return to the prosaic task of rebuilding the city. After the most eloquent Jesuit, one Father Malagrida, made an unfavorable comparison between the prime minister and the devil, charges were trumped up to send the rabble-rousing father to an auto-da-fé. Enlightened despotism was, after all, still despotism, and Portugal was one of the more backward places in Europe. But the removal of his fundamentalist opponents, one way or another, allowed Pombal to devote himself to the very Enlightenment business of alleviating suffering and promoting civil society. His statue stands today in the central Lisbon whose reconstruction he oversaw in a masterpiece of city planning of which New Orleans can only dream.

It's hard to find an attack on the Enlightenment that withstands historical scrutiny any better than Ballard's suggestion that it was responsible for Katrina, though the attacks are as old as the Enlightenment itself. Edmund Burke blamed it for the French Revolution, and later conservatives promoted the view that the roots of all state-sponsored evils could be traced there. The young Marx raised the charge that the Enlightenment advanced the demands of a few clever sons of the bourgeoisie to privileges enjoyed by the aristocracy, bringing about not universal liberation, but new and subtle forms of domination from which the world has yet to recover. Here Marx was quite right: The Enlightenment's goals were never as universal as they claimed, and what they claimed as universal was often a disguised way of privileging some classes, or nations, over others. One could reproach the Enlightenment for betraying itself by failing to realize all its promise. Instead, most contemporary left-leaning thinkers are inclined to call the Enlightenment itself into question. In attacking what was recently called 'Enlightenment fundamentalism,' it has become common to hear one or another defender of the Enlightenment called 'a fanatic of faith in the omnipotence of reason,' filled with 'overweening confidence in a human rationality which asserts its own infallibility,' and committed to the 'deification of science and technology.'

Quotes like these can be found in many a current journal,

but contemporary writers who make similar claims may be surprised to know they were gathered in 1959 by historian Peter Gay. He took them from arch-conservative commentators, especially Russell Kirk, whose book *The Conservative Mind* is still a canonical right-wing text. Nor were the criticisms new in Gay's time. Anti-Enlightenment screeds have been fashionable since the Enlightenment began. Right and left critiques of the Enlightenment have differed in tone, but their images of the Enlightenment are remarkable for the similarities of distortion. Postwar German thinkers pulled out the biggest guns. The cosmopolitan refugee Theodor Adorno could not have been more different from Martin Heidegger, who reveled in village virtues and lent his services to the Nazis. Though they disagreed on almost everything, and loathed each other profoundly, both laid the blame for fascism at the Enlightenment's door. In short: If you're looking for something to unite contemporary thinkers across every possible spectrum, you can do no better than to invoke the specter of the Enlightenment monster: a beast filled with icy contempt for the instincts and driven by blind, dumb optimism or protototalitarian lust for domination. The monster is relentlessly cheerful, stupendously gullible, and endlessly naive. If not quite the mad scientist in the cellar, the Enlightenment is the sorcerer's apprentice, a blithe and callow fool who releases forces that overpower us all. If you're seeking minimal consensus, just call the Enlightenment obsolete – at the very, very best.

These are the most important accusations:

1. The Enlightenment held humankind to be naturally good and infinitely perfectable, blithely ignoring all the evidence about human nature to produce a picture that's as pretty as it is removed from reality.

2. The Enlightenment held every problem to be resolvable by reason, arrogantly overestimating the intellect and underestimating the emotions.

3. The Enlightenment held nothing to be sacred and made everything

profane. Its stance is the stance of ceaseless irreverence, ignoring human needs for the holy.

4. When it worshiped anything, the Enlightenment worshiped the technology it believed would solve all problems. But instead of bringing the progress it held to be inevitable, it led straight to Auschwitz.

These claims are supported by nothing more than shreds of historical evidence, always torn from their contexts. The patchwork creature that results is the rationalist whom the Enlightenment itself condemned on empirical grounds, the fanatic about whom it was skeptical, the optimist it loved to ridicule. This is not about nuance. The Enlightenment wasn't simply more complex than the contemporary caricatures of it; it was often diametrically opposed to them. Yet the caricatures have persisted despite masses of work twentieth-century historians undertook to undermine them. Starting, at the latest, with Peter Gay, a virtual industry has been devoted to researching the Enlightenment. Nor need you be a scholar to find evidence that the Enlightenment was not what it now seems. Leave the archives to others; buy a copy of one of the countless paperback editions of *Candide* to see that these critiques of Enlightenment came from the heart of the Enlightenment itself. The idea that life is not as good, and the world not as simple, as we'd like to believe just might have been news to Candide himself, but it hardly needed saying to his creator. Attacking Candide's sort of worldview – 'All for the best in this best of all possible worlds' – was Voltaire's whole point, part of the Enlightenment effort to look at the world as it is, not as we wish it to be, in order to assess our possibilities within it. Yet not only popular pundits, but writers like Isaiah Berlin or John Gray proceed as if the historians had labored in vain.

Where knowledge has so little effect on public opinion, it's time to ask why. The Enlightenment has come to stand for modernity. I suspect that the monster called Enlightenment is a reflection of our fears; in particular, the fear that modern life is in danger of stealing our souls. The disenchantment of the world is one thing, the demystification of human nature quite another. The more your own secrets are uncovered, the more you may feel that there's no self left at all.

Understanding why fear of the Enlightenment has created a phantom far scarier than anything that ever really existed would help us understand a great deal, but my goal here is more modest: to close the gap between the research into the Enlightenment as a historical period and the Enlightenment as a state of mind. It's the latter, of course, that moves contemporary readers, who may want to know when they are being loyal to the Enlightenment, and when they have strayed into mumbo jumbo. Here historical information is crucial, but it needs to be distilled. In the process of distillation, I will inevitably oversimplify. That's what definitions do.

My goal is to take back the Enlightenment from the clichés that surround it: that the Enlightenment held human nature to be perfect and human progress to be inevitable, reason to be unlimited and science to be infallible, faith to be a worn-out answer to the questions of the past, and technology a solution to all the problems of the future. In fact, no era was more aware of the existence of evil; no era took more care in probing human limits and bounds. The Enlightenment took aim not at reverence, but at idolatry and superstition; it never believed progress is necessary, only that it is possible. You can find some eighteenth-century quote that expresses the crudest version of these claims; you can find second-rate thought about anything. But in rescuing the Enlightenment from the clichés that distort it I will focus on the best of its thinkers.

These waters have been deep and muddy ever since the *Berlinische Monatschrift*, an eighteenth-century version of the *New York Review of Books*, asked several renowned authors to answer the question 'What is Enlightenment?' Even historians who specialize in the period seem unable to agree about things that ought to be simple, like its location in space and time: Which country and which century did the Enlightenment come from? One solution to the disagreements has been to emphasize the different shapes Enlightenment took in different places; what we have to understand is not one Enlightenment but several. So it's sometimes argued the Enlightenment was militant and materialistic in France, tamer and pious in Germany, solid and commonsensical in Britain. But as you look closer, counterexamples arise: Voltaire was hardly militant, Rousseau hardly materialistic, Kant hardly tame, and Hume anything but commonsensical. These attempts to put some order into the Enlightenment only succeed in reproducing national clichés.

Though fiercely devoted to proving the Enlightenment originated in Holland, British historian Jonathan Israel's magisterial new studies aim to end such clichés by arguing that the Enlightenment was as international and cohesive as it often claimed to be. In his account, the diversity among Enlightenment thinkers isn't national, but philosophical: Members of the radical Enlightenment were committed to atheism in theology, materialism in metaphysics, and republican democracy in politics, while members of the moderate Enlightenment supported Deism, dualism, and general reform. He acknowledges, however, that there are borderline cases: atheists like Hume who were political conservatives, theists like Rousseau and Kant whose work supported revolution, writers like Diderot whose metaphysical evasions cannot only have been intended for the censor. The concept of radical Enlightenment fits Spinoza best, though even that is complicated by the old and trenchant description of him as a 'God-intoxicated atheist.' But mixed cases like Hume, Kant, and Rousseau are not marginal ones. They show that the hard division of Enlightenment into radical and moderate varieties cannot sustain as much philosophical weight as some hoped. Israel's work is the most thorough and scholarly of recent attempts to define the Enlightenment, but most recent historians still plead for a moratorium. In one famous essay, 'George Washington's False Teeth,' Enlightenment historian Robert Darnton insists on eschewing conceptual analysis and called for a deflationary definition that would restrict the word *enlightenment* to a concrete historical movement in eighteenth-century Paris – only to proceed, in the same essay, to describe the Enlightenment as a worldview that contemporary Americans should use to promote justice. If historians can find no clarity or consensus, no wonder some have concluded that the Enlightenment exists only as a specter invented by Counter-enlightenment polemicists.

Historians may continue to disagree about defining the Enlightenment, but any philosopher who uses the word had better beware. This is particularly true for someone who argues, as I did in the last chapter, that people acting in extreme situations in the name of Enlightenment share something in common with fundamentalists: a desire for dignity, an urge to escape the material conditions in which they are mired for a standpoint that is free of them. Call this idealism. The desire to change the present world according to an idea of something better was never confined to the Enlightenment. Fundamentalists, too, believe that present experience should be changed by ideas that go beyond experience. What's derided as Enlightenment fundamentalism is often just this commitment to idealism. I have argued that derision itself is metaphysically loaded, for it assumes that only material impulses are sane and mature. Get rid of idealism, in this view, and you get rid of all the dangers fanatics may bring. No doubt about it: You can make a desert and call it peace, too. But there is another option. If the yearning for idealism drives people to fundamentalism, they could be satisfied by other kinds of idealism as well. Part of offering an alternative to fundamentalism means providing a robust defense of the moral language of the Enlightenment – the foundation on which Western culture rests. It's a state of mind that's still available, if we insist on taking it back.

Having argued that Enlightenment thinkers and fundamentalists have something in common, it's crucial to say how they differ. Thanks to recent reminders of where we would be without the Enlightenment, this is easy enough. For anyone unsure about how dark dark ages can really be, Taliban Afghanistan has been positively providential. It provided, for a moment, a window on a world in which public execution through torture, enslavement of women, prohibition and destruction of art and music, and surgery without narcotics were all everyday occurrences. Though the U.S. invasion ended some of those practices, recent Taliban victories have wiped out initial achievements in several provinces. When a thirteen-year-old girl can be shot by Taliban raiders for attending school in 2007, it's hard to think the Enlightenment out of date.

That spot of premodernity should have assuaged every post-modern doubt about defining the original Enlightenment project. If the question of what the Enlightenment stood for is still disputed, what it stood against is not. It stood against superstition. Not only because superstition is silly and manipulative, though many an author enjoyed poking fun at the church's inscenation of miracles to draw the presence and dull the minds of credulous crowds. It was easy to ridicule holy foreskins, jewel-encased saints' bones, and vials of what might or might not be blood, but not every superstition was laughable. Witches were still burned in the seventeenth century; and even in Holland, denying the existence of the devil could bring you a very long term in jail. (If sexual temptation wasn't satanic, it was argued, then it would be natural. And if sexual temptation were natural, there would be no reason to restrain any sort of promiscuity.) Superstition was also responsible for less grisly forms of punishment. The belief that natural evils were the result of moral evils led most people to view illness and poverty as just deserts: If you suffered, you must have sinned. Efforts to combat them were therefore limited less by technology than by the suspicion that combating them would violate God's order.

In addition to superstition, the Enlightenment was opposed to torture. As varied as it was gruesome, torture was not only an accepted form of punishment and spectacle, but a standard part of judicial proceedings designed to obtain confessions – presumably to relieve the burden on the consciences of executioners, who regularly dispatched people for committing anything from blasphemy to theft.

The results were often as absurd as what religious scholar Wendy Doniger calls the twisted logic of torture, in which alleged witches were 'hoisted up on the strappado by a rope so that the weight of their bodies, sometimes augmented by dead weights, dislocated their joints. Imperial law forbade the use of torture twice for a single crime, but the witchcraft prosecutors argued they could use it again if they found new evidence. What was new evidence? The fact that the accused had withstood the first torture, since it was so terrible it could not be borne without the use of magic.'

Along with superstition and torture, the Enlightenment took on inherited privilege. In a world where people tended to do what their parents did, regardless of talent or inclination, Enlightenment demands for equal opportunity were demands for basic justice. This was not merely a matter of your chance to choose to be a philosopher if your father was a saddle maker. At least as important was your chance to be ruled by men whose claims to power rested on something approximating merit. For two centuries preceding the revolution, for example, the French government worked by selling offices. The Crown was always looking for money, and its more fortunate subjects were always looking for privilege. Both their interests were met by the sale of offices – from provincial court clerkships to the presidency of the Parlement of Paris – to the highest bidder, whose heir then inherited his father's political position, much like his land. But why should people with skill and energy languish all their lives on the wrong side of the tracks? Why should the fact that their fathers were rulers allow incompetent and venal men to shape the destiny of millions?

These are questions the Enlightenment raised, but they've hardly been resolved. Nor need you go as far as Kandahar, these days, to see the sort of targets against which the Enlightenment took aim. This is one reason why negative definitions are not enough. In the most general terms, the Enlightenment goes back to Plato's belief that truth and beauty and goodness are connected; that truth and beauty, disseminated widely, will sooner or later lead to goodness.

(While we're making an effort at truth and goodness, beauty reminds us what we're holding out for.) But general terms are too abstract. In the chapters that follow I'll begin by sketching the metaphysics that undergirds an Enlightenment worldview. *An* Enlightenment worldview; I won't pretend to outline *the* Enlightenment world-view, or offer a comprehensive summary of the Enlightenment as a whole. Rather, I'll focus on the thought of Immanuel Kant, the only Enlightenment thinker who really offered a comprehensive worldview with a metaphysics to back it up. In the following chapters I will examine central Enlightenment commitments to happiness, reason, reverence, and hope. These are not exhaustive, but they are values cherished by every thinker who was central to the Enlightenment, and I will expand my discussion of Kant's work with examples from the work of others – more to show that he was not alone, than in the hopeless attempt to try to summarize them all.

I emphasize those Enlightenment values more than the more traditional ones of knowledge and toleration. The Enlightenment held that fundamentalism is driven by ignorance, and can therefore be overcome by knowledge. As soon as science destroyed superstition by revealing the real causes of events, it thought fundamentalism would simply disappear. Occasionally this happened by the book. In nineteenth-century Hawaii, for example, women suffered a variety of taboos along with the usual restrictions: Eating together with men was forbidden, along with the enjoyment of pork, coconuts, and bananas. On arriving in the islands, American missionaries worked to convince Hawaiians that violating these prohibitions would lead to no harm. Though their attempts to abolish the lascivious hula were a failure, the missionaries managed to persuade Queen Ka'ahumanu, who had been the favorite wife of King Kamehameha the Great, to sit down to dinner with the men. Contrary to the priests' warnings, no cosmic disaster ensued. The power of the priesthood disappeared in very short order as Hawaiians saw no reason to obey any other traditional sanctions; general literacy, women's rights, and opposition to human sacrifice were immediately strengthened.

Getting rid of superstition is an ongoing project. But though neither Hume's wit nor his depth are matched by contemporary critics of religion, his arguments have become standard, and the fact that they failed to prevent the rise of fundamentalism is often used as an argument that the Enlightenment failed: If people were rational, they would have abandoned superstition once the word got out. But reason, as we'll see, is not just a matter of knowledge. You may substitute knowledge for superstition without satisfying the needs that drive people into superstition's arms. Hume himself would never have expected his critique of religion to make a dent in the worldview of Osama bin Laden. Skepticism on its own is simply cleverness, the sort of thing that impresses other David Humes. The skepticism that begins by attacking authoritarian traditions ends by supporting them: Having destroyed everything else you might hope for, it has nowhere but tradition on which to stand. The only other recourse is the sort of absolute nihilism that tries to convince you that it never mattered where you stood or what you stood for, anyway.

Tolerance is the handmaid of this sort of skepticism, but like most handmaids it is helpless. Confronted with intolerance, it doesn't know how to behave. Good manners require both that it question its own standpoint, and that it refuse to impose on others who don't share it. Tolerance is so well brought up that it can't respond to those who are not. So, for example, torn between demands for gender equality and worries about imposing Western values, it can do little in the face of an Afghani woman but shake its head and mutter: There but for the grace of God go I. Tolerance is the virtue of disappointed old men; it can never serve as a rallying cry. Without ideals of reason, Enlightenment may destroy itself.

I'm inclined to be hopeful, but not so much as to argue that a better understanding of the Enlightenment will lead committed fundamentalists to collapse. Whether in the Middle East or elsewhere, that's not how commitments work. I am arguing that many of the best and brightest young people are attracted to fundamentalism because it provides things not readily available in contemporary Western culture; these things are not, however, antithetical to it, but stand at the roots of that culture itself. To show this we must know what the Enlightenment most valued. Some of its choices were implied by the choices it rejected. It sought a world ruled by merit, not heredity or choice; its democratic commitments were evident in its very style: writing stripped of pedantry and academic jargon that was meant to be read by more than a chosen few. But some Enlightenment values are less obvious. In the following chapters I'll examine, first, its idea that humankind has a right to happiness. This was a clear denial of the view that life is a vale of tears, but also of the view that life is a bed of roses. While it refused to defer all its hopes to heaven, demanding happiness on earth changed the idea of happiness itself. Enlightenment happiness is fundamentally active, part of a life in which people get what they deserve.

Like many Enlightenment commitments, this one can be traced to the principle of sufficient reason, which I will examine in chapter 7. Enlightenment reason has little to do with logic, mathematics, or calculation. It is rather the insistence that the world make sense to us all. Neither authority nor obscurity should cow us into silence; our right to understanding comes from the same source as our right to happiness. To demand reason is not, of course, to reject every-thing else. The Enlightenment never thought cultivating reason meant ignoring the passions, and spent as much time exploring the one as the other. More surprising is the Enlightenment commit-ment to reverence. Both critics and defenders of the Enlightenment often misread its attitude toward religion. Religious institutions gave Enlightenment thinkers much to attack, but with the exception of a few committed atheists, I will argue that it attacked them in the name of reverence. The Roman advice to admire nothing – *nil admirari* – was not its slogan; its scientific spirit was meant to increase our reverence for creation, not to undermine it. Reason is not the end of religion; as we saw, the question is not whether you believe in God, but what you think your belief entails. Do you put your trust in your own natural ability to reason, or do you bow to revelation? Abraham took a leap of faith at Mount Moriah and landed in the arms of an orthodox God, while his stance at Sodom and Gomorrah would make any Enlightenment hero proud.

The final value I'll discuss is the ability to hope. It's a virtue because it rarely comes without struggle; the Enlightenment knew very well just how hard life can be. It savagely attacked the optimism that later critics attributed to it; with the exception of a few extremists, no Enlightenment thinker held progress to be inevitable. They all, however, decidedly rejected the claim that decline is inescapable. Conservative insistence that we're doomed to degenerate is a self-fulfilling prophecy. If you think everything has been getting worse since the old days, you are unlikely to do much to stop the decline. If you insist on the essential depravity of human nature, you are unlikely to do anything more vigorous about it than shaking your head.

I will focus on these Enlightenment values because they provide common ground and common objects. All things considered, most of us want to be happy and reasonable and reverent and hopeful, and we want it with a passion that can sometimes move mountains. Tolerance? Skepticism? These are formal virtues, born of disillusionment and worry. Caution can hold people back, but it cannot get them going – which is why appeals to the Enlightenment that are based on the need for tolerance so rarely move anyone at all.

Values become real when they become embodied, and we are touched by the forms in which they appear. Not even our minds are moved by argument alone, to say nothing of our hearts and our hands and all the other things that keep us going. If the Enlightenment has a body, it's never portrayed as seductive. This is one reason why historical argument hasn't succeeded in undermining suspicion of the Enlightenment. Here philosophy and history need the help of literature, which moves us more because it moves more of us. Tone and emphasis and nuance are literary notions demanding literary means, which is why I will turn to *The Odyssey* in seeking an image for Enlightenment heroes.

Heinrich Heine described the classic picture of the Enlightenment soul in two of its central figures, Immanuel Kant and Maximilien Robespierre. Though he found what he called Robespierre's 'terrorism' timid and pedestrian next to that of the Prussian philosopher, he thought their characters largely the same. Both were dry, prosaic, merciless, and mistrustful ascetics who were meant to weigh cabbages but wound up killing kings – the one in theory, the other in practice. By nature, each was born to be a petty clerk; force of circumstance gave them roles their souls were unequipped to play, and the West has felt the consequences ever since. Thomas Carlyle was similar to, if less witty than, Heine when he wrote of 'that withered, unbelieving, secondhand eighteenth century from which the possibility of heroism was gone forever.' Given such consensus, a portrait of an Enlightenment hero who cannot be reduced to steely fanatic or rule-governed wimp would be worth a thousand proofs.

The devil's in the details, and my conception of reverence or reason may not be yours. The following chapters will offer interpretations of them that strive to command agreement among broadly different communities. But there are points where no amount of interpretation should obscure the ways in which the Enlightenment parts company with even the most moderate wings of fundamentalist camps. One concerns attitudes toward sex, and more generally toward women. The Enlightenment championed the liberation of both, and though its efforts on behalf of women's equality don't meet today's standards, it took the first steps in our direction. By contrast, traditional gender hierarchies and the suppression of sexuality are threads that bind fundamentalist movements in most religions.

An equally important difference between Enlightenment and fundamentalist worldviews is their relationship to criticism – which is close to, but not the same as, general skepticism. The Enlightenment is inherently self-critical, morally bound to examine its own assumptions with the same zeal it examines others.

It's a trait that has no echo in fundamentalist cultures, and has often been missing in latter-day politicians who pick up the Enlightenment's banner. Acknowledging the deception and violence that persist through even the best of Western political cultures is crucial to resisting the enemies of the modern world, who use the contradictions between our ideals and our realities to dismiss those ideals as hypocritical hogwash. (Just one example: Sweden gives the world's highest percentage of its GNP for aid to developing nations – and is also the world's second highest exporter of weapons.) Contemporary critiques of the Enlightenment might have been framed as calls to extend it. To take crucial examples: Demands for inclusion by women and non-European men are based on just the universalism the Enlightenment championed. The Enlightenment did not realize its own ideals – but that's what ideals are all about. This sort of argument could have strengthened the Enlightenment by showing that through its tools of self-criticism, it had the power to right its own wrongs. Instead, those who should have extended the Enlightenment were engaged in extinguishing it.

We still have a chance to get it right. If you're committed to Enlightenment, you're committed to understanding the world in order to improve it. The first step is to demystify the myths that keep illegitimate power alive. In the eighteenth century, traditional religion was the source of most of those myths: separation of church and state was barely imagined, and the state needed priests' threats of hellfire to intimidate anyone who threatened its authority. But this is no longer the case even in the theocratic states of the Middle East. No fundamentalist revival is as much of a threat to Western freedom as the failing educational systems combined with advertising-driven media determined to make us blind or indifferent to the forces that govern our lives. A twenty-first century Enlightenment would extend the work of the eighteenth by pointing out new dangers to freedom of thought within our own culture, and extend social justice by expanding the eighteenth-century attacks on injustice. The eighteenth century had to learn that the son of a saddle maker, like Immanuel Kant, had as much to give the world as the son of a prince; the twentieth century discovered that the daughter of an auto mechanic has as much right to an education as the son of a banker. We are just beginning to ask why being born in Houston should entitle you to more of everything than being born in Nairobi. Contemporary Enlightenment should seek to structure the global economy according to principles that embody the demand for equal rights at Enlightenment's heart.

It would be pointless to ignore the differences that separate Enlightenment and fundamentalist outlooks, but foolish to ignore what might bridge them. In the pages that follow I will talk about both. Yet insisting on any similarities between them at all is likely to produce scorn from those critics of Enlightenment, left and right, who attack what they call the fanaticism of reason. Such scorn, I will argue, is not much more than what Kant would call lofty disdain – not for the Enlightenment itself, but for any worldview that denies that reality is exhausted by the bottom line. Fundamentalist and Enlightenment idealists share a passionate rejection of materialism. Unlike their critics, their tone is never world-weary, because they're committed to the idea that the world can be changed. This idea isn't something they know to be true, any more than their critics know that it's false. You may regard it as a matter of faith – as long as you acknowledge how many other ideas are matters of faith as well.

CHAPTER FIVE

· · · · · · ·

HEAVEN AND EARTH

Not long ago I traveled for the first time to Africa, as part of a meeting at the Goree Institute in Senegal that had been arranged to allow African, American, and European public intellectuals to exchange experiences. With one exception, none of us well-traveled Western intellectuals had ever set foot in Africa, and we were wracked with a mixture of terror and guilt. It's hard to be certain, but I think the terror was produced less by archaic images of the dark continent than by the warnings of institutions like Harvard Health Services, which wanted to shoot up one of our number with so many prophylactic drugs that he reckoned his odds of arriving half-comatose would be higher than the odds of his catching malaria. The terror melted within minutes of arriving on one of the world's most beautiful and calming tropical islands, but the guilt was thereby only doubled. For it was clearer than ever that we were not only rich but ignorant. Our African counterparts had all studied or taught in the West, and usually both, while we arrived knowing nothing more about their part of the world than what we could glean from a guidebook, and a South African novel or two. What could we possibly do that would justify the fact that some foundation had paid for our tickets to paradise instead of donating the money to kids in a Dakar slum?

'Tell us about Kant!' said a very black man wearing a very white caftan.

I'm not making this up, though I had to suppress an expression of joy. I looked dumbly across the table at the man who'd been introduced as a justice of the Senegalese Supreme Court.

'You Europeans should stop being so damned humble,' he continued. 'I'm looking at your vitae and it says you do Kant. Doesn't he have something to tell us about our struggles to build peace here?'

Doesn't he? It was a very tall order, and about the last one I was prepared to fill. Though I'd never bought the idea that colonialism was the fault of the Enlightenment, I hadn't come to Senegal to peddle its wares. Suddenly it was clear, however, that from such a place lots of things we take for granted still look like treasures, and there is an enormous desire to divide up the wealth. *Intellectual* wealth. At its best, it's a desire that coexists with confidence in the value of one's own traditions, along with a sense of their limits. That in itself is an attitude we could learn from, and come to share.

The African example was the starkest I've recently experienced, but by no means the only one. In Belgrade, a brave band of people operate the delightfully named Center for Cultural Decontamination. It was established during the Milosevic regime to preserve a critical voice against the government – with a mixture of Shakespeare performance, workshops about philosophy and history, and discussions about how they all fit together. Walking down the sidewalks of Sarajevo, you still need to watch out for mortar holes, and local hosts are quick to show you where you could have been shot during the siege. University attendance was up, however, when students had to risk their lives to get there. The tenth anniversary of the Dayton Accords coincided with the bicentennial of Kant's death, which was celebrated in Sarajevo with speeches verging on pathos: The city that had exploded into brutal war was reaching out for support from a cosmopolitan tradition that still seemed precious and fragile.

The Enlightenment's virtues are in sharpest focus where they are most precarious. Self-criticism was always one of them. But in Western Europe and the United States, where the gains of the Enlightenment are so widespread they are no longer apparent, self-criticism has morphed into automatic self-deprecation. We no longer remember how much of our lives depends on the movement whose weaknesses we deplore. It's the sort of amnesia that leads to paralysis and confusion.

In chapters 1 and 2 I argued that conservatives suffer from a surfeit of possible metaphysics, veering between a realism that's fixed on the worst aspects of human and other natures, and an absolute idealism that sees nothing but the reflections of its own dreams. Those on the left, by contrast, suffer not from a surfeit, but a dearth, with no general framework at all. Marxism couldn't do it consistently, but it did express two ideas most of us want expressed: that injustice need not be a permanent part of reality, and that hopes for changing reality are not utopian dreams. The collapse of Marxism rendered the left unable to express either. If you want to hear about hopes for change based on ideas, you must look to the right. Does this mean that the left and the right come together, and is this something to celebrate?

I think both have gotten off track. So it's useful to return to the time when *left* and *right* named much more meaningful political cultures than they do today, when they expressed generally coherent views of reality. The eighteenth century is still our point of political orientation for this, among other reasons. In those days people on the left argued for the reality of ideas like universal justice, against which the existing world should be tested – and found wanting. Critics on the right, by contrast, held such ideas to be chimerical and dangerous. 'What kind of a man,' thundered Edmund Burke, 'would expect heaven and earth to bend to grand theories?'

The poet Heinrich Heine complained that the life history of Kant was difficult to describe, since he had neither a life nor a history. Born in 1724 to a saddle maker in the provincial Baltic capital of Königsberg, Kant was saved from a craftsman's life by the local priest, who made sure the quick-witted boy got the education none of his family had enjoyed. He climbed the academic ladder slowly and steadily until he became known as the Sage of Königsberg, where he lectured six days a week on everything from metaphysics to military strategy. Until he reached middle age, Kant was a bright little moon of the German rationalist Gottfried Wilhelm Leibniz, best known to posterity through Voltaire's caricature, Dr. Pangloss. Like Dr. Pangloss, the younger Kant really did believe that reason was in principle capable of unlimited knowledge that would prove this world to be the best one. No other, at least, could be better. But gradually, despite fragile health and a grueling workload, Kant constructed a philosophical system that was rivaled only by those of Plato and Aristotle, and has never been surpassed. Fame touched him lightly. Even after he was sought from afar as Germany's greatest philosopher, Kant never left his native town, where he continued to live according to the rigid daily planning to which he believed his productivity due. His afternoon walk was so regular that his neighbors set their clocks by it. Only twice in his life did he swerve from routine. The second time was upon hearing the news of the French Revolution. The first was when he read Rousseau. Thus despite the rumor that he supported his studies with his skill in the pool hall, and an even more tenuous story involving secret trysts with a society matron, nothing else ever really happened to him. An unlikelier revolutionary never lived.

Yet Kant was just the sort of man to take up Burke's challenge, and he was explicit: Sometimes there are ideas to which heaven and earth should bow. It was Kant, after all, who thought Abraham should have defied God at Mount Moriah. He also declared that Christians recognize Jesus not from the gospels, but from reason's idea of moral perfection. Whatever we know about goodness comes not from revelation, but from our own ideas of the moral law. For the frail little man who never left his Baltic province was called a fearless Jacobin by his contemporary Prussians. A generation later, we saw the same Heine who found Kant's life so dreary compare him to Robespierre. Indeed, Heine thought the philosopher the more daring of the two revolutionaries: Robespierre merely put the French aristocracy on trial, whereas Kant 'stormed the heavens, put the whole garrison to the sword, and left the Sovereign of the world swimming unproven in His own blood.' Farther to the East, Goethe used another metaphor: Kant, he wrote, 'freed us from the effeminacy in which we were wallowing.'

What could a provincial German professor do to earn such distinction? To understand it we must take a closer look at the theoretical debates in which he engaged; what shook up Kant's life were intellectual commotions. Too often these are viewed as debates about epistemology – theories of knowledge that wrestle with questions about how, and how much, we can know. Like most philosophers, Kant did spend time trying to understand what elements make up knowledge. But questions about how much reason and how much experience go into what we know seldom arouse much passion. The more important questions were not epistemological but metaphysical, and they grew fierce in the matter of ideas. At stake were the reality of ideas like universal justice, on the one hand, and chimeras like angels and demons on the other. For the Enlightenment it was just as crucial to defend the first as it was to debunk the second. People were still tortured for consorting with demons, while writers who denied the existence of such creatures could be driven into exile. And on the other hand, the belief that ideas of universal justice make real demands on the lives of everyone, whether commoner or king, seemed just as fantastic to conservatives as supernatural specters seemed to the left.

In the struggle over questions of reality it was the work of Scottish philosopher David Hume that proved most explosive. Kant wrote that Hume awoke him from dogmatic slumber. Backed by the model of modern science, which described what sorts of things were really in the world, the Scottish philosopher proceeded to say what wasn't, which included most of the ideas we hold dear. Hume's questions were deceptively simple. How do you know the sun will rise tomorrow? It can't be a matter of observation, for all you can observe is what has happened before. The sun has risen every day until this one, but what logic allows you to infer that the future will resemble the past? What about your belief that killing one's father is an unspeakable crime? This is not, presumably, a belief you have learned from experience. Is it a matter of logic, and if so, what's the proof? Watch a billiard ball hit another, and you'll surely say the first caused the second to roll. But what exactly is the cause, and how do you discover it, when all you see is the conjunction of two unrelated objects? Hume never proposed that we stop planning our futures, protecting our fathers, or playing pool. He merely wanted to show that our doing all this, and most anything else, has nothing to do with reason. Our lives are held together by custom, habit, and tradition, which guarantee that our lives proceed in ordered fashion by these sorts of unprovable assumptions.

Now skepticism about the limits of human knowledge is nearly as old as recorded human knowledge itself. Whether you read the pre-Socratics or Ecclesiastes, you're liable to conclude that certainties were always hard to come by, and that life went on nevertheless without them. Doubt – even radical doubt – was part of the thinker's territory. Nor did Hume think his form of doubt posed any threat whatsoever to ordinary life. Quite the contrary: Hume himself acknowledged that his doubts were academic. All he had to do was to leave his study and join his friends in a glass of sherry or a game of backgammon to watch his skepticism recede. Known as Saint David in the Scotland whose Calvinism he put behind him, and Le Bon David in the Paris salons where he grew plump and cheery, Hume never took his own doubt as a cause for grief. While he argued brilliantly that nothing whatsoever is certain, he lived as well as if everything were.

What sustained him was conviction in the force of custom and habit. They are, he believed, the source of whatever we take for granted. Custom and habit lead us to suppose that the sun will rise tomorrow, and that when it does we will still regard patricide as a terrible crime. Given how far such beliefs have taken us, continuing to sustain them is a pretty good bet. It's surely the best bet going – so long as we remember it is no more than that.

This appeal to tradition was itself part of tradition, particularly that of the pagan Stoics Hume admired. What distinguished Hume from the Mediterranean skeptics was less the force of his arguments than their context. Before the eighteenth century, human knowledge seemed all of a piece: Metaphysics was no more and no less solid than physics, geography no shakier than geology, history no murkier than biology. If anything separated the harder from the softer sciences, it wasn't the methods that were used to reach conclusions, but the methods that were used to defend them. If your willingness to burn or bury those who disputed your beliefs was a test of those beliefs' certainty, then theology, not logic, was the hardest science of all. But long wars of religion had produced not just theological, but general inclination to diffidence, if only as a matter of exhaustion. All claims to knowledge were human claims, all sciences products of human effort, and like anything human, they were frail and subject to error.

All that changed with the triumph of Isaac Newton. While he was by no means the only force behind the scientific revolution, he was the most visible and dramatic. The great Enlightenment poet Alexander Pope summed up his age's enthusiasm for Newton, which fell just short of idolatry: 'Nature and Nature's laws lay hid in night / God said, Let Newton be! And all was Light.'

Where others saw chaos, Newton saw connections, joining heaven and earth through laws that governed both. Who before him even dreamed that the phases of the moon and the motion of the tides could be brought together and understood through one idea? Newton's work was both a triumph and a paradigm of the scientific method. Like no other, he united contested territories of empiricist and rationalist views about the elements of knowledge, using methods of observation along with mathematics to formulate a small number of systematic laws. Suddenly, all science was not equal, for there was one science that seemed free of mortal failings. Before Newton, everything could be doubted – including, as Descartes showed, your very existence. After Newton, the world could be divided into hard data, and wishful thinking. We entered the modern world.

Newton's physics set the standard for human achievement. Smart kids today may occasionally endure jokes about becoming another Einstein, but in the eighteenth century they'd all have hoped to be another Newton. Hume, among others, was unabashed about recording his wish to become the Newton of the mind. What he meant, presumably, was the wish to discover a few laws just as indubitable and just as far-reaching for the universe within us as Newton had done for the universe without. Hume wanted to follow (what was taken to be) a Newtonian model, and derive his certain truths only from that which was itself certain: the truths of mathematics, and the most exact and scrupulous recording of experience. And following (what was taken to be) that model, he reached bleak conclusions: Look carefully enough at what is, and you'll see it isn't much. It doesn't include much by way of law, either natural or moral, for it doesn't even include the principle of sufficient reason, the idea that whatever happens can be explained. What really is, is really meager. The rest of the cosmos we populate ourselves – with traditions and presumptions and other useful fictions. Whether ideas of justice or beauty or mathematics, they are but human invention, with no more force or validity than unicorns or elves. Thrasymachus could have agreed, but he had far less to stand on, for he had no model of knowledge or reality that could offer much better. Hume had.

Hence Hume struck a nerve, for he seemed to show that reason gives us next to nothing. Causes *aren't* things in the world, and neither are moral principles, and no amount of searching with principles of logic or tools of experience will turn them up there. Kant was forced to acknowledge the thrust of Hume's point. The most important principles that govern our lives are not things we find in the world, but things we bring to it. In contrast to the Scottish empiricist, Kant insisted that those principles reside not in custom and habit, but in reason and understanding. He spent a lifetime setting out the laws and rules they follow.

You may wonder why he bothered. For Hume never left us in *real* doubt about whether to expect the sun to rise tomorrow. So long as our worlds continue to turn as they ought to, why care if our conviction comes from reason or custom? If we want to do no more than rule out patricide, custom will get us all that we need. We may even be pleased that tradition normally extends the prohibition on patricide to cover monarchs, and care little whether it is custom that makes us regard our kings like fathers, or reason that condemns the excesses of revolutions. But things look different when we consider other claims, for on the difference between custom and reason turn all the hopes of progressive politics. Anyone who believes that it's custom and habit that guarantees our beliefs that the world will keep turning, or that all things considered, it's better not to murder our parents, is willing to let custom and habit go a very long way. They have kept us going to this point, and what's even more important, there is nothing else we can depend on. Calling them in question could lead to disaster, for if human reason is as wretched as it seems, we have nothing to put in their place.

This was just the point of Edmund Burke's *Reflections on the Revolution in France*, which became the best-known critique of the revolution, not because it was explicit about its consequences – the book was published before the worst of them – but because it had a systematic view of its causes: the foolhardy substitution of laws of reason for the time-trusted habits of humankind. Burke was a disciple of David Hume, who was just as cheerful a Tory as he was a radical atheist. Though Hume died in 1776, too early to witness his century's political upheavals, he believed, consistently enough, in preserving the status quo. Customs and traditions had stood the tests of time by constraining the drives for power that humankind shares with wolves. In attacking the very idea of revolutionary change, Burke's *Reflections* explored the implications of Hume's views. Demands for revolution, Burke wrote, arise from mistaken political metaphysics, which despises experience in favor of the abstract rights of man.

Burke had been provoked by the steel and blood of Paris, but he focused on the far less tangible forces he saw behind them. He wrote that revolutionaries were at war with nature. Political institutions should never be based on ideas that spring from our feeble and fallible reason, but from the traditions and habits that have nurtured us for centuries. What kind of a man would subject the sublime forces of nature to the pitiful products of human minds? His question was rhetorical, for he thought he knew the culprits. The revolution was driven by bumbling, incompetent professors on the one hand, and desperate, intoxicated adventurers on the other. No one else would be so foolish as to think we can begin the world anew. Abstract principles like human rights are not tools fit to measure a state. Our guides should instead be the solid if sadder guidelines that centuries of experience have provided. Legislators should study human nature as it really is, not metaphysics.

It's advice that should sound more or less familiar, and Burke was not alone. Jonathan Israel argues:

> Practically all late eighteenth- and early nineteenth-century philosophers were convinced, with some reason, that while most failed to see how philosophy impinged on their lives, and altered the circumstances of their time, they had all the same been ruinously led astray by 'philosophy'; it was philosophers who were chiefly responsible for propagating the concepts of toleration, equality, democracy, republicanism, individual freedom, and liberty of expression in the press, the batch of ideas identified as the principal cause of the near overthrow of authority, tradition, monarchy, faith, and privilege. Hence, philosophers specifically had caused the revolution.

Like most conservatives, Burke uses rhetoric that presents his view as less a view than a mixture of common sense and common observation. Ideas and ideologies are something for liberals; conservatives are just realists content to point out the way the world – alas – is. Burke's pleasure in ridiculing the 'bumblers and adventurers' is a good way to obscure the fact that his position, too, is founded on a particular and powerful metaphysics with its own distinctive conception of human nature. You may smile at Burke's particular political conclusions: The rights of man have come to guide us far more than he could have ever imagined, and you are unlikely to share his trust that 'mighty sovereigns' are the best foundation for prosperity. Such claims are so hard to swallow that you may not notice how much of Hume's metaphysics you have already ingested. Every time you accept the claim that *you can't change human nature* or *you have to accept the way the world is*, you are accepting the foundations of the worldview that grounded the ancien régime.

A year after Burke's book on revolution appeared, Kant published his answer in a pamphlet called 'On the Old Saw: That May Be Right in Theory, But It Won't Work in Practice.' (It's disheartening to know that this saw was already old in 1792.) Kant wrote that conservatives like Burke are short on argument but long on 'tones of lofty disdain.' They think it's enough to ridicule radical standpoints without questioning their own. Even more important, they fail to notice how much of our experience is constructed – often deliberately constructed – in order to perpetuate a social system that benefits the very people who say it's inevitable.

> One must take people as they are, our politicians tell us, and not as the world's uninformed pedants or good-natured dreamers fancy that they ought to be. But *as they are* ought to read *as we have made them* by unjust coercion, by treacherous designs which the government is in a good position to carry out. In this way, the prophecy of the supposed clever statesmen is fulfilled.

Here Kant reminds us that the appeal to reality often conceals a deception, for reality is almost as malleable as our wishes and hopes.

Only portions of it are truly fixed – and it is anything but easy to know which ones. This ought to be trivially true, but it's often forgotten in practice. *New York Times* columnist David Brooks, for example, recently wrote that the civil war in Iraq shows – regrettably – that Hobbes was right. 'Iraq has revealed what human beings do without a strong order-imposing state.' He thereby overlooks a detail: The civil war in Iraq didn't actually arise in the state of nature. It's a product of many centuries of unjust coercion and treacherous designs. No one party is responsible for them all. But to invade a country, destroy its infrastructure, frighten and torture its civilians, and then lament that it reveals the bleakness of human nature is to have, at the least, a peculiar notion of causality.

Even more important are the ways in which those who call themselves realists overlook the fact that there can be more than one way to view reality. Your view of what reality is conditions your view of what you can do within it. Custom and habit (and biology and super-ego) are probably enough to insure that we respect our fathers, or at least refrain from killing them; reason isn't always necessary, and some customs are entirely reasonable. But what can custom say about the habits of southern American slave societies that saw traditional paternalism as preferable to the wage relations of the capitalist North? Or the patriarchal traditions that still lead many cultures to treat women as chattel? Ironically enough – since Burke was an early abolitionist – empiricist metaphysics has no basis from which to criticize such arrangements, for its only touchstone is experience. Experience is always someone's experience, the product of particular places and times. By appealing to the (sorry) facts of (past) experience, empiricists turn contingent arrangements into facts on the ground. Anyone who tries to challenge them will look like she's challenging common sense itself.

Kant was prepared to do just that; unlike Hume or Burke, he was not content with a world that went on much as it had before. For while Hume was giving Kant nightmares, Jean-Jacques Rousseau was the source of his dreams. The thousands of pages

Kant left us contain almost nothing autobiographical; Heine wasn't far off in thinking there wasn't that much to say. But in one rare fragment of confession, Kant wrote that Rousseau had taught him to honor humankind. Before reading Rousseau, Kant was a scholar proud of the academic achievement that distinguished him from the humble world of his childhood, and contemptuous of those who did not share his extraordinary abilities. Reading Rousseau convinced Kant that his own work would be less worthwhile than a common laborer's unless it contributed to restoring the rights of humanity. So he set out to construct a metaphysics that would ground the wild French thinker's hopes for revolution against those who championed the old saw that ideas should take a backseat to reality.

For though Hume had publicly longed for the honor, it was Rousseau whom Kant called the Newton of the mind – though his only foray into natural science was a late little text on botany. Kant compared Rousseau to Newton because both of them revealed the glory and greatness of creation: If Newton had revealed the physical order in a universe hitherto thought to be governed by patched-together epicycles, Rousseau revealed a moral order in a world hitherto thought to be ruled by sin and suffering. Where earlier thinkers appealed to metaphysics and theology, Rousseau introduced history and psychology, using them to describe a world in which evil exists, but isn't inevitable. Evil was not the result of original sin, or a necessary flaw in our nature, merely a tangle of understandable errors. Just as Newton had drawn causal connections nobody had suspected, relating the movements of the tides to the phases of the moon, Rousseau linked the fables and food ingested in the nursery with the outcomes of the political order – and showed how both might be changed. The child who is forced to sit still while his nanny drones on will become the adult who does not squirm upon hearing a politician's empty lies; the child who is spoken to simply and sensibly will grow up to do, and expect, the same. And if we are not condemned to endless sad cycles of custom and habit, we live in a world where justice is possible.

Kant's metaphysics was developed to maintain a balance between the actual and the possible, and to insure they have equal weight. As Kant saw it, the alternatives are few. You can declare that ideas are real, and everything else is illusion. This, he thought, was the view of Plato's *Republic*, which went too far in giving ideas a sort of hyper-reality that put everything else in their shadow. You can declare that only physical objects are real, and everything else is illusion. This was the view of empiricists from the early Greek skeptics to Hume, who in denying the efficacy of reason were denying the reality of ideas. You might declare that both objects and ideas are illusion – a position suggested by Bishop Berkeley, and certain Zen teachings, but it's a view that's hard to express and even harder to maintain. Or you can take what Kant calls the critical path, and maintain that reality is made up of ideas as well as objects, which work in different ways.

Objects are what the world is made of, and much of Kant's metaphysics is devoted to explaining exactly what they are. For Kant, objectivity is a literal notion; it's dependent on the concept of objects. *Objective* is a word that makes sense when you're talking of objects, and nowhere else at all. Nothing is objective but the brute and banal things we know through experience. It isn't an object, for instance, if it can't be found in space and time. This rules out God, who cannot be the object of human knowledge because He cannot, by definition, conform to the limits that bind human experience. It also rules out human freedom, which cannot be located in space. We may have rational grounds for believing in both, but knowledge will always elude us.

This leaves things less precarious than they may look, for God and freedom are not alone here. Consider the idea that everything happens for a reason, otherwise known as the principle of sufficient reason. Where in the world did you get that idea? From the moment you learn that spoons drop to the kitchen floor when you open your fist, to the day you are taught the laws of gravity, experience will have strengthened your conviction in the principle. But experience can hardly be the source of your conviction. For unless you pre-suppose the principle of sufficient reason at the beginning of your experience, you cannot even ask the question *Why?* It structures our experience in ways even deeper than the way experience comes structured into causes and effects. Altered states of consciousness provide a window on what experience might be like without the principle of sufficient reason: Whoever has spent a moment watching data float by without caring about the causes or connections between them has an imperfect picture of where we'd be without the prin-ciple of sufficient reason. The principle of sufficient reason cannot ever be known, but it guides our search for knowledge of whatever we do know. Scientists, and children, may come to the end of their investigations without ever finding the reason why something happened this way rather than that. And yet none of their investi-gations could get going unless they took that principle for granted, not as a matter of conscious choice, but as the basis for the structure of reasoning itself. This means that to understand experience we have to go beyond it, working with ideas that experience may very well support but can never confirm. Kant answers Hume by agreeing that the *is* and the *ought* are different, but the *is* has many com-ponents. It's hardly straightforward, and requires patient analysis. Hume thought he was following in Newton's footsteps, and proceed-ing with principles based on mathematics and strict observation. In fact, says Kant, on Hume's account of experience, neither mathematics nor observation could get off the ground.

That insight is Kant's foot in the door. For if hard science cannot function without ideas of reason that are not themselves objective, then objectivity itself has limits. Kant answered Burke's critique of revolu-tion by questioning the general empiricism on which such critiques are inevitably based. Shall we reject ideas for the more dependable data of experience? But there would *be* no data of experience without myriad ideas of reason; science only works through a dialogue between both. Anyone who thinks we should judge ideas by empirical methods assumes that 'we can see farther and more clearly with the eyes of a mole, fixed on experience, than with the eyes of a being that was made to stand erect and face the heavens.' Moles have tunnel vision, like the empiricists who claim merely to be reporting the facts and forget how much they are appealing to facts they have made themselves. Even more fundamentally, they forget that any knowledge we discover at all presupposes the idea that human reason can and should make the world intelligible. This is not a fact we learn from experience but a demand we make on it, yet without such demands we would remain not moles, perhaps, but surely cavemen. You think that what failed in the past will fail in the future? Kant reminds us of how many sheer technological advances have disproved that old saw. His example? Air travel with balloons. If we don't abandon efforts where science hopes we may create technology, how dare we abandon them where morality demands we create justice?

There are many reasons to see Kant's views as a major source of progressive politics. His work offered a foretaste of international law, a vision of an organization of united nations, and a blueprint for social democracy. But none of these ideas are as important as his idea of the idea itself, for without this basic metaphysics, every demand for change can be dismissed as utopian fantasy. As long as your ideas of what's possible are limited by your ideas of what's actual, no other idea has a chance. Every proposal for change will be vulnerable to conservative head-shaking: Things like freedom and equality may be very nice in theory, but the hard data of experience show they cannot work in practice. Kant turned the empiricists' claims upside down. *Of course ideas of reason conflict with the claims of experience. That's what ideas are meant to do.* Ideals are not measured by whether they conform to reality; reality is judged by whether it lives up to ideals. Reason's task is to deny that the claims of experience are final – and to push us to widen the horizon of our experience by providing ideas that experience ought to obey. If enough of us do so, it will.

For Kant, travel by balloon was a modern miracle; he didn't even imagine universal suffrage, though it's clearly implied by his own principles. Ideas can turn out to be more powerful than even the genius who constructs them. Just because it is an abstraction, realizing an idea will involve interpretation. When carried far enough, Kant's principle – Treat all people as ends in themselves and never as means – implies that all people are entitled to equal political representation. Whether Kant himself was clear about all the implications of his work is unimportant. What's crucial is to be clear from the start about the fundamental difference between ideas and their realization as objects in the world.

Is that all metaphysics gets us? If you've worked through hundreds of pages of abstraction to arrive at what looks obvious, you may not be amused. Like many objections, Kant anticipated this one himself. Toward the end of *The Critique of Pure Reason* he imagines a reader complaining, 'Surely the common understanding could have arrived at this without asking philosophers for instruction.' Kant replies that this is not a fault, but a virtue of his account, for it shows that in questions that really matter, philosophers have no more claim to wisdom than anyone else. Intellect may be unequally distributed, but reason is not.

But there is still more to say. Kant's claims about idealism sound like pious banalities until you begin to apply them. Many people will sleepily agree to all of the above in principle, then go on to ignore it in practice. I'd like to recall one piece of reality that has been so radically altered in my own lifetime that it's easy to forget how far we have traveled. True, even women in Western cultures have yet to reach complete equality, and elsewhere they are still subject to massive, often deadly, injustice. But girls growing up in London or New York (not to mention Atlanta, Georgia) in the 1960s didn't bother to imagine becoming pilots or presidents. A decade later, young women with the more modest aim of contributing to intellectual fields traditionally restricted to men were told to set their sights low. When I began graduate study in the late 1970s, one well-disposed advisor told me he would like to think women could do philosophy as well as men did, but given that it had never happened, it was unlikely to happen now. It was quite a load for the few of us who went on to graduate school to carry; male professors dared us to vindicate all of womankind by proving history wrong, and younger women watched us anxiously in their own search for usable role models. Some women answered this sort of pressure by delving into obscure bits of history in pursuit of some fact that would change the data, to find the mistress of Descartes or the daughter of Locke who had been his equal, his muse, or possibly his source. Archives were racked for papers that showed traces of brilliance, or at least originality. Anything was sought that might support the claim that women had been contributing equally to Western letters all along, and it was only sexism that had left their contributions overlooked, undervalued, or even stolen.

Then as now, this seemed to me dead wrong: willfully distorting the *is* in order to attain an *ought*. While the search recovered the work of some unjustly forgotten authors, the women being sought were simply not there. The reasons for this were perfectly under-standable: Only recently were women given the opportunities that make certain kinds of achievement possible. That is a matter of history, and the attempt to rewrite it does nothing but undermine the writer's credibility. (In fact, it may undermine even more: Anyone who can dismiss reality that cavalierly ought not to be allowed to mess with it.) But the actual hardly exhausts the scope of the possible. Straightforwardly acknowledging what was is the first step in determining what will be. We have an obligation to as much truth as we can manage, but only a clear distinction between what's true and what's ideal will allow us to bring them closer together.

These might be truisms hardly worth stating except that highly educated people continue to overlook them. The liberal Harvard professor who focused on the fact that there had been no significant women philosophers in the past was making the same mistake as the feminist colleagues who dredged up second-rate writing to show the opposite. Each was convinced you could infer the future from the past; neither was separating the *is* from the *ought*. Yet nothing about what *was* need determine what *could* or *should* be – as long as the *was* could be explained.

This is important: Not everything that's thinkable is genuinely possible, and distinguishing between the two is what allows us to distinguish between demands for utopia, and for responsible social change. Otherwise one could offer a parallel argument in favor of time travel: That people have not yet performed it is by itself no argument against their doing so in the future. But the explanation of why travel backward was impossible in the past gives us no particular reason to think it might be possible in the future, whereas the scarcity of women in fields like physics or philosophy can be explained as a result of particular social conditions. If we can offer an account of how those conditions can change, we have offered not a sci-fi fantasy but a program. This is not to assume that the *is* and the *ought* coincide; they rarely do. Rather, the distinction allows us to describe a process by which we could get from one to the other.

Kant's idealism emphasizes similarities between science and morality. Both depend on ideas of reason that are not themselves objective – as things we cannot experience, hence ever possibly know. But our obligations in science are very different from our obligations in morality. In both of them we are naturally inclined to look for certainty. You want to know things directly, as they really are in themselves? Without ideas or assumptions that constrain us? Kant thinks the wish is natural, but it rests on a picture of knowledge that would make sense only for God. For the most important fact about human knowledge is this: Whatever the stuff we perceive turns out to be made of, it isn't made by us. Whoever created reality as a whole must know it with a directness and immediacy we cannot even imagine. Even an atheist can agree on a version of this claim. Indeed, it's not far from Foucault's claim that 'Truth is a thing of this world.' One difference is that Foucault, despite a laudable attack on what he calls the politics of inverted commas, insists on putting them around the word *truth* – which hints at a more genuine but unreachable reality. For Kant, truth is neither 'truth' nor Truth. If our investigations are diligent and honest, they will usually yield the real thing. Our dissatisfaction with the limits of our knowledge is dissatisfaction with the human condition itself – and a barely concealed form of the wish to be God.

But if Kant wants us to stop longing to replace God in matters of knowledge, he urges us to imitate him in matters of ethics. Kant's ethics are based on the principle he called the categorical imperative. When you act morally, you act according to a principle that you would make universal, if you happened to be creating the world and choosing its natural laws. Suppose you're in debt and tempted to borrow money you have no intention of returning. A traditional moralist might warn you of the consequences: Remember the doleful end of Emma Bovary, or any number of less scintillating cheaters who got caught in the acts? Kant's tack is different: He directs you to think about form. What if everyone always borrowed money on a lie when stuck in a similar spot? Would you respond to my tale of woe with a loan if you knew that just as surely as the law of gravity prevents things from flying off into space, there's a law of nature that prevents anyone who borrows money from paying it back? Would anyone ever be believed, or would conviction – maybe discourse itself – break down entirely? The success of your false promise depends on the premise that most people tell the truth; lying itself doesn't work, otherwise.

I'll discuss this example, and Kant's ethics more generally, when talking about reason in chapter 7. I introduce it here to emphasize one point: When you're in doubt about a moral decision, Kant tells you to resolve it by playing God. The categorical imperative is an invitation to imagine yourself at the Creation. Every time you act morally, you have a chance to begin a bit of the world afresh. This conclusion is so extraordinary that it's seldom been recognized, but Kant holds the wish to take God's place to be a natural one. It isn't the result of arrogance, but of logic. The moment you think, *This should not have happened*, you have made a reproach: The world is not in order, and one way or another it should be made anew. Since the book of Job, and at any number of points in between, righteous men and women have longed to step in and change a piece of creation. Their good will is in their own hands, so their consciences may be clear; but the success of their good deeds depends on too many others to be under control. When our power to alter an unjust world has reached its limit, all we can do is refuse to be a part of it.

Kant's philosophy is not without its share of tragedy. Many have described it as a struggle to reconcile opposing views. But if Hume and Rousseau are two parts of a puzzle, the one describing the world as it is, the other depicting the world as it ought to be, it's a mistake to view Kant as trying to fit them together. Most accounts of his work leave him sounding like your least favorite uncle, or magazine columnist, recommending tepid moderation. If the parties would stop their extremism and settle for a little of this, a little of that, we could all get along very well.

In fact, I think Kant's metaphysics provide a basis for understanding our current predicament, but not where it mirrors the sermons of Polonius. Kant knew very well that realism and idealism are hard to combine. Walter Benjamin praised the honesty of Kant's dualism, saying later philosophy had been a reactionary rear-guard action to find harmony between reason and nature, where in fact there is none. Traditionalists demand a return to the world where the *ought* seems to be legible from laws written on earth and given in heaven. One postmodernist response is a form of sour grapes: If it isn't legible, it isn't there, and if it isn't there, who needed it, anyway? Kant never tried to flee the modern in any direction. For he saw that the world is irrevocably split: The gap between the way things are and the way they ought to be is too great to be bridged by good intentions. Each one is as real as the other, though the way they are real is quite different. We ignore each at our peril.

Kant's idealism is honest enough to embrace our ambivalence: We find ideals alternately illusory and frightening, too real and too fantastic. We know they are substantial enough to die for – and we know that people die for mistakes. If they make fanaticism possible and frustration certain, why hold on to ideals at all? Far easier to downplay the realm of the *ought* and write it off as wishful thinking, than to insist on its legitimacy. For that would require us to accord the way things should be as much claim on our time and attention as the way things happened to have turned out. Realism thus considered is a form of sloth. If you tell yourself that a world without injustice is a childish wish-fantasy, you have no obligation to work toward it. On the contrary; if you have obligations at all, it is to convince others, by example or persuasion, that they should grow out of similar fantasies and accept the constraints reality offers. Keeping ideals alive is much harder than dismissing them, for it guarantees a lifetime of dissatisfaction. Ideas are like horizons – goals toward which you can move but never actually attain. Human dignity requires the love of ideals for their own sake, but nothing guarantees that the love will be requited. You might love, and fail to reach your object, all your life long.

Resignation to the status quo was the stance conservatives supported, from the Age of Enlightenment through the late twentieth century, just as cynicism about the possibility of fundamental change was their most formidable weapon. Today this blend of laziness and despair is more likely to be found on the left. Heartsick at how many of their own ideals have not only gone unfulfilled, but have been used as a cover for the worst forms of abuse, many conclude that ideals themselves are simply senseless. When times are grim, the wish to go back to what was once the status quo is only natural. The call for realism is a way to prepare us, metaphysically, to give up the rest we have lost. But the idea of human rights, for example, is not invalidated just because it's unfulfilled, or even abused; that's not how ideas work. Their validity doesn't come from their being realized, but this doesn't make them illusory. Not yet real, they could become so, if they are themselves kept alive. (One great function of the arts is to keep ideals alive in a culture that does not yet realize them.)

Kant's kind of idealism urges you to hope, and act, for more than you can ever attain. Worse than that: It promises that you cannot even guide that urge with absolutely certain knowledge. Seeking certain knowledge to guide our moral and political judgments is always a mistake, for knowledge is always knowledge of what is, whereas moral judgment is about what ought to be. This acknowledges what's true about empiricism, while giving it a critical thrust: As claims about the nature of morality, moral claims are quite literally senseless. Moral claims cannot be true or false because they are not matters of truth or falsity, but about what should be true. *Ought* and *is* are so different that what works for one will not work for the other.

Though Kant had much to say about the limits of nature, he was unwilling to draw the limits of human nature – not only because, like everything to do with freedom, they always retain a touch of mystery, but because morality is normative all the way down. Dignity and self-respect are not themselves neutral notions. We can say they ought to be central to any experience we regard as human. Unfortunately, we can't say that experience would be incoherent without them, for all too often we experience a world in which dignity is wanting, and self-respect destroyed. The idea of human dignity is a demand on the world, not a fact about it.

We hold these truths to be self-evident. It's stirring prose, but it's not quite right. For the patrician planter and the slave in the hold were *not* created equal – any more than the baby born to a crack-addicted slum mother is born equal to the child of loving, affluent parents today. The claim of equality flies in the face of painful and urgent realities. It does make sense as a demand. So seen, it changed reality once, when slavery was abolished. And since reality can only be changed by those who see it clearly, it's fatal to claim there's no difference between conditions then and conditions now. Poverty is crippling, but not as crippling as slavery, and getting rid of one can be a step toward getting rid of the other. But our only chance to break the shackles of present reality is to begin by paying attention to it.

Kant is not reality bound, but he is reality based. Imposing ideals on a nation, or a planet, without regard for the details of what's already there would have seemed to him simply childish: Grown-ups remember the claims of reality even when they give the claims of reason first place. Growing up is a metaphor Kant used for his own philosophy, and he returned to it often. To do it properly, each one of us must go through the same process human-kind undergoes as a whole. Our first steps are dogmatic. Like healthy children, reason begins with unreflective self-confidence in itself and its ability to impose its will on the world around it. As children experience their expanding ability, and with it, the expanding intel-ligibility of their experience, they are liable to suppose that both are unlimited. Reason sees its ideals wherever it looks. The fall comes in adolescence, which Kant calls skepticism in the history of thought – a swing from 'boundless trust to boundless mistrust.' The discovery that your parents and teachers can be wrong produces the heady mix of exhilaration and disappointment we know in adolescence. It's a step toward maturity, but those who stop there are lost.

If children are dazzled by the *ought*, and adolescents by the *is*, what stance toward the world should adults adopt? I began the discus-sion of metaphysics by noting that the advice to be realistic is usually the advice to decrease your expectations, a suggestion designed to insure that you get no more from – and give no more to – the world than those who came before you. It's a view that equates maturity with resignation. It urges you to accept the world you are given, for any other standpoint is just the residue of youthful dreams. Is Kant's insistence that human beings have limits anything other than that?

Indeed it is, for in his view the path to maturity is not only for-midable, but often tragic. Grown-ups navigate a narrow way between hope and despair, and it's the recognition of how often we founder that saves this view from sentiment or kitsch. (You can't always get what you want, and it matters.) The demand is precisely not to abandon the ideals of your youth. They are no more naive than they ever were; what you must abandon is the naive belief that they can be completely fulfilled. The abyss that separates *is* from *ought* is too deep to bridge entirely; the most we can hope to do is narrow it. There is nothing naive, much less Venutian, in living like this. For the wish to bring the *is* and the *ought* together may imply a wish to be God, but it makes perfect sense. As we will see, it's a wish that's driven by the deepest needs of reason itself – not a psychological distortion, but a logical demand.

Defending reason's right to make claims on nature validates our deepest longings. Whether or not we actually get them, we have a right to both justice and joy. It isn't childish to wish for a world in which happiness and virtue are in balance. When the righteous suffer, and the wicked triumph, it is reasonable to rebel. What happens, happens, and it may often be execrable. But the demand to accept the world as it is is not a sign of maturity, but a signal of capitulation. What makes you condemn reality is not an inclination to daydream, or fancy illusions; it's the first law of reason itself. The principle of sufficient reason is nothing but the demand that the world should make sense. Where it doesn't, it ought to be changed.

Kant is the only major philosopher who insisted that reason and reality are utterly different – and gave both equal time. Other thinkers tried to resolve the tension involved in living this way by downgrading one side or another. Conservatives like Hume refused to acknowledge the reality of ideas, which led him to a politics that accepts the world much as it is. Hegel, and following him, Marx, saw the conflict between the real and the ideal at the heart of Kant's philosophy. Each tried to escape it by finding the rational real. Preferring the claims of reason to those of reality can lead to any number of political commitments. Their differences will prove important in many a matter of policy. This is Absolute Idealism, and whether it stayed on the right with Hegel or turned left with Marx, it sought to escape the tensions that surge through Kant's work. These tensions, he insisted, can never be reconciled. Living with them demands daily honesty, and courage, at which many will falter.

CHAPTER SIX

HAPPINESS

There once was a man whose life was as good as it gets, in every sense of the word *good*. He was the richest man in the East, and along with all the wealth his era could imagine, he was blessed with seven sons, three daughters, and friends who loved him so deeply they would rush from distant lands to comfort him if he ever needed help. None of this made him self-righteous or arrogant. On the contrary: He was a man of perfect integrity, who not only avoided evil but went out of his way to do good. Aware that it was the same God who made him and his servants, he never abused his power or boasted of his riches. He listened to his servants and upheld their rights. No stranger was turned away from his door. He shared his food with the hungry, and the wool of his many sheep to clothe the ragged. We know little about his wife except that he was faithful to her; we do know that he encouraged the timid, filled the frightened with strength, brought relief to the comfortless, and gave the desperate hope. His life, in short, was just as good as he was; there never was a better conjunction of the *is* and the *ought*.

One day a series of messengers brought a string of bad tidings. Before one had finished speaking the next had arrived: The first announced that warriors had killed his servants and oxen; the second, that lightning had blasted all his sheep; the third, that raiders had looted his camels. But before he had time to reflect on the loss of his wealth, another messenger came to report that a tornado had hit the house where his children were feasting, leaving all of them dead on the spot.

The man stood up. He went through the ritual motions of mourning that prevent us from drowning in grief. He laid his face in the dust and stammered out a prayer. He had lost everything else, but he was determined to hang on to the mixture of dignity and humility with which he'd met life before. The calamities did not end there: His body was suddenly covered in sores, head to toe. But even as he sat on a dunghill, scratching the bloody boils with a piece of garbage, he made himself remember: Blessings are given, blessings are taken, all at the hands of the Lord.

For how can man be righteous? How can mortals be pure? Pain doesn't spring from the dust, no: Man is the father of sorrow. God never betrays the innocent, or takes the hand of the wicked. The children must have been evil; God punished them for their crimes. You may think your life is spotless, but if God were to cross-examine you and turned up your hidden motives, you would know that your guilt is great. Indeed, it must be inconceivable: Cheating your dearest friends, stripping your debtors naked, stealing food from the hungry, spitting on widows and orphans, laughing in beggars' faces — what else could result in so much pain? As a matter of fact, you are lucky that God has consented to scold you, giving you a chance to repent. What's that nonsense? Nothing to repent? You are undermining religion, and crippling faith in God.

With minor changes, the words in italics are taken from Stephen Mitchell's magnificent translation of the book of Job. It's the oldest book of the Bible, and with the possible exception of Adam and Eve and the apple, it's the story that will be most familiar. Which isn't surprising, for it's based on experience all of us know. Not, I hope, in its details; still, the idea of injustice, of bad things happening to good people, has ancient and universal resonance.

But that's not quite true, as these quotes should have shown. I excerpted them in a way intended to make you uneasy. Omitted is

Job's rage, which takes up much of the book; without it he's the meek and patient man the Middle Ages made proverbial. I left out God's speech, which is terrifying, as well as His repeated suggestions that Job spoke the truth – not the friends who are quoted above. The passages I omitted would have been disregarded, and largely censored, in medieval Christian editions. Even the book's translation is a mind-boggling story. The absence of an authoritative original encouraged centuries of scholars to mold the text to their own views. Where the Masoretic Hebrew text announces that Job's sheep were 'burned by the fire of God,' the Greek translators of the Septuagint, unwilling to make God the author of suffering, simply left them destroyed by 'fire.' The King James Bible turned conditionals into assertions: Job's hesitant 'If I have sinned' became 'I have sinned,' period. For seventeenth-century translators, Job's suffering was inconceivable if he hadn't. Elie Wiesel called Job our contemporary, though nobody was ever more classic. Bad things may have always happened to good people, but we've only come to describe it that way since the Enlightenment. Until then, everyone writing about Job – and write they did, in Jewish, Christian, and Muslim traditions – wrote in a voice that echoed Job's friends.

You are likely to take Job's perspective and struggle to under-stand what God has done. Did He make a bet with Satan just to prove His team was best? Then He isn't benevolent. Did the devil make Him do it, as God Himself once complains? Then the world is Manichean, equally divided between the forces of light and darkness. Was He too busy attending to the ostriches and antelopes to notice what was happening to Job? Then He sounds like an over-worked parent, so He certainly can't be omnipotent. However you parse it, traditional religion is in trouble – which is why there were debates over whether to include the book in the canon at all.

The friends, by contrast, take what they believe to be God's per-spective, and struggle to understand what Job has done. Christian commentators picked up the refrain that he'd sinned in his heart. Perhaps Job had done the right things for the wrong reasons, and what's worse than good behavior with evil motives? Perhaps more than his heart was involved here: Those mysterious boils could be due to syphilis, his professions of fidelity lies. And God, who sees the future, knew that if Job suffered, he would sin, and curse God. If all times are the same for God, why not punish Job ahead of time for the sin he was sure to commit? However you parse it, Job is in trouble and should be punished for asking too many questions about things that don't concern him – a line that was easier to maintain when most Christians had no access to what Job actually said.

Jews do not cut sacred texts; once a book has been canonized it is holy and inviolable. Instead, they write more. Hundreds of works – Talmud, Gemara, Midrash – were written to explain why biblical texts that appear ambiguous or unintelligible actually turn out to make perfect sense. Midrash is a collection of tales that imagine events that might have been left out of scripture; had we known all the details we would understand the reasons for the things we first condemned. (Sometimes this works. Compare your reaction to *The boy smashed the window to take something from the store* with *The desperate boy smashed the window of the locked pharmacy at midnight to take the antidote that saved his sister's life*.) Midrashim always come in the subjunctive – if this had happened then that would have been all right – but though they may lack the stringency of hard analysis, they are often more persuasive. Here's my favorite Midrash on Job: The events in the story took place at just the moment when Pharaoh's army was catching up with the children of Israel as they fled toward the Red Sea. To make sure the fleeing slaves all got across, God gave Job to Satan – as a good shepherd leaves the strongest of his rams to battle with the wolves while he leads the lambs to safety. Now Job appears not as unintended sinner (though there are plenty of Midrashim that portray him that way, too), but as unintended savior, a sort of resistance hero in spite of himself. Either way, we can be certain: There was meaning in Job's misery, even if he didn't know what it was.

Few cultures were built without this assumption; think of Adam and Eve in the Garden. The apple is so implausible an explanation of sin and suffering that it can only express the strength of our wish to have some explanation rather than none. (We all have to sweat, suffer, and die because our ancestors did *what?*) The inclination to connect sin and suffering isn't confined to monotheism: The whole city of Thebes is punished with plague for Oedipus's crimes. Buddhists call it the law of cause and effect. Hindus call it karma. There are differences in the systems, but all are systematic ways of expressing the refusal to accept a gap between *is* and *ought.*

In *Evil in Modern Thought* I traced the history of modern Western conceptions of evil. There I argued that one important achievement of the Enlightenment was to separate what had been hitherto known as physical evil from moral evil. Before the Enlightenment, things like earthquakes and illness were not viewed as different in kind from things like murder and crime. All of them caused terrible misery; all were ultimately in God's hands. And because it's more painful to think our misery meaningless than to think it justified, physical evils had to be the result of moral ones. If you suffered, you had sinned. The assumption was so deep it was rarely stated, but then neither was the principle of sufficient reason, from which it seemed to follow. Sometimes arguments were framed to deal with particular counterintuitive examples. (Why were more churches than brothels destroyed in the Lisbon earthquake? Because God hates those who profane His name with false worship more than those poor wretches who merely sin in the flesh. No, that wasn't Pangloss, but a Jesuit who was actually there at the time.) Far more often, the connection between happiness and virtue was simply seen as self-evident.

Some intellectual revolutions are hard to appreciate because they've been so successful we have difficulty grasping what it was once like to think differently. In this case, by contrast, the revolution is hard to appreciate because it isn't complete. The assumption that our happiness is balanced with our virtues is so deep it can be found almost anywhere. It survives in Islamist claims that the December 2004 tsunami was Allah's way of sweeping South Asian beaches clean of underdressed tourists; in Jerry Falwell's claim that 9/11 was God's punishment for the metropolis that spawned *Sex and the City*; and in your suspicion that the grief your teenagers are giving you is somehow related to the grief you gave your parents. Superstitions die hard even in those of us who thank the Enlightenment for undermining them. But undermine them they did, and our conviction today that every physical evil is *not* punishment for moral evil is a conviction we owe to the eighteenth century.

Separating physical from moral evil was a way of disentangling happiness from virtue. Until you disentangle them, the question of a right to happiness cannot arise. You get what you get, and whatever it is, you must somehow deserve it. Or perhaps more precisely: Happiness – like grace – is with God, so nobody can ever deserve it, and not everyone is going to get it. Once we acknowledge that physical and moral evils are truly separate, we've acknowledged that people may get a fate they don't deserve, and have a right to one they do. There are fortunes and contingencies that ought to be changed. It becomes possible to read Job as we read it today.

Like most thoughtful people in the Western tradition, Enlightenment thinkers thought about Job. Voltaire called him 'friend Job,' and, noting that he wasn't Jewish, used him as an occasion for a particularly nasty stream of anti-Semitic remarks. Noxious as they are, they show that Voltaire, unlike earlier writers, had begun to identify with our hero. His *Philosophical Dictionary* lets loose some clever invective at Job's friends' behavior, and is the first widely read book to emphasize that God Himself punished the friends for being wrong. While Voltaire was annoyed at the friends of Job, Kant was outraged at them. In the popular essay 'On the Impossibility of Every Future Attempt at Theodicy,' he called Job's friends dishonest; rather than speaking what they thought was true, they were speaking what they thought God would want to hear in the event that He turned out to be eavesdropping. Kant's own philosophy, he told readers, was just like Job's: Whatever faith he had must be based on morality, not the other way around; and what counted was Job's righteousness and honesty, which not even the worst suffering could destroy.

Kant's attempt to turn the book of Job into the precursor of the *Critique of Practical Reason* is stretched at several junctures, but that's unimportant here. What's crucial is that Kant identifies with Job *in all of his rage*. Kant thinks Job, not God or his mistaken advocates, was right. He thereby opens the way to reading Job as you do. Presumably you were unsettled by the version of Job's story with which this chapter began. You should find the suggestion that Job's children were swept off by a tornado because they were evil as revolting as the suggestion that a million children died in the Holocaust because European Jewry strayed from traditional faith. You should find the charge that Job must have been responsible for the misery that befell him as outrageous as the claim that anybody working in the Twin Towers was responsible for the worst crimes of American imperialism. There are people who believe such things, but insofar as they believe them they do not share a modern moral universe. That universe holds that we have a right to happiness, as long as we don't forfeit that right by doing something, like un-provoked murder, that puts us outside the moral universe we want others to share with us. While there may be good reasons why governments should guarantee no more than our right to pursue happiness, we believe in our right to actually get it, and consider lives lived without much of it to be tragic.

All this, historically speaking, is very recent. Shortly before being felled by the guillotine he had helped set in motion, the French revolutionary Saint-Juste proclaimed that 'Happiness is a new idea in Europe.' It was just a few decades since Rousseau's *Emile* had repeated: Happiness is the goal of every being who senses. If God made us sensitive, He didn't make us to suffer – a fact we should remember before inflicting traditional forms of education on our helpless children. Following and formalizing him in *The Metaphysics of Morals,* Kant wrote that 'God's end with regard to the human race (in creating and guiding it) can be thought only as proceeding from *love,* that is, as the *happiness* of man.' So much for vales of tears.

Let's make it quite clear: Happiness isn't the same as hedonism, as we'll very soon see. Nor is it the same as quality of life, though we owe the Enlightenment a great deal for improving ours. Quality? Life itself was altered when parents began to think that reaching the age of five without dying was a normal thing to expect of their children. But as Rousseau was fond of telling us, anything you've come to expect as normal no longer makes you happy. His critique of false needs was breathtakingly modern: Long before assembly lines, Rousseau described how we are dazzled by new commodities that promise happiness, and deliver nothing but a dull demand for more. While attacking the ways in which we are fooled into losing our independence, time, and money pursuing a phantom of happiness, Rousseau implores us to hold out for the real thing.

Happiness is also not the same thing as cheeriness. *Would you live your life over if given the chance?* It's a question most people ask themselves at one time or another, and it's one measure of happiness with our lot. Eighteenth-century philosophers asked the question often, and to dispel the illusion that the Enlightenment was unremittingly upbeat you need only see how it was answered.

Voltaire, for example, wrote poems in praise of pleasure and luxury throughout his long life, and clearly had a great deal of both. He also had more than an ordinary share of life's deeper joys: at least one real love story, plenty of friends and admirers, and the knowledge that his work had an impact on the wider world. At moments he clearly felt it; not too long after the death of his favorite lover, he wrote that he was so happy he was almost ashamed. Yet for all his bravado, Voltaire was often torn. In the same book that insists the world is a much better place than its detractors complain, he gleefully retells a myth that describes the earth as a toilet where the slops of the universe are dumped. And when asked about living life over, Voltaire demurred. He thought most of us want our lives back when we lie on our deathbeds – not because we love our lives, but because we fear our deaths. The fact that we tend both to curse life and cling to it is one more proof that humankind is mad. Hume agreed it was crazy to complain both about life's brevity and about its vanity and sorrow, but he went beyond Voltaire: None of us would choose to repeat the last decade of our lives, but all of us are certain the next will be better. Hume thought attitudes toward life had become more sanguine in his day, but this only revealed how dismal they had been before.

Rousseau thought such statements were their problem, not his. Men like you, he wrote to Voltaire, create your own misery. How could a man blessed with Voltaire's fortunes find the world wretched, while he, Rousseau, 'in obscurity, poor, alone, tormented by a suffering without remedy, I meditate with pleasure on my retreat and find that all is well.' Not surprisingly, this letter was one of several to which Voltaire did not reply. The question is important, even if you don't accept Rousseau's answer: that happiness can't be found in the jaded and overstuffed Paris salons, but in a country life, preferably in the mountains, where simple upright people cherish what they have. Yet though he insists that every mountaineer in Valais would choose to repeat his life endlessly – even in place of paradise – Rousseau's own choices are not entirely clear. Few people wrote more poignant paeans to happiness, or more enthusiastically, on occasion, of their own. But one of *Emile*'s passages that deserves more probing says, 'The sentiment of happiness crushes man. He is not strong enough to bear it.' Whether because of this belief, or because he really did see a good deal of suffering, Rousseau often repeated that life always holds more suffering than happiness – even in the book he called his brightest, *Emile*.

If Rousseau was ambivalent, what about Kant? His essay 'The End of All Things' includes Voltaire's Persian legend of the earth as a toilet, and adds a couple of other models: earth as a prison, as a madhouse, as a cheap highway inn. He claims to be merely repeating metaphors others have used. But when he speaks in his own voice, he holds that it's certain: Nobody would choose to repeat his life but for the sense of duty that forbids suicide, and most of us would end the lives we have without it. If our only reason for living were the pleasure we get from it, the species would be doomed.

Even those who knew more about pleasure than Kant did could be brutal about its consequences. In his *Philosophical Dictionary*, Voltaire turns kisses into miracles: We might have been constructed like fish, who simply drop their eggs and semen into the ooze. Instead, men and women reproduce themselves by means of a pleasure that nothing can weary. Shouldn't we be grateful to be singled out for delight? The downside, however, is just as unique: We're the only species subject to sexually transmitted diseases so cruel as to make us regret the acts that bring them on.

You cannot appreciate the Enlightenment until you know how dark it could be. These men were not sunny. Even the legendary Leibniz, whom the later Enlightenment found too optimistic, was highly equivocal. He thought people would choose to repeat their lives on two conditions only. First, we'd need some variety; though we might accept the same amount of good and evil the next time around, we'd demand a change in kind or we'd die, literally, of boredom. His second condition is more important: We'd choose to repeat our lives only if we had no knowledge of the life to come, for our picture of the other world must inevitably discontent us with this one.

And that is just the point. Your right to pursue your own happiness may seem trite, and even problematic, but the days when such pursuit was considered subversive are not long gone. The contemporary Western assumption that worldly happiness is the *only* point of living may need rethinking, but a few centuries ago it was not the point at all. Well into the eighteenth century, happiness wasn't really expected as part of the present. It lay in the past, in a Garden of Eden or in another golden age, and might appear in the life to come, but in this one its appearance was likely to be accidental. The ingredients that make for happiness don't much change – a kiss, a song, a full stomach, a baby's smile – and people enjoyed them, then as now, whatever they thought about their right to do so. But such pleasures were always held to be fleeting. *Life is as miserable as death is terrifying:* This idea is repeated as often, and as casually, as the skulls that appear in memento mori still lifes. Neither was exactly a cliché, but each was part of the daily rhythm the Western world took for granted. You may reject the witless hedonism currently peddled by much of America's industry, and find the thought of Paris Hilton as an icon of happiness one of the sadder thoughts around. But unless you really want to return to the idea of life as a trial and a vision of woe, you owe the Enlightenment a debt.

Kant called himself a melancholic, but that's not how others saw him. This tribute was written by one of his students, Johann Gottfried Herder:

> I have had the good fortune to know a philosopher. He was my teacher. In his prime he had the happy sprightliness of a youth; he continued to have it, I believe, even as a very old man. His broad forehead, built for thinking, was the seat of an imperturbable cheerfulness and joy. Speech, the richest in thought, flowed from his lips. Playfulness, wit and humor were at his command. His lectures were the most entertaining talks . . . The history of men and peoples, natural history and science, mathematics and observation, were sources from which he enlivened his lectures and conversation. He was indifferent to nothing worth knowing. He incited and gently forced others to think for themselves; despotism was foreign to his mind. This man, whom I name with the greatest gratitude and respect, was Immanuel Kant.

The passage is all the more moving in light of the background: Kant's review of Herder's own work was a devastating critique. Apparently Herder was too grateful to bear his former teacher a grudge, and less famous men who knew Kant struck the same note.

His charm was renowned enough to earn him the nickname the Gallant Magister in his youth, and he must have kept his melancholy to himself. Yet the question of happiness seems closely tied to temperament, part of the phenomena psychology sums up with the word *resilience*. It's what allows some conjoined twins to be joyous and playful, and some people with Voltaire's fortunes to grumble and fret. According to psychologist Daniel Gilbert's *Stumbling on Happiness*, more than half of all U.S. citizens experience a major trauma like assault or natural disaster in their lifetimes, but only a fraction develop traumatic pathologies. Being spared looks as mysterious as grace. But however you understand the mystery, the value you place on your life is a statement about who you are. Whatever the source of Kant's strength was, it led him to formulate both the questions and the answers more clearly than anyone before him.

Kant argued that happiness isn't a matter of wishful thinking, but a matter of reason's rights. Many Enlightenment thinkers held Christianity responsible for systematically decreasing our expectations of happiness, but Socrates wasn't much better. Kant saw that the problem was older than Christian aesceticism; it goes as deep as metaphysics ever does. Because we long to believe that, appearances to the contrary, the world is the way that it should be, we use one or another trick to fool ourselves that it is. A disconnect between happiness and virtue? Just an illusion, said many Greek and Roman philosophers. When you look closer, they turn out not only to be in harmony, but identical. Epicureans thought happiness was virtue; Stoics thought virtue was happiness. Kant thought both views were attempts to escape the double pain of disconnection: We are neither as good nor as happy as we ought to be.

Each philosophy offers a different form of false consolation. Epicureans would console us for our lack of virtue by arguing that, on the whole, self-interest creates more good than harm. Just as experience teaches that a little wine makes you happy and a lot makes you wretched, we can learn to regulate our desires to lead to the outcome that's best for us, and everyone else as well. Why invent guilt and torment when you can eat your cake without them? But if the Epicurean offers false consolation for our lack of virtue, the Stoic tries to console us for our missing happiness, insisting that the goods of the earth are pleasant but skin-deep. Real happiness lies not there, but in something much deeper: the consciousness of your own good soul. If you know you've done your duty, you need know nothing more. Certain virtue gives satisfaction nothing else can threaten or match: No torment can destroy it, and no reward is sweeter.

The song is sometimes sweet, and the message may be true: It *is* hard to find

> One rich man in ten
> With a satisfied mind.

Did the songwriters sample poor men, or did they proceed with Rousseauean faith? It's a genuine question. Most eighteenth-century thinkers were drawn to one or another form of Stoicism. The same tune, with different lyrics, was offered by Alexander Pope, the Enlightenment's favorite poet. The final chapter of his *Essay on Man*, 'Of the Nature and State of Man With Respect to Happiness,' concludes in part:

> What nothing earthly gives, or can destroy
> The soul's calm sunshine, and the heartfelt joy
> Is virtue's prize: a better would you fix?
> Then give humility a coach and six
> Justice a conqueror's sword, or truth a gown
> Or public spirit its great cure, a crown
> Weak, foolish man! Will Heaven reward us there
> With the same trash mad mortals wish for here?
> Know then this truth (enough for man to know)
> 'Virtue alone is happiness below.'

Kant loved to quote Pope in his lectures, and we know his life was austere – two reasons why his position is often confused with Stoic ones. But his view is both darker (initially) and brighter (perhaps). To begin with, if your mind is really satisfied, you had better beware. Kant was brilliant in tracking human talents for self-deception. To say we do not know our souls as they really are is to say we live in constant temptation: to ennoble our ordinary interests and conceal our base ones, from ourselves as well as from anyone else. Consequently we may – and we must – try to be decent, but we will never know if we succeed. The Stoic who understands this must seek his consolation elsewhere.

Moreover, Kant argues, the Stoic was on the wrong track the whole time. His impulse is the impulse to control, when life is radically out of hand. If we can't determine the external world, thinks the Stoic, at least we can command our own souls. To try to collapse happiness into virtue is to try to seek refuge from the power of fortune. But the refuge cannot last. Suppose you could – despite Kant's arguments to the contrary – really know you were good. It might be the noblest form of happiness, but it's hardly the only one. Just think about Job. Knowing he'd done nothing to deserve his fate made his fate all the more bitter, and harder to bear. A man less good would care less. Job moves from self-pity to outrage as he comes to understand that he isn't unique, but only exemplary. Or should a righteous man be comforted by the thought that his suffering is not merely private suffering, but evidence that the whole *world* is unjust?

Now a real Stoic must see Job's pain as a sign of human weakness: Were Job a little stronger, he would have needed nothing more than the knowledge his conscience was clear. But since we have bodies as well as souls, our senses as well as our higher faculties make claims on the world. Were we airier sorts of beings, we might be able to live without happiness, or at least to produce what's needed for it out of resources all our own. This is not a mature Enlightenment view. Not sensual needs and vulnerabilities, but reason itself demands happiness, provided we've done what we need to deserve it. Being good gives us rights. For Stoics, virtue was defined so as to be synonymous with (true) happiness. For Kant, virtue is defined as worthiness to be happy. It's an extraordinary outcome. Happiness has priority, as it ought to for someone who wrote that we were created in order to be happy. Yearning for happiness is neither a wish nor a weakness, but something you've a right to feel. Just a few decades earlier, Pope concluded that the first and last purpose of the human soul was love of God. In saying that God's purpose was love of humankind – and therefore our happiness – Kant turned things upside down. Job's longing isn't a defect, or the result of an unfortunate flaw, like the fact that our bodies have needs they can't satisfy alone. It's reason that needs to be satisfied, and nothing less than happiness will do it.

The fact that you have a right to happiness doesn't mean you ought to seek it directly. You're inclined to seek it all the time, which is why it cannot be a duty. Like most people, you are likely to devote most of your attention to your own happiness (or lack thereof), and my perfection (or lack thereof). What if we simply switched? Devote yourself to my happiness and your own perfection, and I'll do the same in return. In a world where everyone did *that*, both happiness and virtue would double. It's a beautiful maxim. But even when we forget to act on it, we can remember Kant's first point: Collapsing happiness into virtue from any direction is a form of bad faith.

With the notion of a right to happiness came a set of demands on the present. As soon as even part of the meaning of life is the happiness you may find within it, then creating the conditions for happiness comes to seem necessary. Pleasures are no longer signposts or symbols, but stand finally for themselves. Happiness is no longer a mystery, whether you call the mystery providence or fate. Once happiness becomes a right, human hands need to guard it. Different conceptions of the state will emerge: In one model the state has an active obligation to promote its citizens' happiness; in the other, it's merely obliged to insure that nothing actively prevents it. In arguments over political economy, the differences between these views are enormous. The one puts responsibility for happiness in your hands, the other demands that the community take a share of responsibility, too. But these views look far more similar to each other than the perspective that preceded them: where happiness wasn't a right but a blessing, hence not a matter for human hands at all.

Once happiness was out of heaven, the ideas of what it came to were bound to change as well. Kant was explicit: While reason can tell you that you have a right to happiness, only experience can tell you what will actually make you happy. 'Only the natural drives for food, sex, rest and movement, and (as our natural predispositions develop) for honor, for enlarging our knowledge and so forth, can tell each of us, and each only in his particular way, in what he will find these joys,' he writes in the *Metaphysics of Morals*, then goes on to blast the paternalism that would legislate others' happiness: 'I cannot do good to anyone in accordance with *my* concepts of happiness (except to young children and the insane), thinking to benefit him by forcing a gift upon him; rather, I can benefit him only in accordance with *his* concepts of happiness.'

Kant wasn't the only one whose mind was this open. Their interest in one another's characters – not to mention in other cultures – made most Enlightenment thinkers aware of how varied the experience of happiness could be. But all of them agree on one point. If the Enlightenment demanded happiness, it wasn't about end-state bliss. Even those who imagined an original paradise didn't long for it. Voltaire was the clearest on this score: His Garden of Eden was an uncouth homestead that no man in his right mind would trade for a bottle of good French wine. He believed the longing for a golden age was out of date; paradise, as he concludes in one poem in defense of luxury, is where he is.

What of Voltaire's young rival? Rousseau is commonly misread as proposing a return to the state of nature. Voltaire may have been the first to misread him, from the opening of his sole response to the hapless Swiss genius: 'I have received, Monsieur, your new book against mankind. Reading it makes one feel like marching on all fours.' But this is simply slander. Both in that book, the *Discourse Concerning the Origins of Inequality*, and in later ones, Rousseau is quite clear: The savage may be noble, but he isn't yet free. Rousseau's vision of happiness was not of a man who turned his back on civilization, but one who longed to improve it.

Kant, as usual, put the point in duller but clearer terms. (He once wrote that Rousseau's writing was so beautiful it made him too agitated to think straight, so he had to pause regularly to calm down enough to understand it.) Perhaps there was a sort of garden, Kant said, where humankind had wanted for nothing, and had no knowledge of evil. But if each of us had lost in leaving that state, the species as a whole has gained. However you may yearn for the womb's shelter, you don't really want to return to it. The loss of innocence was the price of reason, and the Enlightenment had no doubt that reason was worth it.

If paradise means a place where all our wishes are satisfied, then paradise is a bore. This is a message the Enlightenment sent out time and again. It's not only a rejection of heaven as a place where good people go when they die. It's a rejection of the idea of heavenly bliss as the point where desire stops. For the Enlightenment, human beings are essentially active. We are made to create ideals we cannot wholly fulfill, set out for horizons we know we will not reach.

We can test this by means of a couple of daydreams. Both Rousseau and Voltaire left records of theirs, and for all the differences in their conceptions of happiness, neither imagined it as a point where you stop. Voltaire's poem 'Le Mondain' shows his first views of paradise: not Adam's sloppy Eve, but a well-dressed lady, a comfortable bed, good food on better dishes, dancing in palaces decorated with trompe l'oeil designs. Though he no longer thought his own life was paradise, his tastes never changed, and when he got older he pictured utopia as a cleaned-up South American version of Paris high life. You can find the vision in chapters 17 and 18 of *Candide*, in which Candide and his companion, Cacambo, reach the mythical El Dorado and finally experience a land where everything is as it should be. There a simple dinner in a poor village includes 'four tureens of soup, each garnished with two parrots, a giant boiled condor, two savory roasted monkeys, three hundred round-billed hummingbirds on one platter, six hundred straight-billed humming-birds on another, exquisite stews, delicious pastries, all served on platters of a sort of rock crystal.' While he is musing, Voltaire adds a simple home whose doors are made of silver, with interior paneling of gold, and a lobby encrusted with rubies and emeralds, set in a public square paved with stones that smell of cloves and cinnamon, all designed with exquisite taste and harmony. Naturally Voltaire's palace is full of the less tangible sources of happiness that filled Enlightenment dreams: a palace of science that replaced law courts and prisons, an urbane and generous king who would rather be embraced than fawned over. ('Of all the astonishing things Candide saw and heard, by no means the least astonishing was the fact that the king's remarks were witty, even in translation.') The author emphasizes the wisdom that pervades El Dorado, though he seems more dazzled by the precious stones. But even as Candide marvels at the bounty of his author's imagination, he only stays in El Dorado for a month. He says he must find Cunégonde, the lover whose absence is the pretext for his travels, but the *Philosophical Dictionary* makes clear this is just an excuse. Its final comment on Eden: 'The worst of conditions is that of a man who has nothing to do.' Adam should be grateful for his exile, for a place where all our needs were satisfied must be profoundly dissatisfying.

Rousseau's reveries could hardly look more different. Book IV of *Emile* ends with a fantasy about what life would be like if its author were rich. Rousseau assumes that laws of psychology stay fixed even when fortunes change, so he begins by acknowledging that if he were a rich man he'd be no better than others. To acquire a fortune one must be self-centered, arrogant, and merciless; once he had acquired it, he would devote himself to pleasure. 'Up to this point I would be like all other rich men.' The difference between himself and the rich, therefore, is not a moral one. Rousseau wants to talk about taste, and he fills ten pages with fancies that give us a window on his ideal of happiness.

He says that he is sensual and voluptuous, but his idea of sensuality is to follow nature's course. 'Nothing is more insipid than early fruits and vegetables. It is only at great expense that the rich man in Paris succeeds, with his stoves and his hothouses, in having bad vegetables and bad fruits on his table the whole year round. If I could have cherries when it is freezing and amber-colored melons in the heart of winter, what pleasure would I take in them when my palate needs neither moistening or cooling?' Similarly, buying hothouse flowers 'is less to embellish winter than to spoil spring; it is to take the pleasure of going into the woods to seek the first violet, spy out the first bud, and shout in a fit of joy, "Mortals, you have not been abandoned; nature still lives."'

The Rousseau who could have anything would have very few servants, and do his own shopping. He likes exercise, fresh air, and the feeling that nothing stands between him and the rest of the world. Voluptuary though he is – at least in imagination – he wouldn't be the sort of man who uses his wealth to buy young girls' favors. 'I could not bear to see my disgusting caresses make them sick to the stomach, or to imagine them describing the dirty pleasures of the old ape in such a way as to avenge themselves for having endured them.' Dressing simply and comfortably, he'd avoid those women who insist on fancy clothing, though if they 'were young and pretty, I could sometimes put on lace in order to spend – at the very most – a night there.' His dream house is painted more precisely than Voltaire's: 'I would not build myself a city in the country and set up a Tuileries at my doorstep deep in the provinces. I would have a little rustic house – a white house with green shutters – on the slope of some agreeable, well-shaded hill. Although a thatch roof would be best in every season, I would greatly prefer not gloomy slate but tile, because it makes a cleaner and gayer impression than thatch. Instead of a courtyard I would have a farmyard, and instead of a stable a shed full of cows, so that I would have the dairy products I like so much.'

And there he would gather a small society of friends: men 'who love pleasure and know something about it,' women who are happier to hold a fishing line than a deck of cards. Every meal would be picnic and feast at once. 'Gaiety, rustic labors and frolicsome games are the world's premier chefs, and delicate ragouts are quite ridiculous to people who have been breathless since sunrise. The serving would be neither orderly nor elegant. We would have the lawn for our table and chairs; the ledges of the fountain would serve as buffet table; and the dessert would hang from the trees.' The friends would pass their time in conversation that was easy and open, striking just the right note between coarseness and falseness. Should that ever flag, they would turn to singing, and dance in the barn 'more gladly than at the opera ball. There would be no importunate lackeys spying on our conversations, whispering criticisms of our demeanour, counting our helpings with a greedy eye, or enjoying themselves by making us wait for our drinks and muttering about our taking too long at dinner. We would be our own valets in order to be our own masters.' Rousseau calls his daydream an essay in true taste, a key to the only happiness that is free from vanity and illusion. 'Someone will doubtless object that such entertainments are within the reach of all men and that one does not need to be rich to enjoy them. That is precisely what I wanted to get at.'

Of course they are not within reach of all men and women, the way things are now, as Rousseau knew too well. He is far from sharing Adam Smith's view that real happiness is the same for everyone, and that the peace of mind of the poor is no different from that of the rich. Smith wrote that 'the beggar who suns himself by the side of the highway possesses that security which kings are fighting for.' Rousseau had been on the highway; his knowledge of servants' perspectives was gained through years of watching high tables from a distance, and being shown many a back door. He isn't ignoring the plight of the poor here, but showing how simple it would be to change it. Not mythical streets of gold and silver, just a better distribution of real wealth, could put happiness within everyone's reach.

If anything reveals why Voltaire and Rousseau were doomed to endless opposition, it's the way they imagine happiness when they let their imaginations loose. It was a match made in purgatory. In the basement of the Paris Panthéon their coffins now face each other down, presumably for all eternity. One wonders what they would have made of the arrangement. But for all they were at loggerheads, their fantasies of happiness have much in common. Both are rich in the pleasures of the senses and community. Neither man is the cold martinet that left-wing critics saw as Enlightenment monster, nor the reckless glutton imagined by the right. Their daydreams reveal neither prude nor vulgarian, neither recluse nor boor. Rousseau's tastes are rustic, which isn't the same as primitive. (He'd decline to have a library or a gallery, 'especially if I cared for books or painting,' since most people who collect them for show do not.) This is happiness, not hedonism. Both men take pleasure in some forms of equality. While Rousseau goes much further, Voltaire uses the occasion to take shots at European court life, and his poor men in El Dorado live better than rich men anywhere else. Both are convinced that happiness is active: It isn't something that befalls you, it's something that you do.

If experience is the only thing that can decide what makes you happy, nothing can decide between these conceptions. Kant would grant each man the right to his own pleasures, leaving Rousseau to enjoy his green shutters and Voltaire the charms of his niece. In general, we all have the right to fill in our own pictures of happiness. But there are some visions Kant rules out, such as in a prominent example from *The Foundations of the Metaphysics of Morals*. Kant imagines a man with talents that could be cultivated with a certain amount of effort. Because his situation is comfortable, he decides to give himself over to lazy pleasures rather than developing the gifts nature gave him. Not yet so decadent as to forget the categorical imperative entirely, he asks himself if his resolution, or lack thereof, is permissible. The categorical imperative tells him no. For as we know from the South Sea islanders, Kant says, it is possible to imagine a world in which people let their talents rust and give themselves over to idleness, pleasure, and reproduction. But no reasonable being could truly will such a world, since our talents are given to us for all kinds of purposes.

There are several pieces missing in this argument. Can a little history provide them? The South Sea islanders were an object of Enlightenment fascination. Some thought they were as close as we'll come to observing humankind in the state of nature, and they were studied – or more often, imagined – with an eye to understanding the essence of humankind. By 1772 a myth of Tahiti was firmly in place, as Diderot wrote archly before going on to contribute to it. His *Supplement to Bougainville's Voyage* began as a review of the travel diary of Louis-Antoine de Bougainville, the first Frenchman to circumnavigate the globe. Arriving on the island in 1768, Bougainville thought he'd found the Garden of Eden. Bougainville's name survives in a flower, but it is Diderot's Tahiti that outlived the report of the man who had actually been there. The philosopher's descriptions of the South Sea islands read rather like descriptions of Woodstock from a distance: free and friendly, innocent and natural, every man sharing what he had, be it wisdom or fruit or women. Since Diderot held morality to be 'a science directed to the common happiness of the human race,' his goal wasn't description, but to show that happiness lay in a moral code opposed to the ones that prevailed in Europe. Nothing you could do that can't be done. The booklet's funniest scene depicts a conversation between an unnamed French chaplain and his Tahitian host, Orou, who begs the chaplain to spend the night with his wife and daughters. He is welcome to whomever he chooses, but would do the family a particular favor by taking the youngest daughter, who is still child-less. When the chaplain demurs, Orou replies, 'I don't know what you mean by religion, but I can only think ill of it, since it prevents you from enjoying an innocent pleasure to which Nature, that sovereign mistress, invites every person: that is, of bringing into the world one of your own kind; rendering a service which the father, mother and children all ask of you; repaying a gracious host, and enriching a nation by adding one more subject to it. I don't know what you mean by holy orders, but your first duty is to be a man and show gratitude.' After much pleading the chaplain gives in to tears and temptation, though he is still heard calling 'But my religion, but my holy orders' at daybreak.

Neither in the eighteenth century nor our own did this sort of polygamy remain as rosy as it looked from a distance. But Diderot's blissful portrait was no flight of sheer fancy. Captain Cook reported a similar scene, in which he declined a mother's offer of her daughter, saying it was harder to withstand the anger of the older woman than the beauty of the younger. Cook's widely read *Journal* was probably Kant's main source of information about the South Sea islanders, and it is still worth reading today.

Cook is nothing if not observant, and his notes are full of detail. In Tonga he found the fish so delicious that he told his cook to follow the native recipe, but his cook 'did not come up to theres.' The musical entertainment they were offered in Lifuka would have been applauded on any stage in Europe, and Cook had to order a show of English fireworks to keep up with his hosts. His comments, generally, are remarkably free of condescension. He was even willing to consider the Maori practice of cannibalism with a degree of tolerance, believing that when they were settled and united they would forget the custom by learning how to treat men as they wished to be treated, rather than as they were actually treated. The captain wasn't particularly prudish. Though he doesn't say why he denied himself the pleasures of the island women, he was concerned for their safety, and he made some effort to keep the sailors with venereal diseases from going ashore. He wasn't always successful. In exchange for leaving the islanders with syphilis, Cook gave them things they could use: not just trinkets and tools, but a host of pairs of animals. The list makes Cook's ship sound like Noah's Ark. Along with twelve sheep there were 'two young Bulls, two Heifers, two young stone Horses, two Mares, two Rams, several Ewes and Goats and some Rabbits and poultry, all of them intended for New Zealand, Otaheite and the neighboring islands, or any other place we might meet, where there was a prospect that the leaving of some of them might prove usefull to posterity.'

Keeping those animals alive on an eighteenth-century schooner was no picnic. On the third voyage Cook even threw in peacocks, 'which my Lord Besborough was so kind as to send me for this purpose a few days before I left London.' Cook sometimes expressed vexation over all the trouble involved, along with the satisfaction he felt in 'fulfilling His Majesty's design in sending such usefull Animals to two worthy Nations.' But did the nations get it? There was the rub. Some did, some didn't, and that got under the captain's skin. With their free and easy ways they must have known where baby cows came from, but many of the islands had no notion of husbandry. If they saw a cow, they didn't breed or milk it, they simply slaughtered it and ate. On some islands he learned to leave nothing but a stray pair of pigs, for 'as this is an animal that soon becomes wild and is fond of the thickest part of the woods, there is a great probability of their escaping' the very natives they were sent to profit.

Cook was as patient and tolerant as eighteenth-century sea captains got. He wasn't an intellectual; he'd only been to the village school. Contemplating a volcano, he found what 'seems to be a feild open for some Philosophical reasoning on those extraordinary Phenomenon's of nature, but as I have no tallant that way I must content my self with stateing facts as I found and leave the causes to men of more abilities.' But like every eighteenth-century European, he couldn't imagine happiness but in motion. Just as Kant found the greatest joy in 'the consuming thirst for knowledge, the restless passion to advance ever further, the delights of discovery,' Cook couldn't imagine forgoing the pleasure of exploring an unknown coast. The French philosopher Turgot went so far as to call inertia humankind's greatest defect, and Hume thought most evils could be avoided with a slight decrease in laziness. Gotthold

Ephraim Lessing, the playwright whose works drove the German Enlightenment, wrote in 1778, 'If God were holding all the truth in the world in his right hand, and in his left the ever-active drive to seek the truth – coupled with the promise that I would always go astray – and told me: *Choose!* I would humbly fall upon his left and say, "Father, give! Pure truth is for you alone."' There were many reasons why Lessing preferred seeking truth to finding it, but one is clear enough: The Enlightenment held movement, not rest, to be the key to human happiness. Investigations of motion in physics and changes in political economy reinforced this general view: Its conception of the good life is never static and never passive.

Thus it was not loose sexual morals, and not even cannibalism that offended Cook's sensibilities. What bothered him was idleness – the refusal to cultivate either the gifts intrinsic to human nature or those the English had brought. He was disturbed to see indifference even in Omai, the Tahitian who sojourned in England without acquiring the desire to apply himself. Omai, said Cook, had a grateful heart and a tolerable share of understanding, but like the rest of his nation showed no interest in new arts or improvements or even observation of other islands. He would probably care for the animals, but that was likely the only benefit the South Seas would take from the European explorers. What kind of a life was that?

Not *every* European agreed with Cook. Several sailors tried to desert, and were brought back from the hills in irons to prevent them from being 'forever lost to the World.' Given what sailors' lives were like then, it's hard to imagine they were grateful. Here Cook clearly violated Kant's principle that you can only make others happy according to their own conceptions of happiness. Kant avoided violating it himself with the help of a trick: It isn't a concept of happiness that prevents you from living like the South Sea islanders, but rather a concept of duty. Respecting humanity means respecting all the things humanity can do, and making it your business to do as many of them as you can.

Many will say we should have recognized a duty to leave the planet alone by letting some of our talents lie. It's a question to which we'll return. Kant's remark about the South Sea islanders expresses not an argument for duty but an Enlightenment vision of happiness that was fundamentally shared by Europeans, the occasional erotic fantasy notwithstanding. This is no surprise. When the eighteenth century proposed that even part of the meaning of life was to be found in the happiness we have in this world, the concept of happiness was transformed. No longer the fruit that was rewarded for striving, it became part of the striving itself. Looking up all day at coconuts might be a source of some forms of happiness, but not the ones that make up meaning. When meaning was no longer centered elsewhere, happiness itself had to change.

Any conception directed against the passivity of religion that promises peace in the hereafter as reward for toil and trouble here had to be a conception of happiness on the move. It was a conception that led to one set of modern problems; a little less movement would do us all good. But it has the potential to solve another. Kant argued that the well-being of the state does not consist in its citizens' happiness, for many people will be happiest in a state ruled by a tyrant, so long as he keeps them amused. What the Enlightenment rejected in the South Sea islands was what it perceived as a stupor, the docile submission to whatever bit of the given is coming your way. And what's coming your way is unlikely to be a breeze or a cow or a coconut, but a new kind of screen you can zap or click to create the illusion that life isn't passing you by.

CHAPTER SEVEN

REASON

1. *All genuine questions can be answered.*
2. *All genuine answers can be known.*
3. *All answers are compatible.*

And therefore:

4. *We must find a single abstract truth that explains all of reality, and the right way of acting in every circumstance.*

These are the formulas Isaiah Berlin often repeated to describe the Enlightenment concept of reason, though he neglected to say which of its thinkers actually held such a dim-witted view. Not Lessing, who was, as we saw, prepared to beg God to let him search for the truth forever without even the hope of finding any. Nor Kant, who began his most important work, *The Critique of Pure Reason*, with the statement that human reason has limits. He thought it was reason's fate to be permanently thwarted: always drawn to questions that transcend its powers to answer. Nor need you be deep, brooding, or German to question reason's powers. Even Baron d'Holbach, the Enlightenment thinker who comes closest to the caricatures, wrote that 'It is not given man to know everything, to penetrate to the essence of things or to go back to first principles.'

If Berlin forgot the first sentence of Kant's first *Critique*, or Lessing's famous vision of God's left hand, he was not alone. For Heidegger, to whom reason was the enemy of what he called thinking, the Enlightenment represented the extreme form of Western thought – reason that hopes to master the universe. In the view of Richard Rorty, the Enlightenment believed that rational inquiry was the attempt to grasp the intrinsic nature of things, to latch onto that unchanging truth that Rorty spells with a capital *T*. For Adorno and Horkheimer, the allegiance to reason made the Enlightenment totalitarian. All agreed that reason is instrumental, calculating, domineering, and condemned to futility. With such different philosophers singing in harmony, who can blame other mortals for joining the chorus?

Nothing seems so easy to get wrong as Enlightenment views about reason, while its claim that reason and happiness are connected draws immediate fire. Dissenters point out that reason has been known to lead to unhappiness, or that people are too unreasonable to be governed by something of which they have so little. Before you join them, take a moment to wonder what reason is. The Enlightenment spent a great deal of time doing so, analyzing the mind, composing diverse taxonomies of activities they variously dissected as reasoning, understanding, judging, deducing, and so on. While they had no access to neuroscience, many of the questions they asked were the same that researchers now ask – and current findings support many of their answers. Rather than blithely assuming that the intellect was infallible, they were dedicated to exploring it, and all their maps of the mind had boundaries. One nearly constant theme was the idea that reason is not omnipotent. Consider Pierre Bayle, whose 1697 *Historical and Critical Dictionary* was called the arsenal of the Enlightenment because later philosophers used its arguments to take aim at tradition. Bayle's metaphors for reason could be gruesome. He compared it to a corrosive powder that begins by attacking the infected flesh of a wound but goes on to destroy living flesh and bone. Reason may begin by refuting error, but it ends by leading astray. Using his intellect more sharply than most people evidently made Bayle more skeptical about what it all came to.

Voltaire was rarely awed by anyone, but he was so enamored of Bayle that he called him simply The Philosopher, and his work always reflected Bayle's influence. Voltaire's *Philosophical Dictionary* said the limits of the human mind 'are everywhere, poor doctor. Look at the grain of wheat I drop in the earth and tell me how it rises to produce a stalk loaded with an ear. Teach me how the same earth produces an apple high up in this tree and a chestnut in the neighboring tree. I could make you a folio of questions, to which you could reply with only four words: *I have no idea.*' But the classic bombardment on the idea that reason is almighty was provided in Voltaire's unforgettable portrait of Dr. Pangloss, *Candide*'s only character who never displays a spark of wisdom (or, for that matter, any spark at all). If that's what it means to believe reason can do everything, it's tempting to conclude it can do nothing. Pangloss is incapable of observation, and never makes a claim of reason that reality fails to mock. His insights are not only false but flat, their banality so painful that Candide can only be excused for overlooking it because he's so very provincial, and so very young. He needs years of travel round the globe to realize that Pangloss's commentaries on their experience add nothing to their understanding of it. Turning away from his teacher's blather to get down to real work is the book's first and last sign that Candide has actually learned something.

Candide is a satire, and one of its targets was classical rationalism, which elevated the intellect as the Enlightenment never did. For Enlightenment thinkers, rationalism was both overweening and authoritarian, and they sought different models for reason and knowledge. As Peter Gay has argued, 'It is no accident that the philosophes chose as their intellectual ancestors, in the study of man as elsewhere, those modern writers who had distrusted reason without exalting unreason: Montaigne, Hobbes, Spinoza, and Locke . . . The philosophes saw psychology as a dual escape — from unreasonable rationalism and superstitious antirationalism.' Kant called his enterprise transcendental psychology to distinguish it from the psychology of particular people. In chapter 5 I focused on Kant's critique of Hume, rather than Leibniz, because Kant had already accepted Hume's critique of rationalism; it was the call that woke him from his own dogmatic slumber as an old-style rationalist. To Hume's criticisms, Kant added his own. The most important was the idea that reasoning cannot, and should not, be a matter of knowing. In assuming it was, the problem was less that the rationalists allowed reason too much range than that they sabotaged its real purpose – as the locus of human freedom.

If despite their attacks on rationalism, they were committed to defending reason, what were Enlightenment thinkers defending it against? More often than not, it's said to be passion. Writing after both the Enlightenment and the French Revolution were over, some Romantics suggested the guillotine reflected not, say, mob hatred, but the triumph of head over heart – their most powerful argument for giving emotions center stage. Unfortunately, even those who appeal to reason often accept the Romantics' terms. In his 1838 Address Before the Young Men's Lyceum of Springfield, Illinois, Abraham Lincoln said that passion 'will in future be our enemy. Reason – cold, calculating, unimpassioned reason – must furnish all the materials for our future support and defense.' Yet the Enlightenment itself was never opposed to passion or sentiment. Examining the passions was nearly as widespread an Enlightenment pursuit as examining the workings of the intellect. It was the French who were most forthcoming in examining their own, and nobody reading the love letters of Diderot or Voltaire – not to mention the frenzies of Rousseau – could think the Enlightenment was short on emotion. 'I forgive everything that is inspired by passion,' wrote Diderot to his mistress. Writing to others, he made clear that such inspiration needn't be particularly elevated: 'There is a bit of testicle at the bottom of our most sublime sentiments and most refined tenderness.' Now Diderot was particularly prescient; Freud found the first anticipation of the Oedipus complex in the French philosopher's *Rameau's Nephew*. But even the more sober Voltaire, in his *Treatise on Metaphysics*, called the passions 'the principal source of the order we see today in the world.'

Nor did Enlightenment thinkers confine emotion to the private sphere: The eighteenth was the century that not only invented sentimental novels, but made it fashionable for readers to weep over them in public. Apart from the thrill he derived from pure thinking, and from discovering Rousseau, Kant left us no record of his private emotions. But committed as he was to privileging reason over sentiment, he took pains to offer long, if rather stilted instructions on how to cultivate the right sentiments. In fact, much like contemporary work from philosophy to neuroscience, Enlightenment thinkers rejected simplistic psychologies that pitted reason against emotion, emphasizing instead that we're generally moved by both.

If reason wasn't opposed to passion, was it contrasted with nature? This opposition, too, belongs to post-Enlightenment myth. Beginning in the nineteenth century, conservative thinkers used rhetoric like Burke's: Reform was impossible because the present order is the natural one, which reason is too weak to overthrow. Like the first charge, this one, too, relies on associations that were carefully presorted. Romantics portrayed reason as cold and often icy, feeling as warm but never hot; reason as hard, and feeling gentle; reason as ruthless, and feeling forgiving. These images of passion were not exactly exhaustive. They included tenderness but not rage, longing but not despair. Similarly, visions of nature included gamboling sheep and Cotswolds meadows, but left out sharks, floods, and lice. But the Romantics weren't unique in their use of natural images that were impossibly benign. Enlightenment visions were often just as one-dimensional, for everybody wanted nature on their side. Opposed to nature? The Enlightenment saw reason reflected in each of nature's corners, as more and more of the world became transparent. Its subtler thinkers asked how far we could know what was truly natural, given our distance from any original state. But everybody wanted nature's blessing for whatever arrangements they considered self-evident. It's an old tradition whose reach, even today, is almost infinite; as historian Lorraine Daston has shown, moral appeals to nature run the gamut from South African apartheid to Sierra Club environmentalism. The Enlightenment may have had no more valid a claim to it than the Counterenlightenment, but both rushed to claim nature as ally. What is natural has always been contested. At the start of the eighteenth century, it included hereditary monarchy, poverty, most forms of illness, slavery, sexual subordination, and feudal property arrangements. At the end of the century, thousands of questions had left such assumptions wide open. The Enlightenment distinguished itself by allying reason with nature, and saw the two as united. It opposed natural laws of reason to conventional and arbitrary ones, appealed to natural rights as a bulwark against convention. For many things count as reasons, but some things do not: *He said so. It's always been that way. Just because.* The more reason is encouraged by making sense of parts of the world, the more it will continue, asking for the point behind the point, the ground beneath the ground.

If reason sought both nature and passion not as adversaries, but as allies, what were its real targets? The earliest attacks on the Enlightenment all reveal the same answer: Reason was opposed to authority, in particular any authority based on revelation, superstition, and fanaticism. Not the natural but the supernatural was under attack, and it was here that the Enlightenment hoped reason and nature could make common cause. Spinoza was especially feared, far less for his abstract and difficult system of ethics than for his earlier biblical criticism, the first modern scholar's look at a text that had been untouchable. The suggestion that scripture was full of contradictions was hardly shocking; beginning with the double account of Creation in Genesis, they were there for anyone who was minimally literate to see. (That was the sort of thing that led the Catholic Church to restrict its reading.) But as long as the text was sacrosanct, those contradictions could be explained. If Ptolemaic physics could invent epicycles to keep a tottering system going indefinitely, all three faiths could develop bodies of scholarship devoted to making sure that enough of God's word made sense that the rest could be accepted on faith. Spinoza exposed contradictions without apology; held belief in miracles to be no more than a form of belief in magic, the prophets to be no holier than any wandering fool in the thrall of imagination; and argued that true reverence required rational devotion. His use of reason to criticize revelation was followed by many others. The message was clear: Philosophy trumps theology, as reason trumps faith.

In the seventeenth and eighteenth centuries nearly any theoretical book that was any good was cut, censored, published anonymously, or, when all else failed, ceremoniously burnt. Seen from a distance, the effort devoted to suppressing obscure arguments against the existence of miracles may look extravagant, but the censors had a point. If you insist that the world is subject to natural law without exception, you deny the existence of miracles. If you deny the existence of miracles, you deny that God can intervene in nature just to prove His authority. If you deny God's chance to prove His authority, you deny that authority of any kind can exist without reason – and you are well on your way to making reason the only authority at all. The Enlightenment's first object of attack was church authority, partly because of its power, and partly because it provided such splendid examples of absurdity. With its statues purported to sweat blood and its doctrines of Trinity and transubstantiation, the Catholic Church offered particularly soft targets, though Protestant theories of predestination were so hard to accept that they came under equal fire. But the main reason for attacking church authority was to undermine every other sort. The mantle of religion invests the state with an aura of authority it cannot otherwise possess. No wonder both church and state reacted with alarm to the Enlightenment demand that they be separated, and with the charge that Enlightenment thinkers were not just impious, but arrogant. Lessing and Kant and Voltaire and Rousseau show us that the Enlightenment was well aware of reason's limits, so the charge that it had none is the kind of slander that's offered more to discredit than to communicate. The Enlightenment never thought reason unlimited; it just wasn't prepared to let the church set the limits.

So the Enlightenment's appeal to reason began as opposition to authority that had been inherited or imposed but never justified. Its first efforts were devoted to undermining superstition by exposing contradictions in scripture, and using science to give natural explanations for things that looked like miracles. But even as those efforts were successful, new challenges arose. How to distinguish scientific predictions about the future from oracles? Medicine from quackery? In those days they still blended seamlessly into indistinct hash, and Enlightenment insistence on separating them made questions about the nature of reason crucial. What was this ability to separate garbage from gold?

Most of us have in mind two models of how reason works. One views reason as seeking truth the way fishermen catch shrimp or children flies. The object is there, the route direct, the process straightforward, the goal very clear: to gather and keep as much of the stuff as you possibly can. (Information, shrimp, flies: What matters is that it's out there, and you want a lot of it.) The other model views reason as a matter of calculation, tallying up the best means to achieve whatever end you have chosen. It's cool, precise, and unwavering. You feed in a goal, and it tells you how best to attain it. Like Google or MapQuest, it figures out the simplest way to get to where you're going, leaving where and why you are going at all to be determined by something else.

What does the determining? The most common candidate is passion. Your desires and emotions create goals. Whether or not they are sensible ones may be helped by the right sort of training, but it's mostly a matter of luck. Reason has nothing to do with choosing the goals themselves, only the course you take to reach them. David Hume offered the most famous statement of this view: 'Reason is and ought to be the slave of the passions, and should not pretend to any office but to obey them.' In Hume's view, reason was good for very little; he called it perfectly inert, wholly inactive, and finally impotent. What makes us move is desire, beginning with the desire for self-preservation. At its most useful, reason can measure the quickest, cheapest, and most efficient form of fulfilling those desires. It cannot do anything else. Should you destroy the whole world in order to stop your finger from itching? Maybe not, but it isn't reason that helps you decide.

Hume's heirs never tire of repeating that calculation won't get us all we want from reason, but they rarely mention anyone who thought it could. We can fall back on poor Leibniz, who spent much of his life dreaming of a universal language that would somehow depict thoughts so clearly that all the world's problems, from war to metaphysics, would solve themselves. After this language was discovered and codified, quarrelers would drop their swords with the words 'Come, let us calculate,' and pick up their pencils. Leibniz died in 1716, early in the Enlightenment, and he got nothing but ridicule for his efforts toward the universal calculus. True enough, calculation is a wonderful thing. It can tell you the distance to the moon or the next gas station, how much concrete is needed to reinforce a foundation, how much medicine constitutes an overdose. Even without the use of numbers, being able to calculate the best means to achieve your ends is the *first* step toward rationality. If you want to win a war, for example, you'd be wise to win over the people whose territory you've occupied. Rebuilding the infrastructure you shattered, or refraining from humiliation and torture, would be good places to start. But this is simple instrumental reasoning, and though being able to do it is a minimal condition of rationality, critics are right to say it isn't enough.

The model of reason as fishnet may look more promising than the model of reason as pocket calculator. Reason's contemporary critics usually picture reasoning as a process of hauling in knowledge, then claim that something about the hauling was a cheat. John Gray, for example, begins by assuming that reason is equivalent to the gathering of scientific knowledge, and goes on to charge that the gathering proceeds by irrational methods. Thus, he concludes, reason undermines itself. 'The origins of science are not in rational inquiry but in faith, magic and trickery. Modern science triumphed over its adversaries not through its superior rationality but because its late medieval and early modern founders were more skillful than them in the use of rhetoric and the arts of politics.' Citing only the eloquent Paul Feyerabend, who denied there were real differences between astronomy and astrology, Gray goes on to expand on his views. Science is irrational because many of its earliest heroes, like Galileo and Newton, saw themselves as defending theology; and many of its later heroes, like Darwin and Einstein, advanced theories that went beyond available evidence and were only later verified by it.

Gray's *Straw Dogs*, from which the above is taken, rests on straw men who could be felled by a whiff of common sense, let alone a basic introduction to the history of science. For the moment, let's ignore its uncritical assumption that theology is irrational, or its confusion between the validity of the theory and the interests of the theorist. Much more important is the fact that not only Darwin's and Einstein's, but any interesting discovery depends on principles and practices that cannot themselves be known. Forget the theory of relativity, which Einstein worked out on paper fourteen years before an experiment could be constructed to test it in space. You can't find out why the cookie jar is empty without assumptions like the idea that the simplest explanation is likely to be the best one, or the principle of sufficient reason itself. The idea that there is a reason why everything happened one way rather than another can never be proven, but without it we'd never prove anything else. You may need to look harder for the explanation that eludes you, but you'll never be able to show it isn't there. The principle of sufficient reason is the basis of everything we do know, not as datum but demand: to seek understanding and not to give up. Once you see this, you might conclude that everything we do, from charting the cosmos to ordering our households, is fundamentally irrational. You might also ask whether our intuitive models of reason are adequate to describe how reason really works.

Once again, there's nothing to be said against information, or gathering as much of it as we possibly can. Knowledge plays a crucial role in Enlightenment then as now. In a study of twenty-five different civilizations, anthropologist Donald Brown discovered that those that were organized by hereditary caste had no tradition of writing accurate descriptions of their pasts. Substituting legends for history, they also had no political science, biography, or realistic portraiture. All these practices reflect commitments to truth that are held, albeit imperfectly, in societies whose structures recognize merit. Truth has a way of subverting hierarchies that are based on authority, which is why they prefer to stick to myth. Even Rousseau, whose theory of education refused to emphasize academic achievement, was clear about the causes of fear: 'The same cause which makes men distrustful and people superstitious: ignorance of the things which surround us and of what is going on about us.' Ignorance of what's happening around them keeps citizens clueless and compliant, so the Enlightenment spread knowledge through mammoth projects like the *Encyclopedia* in order to undercut government efforts to suppress it. Their view of the *Encyclopedia* as an agent of democracy anticipated contemporary claims for the internet; you needn't think that knowledge of the truth can right all wrongs in order to think it can right some. Echoing Rousseau two centuries later, Al Gore wrote, 'Fear is the most powerful enemy of reason. Both fear and reason are essential to human survival, but the relationship between them is unbalanced. Reason may sometimes dissipate fear, but fear frequently shuts down reason.' What would have been the outcome of the 2004 election, for instance, if the 75 percent of Bush voters who believed Saddam provided substantial support to Al Qaeda knew they'd been duped? If the 56 percent who believed the U.S. found weapons of mass destruction in Iraq actually read the news? Would Americans demand more equitable distribution of global resources if they knew the U.S. devotes less than 1 percent of its budget to foreign aid – instead of the 24 percent the majority believes? Simple information is never enough to change the world, but it's always the first place to start.

The two intuitive models – reason as calculator, and reason as fishnet – describe two functions we rely on every day. They are first steps to becoming reasonable, and these steps are not small. Discovering that disease is caused by germs rather than demons, and reckoning that hand-washing is more efficient than exorcism in preventing the spread of illness, are matters of information and calculation that have saved millions of lives. Were it not for this sort of advance in our abilities to know and to calculate, half of those who complain about the poverty of instrumental reasoning wouldn't be around to do so. Reason produced these, and a host of other wonders. Cognitive psychologist Steven Pinker's *How the Mind Works* summarizes this process:

> The human mind is not equipped with an evolutionarily frivol- ous faculty for doing Western science, mathematics, chess, or other diversions. It *is* equipped with faculties to master the local environment and outwit its denizens. People form concepts that find the clumps in the correlational texture of the world. They have several ways of knowing, or intuitive theories, adapted to the major kinds of entities in human experience: objects, animate things, natural kinds, artifacts, minds, and social bonds. They wield inferential tools like the elements of logic, arithmetic, and probability.

And no doubt a lot more. Reasoning is reducible neither to calcu- lating means nor to gathering information. And as much as we need these capacities, by themselves, they would be of little use without the work of another: the ability to choose ends and goals that builds in the desire to realize them.

It was Hume who recognized that this ability is the source of power, but his conception of reason precluded it. Passions, he thought, are the motors that drive us. Certainly much of our lives is spent pursuing goals that are predetermined, in the drives for food, warmth, and sex that we share with other animals. Yet we also have the ability to determine our own ends – in extreme cases, as the gallows example showed, even against all the claims of biology.

To say that reason can work against the claims of biology is not to reinvent the ghost in the machine. Philosopher Gilbert Ryle coined that phrase to describe Descartes' theory that the mind is a different substance from the body, magically acting on it without ever being part of it. Pinker, for instance, a passionate defender of evolutionary biology, emphasizes that 'people in all societies have words for abstract conceptions, have foresight beyond simple necessities, and combine, compare, and reason on general subjects that do not immediately appeal to their senses.' Just these capacities, he argues, make us all into scientists from the cradle. You needn't deny materialism to know how little we'd have without ideas. One of the most exciting discoveries of contemporary neuroscience is called neuroplasticity, the mind's power to change the structure and function of the brain in response to experience. As *Wall Street Journal* science editor Sharon Begley writes, 'Like sand on a beach, the brain bears the footprints of the decisions we have made, the skills we have learned, the actions we have taken.' Neuroscientists can now watch repeated traumas etch neural pathways to turn grief into depression, meditating monks change the level of prefrontal activity by generating feelings of compassion, and violinists increase the shape of their motor cortex through sheer imagination. Some ironies are happy ones: A generation ago, many people feared (and a few of them hoped) that exact knowledge of how the brain works would reduce ideas to the firings of neurons and effectively eliminate them. Now, apparently, more exact knowledge confirms their reality. It's the materialists who are showing how mind changes matter, and they need no immaterial substances to explain it.

Reason's ability to counter nature is something entirely natural, part of what Kant called its peculiar fate. Our concern, therefore, is not reason's substance but its structure. If reason is not merely calculation or information gathering or any of its other operations, but something that moves us to these and other goals, just how does it work? Leibniz thought the principle of sufficient reason was a statement about the world: *For everything that happens there's a reason why it happened this way rather than that.* Kant recognized that it cannot be a fact about the world, but a demand on it: *For everything that happens, find the reason why it happened this way rather than that.* It's reason that allows us to go beyond whatever experience we are given, and allows us to think: *This could have been otherwise, why is it just like this?* The actual is given to us, but it takes reason to conceive the possible. Without that capacity we couldn't begin to ask why something is the way it is, or imagine that it might be better. These abilities form the basis of scientific research and social justice. They are so fundamental that we can hardly imagine functioning without them, and we're very likely to take them for granted. Orwell's police state revised history constantly in order to create citizens unable to imagine a world other than the one they lived in, or a past different from the present. But even a book as brilliant as *1984* doesn't go far enough. The ability to think that experience could be otherwise is deeper than your ability to imagine a world in which we have not always been at war, with whomever or whatever. Your very ability to learn from experience presupposes the ability to question experience – which in turn presupposes the ability to imagine a different one.

This process is so basic we may never notice it directly; when called to your attention, you may conclude it's automatic. In fact it is radically free. As we saw, the Enlightenment always connected reason and freedom: Knowledge was meant to liberate people from super-stition and prejudice; instrumental reasoning, from poverty and fear. Important as they are, those tasks of reason have elements that are both mechanical and passive: Gathering knowledge implies things that stay fixed enough to gather, and calculating how to get from one place to another implies two places that stay still. Recognizing reality and negotiating our way within it are two of reason's crucial tasks. Yet they are less free, hence less human, than the positing of ends beyond the experience that makes those tasks possible. As psychologist Daniel Gilbert concludes, 'The greatest achievement of the human brain is its ability to imagine objects and episodes that do not exist in the realm of the real, and it is this ability that allows us to think about the future. If nature has given us a greater gift, no one has named it.'

In concluding that reason is what makes us human, this is what Kant had in mind. Human beings are beings who are not restricted to the ends dictated to them by biology. Because they can think about futures, imagine things not as they are, but as they could and should be, they can posit ends of their own. This makes them what Kant called ends in themselves. Beings who are able to create their own ends should not simply become means for others.

You might see the principle of sufficient reason as an exercise in narcissism: The idea that there are reasons for everything that happens is another way of saying that reason seeks its reflection in the world wherever it goes. But it's equally true that reason gives us a desire for sense and for justice in one swoop. Its search is driven by an ideal that underlies everything else it does: The real should become rational, the *is* and the *ought* should coincide. Let's return to the first instance of that ideal: If the *is* was the way it *ought to be*, then happiness and virtue would be properly balanced. People who are good for the sake of goodness should lead long, happy lives; people who are obstinately wicked should not. This very basic premise is the basis of all your indignation when corrupt and brutal people flourish, and when righteous people suffer. It's a premise that's very hard to deny. You can say the words: *Anyone who protects children should be slowly and carefully tortured; anyone who commits rape and murder ought to bask on a tropical island*. Can you mean them? Trying to convince yourself that two plus two equals five is probably an easier task. (Recall the inconceivably wicked Sodomites, who butchered citizens for helping strangers.) A world in which good people suffer while wicked people prosper is a world that makes no sense.

It is, of course, the world we often inhabit. Kant said reason was born when we left the Garden of Eden. In a world where everything is as it should be, we have no need to ask why. The gap between *is* and *ought* is the space where questions begin. And while they may stop for many reasons – loss of patience or energy or funding – they only really cease when the world as a whole makes sense. This is one reason to see the problem of evil as the driving force not only of metaphysics, but of many other kinds of thinking as well. Why do the innocent suffer? Why do wicked people prosper? These questions drive us because they hurt, offending a sense of fairness that seems to be as visceral as it is elementary. Babies scream louder when they perceive that treats are not simply absent, but distributed unjustly. Burnout research attributes stress symptoms to the mismatch between your sense of fairness and that of your boss. Totalitarian regimes use gut reactions to injustice to hone interrogation techniques: Sleeplessness makes innocent prisoners rage more, but leaves guilty ones dazed and quiet. Ordinary criminals in concentration camps survived better than prisoners who had been deported on racist grounds. This is partly because criminals were accorded better conditions than other prisoners, but partly because criminals knew they were being punished for something. Those imprisoned because of race, by contrast, were constantly tormented by the dissonance between what they had done and what was being done to them.

So the mismatch between *is* and *ought* can make us wretched. How does reason use it to make things better? Let's follow its structure with an example. Suppose you observe an official who has failed at all the tasks he was appointed to fulfill and is nevertheless rewarded with goods and glory. Reason tells you not only that things could be otherwise, but that they ought to be otherwise. It thus moves you to ask: What accounts for this discrepancy between *is* and *ought*? You seek an explanation: The man has powerful connections who care more about loyalty than competence. Now you might stop there, having explained the original data, but reason is still discontent. A system in which competence is disregarded in favor of loyalty is dysfunctional; institutions ought to be differently constructed. What accounts for the existence of this one? Before you have explained whatever bits of contingency and corruption led to the appointment of a particular constellation of officials, reason leads you further. Why do we have a political system that gives contingency and corruption free rein? At some point you will likely throw up your hands in rage or dismay; you have a sick child, a double shift, an urge to dance, a need to sleep. Reason does not. Left to its own devices, it will keep asking why the gap between the way things are and the way they should be exists at all, until it reaches a point where no gap exists.

That point would be the best of all possible worlds. A world where everything makes sense would be a world without desire – in any case, without desire that is distinctly human. This is not just a problem for political activists who might be bored or lost if they found themselves in the utopia they devote their lives to achieving. In the best of all possible worlds, any creative activity is hardly conceivable. If everything is truly as it should be, why add anything to it at all? Reason leads us to seek a place we could not actually inhabit without becoming unrecognizable to ourselves.

Critics like Isaiah Berlin have pointed out that the world isn't like this: *There is no complete explanation that makes the world transparent, no point at which all questions are answered, all contradictions reconciled.* No champion of reason ever supposed that there was. Kant used the metaphor of the horizon when talking about reason to signify a point that only children think you can actually get to. Ideals function as ideals precisely because they lead us on past all that we know. After they become real they are just one more bit of the world we take for granted. This leads to recurring ingratitude. Once you've learned to tie your shoes, you're no longer proud of it. Once you've earned the home you longed for, you start to dream of a second. Once you live in a culture where healthcare is considered not a benefit but a right, you consider it trivial. There is something sad, and faintly perverse, in this process, but it's built into the logic of ideals. If what they are meant to do is urge us to go beyond our present experience, they will only work as long as they are not present.

If reason urges us toward an ideal that can never be realized, is the structure of reason itself fundamentally unreasonable? By no means. Paradoxical, perhaps, but some paradoxes are brilliant, and absolutely invaluable. By demanding a world that makes sense as a whole, reason spurs us to make sense of every bit of it within our reach: through science and art in the world of understanding; through politics and ethics in the world of practice. Reason uses the thought of a different reality to keep us going toward a horizon of truth and goodness till we've been round the world. By positing goals that are always higher than any we can ever reach, reason drives us to those we can. Evolutionary biologists may see this as a paradox with adaptive advantage. Other people may suspect a design.

This is a model of reason made to fit particular goals. For in one, and one sense only, did the Enlightenment take reason to be unlimited: It isn't reserved for power or privilege. Basing claims on reason was part of denying the rights of authority: Anyone can think for himself, and anyone can fail. The concept of reason was not accidental, but constructed to support specific universalistic demands. Until Kant worked out the details, it made little sense to speak of an Enlightenment model of reason; better to say that many thinkers were working with a commitment to universalism and to conceptions of reason that were modeled and molded to suit one another. It isn't a vicious circle, but it's a circle nevertheless. The Enlightenment looked to reason as a place to ground its claims for universal rights, but we all have emotions, too. At first glance, these seem a more sensible place to locate universality. The young Trotsky thought that in the truly human society, everyone would be an Aristotle, a Goethe, or a Marx, but even the most optimistic among us suspect that we're likelier to feel the same quantity of love than to write the same quality of poetry expressing it. An ideal of intellect was not only an unrealistic basis for political authority, but a dangerous one: How many hierarchical regimes have been propped up by the differences in what people know? Feeling, therefore, seems a more natural base for democratic demands.

But while several Enlightenment thinkers wrote treatises on the passions, few made them the primary basis for political morality: not, or not only, because emotions are unsteady, but because they are passsive. Emotions are something that happen; technically speaking, they are something you suffer. The right sort of practice – psychoanalysis or medicine or spiritual exercise – may help you direct or control your emotions, but emotions are not what does the controlling. Reasoning, by contrast, is something you do. Thus reason became the focus of the central Enlightenment goal, which Kant called growing up. It's easier to be passive than active, which is why we're all too happy to let other people run the world that circum-scribes our lives, while we play, more or less, on the margins. Growing up means taking our lives out of others' hands and into our own; doing it right requires head and heart and everything in between. It can only be directed, however, by a capacity whose nature is active, and whose goal is orientation. Unlike intellectual ability, the capacity for self-determination could be distributed equally, and is in principle available to all. Here two demands for freedom come together: One conception of reason could promote both the internal freedom to control your own actions, and freedom from other people's attempts to control you.

How universal was this reason that the Enlightenment ascribed to all? Some authors used the most radical and general terms from the start: *Everyone* meant everyone, whether the peasant in the village or the nearly mythical Hottentot across the seas. More often, claims to universal equality began on a small scale that had to expand. Once you acknowledge that the right use of reason isn't restricted, there's no natural place to stop. If the son of a saddle maker might reason as well as the son of a baron, why shouldn't a Chinaman reason as well as a German? And if Descartes was right to separate our minds from our bodies, and locate what's most important about us in the former, why shouldn't a woman reason as well as a man?

This was seldom a conclusion the Enlightenment drew, though several of its best thinkers offered theories that could have led there. They were far likelier to ascribe equal capacities for reasoning to distant Native Americans than to the servants who set their tables or the women who shared their beds. The Enlightenment was infected with the same prejudices that blighted nearly every intellectual movement till the late twentieth century. Unlike Romanticism or the Counterenlightenment, however, it contained the means to undermine sexism and snobbery, precisely because it insisted that reason is the thing that counts most. Reason and universal equality go hand in hand. Indeed, since it was harder to say what reason meant than to lay out the lines of universal equality, we might say that reason was picked to be the engine of Enlightenment because it was the part of us that could be most easily universalized.

Both at home and abroad, Enlightenment thinkers believed in different degrees of equality, and it's here that Jonathan Israel's distinction between radical and moderate Enlightenment is most useful. Some members of the moderate Enlightenment, like Locke and Montesquieu, held human beings to be so differently endowed that their writings could be used to justify slavery. Others, like Diderot, were so convinced of our equal abilities to reason that he thought everyone could understand Newton – and he chastised Newton for using an obscure, elitist style when only a month of extra toil could have made his work clear and comprehensible to all. (Anyone committed to writing prose for the general public will know Diderot radically underestimated the amount of labor involved, but applaud his sally nonetheless.) Between these poles was the sort of general view expressed by D'Holbach: 'The savage man and the civilized, the white man, the red man, the black man; Indian and European, Chinaman and Frenchman, Negro and Lapp have the same nature. The differences between them are only modifications of their common nature, produced by climate, government, education, opinions, and the various causes which operate upon them.'

Here having the same nature and having the same reason amount to the same equally unspecified quality. Consider: This was written at a time when Diderot could offend some of the contributors to the *Encyclopedia* by proposing to print their names without titles. Though this was as liberal a lot as France could offer, they were distraught by the suggestion that how well they could reason (or write) was more important than their hereditary rank. Farther from the center of the Enlightenment, of course, the presumption of inequality did much greater damage. Spanish maltreatment of the Indians was the most vast and cruel. Still, Voltaire made sure to devote a chapter of *Candide* to the miseries of an African slave in the Dutch colony of Suriname. In that outpost of the world's most radically enlightened state, slaves were not only routinely imported but routinely tortured, and paid for a failed attempt at escape with the loss of their limbs. This is the price, Voltaire concludes, of eating sugar in Europe.

Insisting that all men are created with the equal ability to reason was one way to argue against the most blatant abuses of colonialism, but many Enlightenment thinkers went even further. Bayle, for instance, congratulated Japan for expelling the European missionaries, and suggested that China do the same. For though they began harmlessly enough with promises of paradise, their real aim was political and military domination. The Chinese were peaceable and tolerant; the Jesuits, Bayle warned, were not. It wasn't far from the claim that non-Europeans were just as good as the Europeans who sought to enslave or exploit them, to the argument that non-Europeans were actually better. Long before Rousseau's abstract and noble savage, the Enlightenment used more or less empirical travelers' reports to argue that the real savages were not to be found in the wildlands, but in Europe itself. Popular novels depicted Tahitians and Iroquois who were full of natural virtues, uncoerced political arrangements, and peace of body and mind. Here fantasies of sexual and other sorts of liberation mixed with fairly sparse information. The Enlightenment often anticipated contemporary tendencies to imagine the Third World in highly idealized terms. But the very last thing it did was to ignore it.

To be sure, in 1754 Rousseau complained:

> Although the inhabitants of Europe have for the past three or four hundred years overrun the other parts of the world and are constantly publishing new collections of travels and reports, I am convinced that the only men we know are Europeans . . . we do not know the Peoples of the East Indies, who are exclusively visited by Europeans more interested in filling their purses than their heads. All of Africa and its numerous inhabitants, as remarkable in character as they are in color, still remain to be studied; the whole earth is covered with Nations of which we know only the names, and yet we pretend to judge mankind!

Was he right to see the age of exploration as just an age of exploitation? Eighteenth-century curiosity was too palpable to be reduced to something that crude. But if not their purses, were they really filling their heads? Did the Enlightenment look to the world beyond Europe to understand differences, or to bludgeon them into similarities?

This is not a question that would have been entirely comprehensible at the time. It wasn't an age of systematic theory, but everybody had a view. You believed that human nature was benign or perverted, universally similar or crucially different; and what you believed about human nature was deeply connected with what you believed about God, morality, and the meaning of life. Not all these worldviews were coherent; most of them probably weren't. But the idea that you might approach another culture just like that, without any interest in what it meant for your own, would have made little sense. I am not sure how much sense it makes today, when much of the desire to explore non-European societies, or embrace sheer difference, stems from discontent with Western culture. Most motives are mixed ones. Captain Cook was passionately interested in describing small differences among the inhabitants of each island he visited – how they looked and ate and coupled and bargained – and was perfectly unembarrassed about giving them gifts that 'proved the splendour of the English crowne.'

So when the Enlightenment studied other cultures, the axes they were grinding were laid bare. They studied Islam in order to find another religion that, like Christianity, made universal claims, in order to underline Christian faults. Bayle and Voltaire argued that Islam was less cruel and bloody than Christianity because it was more tolerant and rational. The Sinophilia that swept the early Enlightenment was not merely a matter of curiosity about a far and ancient culture; studying the Chinese was part of an agenda. The argument that China had more moral wisdom than Europe was already current in 1685. Bourgeois Frenchmen chafing under the feudal restrictions that still left most government business in the hands of the aristocracy praised the Confucian system, where advancement was based on as much merit as national exams could measure. Leibniz thought Chinese philosophy proved there was a universal theology, which could put an end to religious wars. The practice of using bits of crosscultural anthropology to bolster one's arguments was so common it was parodied by the Marquis de Sade. When he wished to defend xenophobia, he found or invented African tribes so hostile to foreigners they rejected their corpses; when he wanted to argue for incest or torture, he offered long lists of cultures where it was allegedly routine. Sade provided a twist on a trope: More often, the point of examining non-European cultures was to point out the defects of European ones. If men in Tahiti or Peking or Canada didn't need Christian laws and rituals in order to be virtuous, why shouldn't men in Paris do without them as well? Enlightenment discussion of the non-European world was never disinterested. On the contrary, it railed against Eurocentrism with a purity no one has expressed since.

By insisting that whatever else divides us, we are united by our equal abilities to reason, did the Enlightenment run roughshod over differences? Absolutely. It not only ran roughshod; it ignored our immediate experience, which is never about abstractions, but about details. Details are what you get without any effort: the irony or the cockiness or the green eyes or the sentimentality that are in your face, so to speak, when you meet. Who you love and long for and cherish will be swayed by details you are free to embellish or ignore. The same is true, with some caution, of whom you avoid or neglect. But when it comes to matters of justice and decency, all the particulars that make individuals who they are, and undergird your reactions to them, ought to be put aside. To do so requires an intellectual operation both complex and disturbing, for it is likely to disregard what makes you care most (or least) about the people you know. This perspective is by no means all there is to being human, but it's the perspective that is moral. When making moral choices we should perform an abstraction: from the rich self embodied in the world to the boundary conditions that set its limits. Disregarding all the limits you normally cherish is the only way to get past the temptation to treat justice as a matter of helping your friends and hurting your foes.

This brings us to the basic rule of Kant's moral reasoning: However else I see you, I should see you as an end in yourself. Kant called this the categorical imperative, which is nothing other than a formal version of the moral law. *Do unto others as you would be done by*. If you can think that, you can put yourself in my shoes and recognize that I could step into yours at any moment. Perhaps you treat me as a means to your ends today, but we both know it could be otherwise – and resolve to proceed with respect. Is this instrumental reasoning or is it just a matter of decency? This time they come together. Treating me as an end in myself even if you find the ends I've chosen silly or vulgar makes it likely that I will do the same for you when I have the chance. But even when the chances for reciprocity are close to zero, you may decide to do it because you think it's what human beings deserve.

The categorical imperative doesn't ask why you do it. It gives you a guideline to test the rightness of your actions, not your motives for undertaking them. Since Kant thinks we're inclined to self-deception, we'll always incline toward endowing ourselves with better motives than the ones that really underlie our actions. If we'll never know for sure what moves us, it cannot be the thing that matters. Remember his first example: You're in trouble, and tempted to borrow money you can never pay back. The categorical imperative directs you to ask: If you were designing a world and all its laws of nature, could you include a principle that lets everyone make that kind of false promise? Of course not: Such a world wouldn't work. Instrumental reasoning can tell you that much, if you follow it from God's eyes. What you want, it turns out, is not that everyone should make false promises, but that everyone but you should not. You want to eat your cake and have it, too, enjoying the loan you snookered without ever having to worry you might get snookered in turn. You want, that is, to treat me as a means to your end without ever being treated as an end to mine.

Once you're forced to see what you're proposing, you will see it's at odds with your general commitment to decency.

But I'm not designing a world – only trying to manage a little piece of it. Isn't it immodest – put mildly – to act as if my scrubby deeds made a difference?

Perhaps. But it's disingenuous, and sometimes slimy, to act as if they don't. There are deadlier sins than pride. One trick in the town of Sodom was to deconstruct responsibility. When a brick-layer set out a row of bricks, each Sodomite helped himself. 'But I took only one!' each would say when accused. When a greengrocer spread out garlic or onions, every Sodomite snatched a piece; surely such a trifle wasn't worth making a fuss? By systematically inverting the categorical imperative, they robbed their neighbors blind – while making them feel shabby, to boot. It's unlikely that Kant knew all the legends connected with Sodom. But though the thought-experiment he urges us to make in moral reasoning may sound inflated, it's also a way of showing how small things count – adding up, for better and worse, to the shape of the world as a whole.

The categorical imperative is Kant's prime example of moral reasoning, and three objections are often made to it. The first is that we don't usually formulate rules to guide our actions, nor need we. Our decisions are too many, too quick, too demanding to be subject to constant reflection; far better to be guided by a set of general habits that steer us right. This is true; most decisions are made according to principles and customs we need not deliberate. Kant cheerfully acknowledged that his categorical imperative was just another formulation of the Golden Rule. What it adds to the Golden Rule is a more detailed description of a process that anyone can follow, and show to anyone else, for the Enlightenment opposed reason not just to authority, but to the private intuition that is used to support it. Private intuitions may claim any content at all, be it the voice of the Lord or your hunch that something is right, but they all have one thing in common: They are yours alone, and nobody else can test or verify them. Indeed they are only partially communicable. The point is not that we should spend our lives following deliberate formal procedures, but that when we need to decide or justify complicated or controversial actions there is a public procedure with which to do so. *God told you to invade another country? Nothing I say could disprove it. I can, however, respond as Kant did to Abraham: There's no way to be certain that the voice you hear is the voice of God. But if you want to figure out whether an action is right or wrong, here's a method you can follow.*

The second objection rests on a different misunderstanding. It claims that reason is too rigid to respond to the complexity of moral life; it can only give us strict, unbending rules that may lead to conclusions we abhor. One such conclusion is often drawn from Kant's last essay, which seems to imply that lying is so wrong it is not even permitted to save the life of a refugee threatened by a madman. Now there are many ways to read that essay. Some use it to prove that the elderly Kant suffered from Alzheimer's disease. I prefer to read it as an expression of despair about our ability to control the consequences of our actions in the face of bad luck. Those who think it shows that Kant's moral reasoning produces simple, inflexible laws pay scant attention to what Kant actually says in his main discussion of lying. Here's an example from his *Metaphysics of Morals*:

> An author asks one of his readers, 'How do you like my work?' One could merely seem to give an answer by joking about the impropriety of the question. But who has his wit always ready? The author will take the slightest hesitation in answering as an insult. May one, then, say what is expected of one?

Far from arguing that lying is always forbidden, this example leaves everything up to the judgment of the reader. Even ordinary moral dilemmas work as invitations to think for yourself. For reason works not by rules, but by principles – in this case the general reminder that moral decisions oblige us to take up the perspective of the universal. Universal does not mean one rule for all situations: Whether that general rule fits this situation depends on all the particulars of the situation itself. The demand to universalize is just the demand that whatever the particulars of a situation turn out to be, the right action cannot be different for you and your friends than for anyone else in similar circumstances. The categorical imperative is not an attack on nuance, but an attack on exceptionalism. If other countries should obey international conventions, any country that wants to defy them must present grounds to show its defiance justified. 'I'm bigger than you and can get away with it' is not the sort of justification that counts.

The categorical imperative is often seen as a machine meant to do our moral reasoning for us, generating right answers like a factory generates products: raw material in, finished result out. Most criticisms assume this is the model, then attack the model for failing to work. In fact the images Kant uses are very different. Moral reasoning proceeds like the judge at an endless trial, or a child in the process of becoming mature. These are not marginal cases: One is a central figure of civil society, the other of private life. In the realms of human experience that count the most there is neither certainty nor knowledge nor prediction nor rule.

In suggesting we should look to law as a model for reasoning, Kant reminds us that we put our lives and our freedom in the hands of men and women who must rely on their judgment when they apply general principles of law. We (and some of them) might wish that laws could be applied like syllogisms, but with a little ingenuity you can even think of traffic violations that cannot fit this pattern, and no case that matters much can be decided automatically. Partly this is due to the indeterminacy of empirical concepts themselves. As Pinker points out:

> Many everyday concepts have fuzzy boundaries, and the mind distinguishes between a fuzzy boundary and no boundary at all . . . 'Adult' and 'child' are fuzzy categories, which is why we could raise the drinking age to 21 or lower the voting age to 18. But that did not put us on a slippery slope in which we eventually raised the drinking age to 50 or lowered the voting age to 5.

Even beyond the fuzziness of the concepts that go into them, indeterminacy is part of law. There is no rule for applying rules. If you had one you'd need a rule that told you how to apply that one, and the next, and the next; this is one slippery slope that no one can climb. Nor need we. For imagine the alternative: If rules were not open there would be no law at all, for there would be no generalization, just a series of fiats concerning particular cases.

Legal theorists disagree over just how indeterminate law really is, and what the consequences of that indeterminacy are for judges whose decisions shape people's lives. Despite occasional polemics, few really believe that legal decisions are determined by what the judge had for breakfast. Most would agree with British legal philosopher H. L. A. Hart that legal rules are open textured, but not wide open. The law narrows the set of decisions that are possible, but the judge relies on judgment to choose an interpretation within that set.

Why suppose that rules that don't get you absolute certainty get you nothing worth having at all? Hart wrote that skeptics are disappointed absolutists. American philosopher John Dewey would agree. He thinks our longing for certainty pulls us toward rigid, readymade rules in many situations. In medicine, he writes,

> . . . such pretensions are known as quackery. But in morals a hankering for certainty, born of timidity and nourished by love of authoritative prestige, has led to the idea that absence of immutably fixed and universally applicable ready-made principles is equivalent to moral chaos . . . [There is] another manifestation of the desire to escape the strain of the actual moral situation, its genuine uncertainty of possibilities and consequences. We are confronted with another case of the all too human love of certainty, a case of the wish for an intellectual patent issued by authority.

To say that rules are indeterminate doesn't mean we can do without them. But as Dewey continued,

Rigid moral codes that attempt to lay down definite injunctions and prohibitions for every occasion in life turn out in fact loose and slack. Stretch ten commandments or any other number as far as you will by ingenious example, yet acts unprovided for by them will occur. No elaboration of statute law can forestall variant cases and the need of interpretation.

These kinds of facts led Kant to say that judgment cannot be taught but only learned – preferably by watching others use it, or fail to do so. Judge Benjamin Cardozo wrote that this is how 'courts have gone about their business for centuries':

> Logic, and history, and custom, and utility, and the accepted standards of right conduct are the forces which singly or in combination shape the progress of the law . . . If you ask how he is to know when one interest outweighs another, I can only answer that he must get his knowledge just as the legislator gets it, from experience and study and reflection; in brief, from life itself.

Looking at legal cases helps to reject a false dichotomy: Either there's an absolute rule that guarantees right conclusions, or you might as well flip a coin. Either alternative is a way of opting out of the mixture of hard work and risk that moral reasoning requires. We don't refuse to listen to doctors because their judgments are uncertain; we look for a doctor whose judgment we trust. We may appeal a judge's decision, but few of us believe anarchy is a solution to the problems presented by the indeterminacy of law. Moral clarity involves no more and no less work and judgment than we are forced to accept in the rest of our lives.

But you needn't visit a courtroom to know that judgment is required in the simplest cases. Think of how many questions you must teach a child to answer before you let her cross a street alone. How far should she stand from the corner? When is staying on the sidewalk necessary, and when does it simply obstruct all the relevant vision of a person not yet four feet tall? How can you help her decide when traffic is moving or stopped? You have taught her to look left and right before moving; how many times should she do so before it becomes not cautious but paralyzing?

Rousseau was said to have discovered childhood as a stage of human life, with its own shape and demands. Kant used the image of the growing child as a metaphor for Enlightenment as a whole. He thought Enlightenment less a matter of knowledge than courage – to depend on your own reason against all the forces that want to convince you it's more convenient to depend on theirs. His 'What is Enlightenment?' is the most famous Enlightenment essay ever written, and it says that maturity lies in the path between thoughtlessly accepting everything authorities tell you and thoughtlessly rejecting it. This may sound again like Polonius, or the banalities you get from the glossy magazine in the dentist's waiting room. In fact, it's a course that demands considerable nerve, for it recognizes that calibrating the right path is a matter of judgment, which cannot be learned by rule. Far from glorifying the intellect, Enlightenment signals awareness of its fragility.

Kant was explicit in saying children must make mistakes, totter and stumble and bruise. Otherwise, says this essay, they'd remain in the baby carriage of permanent immaturity. They cannot learn to walk without learning to fall. His metaphors are moving, but then there wasn't much traffic in eighteenth-century Königsberg. If you wish you had a rule that your child could follow to step into the street safely, how much more for the times she must decide what to study or how to work or who to love. Helping a child learn to use her own judgment will be all the more remote from rule-following the harder the cases get, but that's just what maturity means. Perhaps the surest sign of having attained it is the ability to recognize maturity in others; the sort of thing that lets you know you can trust her judgment. The Enlightenment gave reason pride of place, not because it expected absolute certainty, but because it sought a way to live without it. Rules can be taught, judgment cannot. It can be learned through the right sorts of experiences, but they, too, can only be directed by the most general of rules, which judgment again will need to apply. The idea that rules and reason should go together created the ever-recurring fantasy that mathematics could become the model of the mind. The longing is an old one; Plato thought mathematical knowledge the highest sort. What we remember from Plato, however, are not the mathematical examples that punctuate *The Republic*. What haunts us are things like the myth of the cave.

Still, every so often a philosopher proposes a method he swears will lead philosophy, and human reason in general, to a system of truths as certain and transparent as the simplest mathematical equation. René Descartes hoped to undermine the Scholastic science of his day by proclaiming: 'Whatever I perceive clearly and distinctly is true.' Rather than the authority of ancient wisdom, which the Scholastics used to back their arguments, Descartes wanted his readers to rely on their own perception. But critics immediately questioned his own model; could Descartes tell us how to decide whether a perception is clear and distinct, or was it merely a subjective feeling? As Descartes wrote in his *Principles of Philosophy*, 'I call a perception "clear" when it is present and accessible to the attentive mind – just as we say that we see something clearly when it is present to the eye's gaze and stimulates it with sufficient degree of strength and accessibility.' His research into optics notwithstanding, Descartes' appeal to the 'natural light of the mind' was as indeterminate as religious appeals to revelation. In his *Rules for the Direction of the Mind*, Descartes suggests that we learn about clarity by studying particularly clear objects, like those of arithmetic and geometry. But what, besides mathematics itself, is ever that certain or clear? Those rules produced so little by way of counsel that Leibniz compared them to the rules of a chemist who advises, 'If you take what you need and do what you should you will get what you want.'

The philosopher Stephen Toulmin believes that if Montaigne

rather than Descartes had been the founder of modern philosophical tradition, then not mathematics and physics, but literature and politics would have shaped the secular worldview. I'm all for dethroning Descartes, not only for his commitment to mathematics as the key to the essence of reality, but for his – not unrelated – obsession with certainty, which put epistemology at the center of modern philosophy. But as Plato's longings show, the search for a mathematical paradigm isn't a modern accident. It's easy enough to understand the desire for it: What a relief it would be to be able to direct our behavior (or at least our children's) with the certainty you get from arithmetic: Follow these rules and *nothing will go wrong*. Like most ideas attributed to Enlightenment simplemindedness, this one was roundly criticized within the Enlightenment itself. It was the systematic Kant, not the literary Rousseau or Diderot, who began his work by denying mathematics can be a model for knowledge as a whole. But even he was occasionally dazzled enough by the model to mangle some of his concepts for the sheer sake of numerical symmetry: twelve categories, three analogies, four paralogisms. While calling *think for yourself* the heart of the Enlightenment, Kant didn't leave it at that; he offered three rules for doing it well. Those rules are very good ones; think logically, think consistently, and think from others' perspectives. But though they may stop you from thinking badly, they cannot, by themselves, assure a result.

This leaves us with two alternatives. One keeps the idea that all reasoning should resemble mathematical reasoning, and drops the idea that reason can reach very far. Then the fact that people respond to Plato's stories more deeply than his arguments would be testimony to our irrationality: We are moved more by intuition or image than by reason, and destined to stay beyond its scope. The other alternative questions the assumption that being reasonable and being mathematical are the same. Reasoning, from this perspective, is a much broader process than any formal procedure can render. It would forgo the security and necessity mathematical models may provide, but also the mechanical overtones. In fact, most recent research leads us away from stark dichotomies. It wasn't until our mechanical abilities were sophisticated enough to try to construct robots that we realized how much we rely on assumptions that cannot be programmed. Simple decisions about which information is relevant and which can be safely ignored are beyond the grasp of the computers we now use. (You needn't build a robot to appreciate this; just try Googling something in a hurry.) Neuroscientists' experiments reveal that emotions are central to proper reasoning, while evolutionary biologists explore the ways in which the emotions adapted to work in harmony with the intellect. Like other forms of slavery, Hume's desire to yoke reason to the passions is obsolete. Both reason and emotion combine to guide us, as both nature and nurture combine to form us. Abandoning the idea that reason is formal is a way of abandoning the idea that it's pure. While learning to use our reason is not as rule-governed a process as some have hoped, it is also not as limited as some have feared.

The final objection made to the categorical imperative goes to the heart of reason itself. Why should you follow rules at all? What makes anyone take up the universal perspective? You don't like my shoes; why should you go through the motions of stepping into them?

There are all sorts of arguments for treating people decently. Doing so makes it more likely you'll be treated decently yourself. Acquiring a reputation for treating people as ends in themselves makes it less likely they will treat you as means to their ends in turn. The problem with such arguments is not just that they don't always apply; there are always people in the world willing to take advantage of others' good natures. More problematic is the fact that these are the wrong kinds of arguments from the start. An instrumental reason for behaving morally is only so good as long as it works; when it isn't in your interest to be decent, what interest can get you to do so? On the other hand, a moral reason for being moral is perfectly circular; it will get you nowhere if the question is why you should be moral at all.

You are, of course, always free to decline. Don't want to grow up? Nothing can be done to force you. Peter Pan may inhabit the realm of magic, but there are plenty of ordinary ways to stay juvenile; determining someone to be self-determined is a contradiction in terms. Self-respect leads most people to follow some version of morality, for respecting other people is part of respecting yourself. If you respect humanity you respect humanity, whether your own or your neighbor's. I argued in chapter 3 that each of us can be moved by an image of someone we believe not only behaved morally, but was willing to risk her life to do so. Describing such people creates not only respect, but a desire to emulate them as a way of respecting ourselves. (Take a moment to contemplate your hero's finest hour. Can you be certain you would *never* try to follow her – and still respect yourself?) Conversely, the spectacle of someone who consciously decides to be immoral evokes a kind of disgust. Dostoevsky's *Notes from the Underground* traces a character who decides to prove his freedom by acting for no other reason than to trounce moral law; he is not only miserable, but filled with self-loathing. Sade's expression of radical nihilism was even greater, and his self-hatred went so far as to request that his grave be unmarked in order to erase every trace of himself from the earth. Our biggest threats, however, don't come from those who are consciously at war with morality, but from those who choose to ignore it. Most of Thrasymachus's challenge is still likely to cause trouble, and most of Socrates' response is still right. Moral action involves the choice to take up an ideal perspective that cannot be justified from the outside, but only through the lives – and deaths – of those who are committed to it.

The Enlightenment focus on those parts of the self that are universal and moral was a part of Socratic tradition. It escaped no one's attention that the differences between a slave in Suriname and a saloniere in Paris were vast and important. In emphasizing what united them, the Enlightenment makes a demand: to perform an act of abstraction that requires both intellectual and moral strength. It's a matter of shifting your focus: disregarding as historical accidents the things that divide us in order to look at what might not.

But *is* it an accident that one of us turned out to be a slave and the other a saloniere? Can we make sense of ourselves without all the accidents that go into making up a life? Many critics ask such questions to show the Enlightenment self is ultimately empty. Once you abstract from the fact that you were born there and will die here, with the parents and talents and hopes that shape your present and limit your future, there's too little left of you to be worth discussing at all. Enlightenment focus on reason may provide a human framework, but filling it in requires just those elements of tradition and context, contingency and passion that it wished to do without. Yet without those elements, what we are contemplating may be models of rational beings, but hardly human ones. Some critics see those models as worse than bloodless; the next step is bloodstained. Carried far enough, the absence of a full-bodied self threatens to be not only barren, but sinister: the Enlightenment subject as dictator, calling his own pale virtues universal, the better to force them on everyone else.

An unforgettable image in contemporary philosophy took the abstract self to the limit. When we think about justice, John Rawls suggested we think about it from a standpoint he called the original position. How would you design a society if you didn't know who you would turn out to be in it? You might be poor, so you shouldn't design a society that favors the rich; you might be a man, so you shouldn't design a society that favors women. If you force yourself to imagine that you might turn out to have any race, and hold any faith, the society you create will not privilege any of them. So far this thought experiment is a way of giving body and drama to the idea of a social contract that many Enlightenment thinkers held as well as expression to American dreams: sons of dukes and peasants were drawn across the Atlantic by the hope of beginning afresh from nothing, building new selves and a New World while casting off whatever baggage had defined them. Rawls, however, went further than either European social contract theorists or American dreamers. In his just world, nothing we inherit counts. You no more earned your native intelligence than your neighbor earned his trust fund. Not only questions of social origin, but everything else we are born with is irrelevant to fundamental moral and political decisions. You may be willing to gamble: Why not design a world full of vast economic differences on the chance you'll turn out to be Donald Trump? In the original position you're asked to abstract not just from class, race, and gender, but from everything you know about your psyche as well. You may be a person who takes risks in this world, but perhaps you'd be timid and anxious in another. You may care about astrophysics or public-health policy, but you might have been Madonna. Or a monk. When thinking about justice you should imagine yourself inside any of these skins, or none of them; the principles you choose should be valid for all. What matters morally are the two powers of reason with which we are born: the capacity to develop a sense of justice, and the capacity to form some conception of the good life – whatever we determine our own good to be. To many critics, this picture shows what's wrong with putting reason first. These abstracted beings may indeed be rational, but any principles that applied to them would make no sense for us. All the features that make up humanity are missing: Their freedom's just another word for nothing left to lose.

If the figures of the original position were meant to describe human nature, there'd be good cause for alarm. For of course this is not who we are. It's not the similarities but the differences between people that make each of us interesting. That's what, after all, we call individuality. Even saying this is saying too little. What's given about people are the details, which is what makes details seem real and everything else invented.

But what Rawls proposed was not a description but a demand. Taking up the moral perspective involves a decision to disregard, for a purpose, not only many of the things you care about, but the things you first perceive. Several centuries of abstraction have taught you that the Mongolian shepherd or the queen of England is a person like you, but what you first noticed were the differences. The shepherd's attachment to his Khonch Nokhoi is no less central to who he is than the queen's attachment to her corgies; the yak's milk drunk by one and the music heard in the nursery by the other, the way he got married and the way she gave birth are as crucial to their identities as the fact that each is endowed with a set of rights that should not be violated. Arguments over which of the two is more fundamental miss the point. What's different about the queen and the shepherd and you is just as real, and significant, as the things that unite them. We simply have to do more work to perceive the one than the other.

This makes Enlightenment heroes fundamentally torn, even fragmented. They cannot stay quite still. They must alternately distance themselves from what's given, loved, and loathed, and return to it. Both perspectives are real ones – but achieving one requires an act of thought and will. It's an act that grows easier with maturity, and may be impossible without it. Neither young children nor young civilizations have learned the kinds of abstractions needed to do it, which is why it can feel unnatural. What's disdained, however, isn't nature itself, but contingency: the fact that nature makes no claims to justice at all. Natural contingency dominates our lives: whether it's a matter of babies born with wounds that never heal, or the less tragic but more common fact that having the right friends in the right places at the right times can reward you in ways having nothing to do with your merits. Reason is a way of fighting back against contingencies, from injustice to illness, that stand in the way of satisfaction and sense. Will it always win? Of course not. But do you really want to give up the contest from the start?

CHAPTER EIGHT

REVERENCE

We are first to consider a book presented to us by an ignorant and barbarous people, written in an age when they were still more barbarous, and in all probability, long after the facts which it relates, corroborated by no concurring testimony, and resembling those fabulous accounts which every nation gives of its origin. Upon reading this book we find it full of prodigies and miracles. It gives us an account of a state of the world and of human nature entirely different from the present: of the arbitrary choice of one people as the favorites of heaven, and that people the countrymen of the author . . . I desire anyone to lay his hand on his heart and declare wither he thinks the falsehood of such a book would be more miraculous than all the miracles it relates . . . So that, on the whole, we may conclude that the Christian religion not only was at first attended with miracles, but even to this day cannot be believed by any reasonable person without one. And whoever is moved by *faith* to assent to it is conscious of a continued miracle in his own person which subverts all the principles of his understanding and gives him a determination to believe what is most contrary to custom and experience.

— DAVID HUME, 'OF MIRACLES'

. . . . .

Few people ever wrote as well as David Hume, which is why he is quoted so often. Were there a Nobel Prize for irony, this description of the Bible would deserve it. Yet before you conclude, as many have done before you, that texts like these make Hume's work one of the high points of the Enlightenment, consider what sets him apart from it. His scorn for reason, for one thing; while no Enlightenment thinker thought reason was infinite, no one but Hume thought it was infinitesimal. His politics, for another: The view that race and class distinctions were natural and legitimate put him at odds with the majority of Enlightenment opinions. And while attacking religion was the favorite sport of many Enlightenment thinkers, most remained merely impious; Hume was truly irreverent. Where to place David Hume is not merely of interest for scholars of Western intellectual history, it's a matter of defining Enlightenment itself. Historians who follow the tradition that assigns him to the Enlightenment know he opposed most of the Enlightenment's crucial tenets. Why continue to include Hume? Those who do so assume that hatred of religion was the glue that held the movement together: The Enlightenment thought nothing was holy, and its triumph is a world in which everything is profane.

However you catalog Hume, this chapter should convince you to put his fellows elsewhere. He was as brilliant, eloquent, and disturbing an atheist as ever put pen to paper, but he was a thoroughgoing atheist. Most leading figures of the Enlightenment were not. The view of the Enlightenment as thoroughly irreverent has somewhat more basis than the other charges made against it. The Enlightenment seemed never so happy as when attacking religion, whether it was the veneration of jewel-encrusted saints' bones or wafers that changed their substance, the vanity of the God of the Old Testament or the resurrection of the God of the New, the cruelty of biblical heroes like David or of a doctrine that consigns babies to eternal torture. We saw that the Enlightenment's first target was church authority, in its day the basis of all political authority, bolstered with webs of superstition and absurdity waiting to be swept away. Most any theological question was fair game, though different thinkers played the game very differently. Despite the outrage Spinoza's patient deconstruction of the Bible provoked, it seems positively deferential when compared to Bayle. The Bible offered bawdy analogies for the taking; in Bayle's hands Abraham became a pimp and David a serial killer. No one else in either Testament fared any better. Voltaire did his best to outdo the master where he could. Here is his account of the difficulties a Jesuit would face if he tried to explain Christianity to the emperor of China.

> *The Emperor:* I don't understand you. You have just told me that she was the mother of God. So God slept with his mother in order to be born of her?
>
> *Frère Rigolet:* You've got it, your Sacred Majesty; grace was already in operation. You've got it, I say; God changed himself into a pigeon to give a child to a carpenter's wife, and that child was God himself.
>
> *The Emperor:* But then we have two Gods to take into account: a carpenter and a pigeon.
>
> *Frère Rigolet:* Without doubt, Sire; but there is also a third, who is the father of these two, and whom we always paint with a majestic beard; it was this God who ordered the pigeon to give a child to the carpenter's wife, from whom the God carpenter was born; but at bottom these three make only one. Now you see that the pigeon who proceeds, the carpenter who is born of the pigeon, and the father who has engendered the pigeon, can only be a single God; and that a man who doesn't believe this story should be burned in this world and in the other.
>
> *The Emperor:* That is as clear as day.

When the riotous mockery was over there was plenty of room for outrage. Millions had lost their lives during wars of religion. Voltaire made several lists purporting to calculate the total of Christianity's victims, which he variously estimated at 9,718,800 and 9,468,800. He also spent several of his last years in rage over the case of one Jean Calas, a cloth merchant in Toulouse, whose son was found hanged in the father's shop. The family originally described the hanging as a murder – understandably enough in the days when suicides were not only denied church burial, but dragged naked through the streets. Jean Calas' lie, said Voltaire, was an act of paternal piety. The public saw the matter differently, for the Calas family were Huguenots, and most French, who were Catholic, thought Huguenots capable of anything. Calas had murdered his son, they said, because he was about to convert to Catholicism. The son was celebrated as a martyr. After a trial in which even torture failed to produce a hint of confession or evidence, Calas was broken on the wheel and burnt at the stake.

Voltaire turned what might have been an obscure provincial case into a European campaign, collecting money and hiring lawyers for the Calas family as well as writing reams about the story. Either way, he believed, the case showed fanaticism at its vilest. If a father would hang his son to prevent his conversion, so much the worse for Protestantism; if educated judges could sentence a man to be torn on the wheel for a crime he never committed, so much the worse for Catholicism. Calas was posthumously exonerated, which restored his family's fortunes, but his champion remained profoundly shaken. Religion, said the *Philosophical Dictionary*, 'far from being healthy food for infected brains, turns to poison in them. What can we say to a man who tells you that he would rather obey God than men, and that therefore he is sure to go to heaven for butchering you?' Not much, as it seems. Few twenty-first-century readers will view this passage without a shiver, and anyone who has read the last will and testament of Mohammed Atta may long for the likes of David Hume. Voltaire is surely right that when the disease has gotten this far it is usually fatal to someone.

Between scorn and rage it's easy to conclude that a war on religion was not only the Enlightenment's point of departure, but the fire that drove its engine from the start. Both its friends and its foes were quick to see the battle as one between God and His ministers on one side, and the rest of humankind on the other. If the Enlightenment wished to hoist human dignity, exalt our natural faculties, and liberate our capacities, it would do so at divine expense. If tradition wished to reply, it could do so only by humiliating humankind.

Even Alexander Pope joined the front by cutting off certain kinds of questioning – not merely by declaring Enlightenment questions to be unanswerable, but by declaring the questioners to be mad, vile worms. And language like that reinforced the idea that Christianity wished to produce a species made to stoop, if not crawl, permanently shivering in fear.

Vile worms or vain priests: From a distance the battle lines seem drawn. If you wanted to protect the sacred, you must mortify the human; if you were devoted to the human, you must reject the divine. Today most defenders of the Enlightenment accept the idea that the divine and the human are fundamentally at war. We can lay down arms, hope for grace and forgiveness, or we can kill God and declare victory for humanism. The Enlightenment was out to reduce fear; religion seemed to feed on it. For however lofty it sounded, prayer was an exalted form of the rites used by any village heathen to ward off the evil eye. Fainter souls might recoil from the comparison, but strong ones would embrace the modern paganism at the Enlightenment core.

Seen a little closer, the picture gets blurred. For most Enlightenment attacks did not attack religion as such, but the ways that religions undermine their own stated goals. Religion meant to proclaim deepest truth thrives on contradiction and hypocrisy; faith meant to promote peace leads to slaughter and woe. Anybody who opened the Bible could find a tangle of deceit and murder, rape and mutilation, savagery and betrayal; anybody who looked at history could see it all reflected in men who slaughter one another over obscure points of doctrine. If Christianity produced the opposite of what it intended, what could be expected from such an ill-conceived faith? If you want to produce virtue you must conceive of humans as beings who are capable of it. Miserable sinners produce miserable sins, and the prayer and ritual they are told to practice only make matters worse. Though it was grist for his mill and he used it, even Hume seemed positively offended by a religion that saw its God as driven by 'the lowest of human passions: a restless appetite for applause.' Seen in the clear light of reason, prayer and revelation were a bust.

Reason's light here was a moral one that relied on arguments about decency: A religion of justice should not promote bloodshed and cruelty, a religion of truth should not rest on superstition and lies, a religion of awe cannot cultivate traits that are foolish and vulgar. Traditional religion did violence not just to our nature but to God's, leaving both without dignity. The God of the Bible doesn't deserve to be God; He is too brutal, too vain, and too petty to meet our real notions of the divine. Note Voltaire's plea: 'May this great God who is listening to me, this God who can surely neither be born of a virgin, nor die on the gallows, nor be eaten in a piece of dough, nor have inspired these books filled with contradictions, madness and horror – may this God, Creator of all the worlds, have pity on this sect of Christians who blaspheme Him.'

This God was hardly less offensive than the Baal who demanded human sacrifice, or the Cronus who ate his own children. What was needed, Voltaire held, was a religion purer than Christianity, as Christianity had been purer than those pagan rituals seem to us. Kant carried the argument all the way home. A genuinely religious standpoint views God to be so great He is beyond our grasp; thus we should not even speculate about His nature. This thought produced the only praise that he (or most any Enlightenment philosopher) ever had for the Jews: By refusing to picture God, or even to use His name, Judaism preserved a sense of holiness that gives God His due.

What traditional religion did to God's nature, Enlightenment thinkers added, was no better than what it did to ours. If it projected our lowest instincts onto the divinity, it expected even less of us, with predictable results. (Call me a vile worm long enough, and don't be surprised at what you get.) Many authors contrasted the brave and noble Romans with the cringing, apologetic creature Christianity was meant to foster. But when it came to worship, all had one thing in common: Pagans and monotheists alike tried to move God with carrots, and expected him to move them with sticks. Each treated Him like a rather dim tyrant whom one bitterly resents but cannot live without. Words of praise? Just attempts to wheedle the master: If I tell you that you're great and merciful long and loudly enough, perhaps you'll be great and merciful with me. The only difference between pagan and monotheistic prayer lay in differing degrees of honesty. The pagan slaughters a bull and begs for the rains to come when he needs them. The monotheist devises a series of rituals to thank God for doing what it's hoped He'll continue to do. There was more than a little anti-Semitism in Enlightenment descriptions of God as an oriental despot, but they knew that Christianity had vastly increased God's power. What sorts of carrots, or bulls, could you possibly offer a being who can give you eternal life and death?

The idea of a God who must be propitiated to help us when we're needy is a debased image of God, and makes us appear even worse. If this is the divine image, both sides look pretty ugly. While portraying God as a vain and brutal tyrant, it turns us into small children or vicious criminals, kept in line with a series of laws we neither grasp nor respect. All we understand is the punishment behind them: Follow this rule, you'll live forever in pleasure; disobey it, you'll die forever in pain. It's not only impossible to imagine that anyone, even a patriarch, could give God lessons in ethics; in this view, God doesn't even try to give them to us. Perhaps for that reason, Abraham at Sodom failed to interest Enlightenment thinkers, though he would have bolstered several of their views. The silence is particularly striking since Voltaire found the story of the Sodomites trying to rape two angels 'the most extraordinary in antiquity.' But his interest was confined to questions about the existence of incubi and succubi, and whether they were more seductive than ordinary men.

The Enlightenment was making an argument not about the truth or probability of religion, but something far more striking: Traditional religion is immoral. This is an extraordinary reversal,

for much of the eighteenth century was convinced of the opposite:
Without religion there would be no morality at all. Bayle devoted
considerable energy to arguing that an atheist could be moral,
Voltaire devoted no less to defending Bayle's claim that a society
composed of atheists is possible. Most people thought it was not.
Even if an occasional pagan exhibited undeniable virtue, a whole
society of them seemed inconceivable. Without a watchful avenging
deity, people would not behave well enough to share the same space.
The *Encyclopedia* argued both sides. Though the entry 'Irreligion'
insisted that morality can exist without religion, the entry 'Virtue'
attacked the 'sophistry and false reasonings of Bayle' with this
interesting argument: The atheist's virtue has no solid foundation,
for he violates the first of his duties – gratitude toward the Creator.
Nearly everyone held some form of religion to be the foundation
without which morals would collapse. (Just look at what Adam and
Eve did when they were given the run of the garden.) Given the
bleak estimations of the value of life that survived into the eighteenth century, hell was considered particularly crucial. For without
it, wouldn't many people be happy with the death that released
them into the void? Then wicked souls, presumably immune to the
longing for heaven, could do what they wanted and simply escape
into nothingnesss at the end of their blasted lives. Traditional religion
kept the notion of hell alive and vivid; good behavior driven by its
image was the best that could be expected from vile worms such
as we.

The claim that traditional religion was unethical was thus far
more devastating than attacks on its veracity. Starting with Doubting
Thomas, Christianity had its skeptics, and – more or less gentle –
ways of handling them. It was perfectly clear that essential articles
of their faith, beginning with the divinity of Jesus, violated normal
expectations about how the world tends to work, but the church
managed to get most to take the requisite steps nonetheless. The
church had also dealt more or less successfully with accusations of
corruption: From sleazy popes to unscrupulous village priests,

everyone knew that church members didn't always practice what they preached. The French, in particular, were never sorry to find instances of moral turpitude in church officials, and Hume carried the lampooning to his deathbed. When Boswell asked him there if he still rejected religion, Hume replied that 'when he heard a man was religious he concluded he was a rascal, though he had known some instances of good men being religious.' Yet individual corruption was never the center of Enlightenment critiques of religion. The claim was not the gap between preaching and practice but that what was preached was all wrong: The doctrine itself was corrupt to the core.

The most extraordinary argument was offered by Kant. He asked you to imagine what would happen if you got the knowledge religion claims to give you: There *is* personal providence at the hands of a God who reads all the secrets of your heart all the time, and controls the laws of nature as He will. Now you know what you thought you wanted: Virtue will always be rewarded with happiness, somewhere or another, and vice will be punished with hell. What does this certainty do to your soul? To begin with, it leads to self-righteousness. If you're certain that happiness and virtue are properly connected, you must believe your own good fortune to be due to your merit, and my bad fortune to be all my own fault. Self-satisfaction and arrogance inevitably result; even if you happened to deserve your good fortune beforehand, you are likely to act in ways that insure you don't deserve it afterward. So knowledge of traditional religion produces smugness, if we're lucky, and Inquisitions, if we're not.

Kant's point goes even deeper. If we knew that acting morally led directly to happiness, we would not only be self-righteous, we couldn't be righteous at all. Everything we did would be sheer calculation, strategically planned to make sure the boss hands out the rewards we crave. Our behavior would doubtless improve; few men would imitate Don Giovanni if they really thought they were headed for hell. But good behavior isn't the same thing as moral behavior.

If you only act for the sake of rewards and punishments, are you any better, or freer, than a well-trained dog? Kant thought you were not. Moral actions must be free actions, and freedom turns out to depend on our limits: Not knowing whether your moral actions will be rewarded is crucial to morality. Kant concludes his argument with a brilliant twist. We may have faith in providence, but thank heaven we have no knowledge. It's possible to detect a note of irony here, but even more a measure of awe. Providence, he says, is no less generous in what it denies us than in what it gives us. This is not the sort of humility that simply accepts our limited fate; Kant thinks we should rejoice in it. Keeping us guessing turns out to be essential not only to God's greatness, but to our humanity.

The second Enlightenment objection to traditional religion is even more surprising than the first. In picturing God without glory, humankind without honor, traditional religion was itself irreverent. Voltaire called the Christian image of God blasphemous; Kant thought it idolatrous. A God who could be bribed with behavior that was good for the sake of reward was no better than a god who could be bribed with the smoke of a sacrifice. Not indifference, but indignation fueled Kant's fire.

Fanatics think they are avenging the Divine Majesty; in fact, Voltaire wrote, they are insulting it. Not because their God looks more like a Mafia boss than a God of justice; that's only a problem of ethics. The critique goes even further: In the accounts of traditional religion, God is not only a gangster, but a bumbler. If He were omnipotent, wouldn't He create the best world possible? And in a world that works as it ought to, what need would there be for miracles? The problem with miracles was not, as Hume argued, that they cannot meet reliable standards of evidence. The very notion of a miracle was incompatible with our notion of majesty. If what God created was good in the beginning, why need He come back to fix it later on?

Such an argument could be underhanded; it's all a matter of

tone. In fact, most of those using it were perfectly sincere. Here's the opening of Voltaire's *Philosophical Dictionary* on miracles: 'A miracle, according to the real meaning of the word, is something admirable. Then everything is a miracle. The marvelous order of nature, the rotation of a hundred million globes around a million suns, the activity of light, the life of animals – these are perpetual miracles.' Anyone who writes this way is less likely to reject religion than to look for another, and that's in fact what happened. The Enlightenment invented Deism, or what it more often called *natural* – sometimes *rational* – religion. The terms themselves were clever propaganda. Emphasizing the link between reason and nature was a way of elevating both, and undermining their opponents. If Enlightenment religion was natural and reasonable, traditional religion must be both unnatural and mad.

Natural religion came in several versions, but this much was crucial to each of them: It offered religion stripped of doctrine, down to common denominators based just on those truths that could be known by anyone, from Königsberg to Constantinople, who was willing to reason. They needed no revelation to believe in a good and wise Creator, and a creation resonant with natural and moral order. Thus instead of serving as a force to divide us, natural religion would unite. It offered the hope that agreement on doctrine could prevent the wars of religion that had devastated much of the seventeenth century, but it offered something more. Religion, they thought, had been mired in the foxhole, retained as the cry of desperate men. (Voltaire was so convinced of this that he ridiculed Satan's strategy in tempting Job, for making people miserable is the best way to lead them to God. He remarked that the devil has grown savvier since Job's day, and learned to shower those he wants to win over with wealth and privilege.) But reverence, not wretchedness, should be the source of true religion; not original sin, but our capacity to advance toward something resembling the image in which we were originally made, and which Christians believe God Himself chose to take shape in. Aren't these more rational, more natural, more *religious* forms of faith than the superstitious mumbo jumbo offered by the keepers of the faith?

Natural religion expressed the breath of wonder that the age of Enlightenment exhaled. All too often, myths of modern thought view the rise of science as a threat to religion, but no one saw it that way at the time. On the contrary. Every new discovery revealed a world of marvels, every scientific advance was a window on God's glory. The God of Ptolemaic cosmology was merely an amateur. How much greater was a God who could design a world with the simplicity and elegance of Newton's? Though embarrassed historians later tried to detach Newton's religious assumptions from his science, the eighteenth century never celebrated his discoveries without the theology they engendered. Not pure physics, but physicotheology was the point of Sir Isaac's labors. The adulation felt for the great man was not a matter of pure science, even had there been such a thing at the time: Few people cared about the laws of motion or gravity for their own sakes. What produced Newtonian excitement was the discovery of order in place of chaos, the framework of a cosmology so perfect you no longer had reason to question it: With a design so intelligent, how could you doubt the designer? Science came not to bury God, but to praise Him. The more we understand the order of the universe, the better we can admire God's wisdom – and His benevolence in endowing us with the gift of reason with which to grasp all His majesty. King David could write psalms in his day; in ours, said Kant, we can only be silent. For what could the psalmist know of the wonders of creation? Modern science, by comparison, leaves us in a state of awe and admiration too great to express. The more science learned about the wonders of the universe, the more wonder-working its author was bound to seem. Bound; for the argument from design seemed less of an argument than a piece of hard data. Theoretically speaking, monkeys on an infinite typewriter could create the works of Shakespeare. But if you had to bet on hypotheses about the author of *Hamlet*, wouldn't you go for the explanation that was simplest?

Natural religion seemed to offer a demonstration of God's existence that was finally worthy of Him. No more proofs bent over tortured bits of logic, no more witnesses to weird revelation, no magic events that violate God's laws; just one quick inference from a marvelous creation to a marvelous Creator. It was the only argument, Kant said, that received the same respect from the man on the street and the scholar alike. The God of the philosophers wasn't a personal one. We worship Him not with an eye to boons He might grant in the future, but to the ones we've been granted in the present. This type of worship does both sides honor. Who needs a God to intervene in the world when we have one who made everything as it should be from the beginning?

To be sure, it was virtually impossible to be openly atheist in the eighteenth century, and every text was written with an eye to the censor. Given that fact, could Deist expressions of reverence be genuine? Many incline to doubt it, and to view Enlightenment professions of faith as pragmatically driven equivocations. Enlightenment thinkers, it's sometimes claimed, cloaked themselves in a mantle of vague general devotion that was necessary at the time, but their true beliefs were godless to the core. From a distance natural religion may seem easy to dismiss. Both atheists and traditional believers tend to view it as a watered-down version of the real thing, a way of hedging one's – temporal or infinite – bets. Natural religion was a fainthearted substitute for the true religion it had neither the will to embrace nor the nerve to reject.

They *were* all writing for the censor. Still, it's hard to doubt the authenticity of a moment like the one in which Voltaire asked a visitor to join him in watching the sun rise near his home on the Swiss border. After a long climb, Voltaire took off his hat and prostrated himself before the glorious view. 'I believe!' he exclaimed. 'Powerful God, I believe!' Then he rose and told his guest, 'As for monsieur the son and madame his mother, that's another story.' Both the awed and the arch tone ring true. Voltaire is particularly important for this part of our story, for if anyone embodies Enlightenment impiety, it is he. No one battled religion with as many different arms. Rousseau's religious enthusiasm is impossible to avoid; it annoyed and embarrassed his Parisian supporters as today's New Yorker might cringe at expressions of red-state zeal. But Rousseau was an untutored boy from the country, Calvinist country at that, and his piety was dismissed as a bit of backsliding: toward his provincial roots, according to his contemporaries, toward romanticism, according to later historians inclined to equate Enlightenment with the absence of faith. Kant's arguments for rational religion were as impossible to overlook as Newton's, but later readers were inclined to dismiss both out of charity, forgiving the Prussian philosopher stuck in a backwater on the border for lapses in the direction of his mother's Pietist faith. Voltaire, however, was originally Catholic, usually French, always self-conscious, and inevitably skeptical. Even before he died, contemporaries called their own era the age of Voltaire. Could the ultimate scoffer's commitment to religion be genuine? If so, it's hard to dismiss that of others.

Most historians now agree that Voltaire's reverence for the God of the Deists was deep and unfeigned. He hated the Catholic Church with the passion only Jesuit schooling seems to inspire, and could be merciless in attacking any number of other religious institutions as well. But his reasons for doing so were neither irreverent nor indifferent; he rather held religion to ethical and religious standards, and found it sorely wanting. His commitment to natural religion is expressed in so many contexts that some scholars have gone so far as to call him mystical. Others hold him to have been such an engaged Deist as to doctor at least one text of a dead man to turn it from an atheist to a theist tract.

The most recent and learned discussion of the subject is found in Jonathan Israel's study. Unlike many earlier historians, Israel doesn't dismiss the religious statements of men like Kant or Voltaire as polite or cautious subterfuge. Enlightenment religion, Israel argues, was real. To explain the gap between the myth of Enlightenment godlessness and the expressions of worship that stream through the texts, he relies on a distinction between two wings of the Enlightenment. Radicals like Spinoza, Bayle, and Diderot really were atheistic scoffers who scorned the weak-kneed consolations of natural religion, along with every other half measure in politics and morals. Members of the moderate Enlightenment, by contrast, were what the left once derided as wishy-washy liberals. They believed in God a little, tolerance a little, equality a little, but took care to rock no boats. Their faith in religion was genuine but tepid – like their faith in everything else. Perhaps the two groups had begun from the same basic principles, but the one carried them to all logical consequences, while the other let civic cowardice or bourgeois comfort stop them short.

Israel's categories fall short of his impressive scholarship: Hume, we saw, was a religious radical and a political conservative; Kant and Rousseau were deep believers, but politically far to the left. My task, however, is not to question an account of the history of philosophy, but the logic behind it – in a set of categories that are still at work today. Do the principles of the Enlightenment lead naturally to atheism? Were believers simply too timid to draw proper conclusions? After arguing boldly against the old-fashioned claim that morals and civilization would collapse without religion, did they succumb to it in the end?

These questions were first raised in the pantheism controversy of 1784, when the terms *nihilism* and *leap of faith* were used for the first time. The young German philosopher F. H. Jacobi was a devoted Humean who showed how the Scottish empiricist's principles could be used to support faith rather than skepticism. Jacobi argued that the use of reason inevitably led to nihilism; the only way to avoid it was to jump into the orthodox fold and leave reason behind. The Jewish philosopher Moses Mendelssohn, known in his day as the German Socrates, was so disturbed by this attack on the central ideas of the Enlightenment, and its German icon, his friend Lessing, that he expended his last energies on a series of passionate counterattacks. The debate became a scandal shadowed by accusations of bad faith, anti-Semitism, and even manslaughter, but arguments about whether Enlightenment principles destroy religion and morality have been going strong ever since. *Something* about religion and ethics seems connected, even if you reject the old view as debased and debasing. You don't need to hold that the fear of hellfire is all that stands between us and anarchy to hold that religion is somehow tied to moral life. It's an assumption made by thoughtful believers and atheists alike. Even as serious a contemporary author as Stephen Jay Gould argues that religion and science should be allowed to rule their separate spheres because we need religion 'to define meaning in our lives and a moral basis for our actions.'

Abraham didn't. His argument with God shows why Gould's well-meaning attempt is deeply confused. If we needed religion as a basis for morality, religion would presumably command and justify courses of action. We have seen that though it often tries to do so, their real justification must be elsewhere. Religion is not connected to morality as foundation; contrary to many assumptions, it provides neither justification nor sanction. Then how are religion and morality connected? Why did Enlightenment thinkers who were willing to risk their livelihoods, and sometimes their lives, to challenge traditional religion insist on maintaining ties to religion after all? What was really at stake?

The Enlightenment denied piety to make room for reverence. If piety is a matter of fear and trembling, reverence is a matter of awe and wonder. There is only one book-length study in English on the concept of reverence, and its author, the philosopher Paul Woodruff, suggests one reason why. Reverence itself is virtually ineffable. It's what gives rise to the feeling expressed by Wittgenstein: 'Whereof one cannot speak, thereof one must be silent.' Reverence is what you feel when you feel overpowered, struck dumb by the realization that some things are beyond human grasp. Why should human language be able to contain it?

Music, if not silence, is its deepest expression, though not every piece of music will do. In 1977 the U.S. launched the *Voyager* space-craft bound for the stars with a message to whomever might eventually find it. But what message should be sent from the Earth as a whole? Like most committee decisions, this one was a mish-mash. When those extraterrestrial beings about whom we know nothing decode the instructions for playing the gold-plated copper phonograph record that prefigured the CD-ROM, they will hear greetings in fifty-five languages and sounds including humpback whales, Peruvian wedding songs, and Chuck Berry. One dissenting observer later printed his proposal: 'I would vote for Bach, all of Bach, streamed out into space, over and over again. We would be bragging, of course, but it is surely excusable for us to put the best possible face on at the beginning of such an acquaintance. We can tell the harder truths later.'

Which truths, exactly? That we are rarely that beautiful, almost never sublime? That though most religious traditions place us in God's image, only a few of us ever approach it? All that, to be sure, and something more: Few of us realize how short we fall, which means that not just great art, but reverence itself is in limited supply. The very word is likely to produce misgivings, like New Age discussions that begin with the word *spirituality*. Even those of us with a high tolerance for what others call kitsch may find the word too sweet or too tinny, something that's devalued the more often it's invoked. Traditional religion did it with poetry, but writing good poetry about particulars is comparatively easy. Once you abandon the guardrails of traditional faith, the force that was behind it veers off, inarticulate.

Woodruff thinks that reverence blossoms in cultures where traditional worship is waning. His discussion focused on the ancient cultures of Greece and China, and argued that attention to reverence flourished there as faith in the old religions drew to an end. It's easy to apply his reflections to the eighteenth century. As faith in traditional Christianity grew harder to maintain, Enlightenment thinkers were all the more eager to preserve the kernel they held essential. Indeed, we have seen, their keenest argument against religion was that it was irreverent. Their wish to maintain a distinction between sacred and profane was not a recognition of mystery, but of limit, with the profound understanding that creation, wherever it comes from, isn't ours to dispose of. Natural religion's image of creation was much clearer than its image of a Creator. Whatever else you believe about the world, only one thing is crucial: It wasn't you who made it. This points to one difference between reverence and respect: Respect is something you should feel for yourself along with others; reverence is the feeling you have for something none of us will ever reach.

It's a feeling that can be abused in traditional societies, which attempt to fix hierarchies by claiming they're sanctioned by God. Delphic mysteries, coronation rites, and military ceremonies are all efforts to evoke reverence for political institutions by giving them an aura of something more than simple power relations. But as Woodruff shows, reverence is the one thing that's traditionally managed to restrain naked power, which is why we want our leaders to have it. If reverence is awareness of human limits, it's what creates humility. 'To live in the knowledge that you are not divine – that you are mortal – is to have good judgment, and to have good judgment in action is to pull back from every sort of excess, especially excess of power.'

You can have reverence for God or nature, but also for ideals of justice or beauty or truth. Kant's gallows example works because we feel reverence for those who defied death in service of an ideal we cherish. To be reverent is to be aware of the contrast between all the things that you aspire to and all that can bring you down: failure and weakness and madness and, should you somehow avoid all the others, death. Our reluctance to desecrate corpses is visceral, not utilitarian. It springs from a sense that cherishing life and feeling awe before death are too close to each other to take risks.

The attempt to tame reverence into doctrines and practices is as precarious as it is natural. One moving effort to shape reverence is the institution of the Sabbath. Jewish tradition understands the commandment *remember the Sabbath day and keep it holy* as a demand to show reverence for Creation. If God rested on the seventh day to contemplate the goodness of His work, we ought to follow Him by reminding ourselves that life itself is more important than all the business with which we usually fill it up. You needn't be a theist to agree to that statement; you're likely to find it self-evident, and probably banal. But precisely the simple truths are those that are easiest forgotten, and Jewish tradition sought a way to capture them. Reverence, like any feeling, cannot be commanded, but a series of laws were devised to mark off a space in time in which it could be encouraged. On the Sabbath, human forms of creation are forbidden – whether baking a pie or running a warehouse or writing a sonnet – to recall all the better what humans cannot produce. Making love is expressly encouraged, along with good food and wine and company. Only what gets in the way of gratitude is proscribed. It's a marvelous recognition of human frailty: While we're apt to forget the truths that are most essential, simply intoning them gets sappy. (Just imagine a society solemnly gathering once a week to repeat, *There are more things in heaven and earth than are dreamt of in my philosophy*.) Instead, a set of rituals was devised to structure your life so you might have a chance to feel it.

Yet reverence refuses to be captured, as anyone who has tried to do it will know. Rituals become ritualized, and the structures that were meant to further reverence can also obstruct it. The Orthodox Jew who hit on the idea of eluding the prohibition on using electricity by connecting automatic timers that would light his lamps after sundown was being pious, but it's hard to call him reverent. This is not an argument against ritual or ceremony; I think we need more of them. It is a note of skepticism about whether ritual, however brilliant, can fulfill its deepest goals.

The dangers of institutionalized practice are, however, hardly as severe as those of institutionalized dogma, and here one example must serve for many more. Rush Limbaugh isn't the finest example of doctrine, but he's been one of the more influential, and he has used many words of the sort I have just used, to alarming purpose: 'I am in awe of the perfection of the earth. The more I learn about the interaction of all the life forms on the planet and the more I witness, the more awestricken I am. We humans had nothing to do with the earth's creation; we are only a part of it.' Neither Greenpeace nor Rousseau could raise an objection. But Limbaugh continues: 'I refuse to believe that people, who are themselves the result of Creation, can destroy the most magnificent creation of the universe, and that after hundreds of millions of years the last two generations of human existence are going to destroy the planet. Who do they think we are?'

It's an incredible argument: Creation is so marvelous it needs no environmentalists. For those who want it, both Noah and Babel provide good biblical authority for ways in which human arrogance could destroy the world. While in these times we may be grateful that he doesn't welcome environmental disaster as a herald of the Apocalypse, Limbaugh's logic is a frightening reminder of how reverence turned dogmatic can be abused.

Like anything that underscores the inadequacy of language, reverence is easier to approach by saying what it isn't. It has more than one opposite: scorn, disrespect, and most important, envy, one of the deadlier sins. *Nil admirari* is what the Romans called the attitude that admires or worships nothing; the poet Horace recommended it as a way of avoiding disappointment, if not of attaining happiness. Reverence is not the reverse of that, for it's usually rare, and one of its elements is surprise. Like love, you cannot will it: If you don't feel reverence toward an object, pointing out its admirable qualities will not help – though without those qualities reverence is impossible. You may feel admiration for all kinds of spirit you cannot achieve: Yogis and sports stars take something about human bodies to the limit, but admiration for them falls short of reverence. Like love, it overwhelms you, and if moments of love and lovemaking can be reverent, it's because you know you're in the grip of something vaster than you are.

If reverence contains admiration, it also contains gratitude. That's the impulse behind the argument for design, which even Hume found tempting as he demolished it. He showed the argument itself to be fallacious, but that didn't prevent Voltaire from feeling reverent in the face of an Alpine sunrise. What you feel in such a moment isn't the kind of gratitude you feel for a gift from a loved one, but closer to what you feel for an unexpected act of kindness from a passing stranger. That is gratitude for Being itself, and for the fact that you're alive to experience it. It's an experience not simply of pleasure, but of silent celebration. These are feelings that enlarge us, and make us better than before.

This view was shared by many Enlightenment thinkers who shared little else. One recent essay bemoaning the scarcity of gratitude in modern life begins with rehashed clichés: 'As heir to the Enlightenment, cultural modernity values autonomy, achievement, efficient production, creative innovation, clear-headed rationality, and the expansion and actualization of the self.' For gratitude, conclude the authors, we should look to 'ancient sources of religion and faith.' In fact, the eighteenth century was passionate about the subject. For Hume, ingratitude was the most horrible and un- natural crime that human creatures are capable of committing; Kant, a little ruefully, agreed that 'ingratitude is one of the most odious and hateful vices, and yet our species is so notorious for it, that everyone holds it for likely that he may create enemies by his benefits.' Ingratitude may be wrong, but it's neither perverse nor accidental, for it is a reluctance to acknowledge your debts. You can't be truly grateful for an act of justice; what you feel is satis- faction when you get what you deserve. Gratitude is thankfulness for acts of goodness you do not. As such it requires you to acknowl- edge your dependency – the reason why Aristotle, who thought it unfitting for magnanimous men to receive as well as give, didn't like it. But Enlightenment thinkers opposed him. For Adam Smith, whose *The Theory of Moral Sentiments* analyzed the subject at some length, gratitude was both a natural passion and a vital civic virtue.

Though Smith held self-interest to function as the framework of civil society, he thought gratitude was crucial in holding it together, for it interests us in the happiness and misery of others beyond ourselves. While these philosophers focused on gratitude toward other people, what makes it a moral emotion has nothing to do with reciprocity. (Otherwise, as cynics argued, it is nothing more than the thank-you note grudgingly written by the child who calculates it will bring him more of the same.) Real gratitude requires acceptance of your limits: You are not entirely independent, but beholden, if only to the past. While emancipating itself from a world in which people's choices were virtually determined by past traditions, the Enlightenment was careful to acknowledge them. Though it encouraged the conditions that made the idea of fashioning yourself possible, it also recognized that you cannot do it alone. A century later, German sociologist Georg Simmel called gratitude 'the moral memory of mankind.'

After Voltaire stopped daydreaming about the dinner and diamonds of El Dorado and turned to its religion, he has Candide and his guide Cacambo meet the kingdom's wisest man.

> The conversation was a long one; it turned on the form of government, the national customs, on women, public shows, the arts. At last Candide, whose taste always ran to metaphysics, told Cacambo to ask if the country had any religion. The old man grew a bit red. – How's that? he said. Can you have any doubt of it? Do you suppose we are altogether thankless scoundrels? Cacambo asked meekly what was the religion of El Dorado. The old man flushed again. – Can there be two religions? he asked. – I suppose our religion is the same as every-one's; we worship God from morning to evening. – Then you worship a single Deity? said Cacambo, who acted throughout as interpreter of the questions of Candide. – It's obvious, said the old man, that there aren't two or three or four of them. I must say the people of your world ask very remarkable questions. Candide

could not weary of putting questions to this good old man; he wanted to know how the people of El Dorado prayed to God. – We don't pray to Him at all, said the good and respectable sage. – We have nothing to ask Him for, since everything we need has already been granted; we thank God continually.

It's a passage that should be required reading before discussing Enlightenment standpoints toward the sacred. Voltaire's tone is always cocky, and often simply snide. But what he imagines in imagining the best of all possible worlds is a world where natural religion is self-evident – for all but a thankless scoundrel. Without superstition and dogma, sheer gratitude can shine.

And this is a standpoint Enlightenment needs – as even the sauciest of its thinkers knew. We saw its vision of happiness: the bold and restless striving to advance beyond what you've already been given. We noted its conception of human reason: the refusal to accept the given as such. Reverence is the moment you are simply thankful for it. When you put them all together, what you have is not a zero-sum game. You needn't mortify the human to feel reverence for what goes beyond it, nor scorn religion to dignify humanity. Whatever else the idea of God may be, or not be, it's above all the idea that human beings have limits – but to understand limits as fetters is to misunderstand what it means to be human. Kant conveyed what we need in the balance. 'Two things fill the mind with awe and wonder the more often and more steadily we look upon them: the starry heavens above me and the moral law within me.' The first, he continued, strikes down our self-conceit. Any sky that's sufficiently clear to reveal enough stars will remind you of your place in a universe that dwarfs you. Yet the moral law you know you could follow if you were willing to stand up for justice lets you know how tall you can stand.

Isn't this all a rearguard action? Touching, even noble if you like, but ultimately simply sad? These fellows who grasped for the dregs of religion after the cup was drunk dry were tenacious, but self-deceived and finally craven. Appealing to a vague oceanic feeling when there's nothing behind it is, as Freud taught us, the tactic of cowards who cannot face facts: Religion is dead, and with it, whatever else that followed from it.

It's a view that major thinkers might responsibly have held in the 1930s, but I was astonished to hear it recently proposed by several Nobel laureates, among others, at a scientific meeting in California. By any empirical data you care to measure, religion is alive and growing. To understand its vitality we must discard the idea that religion is the basis of morality, or even reverence, with its view of these as mere offshoots of particular beliefs. On the contrary: Religion is a way of expressing reverence, and morality, that are felt rather than articulated across every culture we know. It's often argued that one or another movement – Marxism, or the Enlightenment itself – is a secularized version of religion, as if religion were needed to instill the original perceptions *to which it is a reaction*. They include the most fundamental human truths: that natural evil, most particularly death, is part of the world we inhabit; that moral evils, like brothers feeling murderous envy for brothers, are always a threat. Perhaps these would be less baffling were it not for surprising acts of goodness – saving dumb animals from a deluge, risking one's life for the sake of strangers – and in all this confusion we seek meaning and hope. Nobody needs religion to convince them of experience that is universal, anywhere outside the Garden of Eden. These are not religious experiences in any doctrinal sense, though religion is a way for many to make sense of them. What the Enlightenment called natural or rational religion was not a denomination, but a core that is common to each of the major religions alive today. The religious idiom is enormous and powerful, having influenced what we do for millennia. But to suggest that it's what's basic is to take the language for the thought behind it. Reverence and ethics are prior, containing the recognition that the world we are given exceeds human limits, and the determination to overcome the limits that make no sense. Religion may provide a structure in which those urges can be balanced, but it isn't the force that created either.

Supposing you're right about priorities, and it's reverence, not religion, the Enlightenment tried to preserve. Still, even if reverence isn't derived from religion, it survives as an afterglow, and in religion's absence it will die down sooner or later. Enlightenment thinkers still felt it because they were children of institutions that preserved it. However imperfect Jesuit or Calvinist or Pietist schools may have been, they imparted traditions that nourished even those who rejected them. Those who come later will lose even that.

This is the hardest objection to answer, and Nietzsche made it harder when he described the man in the marketplace who cried without stopping:

> 'I seek God! I seek God!' As many of those who did not believe in God were standing together there, he was met with considerable laughter. 'Have you lost him, then?' said one. 'Did he lose his way like a child?' said another. 'Or is he hiding? Is he afraid of us? Has he gone on a voyage? Or emigrated?' Thus they shouted and laughed. The madman sprang into their midst and pierced them with his glances. 'Where has God gone?' he cried. 'I shall tell you. We have killed him – you and I. But how have we done this? How were we able to drink up the sea?'

The man gone mad with grief over the death of the old order is already obsolete. He's outnumbered by the men in the marketplace who can only react to terrible news with terrible jokes. Who are they? Nietzsche later calls them the last men, and they express a modern nightmare: what's left over from the Enlightenment when the energy of irreverence is gone. Bayle and Hume had wit and vigor, which gave their assaults on religion a tinge of respectability. Each of them produced blasphemy that was brilliant, signaling at least the respect one owes to a formidable adversary. After a couple of generations of attacks like these, nothing of the sacred will be left. 'One is clever and knows everything, so there's no end of mockery. One argues, but is soon reconciled – better avoid heart-burn. "We have invented happiness," say the last men and blink.'

Pick your own emblem of nihilism; mine is the cartoon series *Beavis and Butt-head*. This satire of contemporary culture caught its gist so perfectly that 99 percent of college students surveyed at Duke, Harvard, and Stanford were more successful in identifying its heroes than all the major figures of American history. If you missed it, all that's left now are MTV reruns. But while the series was blissfully transient, the mood it expressed was not, and current productions like *South Park* would be hard to imagine without it. Programs like these make Nietzsche's last men look heartrendingly tasteful: If only their characters confined their bodily reactions to blinking! The Russian students who called themselves nihilists in Nietzsche's day were, by contrast, wellsprings of idealism. While they were unclear about what new values could be found to replace the old ones, they were still kicking and screaming about their loss.

It's hard to imagine Beavis and Butt-head kicking or screaming about anything. Everything related to values – desires and goals and aims and dreams – has disappeared from their world. They evince occasional interest in sex and money – without any discernible desires, after all, they wouldn't even be related to the human – but rarely enough to move them to pursue either. Such figures are the the limiting case of our gallows experiment. Not only can we imagine nothing that could make them heroes of resistance; we can scarcely envision them at the brothel.

Their world is never graced by a shadow of reverence. There's so much trash – sometimes masquerading as satire of trash – on the airwaves that it's hard to say what's worse: The blunting violence that's called action? The lackadaisical transformation of sex to commodity? The shows that invite people to degrade themselves for a few dollars or minutes of fame? All of them chip away at human dignity; all of them went further than Nietzsche's grimmest dreams. He wrote that a noble soul has reverence for itself. You needn't go that far to believe that a noble soul must have reverence for *something*. Reverence cannot be produced, but it can be inhibited, and what was a cartoon in one decade can be a reality show in the next. What restrains our expressions of reverence isn't a lack of piety, but something that is far more pathetic: an excess of embarrassment. We will only cease to be embarrassed by reverence when we cease to be embarrassed by hope.

CHAPTER NINE

· · · · · · ·

HOPE

If you want to get to the bottom of human nature, what's the best vantage point? Its most primitive form or its most developed one? People who think we've been corrupted by civilization look to the first for a glimpse of our original state. But if they look long enough, they will find enough examples of senseless cruelty and mutilation to wean them from nostalgia for the early days of humankind. Then consider the alternative; perhaps you think that civilization improves us. Take a moment to consider its softer vices: the tendency to hate those to whom you're indebted, or to take quiet satisfaction in your friends' bad luck. If you're still not convinced, have a look at the international situation, where highly developed cultures have committed themselves to perpetual barbarism, combining the vices of civilization simultaneously with the vices of nature. But don't look too long at any of this or you're likely to contract another vice yourself: misanthropy, or hatred of humankind as a whole.

This attack on 'modern optimism' was published in 1793. Kant's *Religion within the Limits of Reason Alone* describes human nature in both savage and civilized states in a way that seems to cover all the options. All right, I was paraphrasing. Want a dose of the real thing? 'But if we are not yet content, we need but contemplate a state which is compounded in strange fashion of both the others, that is, the international situation, where civilized nations stand toward each other in the relation obtaining in the barbarous state of nature (a state of continued readiness for war) – a state, moreover, from which they have taken fixedly into their heads never to depart.' Progress? asked Kant in the same passage. 'The history of all times cries loudly against it.'

This claim is much older than the eighteenth century. Versions of it were recorded in Egyptian hieroglyphics. The idea that we are bad, and getting worse, feels remarkably comfortable across most cultures. (One thing that has not improved over time is our view of human nature and its prospects.) Most peoples have a myth of a golden age from which we are in decline, but in the absence of evidence about whether the state of nature was violent or utopian, the idea of an original paradise is more likely to be the product of longing than anything else. If you imagine your childhood as golden, or your present as gray, you're more likely to imagine the state of nature as a protected, fruitful garden to which we can never return. The past looks simpler just because it is over and done with in a way the present is not.

All caricatures to the contrary, the Enlightenment could be just as gloomy as any other age, and sometimes even gloomier. Its first icon, Pierre Bayle, thought all of human history was 'the history of crimes and misfortunes.' Kant's discussion of the hidden vices of civilization is particularly chilling: For someone who believes ingratitude is the vilest emotion, zeroing in on our inclination to hate the people who help us faces humankind at its worst. But Kant, you'll remember, called himself melancholy. What did cheerier writers think of human nature?

Here again, *Candide* is a wonderful source; for although it is short and satirical, every event it describes could be found in an eighteenth-century newspaper. The book begins with the senseless slaughter of the Seven Years' War, continues through the autos-da-fé of the Inquisition, and makes detours to describe objects of

Voltaire's special wrath, like the execution of a British officer for failing to win a battle. Countries like England and Holland, to which the French still looked for models, are as inhuman as backward Westphalia. The New World brings no respite from the Old. None of the engines of progress work; wealth and high culture end in boredom and gloom. Education is humbug personified. When Candide gives up on his plans for understanding the world, the only progress to be seen is the progressive abandonment of his hopes. If this is a bright view of human nature, do you need to see a dark one?

Yet for all his acute attention to the variations on savagery the world can offer, Voltaire didn't think human nature was fundamentally corrupt. 'Man is not born evil; he becomes evil, as he becomes sick,' he wrote in the *Philosophical Dictionary*. Those who say we're inherently ill are sick physicians hiding the fact that they can't cure anything themselves. Voltaire's sick physicians are priests, since his goal was not to defend a utopian view that we are all naturally good, but to attack a Christian view that we are all naturally evil. Without understanding the religious context of Enlightenment views of human nature, we cannot understand them at all. This context is key to understanding Rousseau. He was not the only Enlightenment thinker whose conceptions of human nature and its possibilities for improvement were saner than usually supposed. But though his views on this score were not so different from his fellows, he's the one who is generally blamed for believing that human beings were perfect in the state of nature, to which we ought to return.

Let's set the record straight. Unusually attuned to the nuances of crimes and misfortunes, Rousseau never overlooked the darker forces within human nature. On the contrary, he alienated any number of people by rubbing their noses in it. He examined the rotten core of culture with more insight than any had done before him. (The arts and sciences, he wrote, exist to weave garlands of flowers around the chains that bind us.) His relentless determination to see human nature for what it is extends – at least sometimes – to his own flaws, and his autobiography contains what may be the first confession of sheer malevolence: For no reason he could fathom, he told a lie that ruined an innocent girl's life. If anyone knew how bad we could be, it was Jean-Jacques Rousseau.

Yet he offered an insight that was the basis for what Kant would call rational faith. We are active beings, not just observers, and we are bound to act as well as we can. We cannot act morally if we act without hope. (If decline is inevitable, it hardly matters if you do something to hasten it.) Are we in fact declining from a better state, or going forward from a worse one? If nothing can decide that question, shouldn't we consider a different one, namely, which standpoint gives us better prospects for going on? Rousseau, as usual, put the point memorably: 'Let us begin by setting aside all the facts, for they do not affect the question.'

You can see why he drove people crazy. Rousseau was never a man to avoid rhetorical flourish, but what he meant here was more reasonable than it sounds. We have no access to humankind in its natural state. Like other ages, the Enlightenment looked for evidence to support its intuitions. Its explorations were undertaken for gain and glory, but also for knowledge that might settle the question: What are human beings naturally like? The great voyagers knew that their painstakingly written travel journals do not settle the matter. Tribes who were close showed deep differences, so even Captain Cook was regularly frustrated: On one island he was welcomed by fair and generous traders, on another the islanders stole every button that wasn't placed under armed guard. He found the Maoris brutal, their Tahitian neighbors gentle. Which were more natural? It became clear soon enough that there was nowhere we could sail to that would reveal what we were naturally like. Any place we can reach, any time we can access, has already been touched.

Look for a people without recorded history, and you've no way to know which influences have swayed them; where the influences are recorded, the search for a primitive state is fruitless from the start. More important, we observers are hopelessly partisan. Rousseau was the first to point out how deeply we read the data through the screen of our wishes and fears. His own vision of the state of nature makes warfare seem perverse; that of Hobbes makes it seem normal. If you want to establish an authoritarian government, your best chance is to convince your fellows that humankind is naturally brutal and needs a strong leader to prevent it from tearing itself to bits. If you want to establish a social democracy, you will magnify every instance of natural cooperation you can find. Even while journeying to the Amazon in the hope of finding tribes who resembled the inhabitants of Rousseau's state of nature, Claude Lévi-Strauss, the most sophisticated anthropologist who tried to test the philosopher's theses, knew that empirical methods wouldn't decide them.

This is not to say there is no fact of the matter (though there may be more than one), or to suggest that human nature is entirely constructed; it is to doubt that any method could determine which parts are constructed and which are not. Given that we cannot discover the facts, and given how much we project our values onto them in this case above all, Rousseau proposed radical honesty. Instead of giving out stories designed to serve a particular world-view as the truth about human nature, why not lay your cards on the table? Not certainty but plausibility should be the test for accepting a story, provided it supports a view you have other grounds to defend. Kant called the state of nature a regulative idea. We can never know what it was really like, and we ought to stop trying. Rather, the idea is a tool that can be used in various ways. Does that make it wishful thinking? Only if you blur the boundaries between truth and fiction. If you acknowledge that your story is just that – a plausible account designed to further the moral and political viewpoint you're defending – then no fallacies are committed in any direction.

Though sometimes carried away by the force of his own writing, Rousseau was quite clear about what it came to. And while Kant called him the Newton of the mind, Rousseau's second *Discourse* is less a scientific treatise than a counterpoint to Genesis. That's crucial for understanding this most often mentioned and least often understood Enlightenment treatise. Rousseau did not believe human beings are born naturally good. He believed they are not born in original sin – whether the biblical kind or a naturalist version like that of Hobbes. In Rousseau's account, every child is born without stain, like his earliest ancestor in the forest. *In the beginning* neither have moral traits, though each has a natural tendency to pity other creatures' suffering. The tendency is so widespread and unreflective that it's found, he said, in beasts: 'One daily sees the repugnance of horses to trample a living Body underfoot; an animal never goes past a dead animal of his own Species without some restlessness.' Rousseau's analysis of animals' emotions was hasty; animal reactions to death are probably complex instinctive mixtures of pity and fear. Still, much in his casual observation of domestic animals has been borne out by research on wilder ones: There is no doubt that apes and monkeys display empathy for their own and other species. So do elephants, and according to the most recent research, ordinary rats. But though pity may give us a natural foundation for moral virtue, it is not yet virtue itself, but a simple emotional reflex that precedes virtue.

The picture of isolated noble savages inclined to avoid suffering doesn't reflect modern experience, which is indeed better described as a state of perpetual war. Rousseau thought Hobbes projected backward: What he saw as the state of nature reflected the vices of civil society. To maintain that his own story is equally plausible, Rousseau must show how we might get from one point to the other, from the world he imagined to the one we now know. Without original sin, and with natural reflexes that promote benevolence, how did the peaceable savage descend to the depths that we see? In Rousseau's account, the Fall was not a plunge, but a stumble. No deliberate disobedience, or innate depravity, but a series of natural contingencies led to our doom. Bad weather or poor harvests drove the originally independent savages to live in simple communities.

These might have been benign had not culture and human sexuality, born in the same moment, combined to set us in a cycle of other-directed vanity from which we have never recovered. Animals want to copulate; humans want to be desired. Both are driven by the biological urge for procreation, but the second gives human sexuality its particular shape. Once it is born, the rush to distinguish ourselves from our fellows is set in motion, creating a momentum far beyond our original goals. What began as a harmless dance to impress your bride can end in the wish to pick her up in a Lamborghini. The Fall was not a moment, but a process, for human nature isn't static; it has a history. And while that particular process wasn't inevitable, it must be intelligible. We became wicked without willing it, not because of anything essential to our nature but because of a couple of accidents. They all seemed like good ideas at the time.

So wouldn't we be better off without civilization?

Without the civilization we now know, for sure.

Then Rousseau does want to go back to the state of nature?

He knows we cannot.

So what does he propose as a remedy?

You don't call the doctor when the patient is dead.

Then he's bleaker than Hobbes.

Only on bad days. That's what he wrote in 1756, after scores of readers, enraged by his desolate description of French society, wrote to ask for a cure. Seven years later Rousseau published *Emile*, the book that proposed a remedy for the sicknesses of civilization. A child who is carefully raised, he proposed, will not succumb to the slick seductions of civil society; moreover, he'll be better off than the noble savage. The savage wasn't enslaved, but he wasn't really free; he was not immoral, but he had no morality, either. Pity without reason may be better than reason without pity, but best is surely having both. Better to live alone in the forest than endure the backstabbing chitchat in Paris; best of all, however, is not isolation, but fellowship in a small community of equal and virtuous souls.

Like the Prussian philosopher he influenced so deeply, Rousseau was concerned with growing up right. Infancy may well be better than adolescence – for the race as a whole, as well as for each of its members – but maturity is better than either. As we are now, we are prey to culture's most destructive forces. How does culture enslave us? Rousseau counts the ways: from the banal but crucial (it provides us with income) to the psychological (it gives us a precarious sense of self-worth as we see ourselves reflected in others' eyes) to the sublime (for many of us, the moments of awe provided by deep aesthetic experience are so powerful that we're prepared to ignore other, moral areas, in order to enjoy them). Emile's education will force him to be free; thinking for himself in childhood is exercise for doing so as a man. Because Rousseau knows how easily we refuse to think for ourselves, his training can seem harsh. But if Emile is educated wisely, he may grow up not only to read books, but to write them, 'not in order to pay court to the powers that be but to establish the rights of humanity.' Emile should be raised in the country, but not to be a bumpkin; at least twice in the book we are told that Emile will become a philosopher.

Rousseau's own life story nourished his views of progress and hope. *Emile* maintains:

> We know the first point from which each of us starts in order to get to the common level of understanding. But who knows the outer limit? I know of no philosopher who has yet been so bold as to say: this is the limit of what man can attain and beyond which he cannot go. *We do not know what our nature permits us to be*. [italics added]

Though he was writing of human nature in general, his own life must have stamped a sense of infinite possibility on everything he saw. In an age that was only beginning to question the assumption that your life will always be bounded by the limits of your father's, Jean-Jacques left his Geneva home at fifteen, when chance caught him outside the gates at sundown. He took his chances as a wanderer ever after: crossing the Alps to Italy on foot and back again, changing religions twice, making his way as, among other things, a sign painter, a house servant, and a diplomat's assistant. For some time he passed himself off as a music teacher, though he had never studied music or composition. One of his best interpreters, Jean Starobinski, calls this an example of Rousseau's constant attempts 'to satisfy his desire without accepting the limits imposed by the human condition,' and condemns it as 'magic behaviour.' What Starobinski overlooks is how well the magic worked. By pretending to be a musician, Rousseau actually became one. His fraudulently won skills attracted not only enough pupils to make a living, but the attention of the king of France, who liked Rousseau's opera *Le devin du village* so much that he offered him a lifetime pension to live at court and compose. Rousseau turned the offer down, another story entirely, but the point of this one is unmistakeable: Rousseau did all right by rejecting 'the limits imposed by the human condition.' His call to strain our own limits is based on certain knowledge of how far he got by straining his own. The idea that a half-literate printer's boy with nothing particular going for him but the courage to think for himself should become a man who baffled the best minds of Europe was even harder to imagine then than it would be today. If Rousseau could do all that, what do we really know about our own possibilities?

Rousseau had it easy, for like all Enlightenment thinkers he still believed in progress. How much did they have to complain about in 1762? Since then we've become sadder and savvier. What the twentieth century gave us was educated barbarism. Look at Auschwitz, look at Hiroshima.

Before you conclude that the barbarism our age produced is worse than any other, take a careful look at the past. The twentieth century had no monopoly on savagery and misery. Population growth left it holding the record for absolute numbers, but not for relative ones: Two-thirds of the population of Brandenburg, the heart of Prussia, was wiped out in the course of the Thirty Years' War. Was anything much crueler than a Roman crucifixion, with its stunningly sadistic prelude that forced the condemned man to carry the instrument of his own torture through a jeering crowd gathered to watch him expire? Two thousand years of turning a horror into an emblem have inured us to it, and the ritualized genuflection before the Holocaust threatens to make the gas chamber seem as normal as the cross. But there's no clear scale on which to weigh these two evils, and any attempt to find one soon becomes revolting. Was the Holocaust worse than the crucifixion because it killed more people? Was the crucifixion worse than the Holocaust because the last hours were more bloody? Trying to answer such questions shows how little they deserve to be asked. Some evils are so great they can never be lesser.

You've left out technology. The Enlightenment created the instruments that made real destruction vaster than earlier times could imagine.

This is the only critique of Enlightenment that didn't occur to the Enlightenment itself, for they never really imagined the dangers technology could unleash. Though Rousseau thought we could live without most of the contraptions we covet, praise of simple living is not yet awareness of the perils of technology. But when you think of the risks technology poses, presumably you don't mean the technology that improved by 50 percent your chances of living long enough to worry about them. Nor do you mean the technology that ended the days when toothaches were torture and sore throats were deadly; when women's lives were exhausted between grinding chores like washing clothes by hand, and anxious hours at sickbeds keeping children's fevers down with wet rags; when music was limited to people with private concert rooms, and art was something you had to take a ship to Italy to see. Take stock for a moment: For every high-tech advance you find superfluous, there's another you find essential. Deciding which elements will enhance our lives and which will threaten them is a matter of good judgment. This means using Enlightenment skills to solve problems it couldn't imagine.

But there is no straight line that runs from the Enlightenment to technology to the Holocaust. It's no surprise that Heidegger tried to draw one: Though his murky language makes this less transparent than it should be, there was no better way to get off the hook. If the Holocaust was just the inexorable excess of modernity, private decisions to support or oppose the Nazis made no difference. Heidegger never tried to explain the fact that he joined the Nazi Party, played a brief leading role as one of its prominent educators, or turned his back on his Jewish mentor and students. Why should he? What happened in the camps was just the outcome of the modern nihilism he'd always warned about, the manufacture of corpses no different in kind from mechanized agriculture. This is a way to avoid responsibility, but hardly a way of understanding it. Protesting one's innocence by proclaiming the Enlightenment's guilt may reveal something about one's character, but nothing about the subject under attack.

Even without Heidegger's sort of motivation for doing so, decent thinkers have defended similar views. There are two related claims here. The first holds the Holocaust to be the product of an Enlightenment notion of reason; the second holds it to be the result of Enlightenment-based technology. John Ralston Saul's bestselling *Voltaire's Bastards* is a good example of the view that the Holocaust was the culmination of modern rationality:

> It wasn't lunacy that made this possible, nor was this the simple product of traditional anti-Semitism. It was more like the profound panic of a world somehow abandoned to a logic which had cut the imaginations of the perpetrators free from any sense of what man ought to do vs. what he ought not to. The Holocaust was the result of a perfectly rational argument ... There is, therefore, nothing surprising about the fact that the meeting called to decide on 'the final solution' was a gathering mainly of senior ministerial representatives. Technocrats.

Like many others, Saul assumes that reason cannot be moral; it has nothing to say about which ends are right or wrong, but only about the best means to achieve them. We saw this view in Hume's claim that reason is a slave to the passions. In this case, however, the slave was dysfunctional, for it's well known that exterminating Jews violated all demands of instrumental rationality. Had the Nazis not diverted troops and trains from the front in order to murder Jews from all ends of Europe, they might well have won the war. The idea that the Holocaust was the product of an Enlightenment conception of reason not only rests on a simplistic conception of reason; not even the simplest conception works.

To hold technology responsible for the Holocaust is about as useful as holding airplanes responsible for 9/11, but unfortunately there are thinkers who seem to do both. In his *Al Qaeda and What It Means to Be Modern*, John Gray writes that

> Al Qaeda is an essentially modern organization. It is modern not only in the fact that it uses satellite phones, laptop computers, and encycled websites ... The attack on the Twin Towers demonstrates that Al Qaeda understands that 21st century wars are spectacular encounters in which the dissemination of media images is a core strategy ... Without fixed abode and with active members from practically every part of the world, Al Qaeda is 'a global multinational.'

They're supposed to use carrier pigeons? Operating with laptops and satellite phones makes Al Qaeda no more modern than the fact that when Bin Laden gets sick, he summons not a faith healer, but as good a physician as he can get to pay a house call to a cave. Contemporary technologies are as neutral as more primitive tools; the same hammer that built a frame can smash it. Using modern means to promote radically antimodernist causes does not make a movement modern, for the medium turns out not to be the message. Even today, decisive blows are struck by primitive means. Not nineteen lasers, but nineteen box cutters were enough to topple the World Trade Center. And as we'll see in the next chapter, while the murder of millions of Jews was made efficient with modern technology, the most successful resistance to it was made by a group of unarmed women.

To believe that technology is a neutral tool is not to believe that every technological development is an advance. Not everything that calls itself progress is progress, and the growing awareness of the damage some technologies have done to the environment should make us weigh new developments more carefully than our forebears did. At the same time we should remember that many technological advances that met initial resistance, from movable type to infant inoculation, turned out to be unqualified successes. There is no clear metric on which to balance losses and gains. Like most important questions, these will be settled by piecework, case by case, rather than by general principle.

Suppose, for the sake of argument, we grant that we haven't actually become worse over time; better technology has just worsened the effects of what we always were. Yet progress has made us worse off in one way: Science has taught us how bad we really are. Rousseau could afford to set aside the facts because there weren't very many of them; had he actually met Hobbes they could have debated nothing but the merits of competing myths. Today we have not stories but science. Biology, ethology, psychoanalysis, anthropology, evolutionary psychology provide information about human nature that cannot be dismissed.

Nor should it. As anybody who believes in the possibility of progress would predict, we have learned quite a lot since the eighteenth century. The difficulty is not that current theories claiming to offer the key to human nature compete – that's what theories are supposed to do – but that conscientious procedures yield impossibly competing data. There is still too much disagreement about which procedures for gathering data are legitimate; which subjects are revealing (New Yorkers, rats, bonobos, chimpanzees, infants, Kung bushmen?) and under what conditions. There are too many choices, too many perceptions, and above all, too many interests to decide what counts as data that ought to count. This is not material about which anyone is neutral. I am not claiming that all knowledge is driven by interest – a claim that is true but banal in its weakest form, and false in its strongest – still less that there is no scientific truth. I am saying that it is as pointless to talk about evidence for the question of whether human nature is good or evil as it was in Rousseau's day. There is too much evidence, and too much at stake.

Consider the clearest advance here: The publication of *The Origin of Species* was the most important thing that happened to the study of human nature since the Enlightenment. Anthropology was nascent in the eighteenth century, but evolutionary theory wasn't even on the horizon. If any fact cannot be set aside, it's the fact that we turn out to be continuous with the rest of nature. But since the dissemination of Darwin's discoveries, evolutionary theorists have been arguing about what they mean. Did they answer the questions about human nature that the Enlightenment raised?

Many who think they do created the subject of sociobiology, the broadest attempt to explain human nature through a small set of scientific-sounding concepts. Initiated by the biologist Edmund O. Wilson in 1975, sociobiology aroused so much wrath that its supporters renamed themselves evolutionary psychologists to avoid the stigma that early statements of their views produced. Cleaned up and nuanced, the movement has deeply influenced popular assumptions about who we are. At its most basic, evolutionary psychology sees reproduction as the bottom line: Whatever we do is driven, one way or another, by the urge to perpetuate ourselves. However exciting and complex biological and cultural developments may be, all are strategies for maximizing reproductive success in the various environments where we find ourselves. Males want to reproduce as many versions of themselves as possible; females, whose reproductive capacities are biologically limited, seek quality rather than quantity. Just as male peacocks developed feathers to distinguish themselves in the eyes of peahens looking for the flashiest bird on the block, male humans work at achieving the status that signals to female humans they'll provide for their offspring. Everything we do is a variation on that. Whether at the level of the gene pool or the species, everyone's interests are served by these structures, and it is therefore those interests that determine them.

Though contemporary evolutionary theorists are at pains to avoid the more dramatically reductionist claims, their views work together to insinuate them. Not even the most passionate socio-biologist denies some difference between our reproductive strategies and those of a chimpanzee. The man who composes a sonnet for his beloved has done something other than beat his chest and offer a morsel of meat. Yet the tenor of discussion suggests that the additional value provided by human activity is superficial. What we *really* are is the chest-thumping ape; what sonnets and symphonies provide is just packaging.

This standpoint should be familiar; we've seen other versions of the claim that separates the world into ideas and material, and holds the former to be a shadow of the latter. The view is not only dualistic, but decidedly hierarchical: In the relationship between nature and culture, it's nature who's boss. If you don't accept that dualistic starting point, you are unlikely to agree that the sonnet is less significant than the screech, even if you accept the basic evolutionary insight that the two are continuous. (Imagine a geologist who maintained that the earth is nothing but its strata. You might grant him that it's all muck underneath, while insisting that surfaces count: Whether the superfices appear as Norwegian fjords or tropical islands is not a trivial matter.) But suppose you agree with the most militant Darwinians: Anatomy is destiny, biology is primary, and whatever joined them later is of secondary importance. Even this doesn't commit you to what primatologist Frans de Waal calls the 'veneer theory': 'We are part nature, part culture, rather than a well-integrated whole. Human morality is presented as a thin crust underneath of which boil antisocial, amoral, and egoistic passions.' The word *veneer* is well-chosen to describe a number of views that hold that biologically determined drives to reproduce ourselves are what is natural; culture is the transparent and thin attempt to further, while glossing over, that reality.

This view has been convincingly questioned by a number of primatologists whose lives have been spent studying our closest kin. In the process, they argue, they've uncovered facts that cannot, and need not, be set aside when we think about morality. Frans de Waal's work is the most philosophically far-reaching. His research on a wide variety of apes and monkeys led him to conclude that 'we are moral beings to the core.' This research is important because it begins at the bottom. It shows that even if you accept the idea that culture is trivial (or anyway, recent) and that most of what's essential to human nature is beastly, we are far better off than is thought. De Waal argues that moral ability is parallel to language ability, in which nature and nurture can never be completely disentangled. We are born with capacities that are continuous with those of other animals, particularly those apes with whom we share 99 percent of our genes, but those capacities only come to fruition under particular cultural conditions. The emotional responses to others' suffering that we share with apes are building blocks of the complex structures of human morality. Such building blocks are crucial in showing that we really can do what we think we ought to do. De Waal insists that the *is* and the *ought* are not at war. They may be logically separate, but if every attempt to be moral involves a struggle with our own deepest natures, most of us, most of the time, will fail.

What are the emotional blocks of morality? Apes sympathize, demand fairness, internalize rules and punish those who violate them, and know how to make peace through negotiation when conflicts arise. There are rhesus monkeys who starve themselves rather than deliver painful shocks to others; chimpanzees who hug their fellows when they've suffered a beating; macaque monkeys who distinguish between normal baby monkeys and those with neurological disabilities, allowing disabled monkeys misbehavior they would punish in healthy youngsters. Female bonobos step in between their males not only to stop fights, but to sow the seeds of long-term resolutions, and even to climb trees to help wounded birds fly. In all these ways, primates show the capacity most basic to moral development: the ability to put oneself in another's shoes. The sense of justice, the feeling of sympathy, the urge to share, the capacity for gratitude all start right there.

When we call apes kind or generous, are we projecting our own categories into the wild? De Waal notes that worries about projection only arise when we view animals positively; we're perfectly happy to call them aggressive, but balk at calling them sympathetic. He underscores the inclination to interpret the data in the worst possible terms. 'The standard trick is to present mean and selfish acts as proof of our true character, and to either overlook kindness and sympathy, or demonstrate a hidden agenda behind it.' This is as true for animal as for human behavior.

> If animals do show tolerance or altruism, these terms are often placed in quotation marks lest their author be judged hopelessly romantic or naive. To avoid an overload of quotation marks, positive inclinations tend to receive negative labels. Preferential treatment of kin, for instance, instead of being called 'love for kin,' is sometimes known as 'nepotism' . . . In the ultimate twist of irony, anyone who fails to believe we are fooling ourselves, and feels that genuine kindness actually exists in the world, is considered a wishful thinker, hence accused of fooling him- or herself.

There is no particular reason to think our better capacities are defensive or derivative. Cynics argue that the urge to share, for example, is a way of keeping peace with potentially hostile beggars. I give you a piece of my pie in order to prevent you from ganging up with your friends and taking all of it. History certainly provides examples of this kind of strategy: Bismarck's reforms were a model of the kind of welfare initiated under pressure from workers' movements that might have otherwise become militant. But the fact that life sometimes works that way doesn't imply that all impulses to share are forms of self-protection. By revealing patterns of generosity in dominant apes, those alpha males who have nothing to fear from anyone, De Waal showed that the impulse to share can be as primary as the impulse to hoard. In maintaining that altruistic impulses are genuine, De Waal never denies the reality of aggressive ones. Chimpanzees attack others, and sometimes practice infanticide and cannibalism. Precisely for this reason, he argues, their abilities to restrain destructive urges and reconcile conflicts serve as models for our own. Like us, they are both 'fundamentally brutish and fundamentally noble – a more complex picture, perhaps, but an infinitely more inspiring one.'

With a book titled *Good Natured*, De Waal is clearly partisan. Rousseau thought that given the unavailability of the facts, we should regard human nature as neutral. De Waal believes that human nature is positively good. He argues that decades of empirical observation show that evolution itself produced the bases of morality. Far from undermining morality, Darwin can be used as part of a view that's brighter than the Enlightenment's best dreams. We are creatures so social that we need no original social contract, since nature created the means we can use to live together; we are built to find altruistic behavior rewarding. There was no time in which we lived without one another and came to agree that we'd like to try a change. In this view, Hobbes and Rousseau and the author of Genesis are equally wrong in supposing that humans ever existed one by one, or even two by two. Humankind and sociability developed together. As clear about his agenda as he is about the evidence that counts against it, De Waal is happy to wear his partisanship on his sleeve.

On this sort of view, children and chimpanzees have firm intuitions of fairness that start with their own cases: If I give Johnny a grape for doing no more than you did when you got a cucumber, injustice has entered your world. Primatologists and parents of more than one child know the outrage that follows such violations of distributive justice. Like most other things, first stirrings of moral attitudes begin at home. But most of the time, we grow. We learn more about ourselves and more about others and what unites and divides us. As we generalize from our own case to others', we move from indignation about grapes to indignation about fair wages, from concern for getting what we deserve to concern for just deserts in general. The sober-faced baby earnestly dropping her spoon to the floor, over and over and over, is taking the first step to discovering the law of gravity. Yet nobody would imply that Newton's achievement is reducible to the baby's, or his theoretical efforts a marginal addition to our basic urge to drop.

Of course children learn through self-interest, a much better teacher than sermons. Rousseau thought this true of learning in general, and proposed that children learn geometry by calculating the right angle to place the ladder to reach the cherries, astronomy by finding their way home on a starlit night. Most of us learned the golden rule from parents and teachers who told us, more often than ought to be necessary, that anyone who doesn't want Johnny to hit her shouldn't start by hitting Johnny. Like the budding scientist, the young moralist's first steps are small. But in the process of moving from the kindergarten to the categorical imperative, the child learns as much as he does in moving from the kitchen to the laboratory. What is learned, in both cases, is no veneer thinly covering over original impulses whose reality goes deeper. The fact that neurologists can watch our brains change in both cases confirms that even if you measure reality by substance, the changes are as substantial as anything else in the material world.

Even further, one leading neurologist, V. S. Ramachandran, has described the mirror neurons that react equally to pain in one patient and the observation of pain in another as 'Dalai Lama cells.' 'These neurons (mirror neurons) were dissolving the barrier between the self and others – showing that our brains are actually "wired up" for empathy and compassion. Notice that one isn't being metaphorical in saying this; the neurons in question simply can't tell if you or the other person is being poked. It's as if the mirror neurons were doing a virtual reality simulation of what's going on in the other person's brain – thereby almost "feeling" the other's pain.' If research continues to support the idea that we are hardwired for empathy, it would be powerful confirmation of the naturalist view the eighteenth century acquired without access to primate or neuro-logical research. Moral sentimentalists like Hutcheson, Smith, and Hume argued that we are naturally endowed with feelings of sympathy and concern for others that move us to act in their behalf. Strict Kantians may hold that without being founded on principle, such actions are not fully moral, an objection that has been raised to De Waal's claims about the moral capacities of apes. But defenders of moral reasoning need not be so austere. For ordinary purposes, whether benevolence is grounded in feeling or reason is less impor-tant than showing it to be one natural part of our approach to the world. What's crucial is to show that, often enough, feelings and reason converge in moving us to act benevolently, and to take pleasure in those actions themselves – not the rewards we calculate they may bring us.

Why not conclude that the baby improves her calculations? As she grows she learns to anticipate later needs, and reckons that sharing her pie now is likely to net her a slice in the future.

No doubt she does, and it very likely will. Expanding your ability to calculate rewards and expanding your sense of fairness both require complex intellectual processes that develop together. Both explanations work, and as Kant taught us, nothing can decide between them. Most of the time the shopkeeper who is honest because it's good for business looks no different from the shopkeeper who is honest for honesty's sake. Even the shopkeepers will never know for sure; unless their lives are tested by something as dramatic as a gallows, they will have no more certain knowledge of what really moved them than the chimpanzee does.

None of these studies are conclusive. Where researchers find agreement, it's agreement about our ignorance. We do not even know which apes model our closest ancestors: the peace-loving, erotic, egalitarian bonobos, or the more aggressive, hierarchical chimpanzees. Should future fossil and genetic evidence decide *that* question, we'd be unlikely to use it to decide whether human beings were more naturally peaceful or aggressive, for studies have yielded no clear conclusions about the relative influence of nature and nurture in apes, let alone in human beings. Anthropologist Melvin Konner's *The Tangled Wing* concludes, 'Few rules about the social lives of monkeys hold up. One species in different environments can vary almost as much as different species do. So there are no assurances about what our five-million-year-old ancestors' social structure was like.'

As writer Robert Wright argues in his contribution to *Primates and Philosophers*, two interpretations of the data are always possible.

> When we see chimpanzees behaving in a strikingly human manner, we can describe the parallel in at least two ways. We can say, 'Gosh, chimpanzees are more impressive than I'd thought' – a conclusion we're especially likely to reach if we see their behavior as cognitively driven. Or, alternatively, we can say, 'Gosh, humans are less exalted than I'd thought' – a conclusion we're especially likely to reach if we see that relatively simple and ancient emotions can yield seemingly sophisticated behaviors in chimpanzees and hence, presumably, in humans. The latter conclusion is, in addition to being valid, edifying.

Edifying indeed. The same double interpretation is available all the way down. Suppose you want to know why, in this account, we care about developing good character. The sociobiologist will offer the reply: *In the small villages we used to inhabit, your good deeds were noticed and remembered, so you could be sure of getting a piece of my pie someday if you gave me some of yours now*. If you're convinced that sharing is driven by the desire for hedging your bets, you will find this explanation convincing – at least until you ask why they cared about character in London or Beijing. *The behavior that was adaptive for small towns was carried over into large ones, where it continued automatically even after it stopped producing immediate benefits*. Any problem in the theory can be explained by saying that what no longer serves our selfish interests once served our hunter-gatherer ancestors. But since we have, as we saw, no access to original hunter-gatherer societies whatsoever, this is faith-based speculation. It can be carried on without limit, down to Kant's ultimate example of acting against self-interest, the willingness to die for a principle. Why would good Darwinians do that? *Because even if they lose their own lives they may be maximizing the reproductive success of their kin.* And soldiers who die for their countries? *In earlier times, country used to be kin.* And people who die for something even more abstract? If you are already convinced that every bit of altruistic behavior is a disguised form of self-interest, you will find a way to argue that it could have been self-interest in the old days and went on spinning its idle wheels in ours.

This is not a new form of argument. It must have been around in fourth century B.C.E. China, when the philosopher Mencius felt bound to answer it: 'When I say that all men have a mind which cannot bear to see the suffering of others, my meaning may be illustrated thus: even nowadays, if men suddenly see a child about to fall into a well, they will without exception experience a feeling of alarm and distress. They will feel so, not as a ground on which they may gain the favor of the child's parents, nor as a ground on which they may seek the praise of their neighbors and friends, nor from a dislike to the reputation of having been unmoved by such a thing.' If you believe, like Mencius, that we (sometimes) have natural inclinations to be moral, you will read evidence differently. De Waal, for example, knows that arguments can be marshalled for a bleaker view of human nature. But he asks of those who defend it, 'Do they not see that, to paraphrase Buddha, wherever there is shadow, there is light?' If De Waal's role is to show us the bright side, writers like Robert Wright are particularly good at pointing out shadows. But even those scientists whose partisanship is less clear than either acknowledge evidence in support of both, however they mix the proportions.

'The proper study of mankind is man,' wrote Alexander Pope, the eighteenth century's favorite poet. Though we've been studying ourselves ever since, on the question that seemed most urgent the jury is still out. Are we good? Are we not? Few reasonable scientists will hazard a straightforward answer, and the consensus is rather tame. We have learned that our natures are continuous with those of other primates, and even that has not settled ultimate questions: Most of us behave in ways well described as generous and greedy, kind and cruel. Despite masses of data, the conclusions we draw haven't changed much since Pope's:

> Placed on this isthmus of a middle state
> A being darkly wise, and rudely great
> With too much knowledge for the sceptic's side
> With too much weakness for the stoic's side
> He hangs between, in doubt to act or rest
> In doubt to deem himself a god, or a beast
> Sole judge of truth, in endless error hurled
> The glory, jest, and riddle of the world!

Yet a poet who had slept through the intervening centuries would be surprised by one current trend. Though we have no more evidence than the Enlightenment did for the idea that human nature is basically rotten, we seize on anything that seems to confirm it with positive glee. Given two equally plausible explanations of a bit of our nature, we're inclined to converge on the worst. Perhaps in reaction to earlier excesses of reading nature in moral terms, many scientists seem inclined to the opposite view: Nature and morality are not only separate, but permanently at war. Nature no longer appears as amoral, but positively immoral. In rejecting a kitsched-up version of Rousseau, they embrace a toned-down version of Sade.

Economist Robert Frank described this trend throughout the behavioral sciences: 'The flint-eyed researcher fears no greater humiliation than to have called some action altruistic, only to have a more sophisticated colleague later demonstrate that it was self-serving. This fear surely helps account for the extraordinary volume of ink behavioral scientists have spent trying to unearth selfish motives for seemingly self-sacrificing acts.' Now many altruistic actions serve the actors' own interests – especially if you take our interests to include our satisfaction in having done what we think is right. Morality is usually good for us. Just imagine what life would be like if it weren't: Morality itself would be positively fiendish – a possibility described in Sade's *Justine*, whose heroine never does a good deed that isn't immediately punished. Sade's nightmare notwithstanding, we are generally social creatures. And since most behavior generally aims to produce harmony out of discordant interests, acting morally will generally further the interests of the species as a whole and of most of its members thereby. But the claim that morality generally furthers our interests is a far cry from the claim that we – or our chimpanzee relations – act morally only to further our interests.

Evolutionary psychologists know this well, though they continue to suggest that not only self-interest but selfishness is the bottom line. This can make the disagreements between militant and less militant Darwinians look like a matter of degree. Differences in degree can be minor; they can also be quantified. Differences of tone cannot, but they turn out to be more important. No biologist denies that the development from the ape's screech to the poet's sonnet is as palpable as the development from the infant's babble to the orator's speeches. It would be just as silly to deny the difference between acorn and oak tree. Yet without actually stating it, evolutionary psychologists imply that cultural developments are secondary to the biological urges they believe drive them. A favorite way of doing this is to remind us that human culture as we know it is a mere five thousand years old, while primitive hunter-gatherer societies have been in business for a hundred thousand years. Everything that arises later in human destiny is portrayed as an inessential fillip on a fundamental paradigm. Assertions are less telling here than clever asides; praising Wright's book on Darwin, Pinker says Darwin is shown to be 'the best of a bad lot, namely us.' The result is a worldview that echoes from the resonances that surround it. While none of the views is independently confirmed, or falsifiable, each amplifies the others till the din seems inescapable.

Both supporters and opponents of evolutionary psychology, in particular, agree that the tone is in tune with the rest of the culture. Wright's *The Moral Animal* is so breathtakingly explicit that it should be quoted at length:

> What is in our genes' interests is what seems 'right' – morally right, objectively right, whatever sort of rightness is in order. Indeed, Darwinism comes close to calling into question the very meaning of the word *truth*. For the social discourses that supposedly lead to truth – moral discourse, political discourse, even, sometimes, academic discourse – are, by Darwinian lights, raw power struggles. A winner will emerge, but there's often no reason to expect that winner to be truth. This Darwinian brand of cynicism doesn't exactly fill a gaping cultural void. Already, various avant-garde academics – deconstructionist literary theorists and anthropologists, adherents of 'critical legal studies' – are viewing human communication as 'discourses of power.' Already many people believe what the new Darwinism underscores: that in human affairs, all (or at least much) is artifice, a self-serving manipulation of image. And already this belief helps nourish a central strand of the postmodern condition: *a powerful inability to take things seriously* [italics added].

Wright concludes with one of the more succinct descriptions of that condition currently in print:

> What is to be avoided at all costs in the postmodern age is earnestness, which betrays an embarrassing naivete. Whereas modern cynicism brought despair about the ability of the human species to realize laudable ideals, postmodern cynicism doesn't – not because it's optimistic, but because it can't take ideals seriously in the first place . . . Thus the difficult question of whether

the human animal can be a moral animal – the question that modern cynicism tends to greet with despair – may seem increasingly quaint. The question may be whether, after the new Darwinism takes root, the word *moral* can be anything but a joke.

None of the radical versions of these claims have been remotely proven, as anyone will know after wading through recent books with headings like *Biological Constraints on the Human Spirit* (Konner); *Why We Are, the Way We Are* (Wright); *How Morality Evolved* (De Waal); *Biology as Ideology* (Lewontin); or *The Modern Denial of Human Nature* (Pinker). Yet given a choice between two unproven conclusions, what's taken is always the worst. Pinker, for instance, acknowledges that what he calls the tragic vision of human nature 'has not been vindicated in anything like its most lugubrious form. For all its selfishness, the human mind is equipped with a moral sense, whose circle of application has expanded steadily and might continue to expand as more of the world becomes interdependent.'

What reaches public discourse, however, is not a whiff of moral sense, but the most lugubrious vision of all, in which several sources conspire to show that human nature is a nasty piece of work. Under the headline A ROMANTIC IDEAL FALLS VICTIM TO A DARKER REALITY, David Brooks tells us, 'As Steven Pinker has put it, Hobbes was more right than Rousseau.' This is not because he's writing for a daily newspaper; the idea that we are bad, and getting worse, is *very* old hat. Brooks is right about the tone, even when the notes are distinctly differentiated. When attacked directly, evolutionary psychologists retreat from the grimmest versions of their claims, but the message is inevitably dismal. Though writers like Pinker pay heed to nuance, they encourage the darkest spin.

Perhaps our tendency to take the good for granted makes us notice, and comment on, the bad; what author Gregg Easterbrook calls the progress paradox suggests that frustrations rise with our expectations, and make us feel worse while we're actually getting better. Often political interests deliberately exaggerate damages; fundraisers would get nowhere if they couldn't appeal to scenarios of imminent doom. By themselves, however, none of these explain the pleasure we seem to get in seeing our cups as half-empty. When the evidence for that is just as hard as the evidence for their being half-full, we are no longer talking about science and truth. We need to ask: Are such standpoints useful, and to whom?

French-Israeli sociologist Eva Illouz has argued that early in the twentieth century, massive efforts were made to convince people to act upon self-interest. The attitudes that now seem self-evident were deliberately encouraged by psychologists hired to cultivate the qualities corporate capitalism needs. After examining texts from training manuals to self-help books, she concludes that psychologists, acting simultaneously as professionals and as producers of culture, have not only codified emotional conduct inside the workplace but, more crucially, made self-interest, efficiency, and instrumentality into valid cultural repertoires. Throughout the twentieth century, under the aegis of therapeutic discourse, emotional life became imbued with the metaphors and rationality of economics. Illouz's conclusions may seem extreme unless you recall that dueling was a social practice that persisted into the twentieth century. To be a man was to draw a weapon if you were insulted, not to exercise emotional control in pursuit of self-interest. Remembering a world driven by ideas of honor is not, of course, to plead for a return to dueling. It is to suggest that the view of a world driven solely by self-interest is itself a product of history – and of very particular interests.

Is this tendency to assume the worst a right-wing ploy? Conservatives are traditionally identified with the darker views of human nature. Robert Bork's *Slouching Towards Gomorrah* proclaims, 'Every new generation constitutes a wave of savages who must be civilized.' If you believe that, you're likely to believe that authoritarian forms of government constitute our only hope. If things can only decay, the most we can do is conserve what bits of decency are left. Richard

Weaver's *Ideas Have Consequences* even states that 'to establish the fact of decadence is the most pressing duty of our time because, until we have demonstrated that cultural decline is a historical fact – which can be established – and that modern man has squandered his estate, we cannot combat those who have fallen prey to hysterical optimism.' Like every conservative critic, Weaver exaggerates the hysteria of the optimists – and indeed the optimism of the optimists. The main argument for the idea that we are bad and getting worse is the suggestion that the alternative is the idea that we are good and inevitably getting better. Ascribe this view to the Enlightenment, and you make the choice look easy: Between conservative pessimism and utopian fantasy, who would choose the course that has no basis at all?

Friedrich Engels thought evolutionary theory was reactionary:

> The whole Darwinian teaching of the struggle for existence is simply a transference from society to living nature of Hobbes' doctrine of *bellum omnium contra omnes* and of the bourgeois-economic doctrine together with Malthus's theory of population. When this conjurer's trick has been performed ... the same theories are transferred back again from organic nature into history and it is now claimed that their validity as eternal *laws* of human society has been proved.

It does work like magic: Project your worldview into the state of nature, then use the state of nature to justify your worldview. Engels's analysis of the way Hobbes's convictions were projected into Darwinism is no less perceptive because he ignored the same convictions in his own version of the theory of class struggle. Nor is his view confined to old school leftists. Simon Blackburn put the point in contemporary terms:

> There is no close empirical thought about social conditions in the Pleistocene or on the savannah. Rather, the worst features of noncooperative, fiercely competitive late capitalism are simply

projected back, implying the same different mortality rates for rich and poor as we find in the most brutal economic environments today.

Early Darwinism was indeed used to justify social Darwinism, which defended militarism and colonialism as natural consequences of the violent and competitive struggle for domination that drives all sentient life. German generals supported the First World War with the claim that war was the best way to decide who was fittest to survive, and John D. Rockefeller argued that large, ruthless businesses were 'merely the working out of a law of nature.' Though Darwin himself never thought social Darwinism followed from his views, Darwinism is excellent training for a world where social Darwinism rules. Social Darwinism's roughest edges have been smoothed since its earliest days; in the industrial West, at least, we no longer consign those who lose the struggle for existence to an endless abyss. But as preparation for an economy built on unlimited global competition, evolutionary psychology helps create an atmosphere in which everyone who opts out of the competition seems weak-minded. Echoing Engels, R. C. Lewontin, one of sociobiology's most persistent opponents, described contemporary evolutionary theory as Hobbes's war of all against all converted to a struggle for supremacy between DNA models. The debate around sociobiology was intensely political, and most of the objections came from the left: The movement was accused of perpetuating racist and sexist assumptions that were just beginning to be overthrown. But Engels's suggestion is obsolete, in one sense, for Hobbesian assumptions are no longer confined to archconservatives like Robert Bork. In different forms they permeate discourse at all points on the political spectrum. As we saw in chapter 2, left-wing discourse is increasingly captivated by the view that human relations are fundamentally power relations more or less coated with a veneer of ideology. Nowadays evolutionary arguments can fuel most any political fire. The closer the left moves to Thrasymachus, who thought all moral claims were claims to power, the more irrelevant the distinction between left and right. The view of life itself – the subject of biology, after all – as an unlimited struggle for domination can fuel any political position you like, as long as it disdains anything ideal.

Another option is to sever the connection between nature and morality, and some early Darwinians, including Darwin himself, opposed the leap from biology to ethics. For T. H. Huxley, known as 'Darwin's bulldog,' however, avoiding social Darwinism required constant battle. 'The ethical progress of society depends not on imitating the cosmic process, still less in running away from it, but in combatting it.' The worse modern scientists believe nature to be, the more often they warn against drawing moral conclusions. Rape and aggression are natural, they argue, but we need not follow nature's call. Right and wrong are moral categories that we impose on nature, and with which we may even oppose her. Some evolutionary psychologists argue that to overcome nature we need to know how bad it is. More often, they claim they're in the business of facts, and leave the values to be worked out somewhere else. This use of the distinction between *is* and *ought* is more than a little disingenuous. You cannot derive how things should be from the knowledge of how they are. But if nature doesn't determine our possibilities, it does circumscribe them, though the very nature of possibility means we are unlikely to know how much. The more convinced we are that things are natural, the more likely we are to think them necessary – and hence, like being mortal, unfruitful targets at which to aim. Life keeps getting longer, but it's still too short to waste on struggles that look doomed from the start. So while it may be technically true that your views of what human beings should be needn't be determined by your views of what human beings are, they will be influenced by them in more ways than you can tell. As Clifford Geertz wrote in reviewing a book about the sociobiology of sex,

Is is Is and Ought is Ought and the attempt to derive normative standards from natural facts is a fallacy largely induced by
Judeo-Christian theology, Romanticism, popular superstition,
social science theory, and other collective aberrations. There is
a certain breathtaking charm in this view: the natural may indeed
not be the good, but to write a book that says men and women
are radically mismatched in their basic sexual natures, that sex
is a major disruptive force in marriage and a primary obstacle
to human happiness . . . and expect it all to be taken, at this time
and in this place, as 'just the facts' is so wildly unrealistic as to
suggest a highly uncertain grasp on the ways of the world.

Geertz was so unerring about the implications of tone that one
wishes he had asked why reciting the litany of our crimes and
misfortunes feels good, or anyway, familiar. Every age produces
thinkers who declare it to be worse than what came before. They
might turn out to be right; perhaps we just keep sliding downward
at a pace slow enough to make memories hurt. But as long as we're
unable to know our initial position, we can't say whether we're
declining or progressing. For every advance in one direction, a
fair-minded person can name an advance in the other. (Penicillin?
Modern warfare! Nuclear energy? Environmental destruction!
Gender equality? Abandoned children! Washing machines? Video
games! Human rights? Global exploitation! The seesaw is potentially endless.) Whatever the source of our attraction to whichever
view we take up, it isn't a matter of evidence, for the evidence works
both ways.

Why does it feel so good to assume the worst? What draws us
to the most miserable descriptions of ourselves and our neighbors?
No doubt there's an element of self-protection involved here: Optimists may spend their lives being disappointed, while pessimists
spend theirs being pleasantly surprised. But I think the answer goes
deeper, and history can give us a clue. It was Rousseau, not Hobbes,
whose works were consigned to the bonfires. For though full of

religious sentiment, Rousseau's *Emile* denied original sin. Hobbes most definitely did not, though he was suspected to be an atheist. But whatever his views of divine nature, his picture of the human fits into a long and bleak tradition that has come to seem like home.

At least one theologian has made these connections explicit. Anglican bishop N. T. Wright, formerly canon theologian of Westminster Abbey, writes:

> It may come as a surprise to learn that in all sorts of ways I believe postmodernity to be welcomed. It offers an analysis of evil which the mainstream culture still resists; it deconstructs, in particular, the dangerous ideology of 'progress.' I regard the main function of postmodernity under God to be the preaching of the doctrine of the Fall (the truth of a deep and fatal flaw within human nature) to the modernist, post-18th century arrogance that supposes it has solved the world's problems.

I often wonder where the mainstream that believes in progress flows, since most people I hear think we're headed for hell – despite very different visions of what heaven would be. No matter. Though I share many of this theologian's views about particular moral and political questions, I cannot share his embrace of postmodern insistence on how far our corruption goes: Every attempt at goodness is a form of self-promotion; behind every attempt at moral behavior is another twist on original sin. It's a standpoint that seems comforting even to many who are not religious at all. Oddly enough, many of today's most passionate atheists take Christianity's worst feature, the doctrine of original sin, as a self-evident truth. Some, like Robert Wright, argue that political reformers are doing no more than gesticulating wildly like monkeys to win the battle for status; others, like Foucault, hold political reforms to be no more than refinements of methods of control. Though none go so far as to assert it, all suggest a single counsel: You can stop struggling now that you know it is futile.

Unlike postmodernism, Christianity has had millennia to grapple with the consequences of its belief in original sin. That belief seemed to leave us nothing to do but wait for grace, but Christian life requires an alternative, and whole theologies were developed to answer the question: If we were born in sin that cannot be erased without divine assistance, what do we do in the meantime? This is not the place to enter into discussion of faith and works and all the alternatives in between. I do not think the idea of original sin is primary, nor Christianity the source of it, even if Christianity has made the idea feel familiar, any more than the idea of progress is derived from Christian notions of providence, as some have claimed. We are not comfortable with Hobbesian views because Christianity has cultivated them; Christianity has cultivated such views because they seem like a good explanation of the problem of evil.

As explanation, they work even better for atheists. Belief that we're born a bad lot is much easier for those who needn't worry about why in the world we were born that way. Here again, my goal is not to examine the creative solutions Christian theology applied to *that* problem, but to argue that the problem came first. Religion is, in the first instance, a way to wrestle with the problem of evil: Why is there such a gap between the way the world is and the way it ought to be? As discomfiting as the doctrine of original sin may be in one moment, it's consoling in another, for it gives us a reason why: Humankind is corrupt, and liable to corrode whatever it nears. Better to have something to blame than to feel the universe is senseless – even if the blame falls on us. If it only has meaning, almost anything can be borne.

Our tendency to believe the worst claims about human nature thus has its roots not in science, but in faith. While many of Darwin's claims have been confirmed since 1859, the radical conclusions that are drawn from them have not. Some of evolutionary psychology's proudest defenders are fully aware of the ways in which their claims are not a matter of knowledge. Darwin's brother wrote, upon receiving his copy of *The Origin of Species*, 'In fact the a priori reasoning is so entirely satisfactory to me that if the facts won't fit in, why so much the worse for the facts is my feeling.' Robert Wright believes the Darwin brothers' faith, like his own, is 'not *blind* faith, really, since the faith rests on the theory's demonstrated ability to explain so much about life.' Depends how you like your explanations. Writes Richard Lewontin, 'When we combine individual kin selection and reciprocal altruism, it is hard to imagine any human trait for which a plausible scenario for its selective advantage could not be invented. The real problem is to find out whether any of the stories is *true*.' Pick up any book of evolutionary psychology and count the subjunctives. This *may have been* adaptive, that *could have evolved* like this. Its state of nature is hardly less provisional than the older ones; Rousseau's proposal to set aside the facts turns out to be more unique in its honesty than in anything else.

For all that we've learned since the eighteenth century, nothing we yet know has offered a better answer than they did to the question that drove all these inquiries: Is human nature good or evil? Is humankind progressing to a better state? Where knowledge is impossible – yet where we are continually obliged to act – we may believe just as much as is needed to enable us to act rightly. Hope is not the same as optimism. But since we do not know the future, we should choose the view most likely to improve it. Original sin may feel comfortable, but it leaves us with no prospects save despair or grace. Yet whether sacred or secular, original sin is not an object of knowledge. *What we are* is beside the point here, for nothing we do will reveal our real essence. What most matters, therefore, is *what we should be*. Hence we ought to uphold whatever view of nature, and progress, best supports that. What's the minimum we need to believe about the goodness of the world in order to contribute to making it better? We needn't consider humankind to be essentially benevolent, as the dark views at the beginning of this chapter should have shown. We need only see that the alternative to acting as if it could improve is a belief in original sin. If we accept that, then nothing can help us but grace. If we don't, we may be able to help ourselves.

This is not a matter of wishful thinking, but of conditions on the possibility of morality itself. What we ought to do is indeed independent of what is, but since we are human, not divine, we are prey to despair. Reason tells you to work for ideals whether or not you see your hopes take shape in reality. But if reality never answers, you will one day resign. What takes place is not just despondency but – literally – demoralization. Should that threaten, reason permits not a leap, just a step toward a very abstract faith. This is not about dogma, still less about numbers: trying to balance x examples of human goodness against $x+1$ examples of the opposite. It's a step, not a leap, because we know just enough: We are as good as we need to be in order to act as if we are.

How good is that? Vivian Gussin Paley, whose work on children's moral development won national acclaim, thinks we start very well. After describing a group of kindergarteners who show immense respect and empathy for a severely disabled child they encounter, Paley concludes, 'Walking to my hotel, a curious notion enters my mind. When God promises Abraham not to destroy the wicked cities of Sodom and Gomorrah if even ten righteous people can be found, how differently the biblical tale might have ended had Abraham searched in Miss Eliot's classroom.' Even writers who reject every trace of bathos can turn sentimental when speaking of children. Voltaire's *Philosophical Dictionary* is a remarkable example:

> Gather together all the children of the universe; you will see in them nothing but innocence, gentleness, and fear; had they been born evil, malevolent, cruel, they would give some sign of it, as small snakes try to bite and small tigers try to tear something to pieces. But since Nature has given men no more offensive weapons than it has to pigeons and rabbits, it couldn't have given them an instinct that inclines to destructiveness.

Though many thought about childraising, few Enlightenment thinkers actually did it. Most who went so far as to have children left their care to others. In the case of Rousseau, who left his own in an orphanage, the results were presumably disastrous. Still, their views make room for a kitsch-free argument that occurred to me while corresponding with a philosopher who found my book on the problem of evil too sanguine; in his opinion we were all on a slow road to ruin. After a round of philosophical argument I wrote that my three children prevented me from accepting such a view. Getting up in the morning, sharing their plans, helping them to go on in the world made it impossible to resign myself to a scenario of decay. If one cannot offer them the prospect that their good efforts can make the world slightly better than they find it, one can offer them nothing that matters. His reply was almost wistful: 'I myself have neither much hope nor children to fear for.' I could only feel silent gratitude for the fact that I do. Now I wonder if it isn't an ultimate irony. Evolutionary theory denies that evolution produces progress, or any particular goal at all. It is thus thought to destroy the idea that life in itself has meaning. Does the fact that we reproduce ourselves through children who need us force us to believe in progress after all? Children give us a stake in the future; whether or not we want to believe that progress is possible, we cannot possibly raise them if we believe it is not.

What we need to uphold is not a doctrine of optimism; that way Pangloss lies. Kant's doctrine of rational faith is made for a lonely soul – quite likely himself – who has fought some good fight, spending years trying to abolish social hierarchy, or combat poverty, or simply improve the neighborhood. Put yourself in his place. Since you cannot control the outcome of your actions, and since so many things can go wrong, the odds are high that you will come one day to a point of deepest doubt. Why struggle? What for? None of your hopes has yet borne fruit; reality remains as stubbornly impervious to reason as it was before. Science may advance, but humankind seems set in its cycle of distraction and woe. You may go on anyway, perhaps for decades. There will likely come a point when you cannot.

At that point, Kant says, it's no longer enough to tell yourself progress is possible; you need to see a sign – not a promise, or even a guarantee that you're on the right road, just something concrete enough to prevent you from giving up and turning back. When Kant wrote about progress in history in 1794 his idea of a signpost was minimalistic. A passionate supporter of the French Revolution, he could tell even from East Prussia that things weren't going well. Whether the French Revolution had been good for humankind was hard to determine. (Chou En-lai thought it was still too soon to tell.) But our response to the idea of the revolution, said Kant, is unequivocally good; the fact that disinterested spectators across the world look to the revolution with a feeling of hope for progress was a sign of progress itself. Not the revolution itself; just the hope that it might work. Kant's confidence in progress had no more rational ground than that.

I was reminded of Kant's impulse two centuries later: When the Oslo Accords between Israel and the PLO were signed in 1993, negotiators in Northern Ireland suddenly resumed their own stalled peace talks. Hope is as contagious as despair. The fact that Oslo was undermined, among other things, by an assassin's bullet only supports the analogy; hope isn't knowledge, it is always precarious, and the courage and cowardice of individual men and women make and break history. Still, the poverty of Kant's example should forever give the lie to the myth of Enlightenment optimism. If the only sign of hope he could find to sustain him was the hope felt by distant observers contemplating the French Revolution, Enlightenment expectations were slight indeed.

Today more will be needed to keep us going, but it's not hard to find. Kant himself could have seen progress in the fact that he was no longer condemned to be a saddle maker like his father, as he would have been a generation earlier. And advocates of Hobbes should remember that the war of all against all that he thought inevitable was taking place in Europe – which after centuries of slaughter has united itself into a place of open borders and shared destinies. The institutions that guarantee it may be faulty and lumbering, but they are democratic and self-governing, a far cry from the authoritarian structures Hobbes thought necessary to keep the peace. They might also listen to Luis Moreno-Ocampo, chief prosecutor of the International Criminal Court, explaining his work to his thirteen-year-old son:

> My son is studying the Spanish conquerors in Latin America. Yesterday he says to me, 'They killed 90 percent of the Indians, so today you'd put them in jail?' I said: 'Yes. Exactly. What happened to the native populations in the U.S. and Latin America could not happen today with the I.C.C. Absolutely. Absolutely. We are evolving. Humanity is not just sitting. There is a new concept. The history of human beings is war and violence; now we're saying this institution is here to prevent crimes against humanity.'

So far it can at best punish, not prevent them – but who knows what can happen if the court gains broad support? I want to focus, however, on three other signposts that are particularly crucial for showing how men and women have made progress on the backs of ideas.

The first is the abolition of public execution by torture. In pre-Revolutionary France, you could be executed five ways. If you were noble, you had the privilege of decapitation; everyone else could be hung, drawn and quartered by horses, burnt at the stake, or broken at the wheel. There's an eyewitness account of a man being drawn and quartered in Foucault's *Discipline and Punish*; I won't repeat it here, only note that the same person whose stomach turns upon reading it today might have taken her children to watch the event in any of the capitals of the civilized world. Indeed, she would have paid good money to get one of the better seats. This is a change not just of moral sense but of moral sensibility; it's deep, and it's visceral, and it's not three hundred years old.

Torture was never entirely abolished, and significantly, most Enlightenment thinkers took their time about opposing it. Even

Voltaire, outraged by many features of the Calas case, took a while to be angry about the fact that Calas was tortured. As historian Lynn Hunt shows in her excellent *Inventing Human Rights*, Enlightenment thinkers were only gradually brought to reject torture through the conception of human rights that emerged in the eighteenth century. As the Bush administration demonstrated, progress is neither necessary nor irreversible, and its legalization of torture was the most shameful rejection of Enlightenment principles the U.S. government has pursued. But if all you saw in Abu Ghraib was a return to barbarism as usual, you need to remind yourself what was normal two centuries earlier. A world in which Diderot and Voltaire were not sure whether breaking a man on the wheel in a public square was legitimate is not the same world we live in – though a world in which the torture of prisoners is hidden is still not the world that we ought to achieve.

Signpost the second: Wage slavery is one thing, and exploitation another, but there was no hope of doing anything about either as long as men and women could be bought and sold at public auctions. That they cannot is the work of other men and women whose outrage abolished slavery 150 years ago. Racism is still a scourge, but vital pieces of reality vanished in my own lifetime. As a child of liberal northerners growing up in the South I was taught to support the civil rights movement. When we sang 'We Shall Overcome,' we imagined overcoming the present reality for a world that did not yet exist: a world in which black people could attend the same schools, swim in the same lakes, and live in the same neighborhoods as white people. It hadn't been long since the Red Cross separated blood donated by whites and blacks during the Second World War, or returning black veterans were murdered with impunity. The struggle and sacrifices of ordinary and extraordinary people created a different reality. But for all the hopefulness of the sixties, we did not even bother to imagine an America with black secretaries of state. To be sure, the right has often put people of color in visible spaces of power to mask the fact that the real living conditions of the majority have declined. Accompanied by a stronger division of economic classes, racism has persisted into the twenty-first century. Still, in that time when the faith in progress went unquestioned and everything seemed possible, we did not even imagine things we now take for granted. Nor need you think back to your childhood; ten years ago it was said, half as joke, that Clinton was the first black president. Truth is, the idea that we'd have a chance to vote for a real one in our lifetime seemed utterly utopian. In the face of all the changes many of us still remember, denying the reality of progress is just denying reality.

Signpost the third I've already mentioned. It's even more recent, for a generation ago no one imagined that women would demand, let alone achieve, what has been demanded and achieved in the last thirty years. The many ways in which sexism persists – and in parts of the world those ways are lethal – do not undercut the significance of the ways in which women's lives have changed. Though not nearly complete, those changes are all the more important since they touch the deepest recesses: how we move in private spheres. The changes are intellectual, for they have radically altered beliefs about how men and women should structure every aspect of our lives, but they are changes that go all the way down.

All these instances of progress depend on a belief in what used to be called the rights of man, a phrase invented by Rousseau, popularized in the following decades, and bounced back and forth between the U.S. and France till it was embedded in the foundational documents of both republics. Hunt's book shows how the novel idea that people have rights by virtue of being human became real. Sentimental novels, portrait painting, and separate bedrooms all collaborated with abstract arguments to make the logic seem inexorable: If you granted rights to Protestants, you had no reason to deny them to Jews; if you granted them to Jews, you had no reason to deny them to free blacks; if to free blacks, could slavery continue? Once slavery fell, a few souls even proposed that equal rights applied to women as well. Bits and pieces of culture echoed

off one another till their consequences truly seemed self-evident.
Hunt writes:

> Legally sanctioned torture did not end just because judges gave
> up on it or because Enlightenment writers eventually opposed
> it. Torture ended because the traditional framework of pain and
> personhood fell apart, to be replaced, bit by bit, by a new frame-
> work in which individuals owned their bodies, had rights to
> their separateness and to bodily inviolability, and recognized in
> other people the same passions, sentiments and sympathies.

None of this was a matter of learning new truths. When we decided
to abolish slavery, what did we discover? That slaves were human?
Felt pain? Hated to have their families torn apart? Voltaire's lover,
Madame du Châtelet, is said to have undressed before her servants,
'not considering it a proven fact that valets were men.' But this can't
be literally true. What changed was not particular bits of knowledge, but whole sets of assumptions that embedded the world. That
dignity is central is something you may learn, but not through a
series of propositions.

In our own times we have seen impulses altered, and often
changed ourselves. Racist and sexist language is no longer socially
acceptable. While it certainly, like torture, persists behind closed
doors, the very fact of its being hidden produces change itself. Decent
people have trained themselves, in past decades, to change their
slang and their senses of humor; if you begin by finding a sexist
joke embarrassing you are likely, eventually, to stop finding it funny.
Hypocrisy may be the compliment vice pays to virtue, but compliments are anything but trivial. Does the depth of these changes
make them permanent? Not necessarily. In the reaction to the French
Revolution the very notion of human rights was discarded soon
after it was invented, and it took two world wars, and nearly two
centuries, until it was officially enshrined. Most kinds of progress
come in increments. Even the invention of the guillotine was a
considerable advance – in a world that dispatched its prisoners as

slowly as possible, in open pageants of pain. Three centuries ago the very word *democracy* was a term of abuse; is it any wonder we haven't yet gotten it right?

The signposts I've mentioned are hardly news. Nor is the fact that the past two hundred years presented plenty of things besides progress. But Aristotle said philosophy begins in wonder at the facts we take as given. I'm suggesting that we stop and wonder at the changes we take for granted, and remember how extraordinary they are. There is nothing about them that's cosmetic or trivial, though there's always the danger they could be transient. All the more reason to cherish them and make their conditions clear. Whatever else they're the result of, they're the result of the efforts of men and women who were moved by ideas they were prepared to live and die for. And the same impulses that abolished slavery in America established social democracy in Europe; the same forces that made execution by torture internationally abhorrent led to the establishment of the International Criminal Court. These examples confirm the suggestion that Europe now realizes more Enlightenment visions than the country to which Europeans once looked to find a new world. But if this could change once, it could change once again – if we believe ideas can still be as effective in America as anywhere else.

Here the right has an advantage. Progress in history? What seems to have triumphed, world historically, is the narrative of Ronald Reagan: *There was evil, and it was called socialism, and it was vanquished by the ruthless combination of an arms race and a global free market.* Its erstwhile triumphalists no longer believe that history is over, but they point at plenty of things to suggest it's on their side. What's maddening for the rest of us is not simply the absence of another narrative. Not only have many who call themselves progressive stopped seeking signposts of progress, it spends most of its energy scouting the horizon for signs of failure. One thinker after the next has been busy arguing that what we took for progress turned out to be fraud.

It's a form of argument perfected by Foucault, about whom the philosopher Alexander Nehamas wrote, 'He was always able – indeed eager – to see the dark side of every step toward the light, to grasp the price at which every advance had to be bought.' As an art form, it was brilliant. But before we accept the suggestion that the abolition of torture was deceptive – Foucault was much fonder of suggestions than assertions – we should listen to someone who knew what involuntary torture was like. Viennese philosopher Jean Améry was arrested as a member of the Belgian Resistance and tortured in a Gestapo prison. His account is often cited as the most acute analysis of torture ever written. Reviewing Foucault's *Discipline and Punish*, he wrote:

> It's very hard to speak common sense with men like Michel Foucault. One always gets the worst of it – if only because his structural visions are more *aesthetically* alluring than those of critical rationalism. But to completely deny progress and to shrug your shoulders over all reforms is misguided and – I weigh my words – in the end reactionary. It's superfluous to add that [Foucault's example of] Robert Damiens, whipped on the breast, arms and thighs before finally being torn to pieces by six horses, would have raised no objections to our methods of punishment.

As a goad to trying harder, demystifying is constructive. If you show that the civil rights movement damaged life in American inner cities by providing escape valves for their strongest members *in order to focus attention on contemporary problems of urban black children*, you have done us all a service. If you do it for its own sake you suggest that every attempt to work for equality is wasted breath. If you show that the abolition of torture led to subtle and insidious forms of control *in order to press for justice and transparency*, you have served the cause of social liberation. If you argue that every reform produces more complex forms of domination, can you blame the young for giving up and going home? As we saw, the conviction of general futility is not the property of any political direction. The curious assumption uniting critics like Gray and Kagan is the claim that it's Hegel or nothing: either progress is necessary or it's virtually impossible. This is particularly ironic in view of the fact that – like the materialist view of motivation – this is an assumption central to Marx, hardly a philosopher whom either critic holds dear. While many a critic implies the alternatives are limited – either progress takes place with the force of historical necessity, or it will not take place at all – few are willing to state it outright. I suspect this is not only because the dichotomy, stated clearly, is too silly to maintain, but also because once it is stated clearly it becomes plain that either alternative undermines human freedom. If human history is *necessarily* progressing, it does so without any particular input from the human beings within it. If human nature reveals *no* progress, any effort we make is spinning our wheels – perhaps good for keeping individual hearts pumping, but getting us nowhere at all. In fact, there is a third option: progress is possible and it is up to individuals to make it actual. Yet rather than consider an alternative that is as apparent to common sense as it was to Kant, today's Hobbesian critics take pride in talking tough. So Gray's *Al Qaeda and What It Means to Be Modern* praises Euripides' view that human beings 'can expect to achieve very little. Very likely we cannot revive this pagan view of things; but perhaps we can learn from it how to limit our hopes.' Last time I looked they were limited enough.

I'm arguing for hopes that are not irrational, for their signposts are concrete – as concrete as the evidence for global warming. That's right. Both are real, and there is no way to be certain if humankind is progressing toward a better state or racing toward doom. Which one you take up is a matter of choice, but your choice need not be arbitrary. If you believe that progress is possible, you can do something about global warming. If you do not, you can't change anything but the channel.

PART THREE

GOOD AND EVIL

CHAPTER TEN

THE ODYSSEY

AN EXCURSION

Wine-dark? Well, maybe. Greek light can work wonders, so doubtless there are moments Homer got it just right. But at midday the sea shimmers, turning sparkles bright, nearly silver. Mornings the sea light moves like broadloom, weaving the same endless pattern on the clear bottom sand. The light can turn the coat of a stock-still mule into something rich and shining, turn a spiderweb baked on a stone ruin into crystal rays without end. It's light play so entrancing that days spent watching it will not seem lost. Without shelter the sun is nearly blinding; even drying brown grapes will do for a while. Like everything else the boats are still slow here, and the islands so many that you might be forgiven for thinking them all the world. Few things are more tempting than to lie back on sailcloth pillows, white and floating, hedged by the smell of lemon, jasmine, and sun-washed thyme. Watching figs sweeten, and the waveless sea gleam on.

And that's just the earth, on many a Greek island. Odysseus was offered a piece of heaven as well. Kant thought we have a moral obligation not to fritter away our lives in lazy reverie. But then Kant never saw anything outside of East Prussia.

When we first meet Odysseus he is seated in a landscape so lovely that it keeps gods spellbound, gazing long and hard in wonder before gazing their fill. Calypso's island has everything: rich deep woods ripe with violets and vines; clear, cold springs and smooth-walled caverns; fine birds on the roost – all framed by the never-ending play of sky and sea. The island is but backdrop for Calypso herself, the beautiful nymph whose very voice takes your breath. In the daytime she sings before the great stone hearth where a fire sweet with thyme and cedar is blazing; we are left to imagine what she does with the nights. All this has been Odysseus's own, for seven long years, for the goddess loves him. She saved him from ship-wreck and made him an offer few men could refuse: Stay on the island as her lover and join the immortals. An endless life of sweet-ness without pain or woe.

Yet when we first meet him, Odysseus is in tears. Alone on the shore he scans the horizon, but not for the beauty that amazes the gods. He would settle for a glimpse of hearth smoke, as long as it came from home. What an entrance for a hero! To understand what it means to be a modern hero, we must imagine an ancient one, and Achilles, the Trojan War's Greek hero, is always Odysseus's foil. When we first meet Achilles at the beginning of *The Iliad*, we meet him in rage after Agamemnon took his captured slave girl. The object matters little; Achilles' rage drives the first book, as Odysseus's homesickness drives the second. Both are strong and courageous and loyal (to a point), rich and handsome and noble, skilled in battle, sport, and song. But all that is what any Achean prince had to be; otherwise the poet wouldn't bother to mention him at all. Achilles is all those things, just more so. Odysseus is all those things, just more.

Even the way the wandering hero is introduced remains an open question. *Man of many parts* is one translation; *man of twists and turns* is another. Later writers would reduce the twists to one, and call him simply wily. Homer makes his hero staggeringly complex. Even his flaws are multiple. He can be cruel and impatient and unscrupulous. He acts not only against ideals, but against his own interests often enough to make it hard to understand why earlier readers found him egotistic. One mistake after another keeps him from his beloved home. Then there are the tears, not only at the moment we meet him, but at multiple points after that. Twenty-first-century readers may have come to cherish men who cry, but this one goes so far as to whine, and rather often at that. Where a Stoic would push his chin up, Odysseus begins to wail. 'Man of misery, what next?' His complaints are as long as they are repetitive; with every new blow Odysseus launches into a litany of competitive suffering. However bad others' troubles are, he's convinced his are the worst.

But the king of all the gods himself introduces him as the wisest of mortals. He's a bridge between two ages: Born into an ancient code where virtues were straightforward and easy to name, he is the only major hero of the Trojan War to survive it, and hence the one who must found a new order for the age to come. The war itself? Starting with Heinrich Schliemann in the nineteenth century, archaeologists entranced by the poem labored to find traces of something large enough to explain the war's significance – walls or shipyards or earthworks that would have helped provide a clue. They never found anything even close to it, suggesting that later generations may have turned a raiding party into an epic, twenty ships into a thousand, muddy bulwarks into Priam's walls. What matters, then, is how the war was remembered. Until the twentieth century the West remembered it as the first world war. Technology has changed since, but not much else. The war has codes of honor that are clear and often broken; rules of combat that are intricate and often betrayed; motives clear, and mixed between moral outrage and simple greed; and above all, the pain of women forced to watch their men fall and their children shattered. For the Greeks, nothing bigger ever happened, and the wounds were deep enough to keep poets and playwrights returning to them a thousand years later.

Legends put Odysseus at the conflict's beginning and end. He was one of the hundred princes who originally vied for Helen's hand. It was his idea to make the suitors swear an oath: Should the beautiful queen be abducted, every man who did not win her would come to the aid of the one who did. As a way of preventing war among the men who desired her, Odysseus's oath was brilliant. If only it had been sworn by the neighboring princes as well as the local ones, Paris could never have carried her off. Since Odysseus's oath initiated the war, it was only fitting he should end it. Ten years of fighting failed to yield a clear victory: Though the greatest soldiers on both sides had fallen, neither side would give ground. The Greeks remained encamped near the walls they could not breach, the Trojans remained besieged but unyielding. Odysseus devises a plan to break the deadlocked years of slaughter. He's the one who suggests the horse so irresistible it leads the Trojans to their doom. You may wonder: Could a people be so foolish, or a wooden horse so large? The question has never been answered, but that doesn't undermine the story's lesson: Even in military matters it's force of thought and not of muscle that strikes the deciding blow.

It is very hard to find a moral in the Trojan War, which is presumably the point: Any war, for any reason, leaves us wondering later why anyone thought anything could justify the misery left in its wake. Whether ignited by a bride or an idea or a piece of territory, every war becomes a vicious, futile trap that men should avoid from the start. The Trojan War was no more senseless than any other, but it's easier to understand if you view the face that launched a thousand ships as a face that was put on the effort. True, they had all sworn an oath years before. But it's hard to imagine men leaving their farms and their families to defend the weak-kneed Menelaus's honor if they weren't defending something else as well. When Paris came for a visit and left with Menelaus's wife and a largish chunk of his fortune, he violated what international law existed at the time. Much of *The Odyssey* concerns the moral code surrounding guests: The difference between barbarism and civilization turns on how strangers are received. Civilized cultures wine and dine and give them gifts before even asking their names. Barbarian cultures eat them alive. There isn't much middle ground. No moral principle is so often repeated, nor weighted with such authority. Zeus is the protector of guests' rights, and of hosts' rights as well. Thus Paris's crime in stealing off with Sparta's queen and its treasure was not merely sleazy but heinous. The ships that followed to bring them back to Greece were standing on principle: If wrongdoing was ever to be punished, the line must be drawn right there. Of course, Menelaus's allies were surely hoping for plunder as well. Motives usually come in mixed packages.

So the war was Odysseus's war. His oath launched it, his strategy ended it, and anyone following the battles closely can see him at crucial points in between. Whether in combat or planning or negotiation, his hand cannot be missed. Odysseus will forge new heroic virtues, not because he couldn't master the old ones, but because he saw they were no longer enough. This is crucial for his role as bridge-head between two ages, and Odysseus's hand in the war effort is not only to his credit. Homer ended his story without lingering on what happened to the losers after Troy fell, but later writers lingered, and they were quick to accuse. Writers like Euripides, for example, made him out to be a colder-blooded villain than anything Homer imagined. But even if he wasn't central to the war's worst atrocities, Odysseus was so central to the war effort at large that those atrocities were also his fault. Even in an era that valued martial virtues, this was a heavy burden to bear.

And he lived to tell the tale. Achilles and Hector died on the battlefield and were laid to rest with the glory that made their comrades envy their deaths. Agamemnon was murdered the day he came home. Odysseus's survival makes us mistrust him; how can he be a hero if he always squeaks by? Nor is his departure from Troy particularly glorious. Odysseus was called a sacker of cities, a somewhat obscure way to describe a common pirate. After leaving the ashes of the great heroes scattered on the Trojan plain, Odysseus wants to bring gifts back to Ithaca, so he burns and loots the city of Ismeros on the way. True to form, even Odysseus's piracy is well considered. He loads up a modest store of treasure and enslaves a modest number of women before urging his men back to the ships. Foolish and mutinous, they gorge themselves on wine and cattle. The remaining islanders have time to regroup and rearm, and the sailors' excess is duly punished; many lose their lives before Odysseus and his remaining crew row out to sea again. Even piracy, apparently, should be temperate, and this is only the first of many scenes in which Odysseus's self-control will save him, while his men's self-indulgence spells their doom.

The next is only narrowly averted. They sail to the Land of the Lotus Eaters, where a sweet fruit makes men forget where they came from, and wherever they wanted to go. It might be hashish, it could be cable – whatever it is that takes your desire for movement and leaves you happy to tarry, watching the world go by. Heroes are fundamentally active, so the life of a sluggard never really tempts Odysseus. But the lotus promises relief from memory, and what a lot this crew has to forget! Grief at the losses they've suffered, shame at the losses they've caused; ten years of war and camp life and storm could make the prospect of oblivion seem like bliss. Odysseus never seeks it. Like Captain Cook in the South Seas he drags his men back to the ships and ties them to their benches with their eyes streaming tears, forcing them to remember the way home.

They stop at the land of the Cyclops, giant brutes who know neither bread nor wine nor council. The giants have not yet learned to plant or reap, trade or build, to gather in communities or to listen to the gods. Each lives alone in a cavern, his one eye seeing as much as one eye can. If the Lotus Eaters remind us how close we come to forgetting where we came from, the Cyclops remind us that sheer barbarism is never far away. It can coexist in the same time as culture, and the line between the two is easy to cross. Odysseus almost does so, and his adventures on that island show how much he still has to learn, for the trouble he met there had no need to happen. He takes his finest fighters off exploring. While his men want to grab the lambs and cheeses and run for it, Odysseus wants to find out what the land is like, whether the natives are 'savage and lawless, or hospitable, god-fearing folk.' This is part of what makes him a hero, but need he stay in the giant's cave waiting, having intruded on his property and eaten most of his stores? Odysseus's bravado costs six lives, for the giant mocks the gods and their laws. Far from being impressed by the fame of the war heroes, the giant is happy to bash their brains in and swallow them whole for dinner.

Odysseus saves himself and half his crew by a ruse. The primitive giant has never seen wine; Odysseus gets him into a drunken stupor and gouges out his eye. This is better than murder, for the death of the giant would leave them trapped in the cave by a boulder too heavy for humans to move. Odysseus and his crew leave in the morning, when the Cyclops opens the door to let his flocks out, with a tenderness that reminds us that not even monsters are always monstrous. But first comes a trick so silly that, like the Trojan horse, it makes you wonder who on earth could be fooled by it. When the Cyclops asked for his name, Odysseus had answered, 'I'm called Nobody.' The point of the dodge is clear the next day, as the giant bellows in pain that *Nobody hurt him*. His fellow Cyclops turn away. Why should they come to his aid if his troubles were caused by nobody, but sent by fate or the gods, against whom resistance is pointless? It's not the last time Odysseus is in a quandary about whether to reveal his name and origin. His suppleness is decidedly unaristocratic. Odysseus is as convincing a beggar as he is a king because he cares so little about the difference between them.

But care he still does, enough to risk all their lives rather than stay anonymous. The moment he and his crew are safely shipboard, Odysseus shouts a taunt that makes the blinded giant throw a mountain, causing a tidal wave that nearly sinks the ship. Heedless of his crew's pleading, Odysseus shouts again: *It was Odysseus who maimed you, Laertes' son from Ithaca*. The risk he takes is so foolish it sounds like teenage swagger. Odysseus is on the cutting edge of the modern, and the epic heroes he grew up with depend on their names. There was no glory without a signature. Sometimes he locates himself in what he makes himself to be, but he cannot help but look back to a frame in which his nature is decided by father and fatherland.

What does Circe stand for? Roget's *Thesaurus* lists *Circe* as a synonym for *lustful*. She is the witch who does what men most fear, beguiling them with a lust so dark and potent that they lose not only their reason but even their human form. To say she uses a magic drug is to say we don't know how she does it, but the course is quite clear. Circe is eros built as a snare. Her low, luscious voice sings out from her palace in the glade, tempting men to come closer; her welcome is as quick and light as a cat's. Her cups are golden, her wine is sweet, and her bed, we're told, is flawless. Men lose themselves in desire and longing, their bodies overwhelming every other part of them till all that is left is what they have in common with panting, snorting pigs. (Poet Derek Walcott's version of *The Odyssey* suggests this could only be achieved by a woman who thinks all men are swine to begin with.) Before erotic power like Circe's, even men who have fought wars and vanquished giants are stammering and helpless.

Only Odysseus can tame a force that strong, and Circe knows it: He's the only mortal she cannot enchant. She wants him all the more, and calls him to her bedroom after she's turned his men to swine. He makes her swear oaths, and disenchant his crewmen, before giving in to pleasure, and for one long moment Odysseus has it all. He remains perfectly human while feasting in senses, as Circe's maidservants pour him cups of wine on crimson and silver tables, bathe his sea-washed body, and rub it sleek with oil. After their stint in the pigsty, his men are younger and handsomer than ever, and they settle in for the unbridled feasting that lasts for a year. For Circe's words are no less seductive than everything else she offers:

> Now you are burnt out husks, your spirits haggard, sere
> Always brooding over your wanderings long and hard
> Your hearts never lifting with any joy – you've suffered far
>   too much

'As we were men,' Odysseus recalls, 'we could not help consenting.' Who could resist it? Even strengthened by the drug that helps him withstand her, Odysseus gets sufficiently tangled in Circe's charms to make him forget his own goal for a year. It's his comrades who call his luxurious repose madness, and remind him of his bed at home.

To get there he must go through hell. Even Odysseus shudders at the prospect; in tears, in despair, he asks for a guide. No one has ever sailed to the land of the dead and returned. But Circe reminds him that he's the royal son of Laertes, born for adventure. He need only spread his sail and follow her directions, pouring libations here, turning down rivers there. By the time he crosses the Styx he knows what to do. Hades' ghosts come alive, just a little, when they drink sacrificial blood, so they crowd around Odysseus when they see he has killed black sheep, as Circe instructed.

One of the ghosts is the hero's mother. He weeps to see her phantom, and longs to embrace her, whom he last saw alive when he sailed for Troy. But Odysseus no more gives way to emotion in this case than anywhere else. He will not let his mother's ghost see him till he has followed instructions exactly and given the first drink to Tiresias. While Odysseus is the only mortal who will see what it's like to be dead, Tiresias is the only mortal who ever lived both as man and as woman, surely a great source of wisdom. But though Tiresias knows things that will help Odysseus on his homeward journey, there was no need to go all the way to hell to find them out. What Odysseus gets in Hades is another kind of lesson. He meets the shades of the great fallen heroes, and learns that this kind of heroism has come to an end.

His comrades in arms all pass before him: princes and warriors sublimely majestic, unequivocally grand. Ithaca is rather a backwater, and these nobles are greater than Odysseus; each played the role he was born to with unwavering splendor. Now they have a chance to reflect on it. Agamemnon is infinitely bitter; in place of a homecoming after ten years at Troy, he was killed at a banquet by his wife and her lover. The wretched death without honor or mercy casts its shadow over everything he lived for, and nothing suggests his ghost will find redemption. Far more important, however, is Odysseus's encounter with Achilles. Achilles' first words set the tone clearly: What brings his reckless friend to the house of death, 'where the senseless burnt out wraiths of mortals make their home?'

Odysseus moves quickly to comfort, and his words ring convincing: No man is greater than Achilles, never was, never will be. In life his comrades honored him like a god, and now, Odysseus sees, he lords it over the dead. Achilles lived the life and died the death for which every hero yearned. What cause can he have to complain?

> No smooth words about death to me, shining Odysseus!
> By god, I'd rather slave on earth for another man
> Some dirt-poor tenant farmer who scrapes to keep alive
> Than rule down here over all the exhausted dead

The ghost's words are the eulogy for the old order. The right sort of death, and the right sort of funeral, were so crucial to what it meant to be a hero as to put most else in the shadows. The idea that the meaning of your life is whatever happens after it was not a Christian invention; though ancient cultures viewed death differently, they still viewed it as central. Death, as we saw, still merits reverence. We no longer honor corpses with sacrificial victims, but we hold their mutilation in horror, and we still see the heroic death as central to heroic life. We may call someone happy before we know her end, but we'll hesitate to call her heroic. More than our lives, our deaths seem to reveal who we are. A hero who dies in the bedroom must have become faint- (or anyway, less than whole-)hearted.

Agamemnon's speech is built on this assumption. He'll be enraged for eternity – not because his life has ended, but because it was robbed of the right sort of ending. But Achilles' lament goes much further. No death was more valiant, no funeral more grand – yet he would prefer the low life of a bondsman to any death at all. To savor every breath while you have it, to shun every fruitless last stand while you can – such advice from the dead to the living can only come from Achilles, who spent his last days as a hero because he scorned counsel like that. This is a man who ate his fill of the fruits of victory before discovering they were sour. If Achilles says it wasn't worth it, it is time to rethink what heroes should be.

What other lessons does Odysseus learn in his wanderings? The encounter with Scylla and Charybdis, for example, brings the message that sometimes there are no good choices; steering a course toward the lesser evil may be the only thing that makes sense. The ship must pass a narrow strait bounded on one side by Scylla, a yapping six-headed monster whose giant tentacles pluck from every ship a man for each of her triple-fanged jaws. On the other side lies Charybdis, the whirlpool who sucks in the tide and vomits it up like a cauldron, drawing whole ships under in her yawning mouth. Circe tells him the choice is simple: Hug the cliff of the monster Scylla, for it's better to lose six men than to lose them all, and the ship as well. It's the sort of clear utilitarian calculation some philosophers like to contemplate. Odysseus's instinct is to fight, and he asks Circe how to run from Charybdis and strike Scylla when she raids his men. 'Old contender!' Circe chides him. 'Will you not yield to the immortal gods?' Scylla is eternal evil itself, the horror, pain, and chaos that will never die. Her mother is Brute Force, and no power can fight her. All that makes sense is to flee. Should Odysseus slow down to break out arms against her, she will simply pluck off six more men. The message is hard and clear: When the evils are fixed by laws of nature, railing against necessity is fruitless, and likely to cause more evil. False notions of heroism that refuse to make sacrifices only lead to greater sacrifices. Mature heroes choose lesser evils over fruitless last stands.

What song do the Sirens sing? Short as it is, Odysseus's encounter with the Sirens is rightly seen as central. Nowhere is Odysseus more himself. He must sail past the creatures whose song is so besotting that their island is littered with the bones of sailors who could not help but leap. No mortal is unmoved by their song, and none of Odysseus's temptations is greater. His choices are few. Knowing the danger, he could refuse to listen altogether, and stop his own ears with the beeswax he puts into the ears of his crewmen to keep them from jumping ship. But this is not a man who makes his life easy. He protects his crew from temptation, but lets himself feel its full force. Having ordered the sailors to tie him to the mast, Odysseus will listen to every sweet note, feel the pain of all he's missing. In the moment he hears the Sirens, Odysseus, like anyone, is tempted to be a romantic hero, throwing caution to the winds and himself into the waves, willing to go to the depths forever for a moment that feels whole. Much as he begs the crew to untie him, they row on. They will never understand his pain.

The Sirens do. That is, in fact, the secret of their seduction. What they have to offer is not any old music, but the lure of understanding.

> Come closer, famous Odysseus, Achea's pride and glory!

This is flattery, of course, but it's much better than that.

> We know all the pains that the Greeks and Trojans once
>   endured
> On the spreading plain of Troy when the gods willed it so
> All that comes to pass on fertile earth, we know it all!

For many souls, nothing is more tempting – and elusive – than the promise of being known. Even those who love you may not be able to offer it. Penelope can wait for Odysseus, but can she know what he went through in ten long years on the Trojan plain? Most of his comrades have died there, leaving Odysseus to map out a new world where his memory is staked. The next generation will take it for granted. Alone on the border between times and spaces, Odysseus must long to be known for a moment, without fragment or explanation, as he longs for nothing else. Of course such a longing is erotic. It's no accident the Bible speaks of carnal knowledge.

But you can't be a hero without paying some price. Odysseus puts himself through the torment of temptation in the struggle for something like truth: not just to know what the Sirens sound like, but to have heard them, tasted a moment of transcendence and be forced to acknowledge that he will be fundamentally lonely all the rest of his way. Odysseus's refusal to stop up his ears to what he is missing may be the bravest thing he does. Critics are not wrong to say it requires an assault on his own nature. More exactly, it requires a recognition of the split between reason and nature that runs through each of us, and can never be entirely healed. A traditionalist would have stopped up his ears and refused to listen entirely; one knows people who do. A romantic would have given in to nature and not cared how many lives were lost with his own. We remember the myth of the Sirens because facing them is Odysseus's hardest task. They force him to face the fact that being fully human means being torn.

He has sailed round the world, tasted and spurned both danger and temptation. Arriving at the place where he started, he might fall to the earth, or weep, or run to the wife and child left waiting twenty years. Instead, he asks questions. Even after the goddess of wisdom herself says he has finally reached Ithaca, he refuses to believe he's found the land he loves. For this the goddess rewards him. 'Always the same, your wary turn of mind,' Athena exclaims, her glances flashing warmly. 'That's why I cannot fail you in your evil fortune – you are so winning, so worldly-wise, so self-possessed! Anyone else, come back from wandering long and hard, would have hurried home at once, delighted to see his children and wife. Oh but not you, it's not your pleasure to probe for news of them – you must put your wife to the proof herself!'

Everything you may love and hate about Odysseus is condensed into his homecoming. Talk about suppressing emotion! After ten years at war and ten years at sea you want him to rejoice, and run, and sing out loud. His reserve is almost maddening. Some of it, to be certain, is reasonable. From the coastline, most Greek islands look equally alluring. Odysseus has been washed up on so many shores, hoping against hope that he'd found the right one; it would be foolish to kiss the wrong bit of ground. Anyone who's ever sought her heart's desire and found a mirage instead will understand his caution. And the voices of the dead have given him warning. Agamemnon's bloody homecoming is always in the background; the wife he has longed for could just as well embrace him or stab him in the back. And even if, as rumor has it, she has never betrayed him, he cannot know who else is faithful. His house is under siege. A hundred suitors have overtaken his estate. They are degenerate and menacing, and though they are rivals for Penelope's favor, they behave like a mob. Willing to plot to kill Odysseus's son, they can hardly be expected to welcome the father's return. Caution and planning and plotting are required to outwit them. Odysseus returns to the palace disguised as a beggar to learn the lay of the land before he retakes it.

Still, readers have puzzled over Odysseus's caution toward Penelope. He cannot really credit Agamemnon's warning after he sees her; there's no lover waiting to murder him, just an impatient crowd of suitors bullying a powerful, heartbroken woman whose very resourceful strategies have reached their end. Is he afraid after all? Or does he want to test her, and win her, all over again? Did she love him for the sake of appearances – the king's fortune, the young lord's physique – or would she stand by him as a ragged beggar? Who has never wondered how far a love goes?

This is a story with happy endings, so we're never really in doubt. Even as a worn-out old beggar, Odysseus outdoes every man in every way. He can invent poetry that's good enough to impress a goddess, string and shoot a bow others can barely lift, and when he finally appears in his own form his presence is so magnificent it puts younger men to shame. Thanks to all his good planning, he needs but two loyal men to slaughter the mass of interlopers. As elsewhere in this story, David trumps Goliath every time. Even in battle, wisdom and skill are better than force. The king and queen win each other all over again, for Penelope is the only woman alive who is Odysseus's match in cleverness, steadfastness, and care. Both have a dignity so radiant that we are hardly surprised when the last trick they play on each other turns into the marvelous symbol of the marriage bed.

All right, she tells a servant, make up his bed in the hall. The suitors who plagued her are slain, the man who has killed them might be her husband. Just like him, she holds back her joy till she's tested to her heart's satisfaction. Her husband is the only man on earth who knows that his bed cannot be moved by anyone but a god. For he built their bed himself, part of a living olive tree inside their courtyard, from start to finish, boring holes and fitting ivory, lopping off leaves, and finishing stone. As Odysseus describes the craft he lavished on the bed, you may come to feel it's his finest achievement; there is no doubt it's a labor of love.

His critics always emphasize the book's oppositions: Odysseus, they complain, is too much reason, and not enough nature. Alienated from his true self by constant battle with natural forces inside him and out, his survival comes at the price of his dreams. But nothing in the critiques prepares us for the extraordinary symbol of reason and nature reconciled in the bed that's alive – and tamed – a symbol of the way marriage itself should unite mind and body, sex and civilization. The bed shows the way Odysseus has it all: a place at the center of civilization built on, not against, rooted nature; a love time has tested, a passion that knowledge has deepened. We're suspicious of happy endings, and terrified of kitsch.

Penelope is key to preventing it here. Her skepticism is the device that allows Homer to introduce the bed, but it is also what gives the lovers' emotions body and soul. Kitsch has neither; it's the distortion of emotion that makes you suspect the genuine article. Imagine an alternative ending: 'Darling!' cries the smitten queen, sinking gently into his arms. 'You're home!' She melts, they weep,

he carries her upstairs in dirt and tatters, and we are left feeling –
nothing. Instead, the poet leads us through Odysseus's attempts to
master his mounting frustration, Penelope's attempts to still her
confusion and fear. Young and impatient and angry, Telemachus
calls his mother cold-hearted:

> What other wife could have a spirit so unbending?
> Holding back from her husband, home at last for *her?*

Penelope is strong enough to withstand her son's reproaches, for
like Odysseus she knows better. The secret signs known only to
them reflect the understanding that some feelings wither when put
on display. Her slowness to catch fire makes you sure it will blaze.
When she kisses him at last, she explains her reserve:

> I could not welcome you with love on sight
> I armed myself long ago against the frauds of men who might
>   come
> Beguiling me with talk.

In holding out for the real thing, Penelope finds not only the right
man, but the right response. When they finally embrace he will see
her as a shipwrecked sailor sees a sun-warmed stretch of land. And
to make their night last longer, the goddess of wisdom commands
the very heavens to hold back the dawn.

The hero does not, of course, have it all, for like all men he is
mortal, and every moment of joy is streaked with the knowledge
that it could end any minute, and will certainly end too soon. Not
even his homecoming is final, for he has another mission and will
soon be on his way. Unlike all men, he could have had it otherwise,
which returns us to the question with which *The Odyssey* begins.
What let Odysseus leave Calypso's island, spurning endless, ageless
pleasure in the arms of a goddess to make his way home?

The question becomes even more acute when we remember
what else the hero saw. Though the order of narration makes this
confusing, Calypso's offer comes *after* the Cyclops and the Sirens

and Scylla and Charybdis and any number of ordinary monsters in between. Odysseus has been shipwrecked and famished, watched crew and companions suffer and fall, and unlike them all he has been through hell. He cannot console himself with sweet dreams of afterlife: No Elysian fields await him, just the company of sad shades so eager for a semblance of living that they'll scramble for a taste of sheep's blood. When he refuses Calypso's offer of eternal life, Odysseus knows what death means. What is still more awesome: He does not even know if he will find his heart's desire. Penelope may not be waiting. Telemachus may have usurped the throne. Another storm sent by the sea god may finally do him in. When he leaves Calypso's island, Odysseus is leaving certain immortal bliss for a future so uncertain that it's positively doubtful. Was there ever a braver deed?

He risks it all, in the first instance, for the woman he loves. This is a man who can have whom he will; Odysseus never meets a woman who doesn't want to keep him in her bed. Besides the lovely nymph Calypso, there's the wilder and darker temptation of the enchantress Circe; later on he will turn down Nausicaa, a girl not only radiant with the first light of maidenhood, but the heiress to a kingdom at that. He is offered every erotic fantasy that can try men's hearts, and he leaves them all behind. (The man is so charismatic he can even turn rejected lovers into allies. Circe, Calypso, and Nausicaa long to hold him, but they all help him, in the end, on his way.) The vision of Penelope that drives him on is not clouded. When he tells Calypso that she is far greater than Penelope in beauty and stature, he isn't merely flattering her. Mortals cannot compare with goddesses in grace or form; Penelope – he knows it – will age and die.

And still she is *his* love, the woman he's willing to die for. Theirs are not the ties of two people whom common histories have bound so tightly they cannot imagine living without the other. On the contrary, Penelope notes wistfully, when they finally unite: The gods have denied them that sort of happiness. The twenty years that separate them cannot be reclaimed. Odysseus and Penelope are simply each other's match, 'two minds and two hearts that work as one,' he calls it, 'their own best claim to glory.'

It would be anachronistic to call *The Odyssey* a feminist novel, but, considering the millennium, the heroes' relationship is astonishingly reciprocal. This is partly because each shares qualities usually assigned to the other sex. Odysseus weeps for home 'as a woman weeps for her fallen husband.' He is flexible, supple, able to fit into the world as he needs to rather than forcing it to fit his will. More than any other Greek hero, all this puts him at ease with women, whether they happen to be goddesses or girls. And Penelope has her share of traits traditionally called masculine; she is steadfast and self-controlled, at once canny and authoritative. They are clearly equal in both wisdom and cunning, as in something more important: Both are equally alive.

Earlier times may not have understood it any better than we do, but they weren't as embarrassed to name it: the life force or spark thought close to divine. It is not. Instead, it's something that makes those who have it fully human, and those who don't look like sleep-walkers. Those who have it can turn the meeting of an aging couple into a dramatic triumph, find meaning and beauty in scrap iron or tomatoes; they can make prose lyric, and poetry transcend. It isn't enough to make someone heroic, but without it any hero will be forgotten. Rousseau called it force of soul; Arendt called it love of the world. It's the foundation of eros; you may call it charisma. Is it a gift of the gods, or something that has to be earned? Watching such people, you will sense that it's both: given like perfect pitch, or grace, that no one can deserve or strive for, and captured like the greatest of prizes it is. Having it makes people think more, see more, feel more. More intensely, more keenly, more loudly if you like; but not more in the way of the gods. On the contrary, next to heroes like Odysseus and Penelope, the gods seem oddly flat. They are bigger, of course, and they live forever, but their presence seems diminished. Even their lovemaking is dimmer and trite. Circe's bed is flawless, and Calypso's island is spellbinding, but their lust for the hero is just that. Both pale before the description of the joys of the marriage bed, where the lovers cannot sleep for reveling in each other's words and arms.

Those who have come close to death will often express it: Knowing that you're finite is part of feeling truly alive. (It isn't, however, enough to produce it; in some people the knowledge of finitude causes nothing more than depression.) The gods of *The Odyssey* aren't alive, just immortal; and with immortality most of the qualities we cherish become pointless. With nothing to risk, the gods need no courage. Where they can get what they want by magic, what's the point of creative achievement? Without mortals to watch, at war and at love, the gods would curse their empty power, and yearn to die of boredom. 'Human limits structure human virtues, and give excellent action its significance,' writes Martha Nussbaum in 'Transcending Humanity,' her admirable discussion of *The Odyssey*. In choosing Penelope over Calypso, Odysseus chooses a woman embedded as he is in the middle of life. His travels offered constant chances to opt out of the human: as a pampered minor god or a satisfied pig. The course he takes is a choice to push human life to its limits, and stay resolutely human. Sheer romance? Without question, though always hard-edged, with the knowledge that human desires form a paradox. You must love as if forever, while knowing that forever would dim the love itself. Wisdom is no less wisdom for being bittersweet. This is part of what makes true love itself adventure – the other object this hero cannot find on Calypso's isle. He's a man for whom an unadventured life is not worth living. Odysseus is not Abraham; though he shows more concern than other Achean princes for the lives of his sailors, he will not risk his own for them, much less for nameless creatures whom he has never seen. But he will take risks, scorn hazard, dare chance – to embrace as much as life ever gives.

· · · · ·

Why turn to *The Odyssey*?

There are plenty of reasons to do so, but one is close at hand. For the *Dialectic of Enlightenment*, twentieth-century philosophy's most important critique of the Enlightenment, *The Odyssey* was the beginning of the end. Its authors, Theodor Adorno and Max Horkheimer, saw the epic as commencing the slow descent of the human spirit that marks the modern. Odysseus, they argue, was the prototype of Enlightenment. The first modern novel showed the first modern man: uprooted, cool, and dispassionate, driven to seek the world and find everything but his soul. His wiles always work, but the cost is immense. Premodern heroes, they wrote, try to control the world through the relatively harmless ritual murder of bulls and goats. Modern heroes sacrifice themselves. Premodern heroes were subject to the tyranny of superstition and brute force; with internalized repression, modern heroes invented something even crueler. Odysseus blinds the Cyclops, but in calling himself Nobody he negates not only his name, but his essence. And the captain who stops up his sailors' ears and binds himself to the mast to get past the Sirens foreshadows the modern capitalist, driving himself and his workers relentlessly through a denatured world. As compensation, he treats himself to an occasional opera ticket; the workers are denied even that.

Anyone who wants to defend the Enlightenment today must come to terms with these claims, for they capture the core of the charges laid against it. At their simplest they are a warning: Those who put mind over matter are likely to lose their souls. These metaphors express the persistent suspicion that reason and nature are not just separate but at war. Anyone committed to reflection over impulse, to paths more circuitous than straight, will deny the claims of nature – his own as well as anyone else's. Men like Achilles and Ajax have straightforward virtues: brawn, passion, loyalty, and courage. Odysseus has all that, and a mind as well. And with minds come indirection and ambiguity, convolution and tangle. What's lost can seem all the more beautiful for seeming simple. Golden ages have no shades of gray.

For Adorno and Horkheimer, Odysseus's triumphs reveal the

empty triumphs of modernity itself. Saying he is Nobody allows Odysseus to escape, but is his life worth the cost? In a culture where naming is magic, the hero disowns his own self in refusing a name. Doesn't this foreshadow the abstract modern self that's no self at all?

But there's another way to see it: Calling yourself Noman is like calling yourself Everyman. In the old order, what counted was your lineage. You were Agamemnon, son of Atreus, or Helen, daughter of Zeus. Divine parentage was useful, but noble parentage was necessary, and whoever didn't have it might as well be nameless, and forever forgotten. Modern heroes like Odysseus are no longer tied to their origins: Anyone can be a hero, and anyone can fail. In an era where human choice begins to matter, why not let go of your name itself, first of all the ways in which your parents fix who you will be?

In the *Dialectic of Enlightenment*, the encounter with the Sirens is an indictment of reason: Through foresight and planning the captain finds a way to have the experience but negate its force. Odysseus suppresses his passion in order to reach his distant goal. He thereby reveals how the modern subject uses reason to dominate nature – his own nature first of all – while leaving a small space for the sterilized version of nature and passion we have come to call high culture. Thus safely bounded, art no longer has the power to move us, but it can function to let off steam. Odysseus appears as a captain of industry whose workers have been deafened in order to toil ever harder, never straying from their course. The image is powerful until one asks the question: So you want he should drown?

Grown-up heroes must make real choices. Odysseus's solutions preserve his commitment to Enlightenment virtue. He knows a great deal about happiness; few people tried out as many forms of it. He's a master of reasoning, practical and instrumental, as good at setting goals as he is at finding the means to achieve them. His reverence has been tested and tempered; the pull of hunger and longing never stop him from following the prohibitions lesser men disregard. And his hope for something other than the alternatives he is given sustains him through each storm. His choices are often marred; virtues are not guarantees. Yet with Odysseus, all four values the Enlightenment cherished are always on display.

As it turns out, Odysseus-bashing has an even longer history than Enlightenment-bashing. If *The Odyssey* marks the beginning of the modern, the attack on modernity didn't have long to wait. 'I do not know how it comes to pass,' wrote Voltaire, 'but every reader bears secretly an ill will to the wise Ulysses.' Voltaire exaggerated slightly, but it's easy to forgive him, for few readers even bothered to keep their ill will a secret. Most of them were perfectly open. 'May I never have a character like that,' said the Greek poet Pindar, 'but walk in straightforward ways.' Pindar was an aristocrat, and an uncompromising defender of tradition. He found Odysseus simply base, a far cry from the early noble heroes who won their wars and their fame with nothing but courage and strength. For Pindar, Odysseus represented moral decay. A world where a cunning upstart from a small and distant island could triumph over the austere and highborn prince Ajax was to him a world gone wrong. It's a world where simple deeds are trumped by slick words, strength by guile, lions by foxes. Pindar was not quite ready to mourn the old world forever, but he would go down fighting the new.

Pindar represented the conservative tradition in fifth-century Greece, but another kind of attack came from the progressive one. Euripides was not inclined to defend aristocratic values, but his tragedies portray Odysseus as the worst villain of all. That his deception and guile are set in the service of higher causes only shows his inhumanity: Far better to commit crimes of passion than to commit crimes for reasons of state. At bottom nothing matters to Odysseus but his own ambition, and to serve it he will shrink from nothing. He will trick the widowed and the lame, break codes of honor, order the death of children without pity or shame. For Euripides' Odysseus, any crime can be rationalized, and they all seem to pay.

Both conservative and progressive fifth-century critics thought that the rise of Odysseus spelled the waning of heroism. The noble age had ended, if men like him prevailed. Pindar made this perfectly clear, blasting Homer for leaving multilayered, ambiguous Odysseus alive, while the straightforward noblemen of old receded into shades. Somewhat later, Stoics objected to Odysseus's repeated complaining, and took him to task for being unmanly. (He might have called them inhuman, for *The Odyssey* reminds us that heroes rarely feel heroic inside.) So the lament that we are losing our heroes is no recent development. Thomas Carlyle, the English writer most committed to the idea of the heroic in history, traced the hero's progression within it. He thought the first heroes were gods; from that high point they became prophets, poets, priests, men of letters, and kings, in dreary succession. Living in the nineteenth century, Carlyle argued that the decline of the hero was only apparent: Each age receives the kind of hero that suits it, and what he called the heroic gift is admirable in all its forms. Who needs gods and soldiers? Shakespeare, he insisted, would be with us long after the British Raj had crumbled, for don't books achieve miracles? It's a thought any writer might cherish, but Carlyle's protestations sound like protestations too much. Something about the flourish with which he defends the very idea of the heroic against the creeping tide of skepticism suggests a rearguard action.

Still, the nineteenth century blazed with talk of great men and women in history and literature, though everyone knew the best heroes were flawed. Charles Dickens never leaves us in doubt about the morals of his stories, but his characters are not cartoons. You might prefer Charles Darnay as a son-in-law, but he pales next to Sidney Carton, whose walk to the guillotine is indeed a far, far better thing than he ever did before, since he passed most of his life as an interesting drunk. The more memorable the hero, the bigger the cracks. Even courage, the hero's signature, is rarely straightforward. *Moby-Dick* took no fearless whalers on board because, Melville writes, anyone who is never afraid is not a hero but a fool.

Nevertheless, were you born in the nineteenth century, you would have known who your heroes were, and you would have known exactly why. Till mass death in the trenches killed classical conceptions of bravery in the field, men looked to be heroes in battle. Women's fronts were no less emphatic for being more diverse: Bringing food to the needy, balm to the wounded, letters to the ignorant were attended with all the rhetoric of combat. Changes in the nature of warfare immeasurably weakened the military paradigm. It was hard to put heroic spin on the business of cowering in a cold, stinking mudhole watching shells fly, and the writers who survived it were not inclined to try. But the impulse to look to the army for models of heroism outlived the First World War and is still with us, however shakily, today. Outside the military, the question *Who are your heroes?* has become not only hard to answer, but almost impossible to ask. If you're like most people I have questioned on the subject, you will pause, look into the distance, and stammer, not sure whether to be more embarrassed by the question or the silence that follows it. After a moment you may venture: 'Perhaps Nelson Mandela . . .' not because you know much about him, but rather because you don't. Naming heroes seems easier when they're distant, if not actually dead; for most of us in the West, Mandela is too far away to come into focus. What happened to make heroes seem obsolete?

In his book *After Virtue*, philosopher Alasdair MacIntyre argues that heroic societies are those in which heroes cannot be detached from themselves; since we can only possess virtue as part of tradition, heroic virtues are no longer available. But in the world of the modern, where your life is no longer determined by the lives of your parents, no one self feels authentic, making the question of identity as precarious as it is paramount. You can think of this as a loss, and you can think of it as an occasion – for the exercise of the backbone it takes to live outside fixed roles. Seen through the right lenses any hero can be unmasked. The proverb 'No man is a hero to his valet' was already proverbial in the seventeenth century. Anyone who takes the boots off a general will find clay feet if he wants to. But valets are no longer with us. In a world where we take our own pants off – or wait to have them removed by a tabloid – we are each our own valet, and all the feet are out in the open. Knowing what they look like makes it hard to look much further. Have we learned too much to believe in heroes? When we all stood in court in costume, it was easier to be vain and vainglorious. Now not even courts are off-limits. We know what sweet obscenities Charles whispered to Camilla on the telephone, what pornographic games the world's most charming president played in the White House. Not the murderous but the puerile impulses in all of us can make the search for something heroic seem ridiculous.

Yet this problem was already confronted by Hegel. 'No man is a hero to his valet; not, however, because the man is not a hero, but because the valet is – a valet.' The valet's view of the world is crude and common, and he will turn up every stone to confirm it. After modeling a hero with proportions too flat to fit into anything but a comic book, he asserts there are no (more) heroes in the world. His picture is not only one-dimensional, but also simply cheap. Straw men are no use even in arguments; how could they be useful as heroes? Petty and ungenerous people seek pettiness and parsimony; magnanimous souls will seek their own kind. Our age, wrote Hegel in 1806, cannot see its own heroes because we look with the eyes of valets. (He called them pedants.) It takes one, in short, to know one. If you are a hero you know that your feet can ache and stink and still climb whatever peaks need to be scaled, and stand there holding forts. If you are a valet you'll see nothing but mud.

Knowing heroes were imperfect, and sometimes even silly, didn't stop earlier ages from maintaining them, but the twentieth century introduced something new. Others may have unmasked the hero and stopped; our age had something to put in its place. Instead of competing with our neighbors to see who could be the bigger hero, we began to compete to become the biggest victim. Tracing this development is worth its own study, but even a glance will suggest that its results have been mixed.

The desire to give voice to victims began in demands for justice.

Earlier accounts of history let victims die a double death: once in the flesh, once again in memory. To insist that victims' stories be part of the historical record, and that the victors' stories be told without cant, was just a matter of righting old wrongs. If victims' stories have claims on our attention, they have claims on our sympathy, our systems of justice, our bank accounts. As an alternative to worldviews in which the survivor of a massacre by Roman legions or Mongol hordes expected nothing more than a lapidary 'Shit happens,' it's a definite step toward progress. We've come to assume that the world as a whole should be just. Where bad things happen to good people, the world is out of joint, and we see ourselves as meant to set it right.

Yet something went wrong when we reconsidered the place of the victim, and the impulse that began in generosity can turn downright perverse. It's visible in the attempts of competing groups to take moral high ground by staking claims to comparisons with the Holocaust. One stumbling block to European integration is East–West resentment, as Eastern Europeans demand that their sufferings under Stalin be acknowledged in the same terms as others who suffered under Hitler. Occasionally this bursts into scandal: When a European commissioner opened the annual Leipzig Book Fair by stating that Stalinism was as bad as Nazism, the vice president of the German Jewish Community walked out in demonstrative protest, fueling debates for months. I think the commissioner was wrong, but for a Latvian born in Siberia, to which her parents had been deported, the instinct was intelligible. References to 'the Holocaust on your plate' by animal-rights organizations are not. The limiting case of this trend is the story of Benjamin Wilkomirski, the Swiss man whose claims to have spent his childhood in a concentration camp turned out to be faked. As German critic Jan Philipp Reemtsma has pointed out, earlier orphans inventing their own histories fabricated noble parents. Anyone could be the son of an errant knight or a wayward pope, and claiming aristocratic origins was the best way to rise. Now that cachet has given way to another;

claiming a more miserable birth than your real one guarantees a new form of status. What's interesting is less the fraud than what makes this fraud possible: What was recently a stigma has been transformed into its opposite. Even a hint of suffering has come to cast an aura that few can resist.

From the Wilkomirski case it's not far to a justice that promises: to each his own concentration camp. We have valorized a set of virtues that I'd rather not have in my world unless absolutely necessary. More precisely: Undergoing suffering isn't a virtue at all, and it's unlikely to create any. Virtue is not about what happens to us, but about what we do with it. Victimhood should be a source of legitimation for claims to simple restitution, but not for anything else – even the legitimation provided by overmuch attention. If we view victimhood itself as a source of legitimacy, we are on the way to untying legitimacy from virtue altogether.

Apart from the longing for justice, there are other reasons for this shift. It's easier to be a victim than a hero, and it's easier to tell if someone else is. Wilkomirski, and others like him, were eventually discovered. All things considered, telling a real victim from a false one is simpler than deciding if somebody's heroism was hollow. What you have suffered is easier to know than what you've done, and harder to demask. It takes a brutally honest victim to demask the victim's status itself. Jean Améry, who survived two years at Auschwitz, insisted that suffering there made no one wiser, deeper, or more human. Rather than growing into the future, 'the victim is nailed to the cross of his destroyed past.' Améry's reference signals the fact that Jesus was the first model for valorizing the victim; but those who tried to imitate him were not heroes, but saints. Nailed to the cross of a wretched past? What healthy culture would trade this stance for the older one?

The shift toward the victim was bound to lash back; other things being equal, people don't want to be nailed to crosses, or keep their eyes fixed on past pain. Nor are many attracted to the dull but safe utilitarianism that finds self-interested calculation the best guarantee for an orderly world. I scratch your back, you scratch mine. Nothing to be said against it, but with sufficient attention to itching and scratching and a little fantasy, we are back in a world where characters like Beavis and Butt-head rule. In a Hobbesian world threatened by permanent war, utilitarian contracts may be objects of longing. But as soon as treaties are signed and bellies are full, this is not a world to which many will aspire.

I propose we restrain our attachment to victims and return to an older model, where your claims to legitimacy are focused on what you've done to the world, not what the world did to you. This wouldn't return the victims to the ash heap of history, but it would bring the hero back to center stage. One of the first heroic virtues is generosity, as well as a certain humility that recognizes the contingency that plays a role in our lives. (There but for fortune could any of us go.) These should allow us to honor caring for victims as a virtue – without suggesting that being a victim is one as well.

That proposal met with protest at a recent meeting of human-rights activists, where I suggested that racist violence among young people might be easier to reduce by pointing to the courage of people who oppose it rather than the misery of people who suffer it. My colleagues bristled at the word *hero*; of course teenagers need role models, and figures of identification, but must we offer them heroes? Their antipathy is understandable. Americans hear the word and think Rambo, Germans hear the word and think worse. The appeal to blood and soil left the earth drenched in gore from Moscow to Normandy. It was Mussolini who wrote that the culture of the hero was fascism's answer to bourgeois egotism; the hero's reputation did no better in the other direction, as the noble impulses that had fought fascism gave way to the tyranny and terror of Stalinism. Both Stalinism and Nazism were dead set against the ambiguities of modernism, and set out to produce art that glorified the human spirit. Neither the art nor the spirt came anywhere close to the glorious – with the consequence that the word *glory* itself has gone out of use. The idea of the hero was not just degraded, but contaminated

– one sure reason to turn to the idea of the victim when looking for standard-bearers. Though less abashed in its use of heroic language than the left is, the right, too, has trouble naming names. The appeal of Ronald Reagan, after all, is the appeal of someone who *played* heroes; had his political life been preceded by a career as an accountant, it would have hardly carried the ring of anything grander. No wonder we've replaced talk of heroes with the (faintly arch) talk of icons. Icons were painted in two dimensions – not because Greek Christians lacked technique, but because they feared that the three-dimensional representation their forefathers perfected looked too human to circumvent monotheist prohibitions on idolatry. A culture that trades heroes for icons has stopped imagining objects of admiration that can be more than symbols.

That aspirations have risks is all too clear. Rumbling bellies surely swelled the ranks of fascist movements in the last century, but just as important was disgust for the pedestrian version of human life the mainstream offered. Too much has been made of parallels between fascist and Islamic totalitarianism, but they do have one thing in common: Both attract followers who are sick of the consumerist plodding and the passive whining that mark the default positions of the cultures that surround them. Weary of a world with no room for heroic action, some boys think striking terror will keep them, at the least, from becoming the victims they despise.

Role models will not tempt them, nor objects of identification, for the very words drip dryness, fruit of a culture that combines mediocre social science with superb technology to create the world they reject. They and their more passive counterparts – those who no longer aspire to anything more than an occasional new gadget – need alternatives whose very cadences show the hero's secret: that every life could be large enough to contain a world.

My return to Odysseus is an unashamed appeal for a hero whose strengths and weaknesses match the modern world. In many ways he's no model at all. I'm willing to overlook the residues of feudalism and sexism as par for any eighth-century course, but I'd do without his piracy and bragging, and some of the whining as well. You may object to his other sins, and that's just the point. Odysseus's achievements are imaginable because he's imperfect. Unlike role models, heroes are full-bodied and hot-blooded. *The Odyssey* is not just a tale about staying, but about being alive.

What makes its hero modern? The fact that the noblest man in Ithaca is a swineherd is no argument for republicanism, just as Penelope's ability to outmaneuver a hundred men on her threshold is no argument for gender equality. Still, there are signs of change that hint at our notions of progress: Odysseus is less impressed than others by distinctions of class and gender, and his ability to transform himself is a way of showing we are not identical with our social roles. But Greek time was not linear, so our idea of progress is absent in this epic – and a good thing that is, for if you believe in progress you must believe we've made some in the intervening millennia. Still, modern is not just *The Odyssey*'s foretaste of unanchored identity, or the appeal to brains over brawn. It's also Zeus's claim at the outset that the gods are not responsible for human fate. In *The Iliad* they were, and without anything we can see as a morsel of justice. Modern is also the recognition that taking fate into our own hands will not end the cycle of pain. Some of the love and death and envy and longing with which Odysseus struggles will always be with us; he is an example of how heroes contend with them. Unlike fanatics, who see only the *ought*, and Pharisees, who see only the *is*, heroes keep both eyes open. Before you reject appeals to the heroic please consider: Are we afraid of them because they end in blood and thunder, or because they end in kitsch? I suspect that we are often moved less by the fear of fascism than the fear of embarrassment – a fear that ought, itself, to be most embarrassing.

Who are your heroes?

Rereading *The Odyssey* reveals that the difficulty of answering is not a problem about modern – or postmodern – life. Plato records an argument about whether Achilles or Odysseus was the better man, and the question is older than he was. Both men are heroes;

few could be more different. Odysseus has an eye for the ordinary that Achilles disdains. (He makes sure everyone eats before battle, while Achilles declares he can run on pure rage.) Odysseus is as democratic as Greek princes ever get. (Seventeenth-century readers were disgusted by the fact that he slept in a pigsty, and missed the fact that the swineherd's welcome is so magnificent it puts nobler dwellings to shame.) Odysseus is cautious where Achilles is brash. (Imagining how the latter would have faced the Sirens is an interesting exercise, but we cannot imagine Achilles stooping to put beeswax in his crewmen's ears, or letting them tie him up.) Odysseus's motives are usually mixed. (Is he traveling to get home to his family, or to see the world on the way?) Achilles' actions are so straightforward that it's sometimes hard to see any motive behind them at all. (When he finally joins the battle, it wasn't the result of deliberation.) Achilles acts with absolute certainty. (His fate has been foretold; he knows he will die at Troy.) Odysseus's certainty concerns himself and his powers alone. (Knowledge of what awaits him is radically incomplete; wherever he seems certain he's certain about no more than himself.) Their encounters with women are as different in number as they are in kind. (Achilles covets one or another slave girl. Odysseus has complex erotic and other relations with a host of women before leaving them behind for the wise, middle-aged love of his life.) Whatever his reasons for wandering, Odysseus is eternally cosmopolitan; no wonder James Joyce made him a rootless Dublin Jew. This gives him depth and loss at once. He is never entirely at home abroad, and he will always be rather abroad at home. It's this that gives him the alienated quality his critics find shifty. You cannot take the relationship between self and world for granted if you've seen very much of it.

Achilles' courage, like his other virtues, is completely natural. His virtues are those of unforced innocence; there is no gap between desire and action that must be explained or filled. Most of Odysseus's deeds are studied — as down to earth as wax in his sailors' ears, as premeditated and violent as his own chains. For Adorno and Horkheimer, he uses force on himself, and misses life in the bargain.

They are right about the former. His encounter with the Sirens is a recipe for disenchantment: how to conquer fear for those who were not born fearless. Perhaps you like your heroes to be naturally valiant, ready to rush into frays without hesitation or doubt. It's one way to convince yourself you needn't be heroic. If heroes can tremble and cry and falter, you could also become one – especially if given instructions that model design. Want to survive a monster? Here are the sort of steps you'll need to do it. It's a matter of preparedness and planning, not boldness and force. Like all Enlightenment projects, demystification is its end. Achilles would have curled his lip and jumped into the sea, sword in hand. Perhaps he could even have taken a Siren down with him.

The Iliad and *The Odyssey* have been called the Greek Bible. Together they formed the central sourcebook for later Greek culture, and with that much of the rest of Western culture as well. We can use them to chart our own fortunes because whatever else has changed since they were written, these alternatives are much the same. Achilles is a romantic hero, while Odysseus – though he undertook the most romantic act in the history of literature – is not. For perhaps the most important difference between them is the difference between a tragic death and a story with a happy ending. A romantic hero who lives into ripe old age becomes a cartoon or a fop. And a man who lives out his time cannot, we imagine, be a real hero. Thought through to the end, the figures of Achilles and Odysseus reveal our ambivalence about the idea of a hero itself.

Heroes give us alternatives to resignation. They show that the limits of life can be probed and extended, that we need not swallow every piece of the frameworks into which we are born. Accept human nature? 'We do not know what our nature permits us to be,' wrote Rousseau. Even if you believe him, knowledge is not the same as conviction. You may sense that the limits of your tribe or your town are not the limits of what's possible. But until you see someone actually overcome them, you're unlikely to believe that it's possible for you. This is why there are all sorts of heroes: Sports players, mountain climbers, and certain kinds of rock stars all hold out the promise of a life lived more, and more intensely, than the ones to which we are told to be resigned. Complete heroes cannot confine their achievement to one arena. They pursue war and love and justice with the same commitment and skill. Like Odysseus, they do not always get it right. Heroes make the difference between theoretical possibilities and real ones, proving beyond doubt that it isn't merely wishful thinking that makes you want to be more alive.

But if heroes are an inspiration, they are also a challenge, and it's a challenge we'd often prefer to forget. The knowledge that some people have made more out of their lives than you have can be unwelcome. This is especially true when, unlike the ambivalent Odysseus, the hero in question is a moral one. You may never have a moment when you want to climb Everest, but you would like to think you could defy a tyrant if you had to. And since none of us ever know if we could do what we should in the extremest of cases, the vision of those who have risked their lives for the sake of ideals can sometimes be so threatening we'd prefer to see them dead.

Why think the only true hero is a dead hero? For a start, there are trivial reasons, like piety. We may undress living people in any tabloid, but we draw the line at seeking clay feet among the dead. The young Rousseau went so far as to say we would remember Socrates as a skillful sophist if only he'd died in bed. Dead heroes' flaws can be forgotten like dead criminals' sentences; there is little point in insisting on either. But the more important reason we view death as central to heroism is less attractive: A part of us wants to resign. The greater the number of people who have done so before us, the lesser the strain on our conscience. And the higher the price of resistance, the more understandable resignation will be. If you have to choose death to combat injustice, most people will forgive you for staying home.

Hans and Sophie Scholl were college students guillotined in Munich in 1943 for writing and distributing anti-Nazi pamphlets.

Their actions were unquestionably brave, even if their only consequence was to let later generations of Germans know that not
everyone capitulated before Nazi terror. In Germany today, most
cities have streets or schools named after them, or the little resistance group they founded, the White Rose. By contrast, the most
successful act of resistance in the Third Reich is the least well known,
and none of its heroes is known by name. It also took place in 1943,
when the Nazi government was undecided about deporting and
murdering Jewish spouses of non-Jews. They decided to test the
waters by rounding up four hundred Jewish men whose non-Jewish
wives had already withstood considerable government pressure to
divorce them. When these women learned that their husbands
were being held for deportation in the Rosenstrasse, they held a
spontaneous demonstration in front of the building. For one long
week these women refused to leave the little street in central Berlin,
as heedless of the Gestapo machine guns trained on them as they
were of the icy February wind.

It's often said that nonviolent resistance worked for Gandhi and
Martin Luther King because their oppressors were civilized; the
governments of Britain and Alabama could be bested by the moral
courage of their opponents, while totalitarian regimes simply shoot
them. But in Berlin's Rosenstrasse, the police backed down. The
men were released. They and their wives survived. And except for
a second-rate movie, all that marks this act is a small clay-colored
memorial in a side-street park even few Berliners know. Seeing it
moves many to tears. But what is tragic is not the heroes, but the
fact that nobody else followed suit. What stopped them was less the
Nazi terror itself than a much older message: Heroic action is futile,
and mostly ends in death besides.

Neither Pindar nor Adorno went so far as to say it, but their
suspicion of Odysseus turns on the fact that he comes out alive.
Earlier it seemed the willingness to lay down your life was a proof
of your freedom. Odysseus is a challenge to live without proofs.
Our willingness to esteem comes at a very high price: We're prepared

to ask no questions and take heroic claims at face value as long as the hero is dead. Then as now, we like our heroes tragic. Nor need you accept the principle to respect someone willing to die for it. You may loathe the style Achilles stands for, but honor the fact that he stood (and fell) for something. By contrast, Odysseus's uncanny (or canny) survival awakens suspicion that he stood for nothing at all. None other than the great romantic hero says this is mistaken; we have Achilles' word that magnificent deaths are hollow. It isn't a message that's suited for anyone concerned to preserve traditional values, so the first poetry Plato's *Republic* proposed to ban was Achilles' speech from hell. Plato thought it so bleak that it would discourage future heroes who might be tempted to imitate him – which is presumably what Homer intended.

With characters like Odysseus we will never know for certain, but we'll suspect that his motives are as mixed as ours. He is unsettling because he is so recognizable, and so close. His strength and his beauty are mythic. But we could, in principle, have his wisdom and his wiles, his loyalty and courage, his willingness to test the borders of the known world. We surely have his flaws. We take risks for sheer bravado, let enchantments of the senses obscure the sight of our goals, for longer stretches of time than we mean to do. We make compromises and hope that what we chose as the lesser of two evils was indeed really necessary; our judgments are uncertain, and still they must stand. Our motives are opaque and our desires often torn. Challenged to act bravely, we are less inclined to jump out of bed and lace up our boots than to huddle on the border and complain. We are quite certain that our troubles are the worst ones, our fates the unluckiest. We long desperately to be at home, and take no end of time to get there. Yet even in showing his failings, his story shows the difference between living and sleepwalking. If Odysseus can be a hero, then so, in short, can we.

CHAPTER ELEVEN

WHAT ABOUT EVIL?

Put yourself, if you can, in his footsteps. You have long laid your life in the hands of the Lord. Told to leave the land of your fathers forever, you pack your bags and go forth. Told to cut off your foreskin and those of your servants, you see to it the same day. Your willingness to obey strange and painful commands without question is what makes you a man of faith. And now the voice you have followed for a quarter of a century tells you He plans to destroy the city of Sodom. What makes you speak up? It can't be piety or reverence or devotion; those are all the things that drove you to obey the Lord without a murmur, much less a protest. Nor is He demanding anything of you at all; you are simply being informed in advance of an event in which no role for you is foreseen. You could be a distant witness and keep your hands clean. When God revealed His homicidal intentions to Noah, Noah nodded and built a boat. (One rabbinical source makes this the reason he's chiefly remembered in kindergartens, while Abraham's intervention merited glory.) What led the patriarch to risk everything to remind his sovereign lawgiver that His plan is manifestly unjust?

Whatever it is, it isn't religion, for religion is everything else that he did. Abraham's credentials as a knight of faith are beyond reproach, but they aren't the source of his sense of good and evil.

That sense may inform his faith, but it is prior to it. Most people lose heart in the face of authority. They yield to priestly orders to shun excommunicated families, crusaders' instructions to behead infidels. Nor need the authority be expressly religious. White coats, officious manners, and the little word *Yale* was all it took to make 65 percent of those tested in Stanley Milgram's famous experiment push buttons they thought were shocking other people unconscious. Where does Abraham get the nerve to challenge the greatest, most sacred authority of all?

No attempt to think ourselves into Abraham's world can be very successful, but even the most limited success should undermine the view that we get our moral concepts from religion. The view cuts across religious and political commitments, and it persists although the Bible itself says it ain't necessarily so. Running for president, both Pat Robertson and Joe Lieberman quoted, more or less accurately, George Washington's claim that 'reason and experience both forbid us to expect that national morality can prevail in exclusion of religious principle.' Would everything be permitted if God did not exist? Many have swallowed the idea without ever defending it.

Nowhere is this assumption more alive than when talk turns to evil, as it's done so often since September 11, 2001. Public discourse was the first thing Al Qaeda's attacks dramatically changed. 'Today, our nation saw evil' was George W. Bush's initial response. It would not be his last; in *The President of Good and Evil*, philosopher Peter Singer counts 319 speeches that invoked the word – by June 2003. Bush's rhetoric was not unique, and many critics were quick to point out similarities between his calls against evil and those of Islamic fundamentalists who were as bent on Bush's doom as he was on theirs.

If the Islamicists' theology was worn on their sleeves, Bush's was only partially covered. Speechwriter David Frum, who authored the Axis of Evil speech, wrote that 'in a country where almost two-thirds of the population believes in the devil, Bush was identifying Osama bin Laden and his gang as literally Satanic.' Many observers have pointed out the apocalyptic language sprinkled through Bush's speeches to appeal to a Christian fundamentalist base while appearing acceptably nondenominational to the rest of us. Before advisors decided the word was incendiary, Bush even promised a crusade against evil. This sort of language, and the rigidity of the oratory, led many to think that the revival of talk about evil must be derived from a revival of religion. Where else would we get the idea?

Ask Abraham. It wasn't religion that told him the destruction of innocent life was an evil great enough to risk his life to oppose. Religion is not the source of ideas of good and evil, but one way to respond to them; it makes more sense to say the fact of evil gave rise to religion than that religion gave rise to the idea of evil.

My concern at present is simply to show how evil can be discussed, and combatted, in language common to all: those who seek their resolutions in religion, and those who seek them without it. Religion can serve as a source of explanation for evil or a solution to it, but it no more invented the concept of evil than the concept of good. Religion is rather a way of trying to give shape and structure to the moral concepts that are embedded in our lives.

It's a point that was missed in the aftermath of what philosopher Richard Bernstein called the abuse of evil, the use of the word *evil* to stifle thinking rather than promote it. Bush's rhetoric was stifling because it was offered as a substitute for explanation, not a demand for it, and because it was demonizing, a way of externalizing the idea of evil altogether as something other people do. The U.S. has often been ingenious in making evils invisible, as critics around the world have been quick to point out. But this was no reason to deny one claim that Bush repeated: Terrorism is evil made visible. Of all the ways to criticize the Bush administration's response to 9/11, refusing to agree with him that the attacks were evil was the most self-defeating. You don't preserve your scruples by abandoning moral discourse to those who have fewer of them. To deny that the terrorist attacks were evil was to fly in the face of the shock and horror shared around most of the globe. In Berlin in the days after 9/11, I saw green-haired punks and stolid bureaucrats lay wreaths before the American embassy together; a banner printed with the word INCONCEIVABLE in sixteen languages roll down the steeple of the city's oldest church; American flags hanging from windows in neighborhoods that were traditional hotbeds of anarchic anti-American feeling. Through my open window rose the strains of a men's chorus singing 'Dona nobis pacem'; never was this proudly insouciant city so helpless and still. Berliners have witnessed enough evils to know another when they see it.

Bad, awful, wrong, and *wicked* are perfectly useful terms of condemnation, strong enough to cover most of the things we abhor. Why did the attacks of 9/11 cross the line to merit the word *evil?* This kind of terrorism deliberately reproduces the worst of nature's rages. As Abraham reminded God before Sodom, moral beings are bound to deal differently with the just and the unjust. Plagues and floods and earthquakes ravage them all without distinction or warning. Before the Enlightenment, they were all known as natural evils; since then we record our belief that nature has no moral categories by calling them disasters. But if nature is blind to moral judgments, contempo rary terrorists defy them. The very term *collateral damage* reminds us that we often fail to maintain the moral distinctions decent people try to draw. But unlike earlier assassins who canceled plots that would have killed bystanders, contemporary terrorists don't even try.

Their deliberate rejection of the basic division between the guilty and the innocent, the implicated and the helpless, allows them to create the dread and panic that is their aim. This is not only the fear of death – now real enough every time you sit next to a man who strikes you as odd on an airplane – but the fear of a world ruled by utter chaos. We know accidents happen, but terrorists aim for a world where accident rules. On September 11, staying home with a sick child and calling in with a hangover both turned out to save people's lives. When the threat of random murder is omnipresent, we live in a world where reward and punishment, life and death, are so arbitrary that their very meaning looms precarious. That's a state where the possibility of community itself is threatened. Rousseau thought fear of death worse than death itself, for in poisoning our lives it undermines our trust, and ultimately, our freedom.

By imitating nature's implacable disregard for the difference between the just and the unjust, terrorism rejects the very basis of morality. (Presumably the fact that it's so basic led Abraham to take a stand.) And this is what made the events of 9/11 not just wrong, but evil. With its brilliant eye for symbol, Al Qaeda targeted two places that have consistently produced forms of evil that were no less devastating for being less spectacular. For much of the world, Wall Street and the Pentagon stand for economic and military over-drive. But though it happened at the Pentagon and Wall Street, what happened that day was inexcusable. To think otherwise is not simply to think that two wrongs make a right. Even more important, it's to think that evil has only one form.

To explain something is *not* to excuse it, though both Bush and his critics suggested otherwise. For this president, condemning terrorism as evil eliminates the need for understanding it; for many of his critics, attempting to understand the causes of terrorism precludes calling it evil. They fear that calling terrorism evil commits us to rule out any course of action but violent military response. This doesn't follow. Osama bin Laden and his closest deputies are not promising candidates for reeducation, and here violent solutions are the only realistic ones. But you can hold even their young followers responsible for their own choices while working politically to make those choices less appealing. The word *evil* by itself need not dehumanize, if coupled with analyses that show how ordinary humans with ordinary motives get caught up in it.

These concerns should not prevent us from talking about evil, but they should prevent us from talking about evil people. Calling actions evil can be polarizing; so be it. Calling people evil is polem-ical. Worse than that, it presumes a knowledge of the human soul, where I have no such right. According to Kant, I don't even know my own. This is not a philosopher's expression of ultimate ignorance, or a matter of general skepticism. On the contrary: We know, in general, quite a lot. We know that our capacities for error are great, and our capacities for deception even greater. We know that our motives are usually mixed, and that we're strongly inclined to see our own behavior in the best possible light, weakly inclined to see other people's in the worst. We also know that we are free. While the odds are against our becoming heroes, we might walk to the gallows after all. Face to face with an unjust sovereign, we may find there is more – or less – to our character than we suspected. Given all that we do know, humility about what we don't know is not an epistemological, but a moral imperative. However well you know me, you do not know my future, nor how I might redeem myself in it. And even after death ends the opportunities for active redemption, there may be reasons for excusing or blaming me that you will never guess. Evil people are irredeemable, and not even God, in some accounts, can be certain of that.

Religion isn't the source of the idea of evil, but it encourages our tendency to think of evil as an all-or-nothing affair. If you believe your soul will end in heaven or hell, then the question of whether your soul itself is good or evil matters – matters, in fact, more than anything in the world. Your purity of heart is your ticket to redemption; your lack of it may make you think your efforts to do good are pointless. If you are not convinced of an ultimate fate, good and evil can come in increments. No one thing tips the balance if there's no balance to tip.

What about sadists and psychopaths, people who take pleasure in causing misery and pain? What do you gain by insisting on them? Movies like *The Silence of the Lambs* and its offspring, and the real cases that resemble them, receive vast amounts of attention. Though few people want to commit gruesome crimes, few people can avert their eyes from them. Like most things, this sort of perversity was already recorded in ancient Athens. One reason for fascination with such forms of evil is not perverse but understandable: We'd prefer to believe evil looks like that than to face the fact that it may look, and feel, almost harmless. For most of us, Hannibal Lecter is neither comprehensible nor tempting, and focusing on his ilk is a form of comfort: Evil is as terrifying, alien, and inscrutable as a black hole worlds away. In fact, a more recent film provides a far better model of what we should fear. Not the mad dictator Idi Amin, but the young doctor in *The Last King of Scotland* shows the innocent descent into evil that threatens us most. Without malice in his heart or cruelty in his dreams, he's driven by the most common of motives: lust for proximity to beautiful women and powerful men, taste for the small privileges and luxuries that lighten everyday loads. It isn't wickedness but thoughtlessness that makes him cause a series of awful deaths *without ever meaning to*. As Arendt's book *Thinking* put it, 'The sad truth is that most evil is done by people who never made their minds up to be or do evil at all.' Focusing on psychopaths is a good way to forget this, and it carries more than one risk. In addition to obscuring how little evil is committed by madmen (social psychologist Philip Zimbardo estimates it at 2 percent), it focuses on the evils for which responsibility is hardest to ascribe. Psychopaths, by definition, are too sick to be entirely culpable. But the problem, wrote Primo Levi, is 'not that evil men did evil things, but that normal men did them.'

In his superb *Trust and Violence*, Jan Philipp Reemtsma puts the point even more sharply, insisting that the most often asked question about the Holocaust makes no sense. Reemtsma answers the question 'How is it possible that ordinary men could commit such crimes?' with the laconic response: who else should do it? There aren't enough sadists to go round.

Don't be judgmental can be an alibi for moral laziness, but it stems from one impulse that is sound. Some judgments do not belong in human hands. To call someone evil is to size up her soul, and none of us will ever be in a position to do that. To call her actions evil is another matter. If you want to encourage people to make moral distinctions rather than throwing up their hands in the relativism of helplessness, here is where to draw the line. Let Abraham be your model. He focused on the action rather than the agent, appealing to the *best* in character: Surely the Judge of all the earth would not violate the fundamental principle of justice? It's undoubtedly easier to assume your partner is well-meaning when your partner is the Lord, but the principle remains useful in less exalted company. Have the courage to judge actions, even those committed by the highest authority; don't have the presumption to judge agents, even those of the lowest appearance.

Kant's profound recognition of the opacity of our intentions never led him to question the role of intention in determining whether an action is good or evil. Modern thought made intention central, and this is far from a theoretical problem. The difference between murder and manslaughter is the difference between killing someone with malice and forethought, and killing him accidentally. Nor is every accident judged the same. Running over a child who darts in front of a car driven by a responsible driver at speed limit is punished very differently from running over a child in the course of a drunken spree. Our intuitions about intention are just as strong – and just as uncertain – in less tragic cases. *I didn't mean it* may serve as excuse when I step on your foot. If the subway is hectic and crowded, or you saw me swerve to make room for a baby carriage, this is all you need to hear in order to nod and forget. If I'm giggling, boorish, and intoxicated, you may well retort, 'I didn't think you *meant* it,' and still have reason to be angry.

Kant's shopkeeper example shows both the depths and the limits of those intuitions. Recall that both shopkeepers engage in identical practices: Straightforward and honest, neither would sell spoiled fruit to unsuspecting children or put a thumb on the scales to deceive blind old men. Perhaps they are equally friendly, chatting up customers and remembering whose health to ask after. But one of them does all this because he cares about honesty and kindness, the other because he knows that appearing to do so will win more business. No question there's a difference between the two men, though their actions may never reveal it. We'd call only one of these men truly good – if we were in the business of passing judgment on their souls.

But we're not. We have no right to do so, and it doesn't even matter. As citizens whose interests lie in having as much decent business as possible, we *want* decent business to flourish. Too much attention to cases like these focuses morality on particular moral situations rather than on whole lives – which we live with intentions that are mixed through and through. Considered in isolation, the differences between the two shopkeepers' intentions seems to matter immensely. For social and political purposes, their intentions hardly matter at all.

This is true enough in cases like the shopkeepers, whose actions link intention and consequence in the same direction. (If you find shopkeepers too prosaic, take your example from politics. A war may be started to defend a people from injustice, or to protect oil prices. You may decide to support, or oppose, a war that does both, but you know the difference between them – even if you will never know which intention was really at work.) It's even clearer when we remember how often intention and consequence disconnect. Good people do bad things almost as often as bad things happen to good people. This is no modern phenomenon; as *New Yorker* writer Adam Gopnik recently put it, 'Shakespeare's continuing appeal to liberal societies, despite his feudal settings, lies in his ability to create characters who intend no harm and end up covered with blood.' Still, something about the twentieth century made what Arendt called the banality of evil impossible to ignore. No single event was decisive in undermining our assumption that evil actions require evil intentions. It's easy to forget the trauma of the First World War in the wake of the horrors that followed it. Greed and colossal lack of foresight are not usually mortal sins, but nothing else was needed to start the war that set in motion all the devastation that resulted. Hiroshima, and even Nagasaki, were said to be necessary to save lives that would have been lost in an invasion of Japan. The claim turned out to be false, since the Japanese were willing to surrender, but thousands of people unleashed the atomic age because they believed it was true, not because they were bloodthirsty or nihilistic. Even the Nazis acted according to a set of moral principles that served to convince them that the most evil of actions were fueled by the best of intentions. You may reject those principles entirely, but you cannot study interviews with former Nazis and conclude they were moved by simple lust for murder and plunder. Nor did they hold moral principles merely in the abstract; even the most abominable actions were accompanied with the insistence on honorable intentions. One Wehrmacht soldier reported by German psychologist Harald Welzer was proud of the fact that he shot only children: 'My comrade shot the mothers, and I saw that the children couldn't survive without them.' Exactly the same reasoning was offered by Hutu women who murdered the children of their Tutsi neighbors. Perhaps nowhere was the disconnect between action and intention so strong as in the history of twentieth-century communism. For seventy years, brave men and women all over the world devoted their lives, and often their deaths, to principles of brotherhood and liberation that turned out to produce the opposite. The estimate of 100 million victims by the authors of *The Black Book of Communism* has been questioned, but no one doubts that communism destroyed legions – and possibly the ideals it was created to defend.

Any one of these examples should make you hesitate to locate the goodness of an action in the goodness of the intention that led to it. Arendt's masterful *Eichmann in Jerusalem* showed how the greatest crime of the twentieth century was organized by a pathetic, self-serving bureaucrat who was in no way demonic, but spectacularly mediocre. In showing how something can be evil and nevertheless banal, Arendt showed how moral condemnation can work together with detailed understanding of the mechanics of evil. Her book caused unprecedented furor. Many historians criticized Arendt's description of Eichmann, though some acknowledged that if Eichmann himself was not as banal as Arendt portrayed him, the Holocaust was made possible by millions of people who were. The controversy over *Eichmann in Jerusalem*, still alive forty years after its publication, is a philosophical controversy disguised as an historical one. I have argued elsewhere that Arendt herself did not entirely realize how thoroughly her thesis opposed centuries of thought about ethics. In insisting that Eichmann was an unexceptional man who was responsible for exceptional crimes, she was not, as critics charged, attempting to excuse him. On the contrary, she insisted that he was guilty, and thought that he ought to hang. As Mary McCarthy wrote in her defense of Arendt, 'The Hue and the Cry': 'Calling someone a monster does not make him more guilty; it makes him less so by classifying him with beasts and devils.' Rather, Arendt was arguing that our intentions are the least of our responsibilities, for if crimes can be committed with all kinds of intentions, we are responsible, finally, for what we do. Perhaps you *didn't* mean it; it very rarely matters. What matters is not 'the possible noncriminal nature of your inner life and of your motives or with the criminal potentialities of those around you,' as Arendt imagined how the court should have spoken to Eichmann. 'We are concerned with what you did.' Arendt's search for a political and psychological explanation is a way of giving depth and body to moral categories, not of getting rid of them.

Were Eichmann and his cohorts psychopathic monsters who were uniquely hateful or vicious, it would be easy to externalize the evils the Nazis committed. Evil would be whatever acts of barbarism are committed by those kinds of beasts. Arendt's analysis unnerves those reluctant to draw the conclusion she explicitly intended: Under the wrong sort of circumstances, most of us are capable of the wrong sort of actions. However you may deplore it, the conclusion has been verified many times over – not only in the acts of genocide that have recurred with sickening frequency in the years since the Second World War, but in a series of brilliant controlled experiments. Social psychologist Philip Zimbardo's profoundly important 2007 book *The Lucifer Effect* examines those experiments and others to prove that whatever historical questions remain about Arendt's discussion of Eichmann, her general claims are indisputable.

In his most famous experiment, Zimbardo took a group of healthy young men who had been intensively tested to rule out any measurable form of psychopathology. He randomly assigned half of them to act as prisoners, and half of them to act as guards, in a makeshift jail in the basement of a Stanford University laboratory. Zimbardo himself took on the role of prison superintendent, while giving the guards few guidelines but the instruction to refrain from physical torture. Within forty-eight hours, each group was transformed. 'At the start of the experiment, there were no differences between the two groups; less than a week later, there were no similarities.' An extraordinarily vicious cycle was set in motion. The student guards set about degrading prisoners through simple sorts of punishments: verbal abuse, sleep deprivation, hours spent in stress positions repeating mindless physical and mental exercises. As the prisoners became increasingly dehumanized, the guards found it increasingly easy to degrade them further. One student who had played the role of prisoner reported:

> The Stanford prison was a very benign prison situation, and it still caused the guards to become sadistic, prisoners to become hysterical, other prisoners to break out in hives. Here you have a benign situation, and it didn't work. The guard role promotes sadism. The prisoner role promotes confusion and shame. Anybody can be a guard. It's harder to be on guard against the impulse to be sadistic. It's a quiet rage, malevolence, you can keep down but there's nowhere for it to go; it comes out sideways.

Zimbardo's conclusion after a lifetime of research is chilling:

> Any deed that any human being has ever committed, however horrible, is *possible* for any of us – under the right or wrong situational circumstances. That knowledge does not excuse evil; rather, it democratizes it, sharing its blame among ordinary actors rather than declaring it the province only of deviants and despots – of Them but not Us.

Nor does Zimbardo exempt himself; he sharply criticizes his own willingness to slip into the role of prison superintendent without regard to the psychological damage it caused his subjects. Without the indignant intervention of the woman he was courting, at whose urging the experiment was ended early, Zimbardo would have gone further in promoting the evils he was committed to study.

Zimbardo's research expands the conclusions discovered by his colleague Stanley Milgram, whose experiments set out to explore how ordinary Germans became accomplices to mass murder. The experiments showed how little is required to command obedience to orders that clash with conscience. Hundreds of subjects, believing they were participants in a study that examined the role of stress in learning, were told to give increasingly intense electric shocks to learners they could not see. The shocks were fake, like the screams of the actors pretending to be learners in the next room, but the results were not: 65 percent of subjects tested were willing to cause electric shocks they believed would cause unconsciousness, and possibly death. Their willingness to follow orders didn't even require the defense of God or country, but only the cause of science. At four dollars an hour, even in 1974, this was considerably less than thirty shekels. Milgram's conclusion: 'If a system of death camps were set up in the United States of the sort we had seen in Nazi Germany, one would be able to find sufficient personnel for those camps in any medium-sized American town.'

Like any major research, Zimbardo's has been subject to criticism. Future work may refine his results, but their main thrust was reconfirmed in 2008 by Jerry Burger, a social psychologist who recreated a version of Milgram's experiments, modified to prevent the damage to which subjects of Zimbardo's and Milgram's were vulnerable. These recent experiments yielded dishearteningly similar results: fully 70 percent of those tested were willing to follow orders they thought were orders to torture.

Neither Arendt, nor the social psychologists whose research confirms her theses, retreated into despair. To the contrary, Arendt thundered against the idea 'that there is a law of nature compelling everyone to lose his dignity in the face of disaster.' Contrasting

Eichmann with Anton Schmidt, a German sergeant shot by the Nazis for aiding Jewish partisans in Poland, she wrote,

> The lesson of such stories is simple and within everybody's grasp. Politically speaking, it is that under conditions of terror most people will comply but *some people will not*, just as the lesson of the countries to which the Final Solution was proposed is that 'it could happen' in most places but *it did not happen everywhere*. Humanly speaking, no more is required, and no more can reasonably be asked, for this planet to remain a place fit for human habitation.

For Arendt, even small numbers matter. After all, she notes, only ten could have saved Sodom. Zimbardo argues that we all underestimate our vulnerability to 'the toxic effect' of bad systems and other situational forces. Becoming aware of this frailty is 'the first step in shoring up resistance to such detrimental influences and in developing effective strategies that reinforce the resilience of both people and communities.' His approach 'should encourage us all to share a profound sense of humility.'

If your reaction to these insights is a quiet murmur – *There but for the grace of God go I* – you have missed the point entirely. Humility is no excuse for resignation; realizing that any of us might collude in evil is just the other side of realizing that any of us might oppose it. This kind of humility, as Zimbardo's continued research shows, is anything but passive; it should function as a call to action. In focusing on what we do rather than what we are, and in showing that most of us are capable of doing the worst, the work of philosophers like Arendt and psychologists like Zimbardo undercuts what former national security advisor Zbigniew Brzezinski recently called 'Manichean paranoia.' He was referring to the second Bush administration, but they weren't the first in history to decide that they were as intrinsically good as their opponents were intrinsically evil, and to assume that any actions they engage in must therefore be good as well.

Then how to proceed? Can we find a definition of evil that

allows us to recognize and measure it? Perhaps somebody may come along and propose an alternative, but I've never seen one that did much work. General definitions of evil are either so broad as to be almost meaningless, or so narrow that they exclude everything but the evil you currently have in view.

The problem is made harder because evil has a history, and its history isn't stable. Here the concept of evil isn't alone. Think about the transformation of the idea of beauty. In one century we moved from viewing beaches as dull wastelands, to seeing them as the world's most desirable properties; in one generation we moved from prizing the voluptuous Monroe, to envying the bodies of half-starved waifs. Or consider the concept of justice, which once involved taking two eyes, and more, if yours was put out. The Bible got it down to one eye; today's injuries are settled by lawsuit. Still, we use concepts of beauty and justice and fill them with meaning and sense – albeit, and rightly, more humbly than our predecessors.

Doesn't evil matter more? If it can't be defined exactly, is there anything to make it more than a tool in a shouting match between Bush and bin Laden? And if that's the case, shouldn't we abandon it sooner rather than later? It's as natural to long for essences as to long for unbreakable promises. They would make our lives simple, provide framework without guesswork, guarantee our decisions, remove the need for judgment. And it may be just as natural to feel that where essences are unavailable, the concept floats away.

But rather than abandoning the attempt to understand evil for want of a definition, I suggest we abandon the search for its essence. In its place we can use the idea of family resemblance proposed by the Viennese philosopher Ludwig Wittgenstein, who was skeptical of every appeal to essence. Instead of supporting a general skepticism about our ability to understand and use concepts altogether, he proposed that we rely on our experience of families. You see when a child is the spitting image of her father, or bears an uncanny resemblance to an aunt. You are more likely to see it in my children, and I to see it in yours, yet both of us know the resemblance is there. The shape of a nose? The angle of an eye? It's often just a shadow that cannot be untangled, but you needn't be my identical twin to be, recognizably, my sibling. Nor do you conclude that the crucial thing holding a family together is an essence that hasn't been found. DNA may help settle paternity suits, but it can never tell you what belonging to a family means.

After Wittgenstein, take a lesson from Donald Rumsfeld. (Just this once.) Shortly after the first photos hit daylight, he declared, 'What happened at Abu Ghraib was not right. But it's not the same thing as cutting off someone's head in front of a video camera.' It's not the same thing. But only if you think that evil has an essence can you draw the conclusion Rumsfeld wanted us to draw – namely, that one of these actions is evil, and the other is simply too bad. The differences are abundant. One of these evils is visible, and the other still is not. One of these evils is the product of ruthless individual will, while the other is produced by a large complex system that makes it easy for individuals to evade responsibility. One of them takes death as its clear-eyed goal, and the other as an unfortunate by-product. One of them reduces people to shivering pale heaps of terrified flesh, in tears on a screen; the other reduces them to naked faceless bodies. What they have in common is a willingness to use methods so loathsome they create enemies left and right. But the biggest difference is probably this one: Since one of the perpetrators is so much more powerful than the other, its effects are likely to last longer. Abu Ghraib confirmed the world's nightmares, creating hatred and suspicion of the U.S., the West in general, and anyone in the future who's inclined to say a word, however sincere, about defending human rights against dictators. For the sake of argument, let's suppose the intentions of the U.S. soldiers who tortured prisoners at Abu Ghraib were better than those of the groups who beheaded hostages. What good are those intentions if the consequences turn out to be worse?

If evil comes in too many forms to reduce to an essence, the only way to identify it is to engage in careful analysis that goes case by case. This sort of analysis isn't unique to understanding evil. Think about beauty. Reading good critics who explain how a particular piece of art, with these particular features, is beautiful, will teach you more about recognizing beauty than a list of conditions that are necessary and sufficient for something to be beautiful. I want to approach evil similarly, by examining three particular examples of it.

Almost any choice of example will be controversial, with one exception: the Holocaust. No minimally informed or responsible person will deny that the murder of six million European Jews was evil. Indeed, accepting this claim can serve as a criterion of responsibility; if you deny it you cannot belong to a responsible political community. Because it is universally acknowledged as a paradigm, I will not use it as example here. Pointing to it has become too simple. If that's what evil is, it's easy enough to avoid. Years ago, the demagogic preacher Louis Farrakhan responded to charges of racism by saying, 'I'm not an anti-Semite. I never put anybody in an oven.' Nice to know how to stay on the side of the angels.

The Holocaust has become the gold standard for determining evil. If focus on it has made narrowing our understanding of evil too easy, it has made the lessons learned too opaque. *Never again!* with a picture of Auschwitz has been used to mean:

Don't let Jews be killed!
Don't appease tyrants!
Don't ignore genocide!
Don't be racist!
Don't trust Germans!

and any number of other messages. While the fact that the Holocaust was evil is perfectly clear, the consequences are anything but. Fascination with it is perfectly understandable; if your idea of moral clarity is pointing to something that is beyond every pale, you need look no further. But the use of the Holocaust has not only given us one kind of clarity at the expense of others, it has also served to externalize evil as something other people do. If you are American, other people might be Germans. If you are German, other people might be those who joined the Nazi Party. If you were a Nazi, other people might be those who gave you orders. Even Adolf Eichmann portrayed himself as a victim.

Bulgarian-French critic Tzvetan Todorov proposed a wonderful maxim: Jews should focus on the universality of the Holocaust, Germans on its uniqueness. His suggestion follows from Kant's general principle: If I worry about your insufficient happiness and my insufficient virtue, the quantity of both is bound to increase. When Germans and Austrians focus on genocide as a universal phenomenon, it's a way of avoiding responsibility. When Jews do the same thing, it's a way of assuming responsibility. It may be Kant, but it's also kindergarten: Todorov's principle is another way of saying we are morally bound to clean up our own messes first. Whether your sister's mess is equal or greater is not, in the first instance, your business. This is a lesson we (try to) teach our children early, and it has deep moral implications. Just run it through the categorical imperative: If you were creating a world, wouldn't you create one where everyone took care of their own garbage before pointing to yours?

Are there worse evils than those committed by the current U.S. government? Without a doubt. The murder of hundreds of thousands of refugees in Darfur is surely more flagrant, and so are kidnapping children for slave labor in China and stoning women to death in Saudi Arabia – which is why they require less discussion here. Samantha Power's relentlessly probing *A Problem from Hell* describes how the recognition of genocide as a unique category of evil did nothing to prevent its recurrence around the world. The ink was barely dry when *Never again* became *One more time*. Her discussion is invaluable, but her examples have a chillingly similar structure. The examples I'll discuss are examples of lesser evils that exhibit a variety of forms. My goal is to show how the word *evil* can work – not only as a call to arms, but as the beginning of analysis.

In the months before the U.S. invaded Iraq I was often asked to comment on American foreign policy by the media in Europe, where I usually live. Because I strongly opposed the war, and because my book on evil had received some attention, I expected to be asked whether I thought the Bush administration was evil. It was a question I dreaded. As wrong as the war seemed to be, calling the administration evil seemed worse than useless, a descent into mud- and venom-slinging that could only make political solutions harder to find. To my relief, the question never came, and I was spared having to weigh out an answer. Five years later, I have no hesitation at all. As the government's actions became increasingly shameless, my own views became increasingly clear.

Are *they* evil – where *they* means Bush, or Cheney, or Rove, or Rice, or some combination of them all? Beats me. If their intentions were good, one can only quote the Berlin critic Kurt Tucholsky: The opposite of *good* is *good intention*. If their intentions were not, then there's nothing left to wish for but mercy on their souls. None of that is my concern. I'm concerned with the consequences of actions committed in the name of the country where I was born and raised, which will affect the world for generations to come.

What's the point of focusing on cases involving a government that is already history? A few years ago, *New York Times* columnist Paul Krugman wrote, 'Someday, when the grown-ups are back in charge, they'll have quite a mess to clean up.' Already the mess is reeking, and every U.S. citizen is needed to help clean up the muddle that's been made of our moral concepts. Moving forward to salvage our ideals requires understanding the ways they were violated, in a collective self-examination that is the beginning of taking responsibility. Here we can learn crucial lessons from postwar Germans. German history is not American history, but it provides us, as Diane McWhorter put it, with 'a rather spectacular example of the insidious process by which decent people come to regard the unthinkable as not only thinkable but doable.' In 2007, the *New York Times* columnist Frank Rich went even further: 'Our humanity has been compromised by those who use Gestapo tactics in our war. The longer we stand by idly while they do so, the more we resemble those "good Germans" who professed ignorance of their own Gestapo.' Postwar German efforts to understand how this could happen spawned several long compound words: Working-through-the-past (*Vergangenheitsverarbeitung*); overcoming-the-past (*Vergangenheitsbewältigung*); and conquering-the-past (*Vergangenheitsüberwältigung*) are names for the painful self-examination that has dominated political and cultural life since the end of the Second World War. It took five decades for the German people to begin to come to terms with the Nazis, and the rest of the world to begin to believe it. It's time for Americans to get started.

Dismissing past crimes in the name of moving forward just lets those crimes fester; ask any German who grew up in the ruins of the fifties. There were cities to rebuild, an economy to reinvent; people bit grim lips and did not talk about transgressions past. The country leaked slow toxins. A decade later, the past was suddenly present, and it remains so half a century later. The U.S. could avoid a great deal of national affliction by learning from those mistakes, and refusing to wash over the crimes committed in its name. At present, movements are underway to consider prosecution for war crimes, truth and reconciliation commissions, or some mixture of the two that refuses to move forward without looking back. Rich supports the impulse to take action against the crimes of the Bush administration with a quote from Dawn Johnsen, whom Obama appointed to run the Justice Department's Office of Legal Counsel. As Rich explains, Johnsen wrote that

> 'We must avoid any temptation simply to move on,' because the national honor cannot be restored 'without full disclosure.' She was talking about America regaining its international reputation in the aftermath of our government's descent into the dark side of torture and 'extraordinary rendition.' But I would add that we need full disclosure of the more prosaic governmental corruption of the Bush years, too, for pragmatic domestic reasons. To make the policy decisions ahead of us in the economic meltdown, we must know what went wrong along the way in the executive and legislative branches alike.

There's no shortage of examples of the recent violation of American ideals, or even those that cross the distance from *awful* to *evil*. The border between the two is unmarked. *Evil* is what you say when, jaded as you may be, your jaw begins to drop when you hear that a line has been crossed: *That*, said Arendt, ought not to have happened. Of course, we become inured; if it happens often enough, an act may seem to cease being evil and become merely bad. In such cases the initial evil may lie precisely in the way it hardens our hearts.

· · · · ·

I think that's the case with a nearly forgotten sideline to the Bush administration's response to 9/11. Until then only people who dabbled in horse racing knew the word *trifecta*. To win the trifecta is to win big-time. Everyone who bets on horses dreams of it: If you bet on Buckpasser, Desert Stormer, and Tom Fool, and they come in the way you called it, you've won the trifecta. According to Mitchell Daniels, then director of the White House's Office of Management and Budget, it was mid-September 2001 when the president first told him, 'Lucky me, I hit the trifecta.'

Recall where you were that September. The ruins of the World Trade Center were still smoking, and whether you were in Paris or Podunk, you had watched the towers fall countless times onscreen, but it hadn't made the shock wear off. The airlines had started to fly again, but thousands of trips had been canceled, and you wondered whether it was decent to worry how your job would be affected when the state of the world seemed in balance. Would there be war? What kind? To what end? When an unknown – to this day! – terrorist killed several people with white powder containing anthrax, you wondered if there were any limits at all. Fear was international: Congress shut down for a week in Washington; in Berlin in October, local election votes were counted by workers wearing masks and plastic gloves. And all over New York City, homemade posters with haunting eyes showed the heartsore longing of those still looking for loved ones – or at least a piece of their bodies.

Hit the trifecta?

Bush left no one in doubt about his meaning, because he didn't confine the remark to private conversation. He liked it so much that he used it in thirteen separate speeches made to largely Republican audiences from February to June 2002. Here is one, dated by the Office of the Press Secretary as 16 April 2002, given to a meeting of the leaders of the Fiscal Responsibility Coalition.

> The recession – no question, I remember when I was campaigning, I said, would you ever deficit spend? And I said, yes, only if there were a time of war, or recession, or a national emergency. Never thought we'd get [laughter and applause]. And so we have a temporary deficit in our budget, because we are at war, we're recovering, our economy is recovering, and we've had a national emergency. Never did I dream we'd have the trifecta. [laughter]

Had Bush's remark been made only once, it might have been dismissed as merely tasteless, the bumbling attempt of an awkward man to shine a little light, however garish, in the darkness. Grotesque substitutes for humor are not as uncommon as they should be. Running for president, John McCain offered one of his own. When asked what he would do about Iran if he won the election, he launched into the Beach Boys' old tune 'Barbara Ann.' Sing it fast and you'll agree: It does sound a lot like *Bomb Iran*. Both would-be jokes were reported in the national press, and can now be found on YouTube, but public outcry was sparse – perhaps due to the assumption that gallows humor is an achievement. As indeed it is – if you're the one standing under the gallows. If you're the potential executioner you should keep your mouth shut.

What made the trifecta remark evil was not simply the way it mocked the endless pain and mortal terror of other human beings. (Bush's capacity to do so was noted during his term as governor of

Texas, when he broke into falsetto to mimic the plea for mercy of Karla Faye Tucker, a young death row inmate he chose not to pardon.) Worse was the repetition of glee about the worst attack on American soil – while simultaneously using that attack as justification for everything else the government did. We all play multiple roles now, but it's tempting to wonder how he managed. Hand on the heart, face locked into solemnity while attacking opponents for 'forgetting the lessons of 9/11' in the morning? Loose-bent knees and homeboy grinning while hamming it up with the base at night? Fortunately, this bit of cognitive dissonance was ended in mid-July 2002, when senior White House advisors told Bush to stop repeating the joke. Their reasons were not fundamental: say, indignation at turning a tragedy into a joke about its expedience. The minor debate that had erupted was about the veracity of the remark, not its decency. *New Republic* writer Jonathan Chait claimed there were no campaign discussions of exceptions for deficit spending. Had Bush actually made a campaign promise to keep the budget balanced unless the country was in a state of war, recession, or national emergency? The question wasn't trivial, since Bush had campaigned on a platform promoting enormous tax cuts – a promise fulfilled – without endangering the Social Security surplus – a promise broken. Bush's three exceptions, charged Chait, were ex post facto excuses made to rationalize a broken promise. Because Chait was right, and White House advisors found no record of any exceptions mentioned on the campaign trail, the trifecta routine was finally squelched.

For more suspicious observers, the remark suggested something more sinister than lying. Not on the campaign trail, but shortly before September 11, Bush had discussed the circumstances in which he'd run a budget deficit. 'I have repeatedly said the only time to use Social Security money is in times of war, times of recession, or times of severe emergency. And I mean that. I mean that.' Five days after the president named his exceptions, they all came true at once. Some critics even went so far as to charge that the White House had deliberately ignored warnings that a terrorist attack was imminent. After all, they argued, the Bush government had several reasons to welcome such an attack. A terrorist strike would mean billions of dollars in new contracts for the defense industry, which had contributed heavily to Republican campaigns in 2000; it would divert money away from the Social Security program the government wished to undermine anyway; and it would generally shore up a presidency already endangered by financial scandals and perceptions of incompetence.

Conspiracy theories should be theories of last resort. Though most of the relevant documents are classified, it's easy enough to explain events without them. The government ignored warnings that Al Qaeda was about to launch a major atttack the same way it ignored warnings that New Orleans levees were about to over-flow. Foresight was never among its stronger points. It has proved outstanding in using events it did not foresee to advance agendas it did. That was the sense of Richard Rorty's statement that 9/11 was America's Reichstag fire. Rorty did not endorse conspiratorial claims that the CIA planned the destruction of the World Trade Center as the Nazis planned the Reichstag fire. Nor was he comparing the souls of the two men who led their countries toward disaster. Rorty's comparison was provocative, but it maintained what no more than hundreds of other critics did: 9/11 allowed the Bush administration to ignore criticism of its own failings and fast-forward a historic program to roll back constitutional liberties, New Deal social programs, and multilateral foreign policies. The government leapt at the opportunity; it didn't create it. None of the consequences of 9/11 is comparable to the deaths of fifty-eight million in the war that Hitler launched six years after the Reichstag fire gave the Nazis a pretext to destroy their opposition. Still, even Hitler refrained from gloating over the opportunity he engineered – much less laughing about it with thirteen different audiences.

When the president of a nation cheapens life and death by joking about them, what's a nation to do but follow him? Shortly after the trifecta remark went public, the Internet recorded explosions of indignation – whether Paul Krugman's about the president, or readers so shocked they accused Krugman of inventing a story they believed impossible in a nation still in mourning. Google *trifecta* today and you'll discover something almost as surprising: *Trifecta* passed into political discourse from Bush's remark about good luck to mean simply *anything that comes in threes*. Former press secretary Ari Fleischer spoke of a trifecta of issues the president wanted Congress to enact. Former chief of staff Andrew Card spoke of a trifecta of challenges to the country. The Homeland Security Council named a 'terrorism trifecta: proximity, pattern, and weapons profile.' The blithe use of the word was not confined to members of the government, but passed easily on to its critics. Are they aware of the awful route by which the word moved from horse racing to politics? Are they aware that continuing to use it coarsens our sensibilities in a way likely to corrode our moral sense? Almost certainly not. The first time I heard a young woman in a Berlin bar say, 'I laughed till I was gassed,' I gasped in shock. Surely I had misunderstood what she said? No, she responded, embarrassed, she'd never really thought about it; perhaps that was an expression that had had its day.

The trifecta remark had no further consequences than to mark down a discourse that gets cheaper every day. No one was killed or tortured or maimed by it. Had Bush refrained from saying it, the world would have looked much the same as it does now. His joke about the windfall the terrorists provided left so few visible traces it has largely been forgotten. However often it was repeated, this statement produced no clear harm. Is that enough to excuse it?

· · · · ·

Direct consequences are equally absent in the second act I want to examine, which received even less attention than the first. It took place on a tiny island at the westernmost tip of Africa, whose beauty is all the more poignant for the poverty that leaves even the most gaily painted of its colonial buildings looking as if they could flake into the sea any moment. The aga khan once built a house here; Senegal's first president, Léopold Senghor, and French writer Roger Garaudy founded a small institute. But Gorée's biggest asset is its heritage of slavery. Historians disagree over how many slaves really passed through the island on their way to the New World, but for countless West Africans, Gorée was the point of no return. Its location – half an hour's ferry ride from Dakar, at the very edge of the continent – and sheer loveliness helped lead UNESCO to declare it a World Heritage site. 'It's the African Yad Vashem,' says South African poet and painter Breyten Breytenbach, director of the Gorée Institute, an NGO devoted to pan-African peace and development. Like Yad Vashem, Gorée is a place of pilgrimage for world leaders who want to display their concern over the evils of the past. The pope, and Mandela, and Mitterand, and Clinton came and went there; the 1,300 islanders watched them with dignity and calm. Gorée is dusty, unhurried, and utterly peaceful. There are no cars and no crime and not much to do but sit under the bougainvillea and baobab trees waiting for day tourists to buy trinkets. George W. Bush's 2003 visit, however, the start of his first African tour, left scars that stirred Goréeans long afterward.

SLAVERY RETURNS TO GORÉE, said the headlines in the Dakar papers, but apart from a small piece in the French newspaper *L'Humanité*, the rest of the world took no notice. Covering the event for *Time* and CNN, reporter John Dickerson did note that audience response to Bush's speech was muted, and the island appeared abandoned, but he didn't leave the docks to find out why. Even Bakari Akil Il, in a withering critique of the speech for Global Black News, didn't guess the half of it. Lambasting a president who did so little to fight racism for 'dropping names such as Frederick Douglass, Sojourner Truth, Booker T. Washington, W. E. B. Dubois and Martin Luther King as if he'd just received a degree in African American studies from Morehouse College,' Akil asked: 'Does anybody see what is going on? Does anybody care?'

Apparently not. What outraged the Goréeans was not the fact

that American and Senegalese police spent the week before Bush's arrival combing the island. 'They can bring search dogs into my house,' said Marie-José Crespin, a retired supreme court justice who lives next to the slavery museum. 'It is post 9/11, after all.' One of the island's most distinguished residents, Madame Crespin was invited to join the few dignitaries imported from Dakar to welcome Bush on the quay. She refused. 'As a jurist,' she told me, 'I'm not interested in meeting someone who has so little respect for international law.' Thereupon Madame Crespin was told she would have to leave her house and join the rest of the islanders to be locked up in a makeshift pen at the local soccer field for the duration of Bush's visit. They would be watched by armed guards, and were advised to bring food and water for the long day under the summer sun. British residents Emma and Andrew Gilmour, who hold diplomatic passports, were allowed to stay in their own house with their four small children – behind armed soldiers posted in their courtyard.

'I have a diplomatic passport too,' says Madame Crespin, 'but I didn't want to take that route. I told the police they would have to take me out by force, in front of my grandchildren. The Senegalese soldiers begged me to change my mind and leave peacefully.' After long consultation a compromise was found: Madame Crespin was locked into one room of her house, guarded by soldiers. 'But only the front room,' she explains, not in the atelier overlooking the sea, where she spends her days making the jewelry that supplements her pension. 'As if I might lean out the window and shoot around the corner.'

What happened to the island's ordinary residents? They were awakened at dawn and herded to the field behind a new metal fence, where they waited in the hopes of being included in the ceremony. Bigné Ndoye is a large, gracious woman who runs a dimly lit shop selling postcards and wooden statues. 'I understand about the security problems. 9/11 has changed things. If something happened to Bush in Senegal, all the Senegalese would be responsible. So maybe we can't shake his hand anymore, like we did with Clinton. I just wanted to see him.' Bigné has visited the United States often, and her praise of the country harkens back to other times. 'I love America,' she told me in excellent English. 'If people work hard, they have things you can't get anywhere else. And it's not like Paris. If you stay out of trouble, stay away from drugs, nobody bother you. I have lots of friends in America, black friends, white ones.' Full of anticipation, she donned her finest clothes on the morning of Bush's visit. 'Not like this one.' She gestured disdainfully at the diaphanous green and gold gown that looked regal enough to me for any occasion, but Senegalese women have standards of elegance few others can match. Outside in the hot pen she bore her heavy festival dress patiently, waiting for the moment when Goréeans would be allowed a glimpse of the leader of the country she wished to honor. The hardest part of the day was not the humiliation, or the hours huddled together on the sand in the sun, or the fact that nobody thought to compensate the islanders for the losses incurred when they were forced to close their shops. 'What hurt was the moment we heard the boat leaving, and realized that not one of us was going to see him. Clinton was talking for the television cameras, but he also spoke to the people of Gorée. Bush was only speaking to the African American voters back home.'

Flanked by Colin Powell on one side and Condoleeza Rice on the other, Bush stood on the quay to deliver a speech condemning the evils of slavery and celebrating America's overcoming of its racist past. 'For hundreds of years on this island peoples of different continents met in fear and cruelty. Today we gather in respect and friendship, mindful of past wrongs and dedicated to the advance of human liberty.' With its residents safely imprisoned, the island had become the sort of ghost town Hollywood uses as backdrop. For those who didn't peer behind the scenes, the words signified nothing more remarkable than the platitudes that are speechwriters' daily bread. Senegal is a small country of ten million people, far from centers of natural resources or strategic importance, and the entourage was on its way to the next country.

Security issues have occupied all recent state travel, and Bush's

visits to European capitals have been criticized for security measures so tight that few residents welcome his arrival. During a trip
to Mainz, not a window along the motorcade route could be opened;
during a trip to Rome, garbage bins were sealed shut. In Senegal,
however, the measures were as radical as the message was false. To
'gather in respect and friendship' in order to celebrate 'the advance
of human liberty' while locking up the natives in a baking pen
under armed guard is beyond racism, or hypocrisy, or brute bullying.
Not every lie is a crime against truth. This one was.

In an island so small and so shaded in history, that kind of event
will resound. Future generations are likely to tell the story as a
larger town recalls the invasion of a horde. The motives were not
malevolent, or even rapacious, as those of other hordes have been.
Yet I wavered between shame and heartbreak as Bigné finished
telling me her story and went off to say prayers. Like 94 percent of
her country-people, she is a Muslim. Senegal presents its Islam gaily:
The brilliant headscarves worn by its women appear as ornament
rather than punishment, and though people pull out their prayer
mats on the streets when the muezzin calls, devotion coexists with
traditional African rituals, and recourse to images and witchcraft,
in times of emotional trial.

Across the harbor in Dakar, beliefs are no different, but conditions are. Concrete apartment blocks and leaky tin shacks are much
more common than frangipani-filled courtyards, and the sidewalk
merchants hawking everything from watches to mangoes do so with
an insistence born of desperation. Poverty cannot dim the colors,
though in the dry season the women sitting on cardboard scraps by
the roadside are covered with dust. Among the wares they have to
offer are pictures gaudily painted on stretched cloth. Some portray
Osama bin Laden wearing a resolute half-smile.

· · · · ·

Jean Améry's classic dissection of torture begins with an admission.
'What happened to me in the vault at Breendonk was certainly not

the worst form of torture. No one put glowing needles under my fingernails or stamped out burning cigars on my naked breast. What happened to me was comparatively benign, and it left no scars on my body.' Yet twenty-two years after being interrogated by the Gestapo in occupied Belgium, where he was arrested for distributing Resistance leaflets, he wrote that 'torture is the worst thing that can happen to anyone.'

What happened to Améry was confined to beatings, with fists and with whips, most of them delivered while he was suspended on an iron hook designed to dislocate his shoulders by pulling his arms backward. It worked; he talked. He accused himself of crimes never committed, in the hope that confession would put an end to the pain by provoking the guards to beat him to death. The Resistance group to which he belonged had been careful; its members knew one another only by cover name. Otherwise, wrote Améry, he would likely have given away all the information his torturers wanted before he slipped into blessed unconsciousness.

The very first blow, Améry wrote, is like a rape, and with it one loses what he called trust in the world. 'With the first blow, against which there can be no defense, and to which no helping hand will respond, a part of one's life is ended that will never awake again.' This is more than a loss of dignity, though dignity is surely at stake. 'Weak pressure from a hand with the right tool is enough to turn the other – along with a head in which perhaps Kant and Hegel and all nine symphonies and *The World as Will and Representation* are stored – into a shrilly squealing piglet at slaughter.' That loss can never be redeemed. Banalities about life's fragility were hardly news to Améry. But after torture, he never 'ceases to be amazed that everything he calls his soul or his spirit or his consciousness or his identity can be annihilated the minute his shoulder joints crack and splinter.'

The deliberate reduction of a human being to a squealing, bawling beast is humiliation – what Israeli philosopher Avishai Margalit says decent societies must avoid. By destroying people's control over their own vital interests, humiliation rejects human beings as human. This is indecent, Margalit argues, because 'every human being has the radical possibility of starting life anew at any moment irrespective of his life's previous course. This freedom to shape one's life is, in another sense, the only nature humans have, in contrast to other animals and things.'

This is a Kantian view. You'll recall that Kant held the basic principle of morality to be this one: *Act so that you never treat other people as means to an end, but as ends in themselves*. On this principle, any form of torture involves humiliation, and is therefore absolutely wrong, even should it have no detectable consequence. But even the kind of torture Améry called benign has consequences that are very clear. Whoever was tortured, he wrote, is forever ruled by fear. Fear, 'and then what are called resentments. They remain.'

Améry's description of the ways in which the memory of torture obsessed him, decades later, with fantasies of revenge he knew were senseless, should be required reading for anyone assigned to interrogate prisoners of war. But did it really take the memoirs of a brilliant self-taught philosopher to understand what common sense must have known? Remember the context in which the torture at Abu Ghraib took place. A month before the U.S. invasion of Iraq, the largest global demonstration on record was organized to protest it. In New York and London and Rome and Madrid and elsewhere, 15 million people took to the streets to demand that the U.S. refrain from the looming attack. In country after country, observers noted the breadth of the crowds: grandmothers mixed with students, hedge-fund investors with poor people, all startlingly united against the war. In New York they were neither deterred by the freezing weather nor the government's sudden warning that everyone should stay home because of a terrorist threat that never materialized. Often for the first time, traditional allies and circumspect diplomats expressed the gravest doubts about the basis of U.S. foreign policy, and many predicted a conflagration that could spread from Baghdad to ignite the world.

If evil actions don't require evil motives, good actions don't require good ones. Forget humanity or dignity. Sheer self-interest should have driven the occupying forces to treat the Iraqi population especially well. Didn't the American government want to prove its critics wrong? In the face of so much opposition, and so many dire predictions, you'd expect a model occupation. Opulent reconstruction programs and kid gloves, with instructions, issued to every soldier would have left the war's critics gnashing their teeth. In place of the expanding crisis we predicted, it could have left enough Iraqis glad to be rid of a tyrant to console the rest for the dubious way it was done. Had the occupying forces cared to win hearts and minds – not just in Iraq, but in the rest of the world that was watching – they would have tortured their own soldiers before harming a hair of the native population. It might not have won the war, but it would have made the failure less devastating. Instead, Seymour Hersh reported, they shrugged their shoulders: Even after the scandal had broken, one senior general tried to deflect investigation with the statement that the abused detainees were, after all, 'only Iraqis.'

We know the rest of the story. Or rather, we know some of it. Books about Abu Ghraib, Guantánamo, and prisons rumored to be worse than either are still being written. It will be years before we know the details, and many more till we know the extent of the damage it caused. Still we know enough now to know it was evil. *Aren't there worse forms of torture than were practiced at Abu Ghraib?* Drawing and quartering, for example? *Not then, but now. Don't other countries do worse things?* Without a doubt. Should we take our standards from them?

Those in the know, from Donald Rumsfeld to Human Rights Watch, all maintain that the abuse made public was the tip of an iceberg, the most harmless part of the abuse that occurred. Scores of Iraqis were tortured to death, and there's nothing worse than that – except perhaps the threat to torture or kill someone's child. According to the ACLU report on the subject, this has occurred, too. Hersh records 'the sexual humiliation of a father with his son, who were both detainees.' He gives no details, but the pictures of naked Iraqi men forced to simulate sodomy are enough to raise the question: Are the same people who thought consensual fellatio occasion to impeach a president really dismissing forced fellatio as a bagatelle? In addition to death, and child abuse, and rape of male and female prisoners, there were untold beatings and mock executions, kicks and electric shocks, and above all a clever array of practices whose goal was not physical pain but degradation and terror.

'There's no way Rumsfeld didn't know,' Hersh reports a congressman insisting after the House Armed Services Committee hearing. 'This is a guy who wants to know everything.' More important, there is general agreement that the guards on duty could never have been so diabolically creative. Many were low-ranking soldiers who joined the army to get the education they could not get in the hamlets of West Virginia or Kentucky – which many had never had a chance to leave at all before shipping out to Iraq. How could they know which forms of (let's follow Améry and call it benign) torture would cause their prisoners the most pain? It's hard to say what is more humiliating: being forced to fake fellatio in a homophobic culture, or having a uniformed woman mock your naked genitals in a patriarchal one. Either punishment, as well as the menace of trained attack dogs, was particularly hellish for Arab prisoners, and every independent study of Abu Ghraib confirms the chain of command. In *Torture and Truth*, Mark Danner concluded, 'When you read the documents, Secretary of Defense Rumsfeld was involved very personally in approving procedures that went beyond the line of what is allowed in military law, and for that matter, in civilian law, when it comes to what can be done with prisoners.' In arguing that Rumsfeld should be investigated for war crimes, Human Rights Watch concluded:

From the earliest days of the war in Afghanistan, Secretary Rumsfeld was on notice through briefings, ICR reports, human rights reports, and press accounts that troops were committing war crimes, including acts of torture. However, there is no evidence that he ever exerted his authority and warned that the mistreatment of prisoners must stop. Had he done so, many of the crimes committed by forces could have been avoided.

In December 2008, the U.S. Senate Armed Services Committee finally released a summary of its own investigation, which found rotten apples all the way up the chain of command: not just Rumsfeld, but Rice, Cheney and Bush, among others, were responsible for the structure created to torture prisoners. As of this writing, the full report is still being declassified.

When the images from Abu Ghraib were released to the media, many people expressed shock. For Philip Zimbardo, it was the shock of recognition. The images recalled the worst of the Stanford prison experiment. In that experiment, college students had forced other college students to strip naked, stand with bags over their heads, and play sexually humiliating games. In both cases, the prisoners were held in pretrial detention; in both cases, the worst abuses occurred on the night shift, a time when the guards felt especially free from the usual constraints on abusive behavior. 'It was as though the worst-case scenario of our prison experiment had been carried out over months under horrendous conditions, instead of our brief, relatively benign simulated prison. I had seen what could happen to good boys when they were immersed in a situation that granted them virtually absolute power over their charges.'

Zimbardo was not the only one to draw parallels between his experiment and the torture at Abu Ghraib. A report prepared by the Schlesinger Commission to investigate the scandal concluded that the landmark Stanford study provided a cautionary tale for all military detention operations, precisely because the study took place under conditions which were relatively benign. 'In contrast, in military detention operations, soldiers work under stressful combat conditions that are far from benign.'

If good kids could turn into sadistic, brutalizing guards under the best of conditions at Stanford, what happens when good kids are put into '80 acres of hell'? As at Stanford, some of the guards at Abu Ghraib broke more, and more quickly than others. At least one retained enough moral clarity even in that stinking, dangerous hellhole to refuse to participate, and to report the abuse to his superiors. Whatever led him to do so was not a higher degree of religious training than his comrades. Charles Graner, convicted of the most sadistic abuse at the prison, said, 'The Christian in me says it's wrong, but the corrections officer says, I love to make a grown man piss himself.' This is no reflection on Christianity, for no religion can claim a perfect record in safeguarding moral values; even Zen Buddhism, according to recent research, was heavily implicated on the Pacific front in the Second World War.

We don't know why people have different moral thresholds; why some scruples melt under fire and others are steeled. For Arendt, the difference in German reactions to Nazism was 'the surprise of [her] life.' Nothing, she wrote, could be expected: No prior knowledge of friends and acquaintances was enough to predict who collaborated and who did not. We succumb to evil at different rates, and no psychological studies have been able to predict them. Some family structures, some forms of education nurture resilience better than others, but every so often a moral hero appears without the benefit of any of them. That's what human freedom means. If psychology cannot anticipate individual reactions, it can anticipate general ones: Put decent human beings under indecent conditions, and most of them will behave indecently. That knowledge, according to 'Psychology and U.S. Psychologists in Torture and War in the Middle East,' a 2006 report in *Torture*, 'informs torture in Iraq. A situation is created – made worse by understaffing, danger, and no outside independent controls – and with a little encouragement (never specific instructions to torture) guards do torture ... The U.S. administration's advantage in the Stanford experiment "situation" is that it provides deniability – there are no orders to torture, but the situation can be predicted to cause it.'

Because of this, Zimbardo rejects the claim that the torture at

Abu Ghraib was the work of 'a few bad apples.' It was the barrel, he insists, that was rotten. Most critics were skeptical of the Defense Department's denial of systemic abuse, but Zimbardo's research allowed him to review the evidence and finally stand as an expert witness for one of the soldiers sentenced in the case. Were those soldiers responsible? Up to a point. But as the architect of a tiny, restricted system who wound up producing evil by designing an experiment that fostered it, Zimbardo refused to leave responsibility to the small fry who behaved in ways the situation was designed to assure. Rather, 'in putting the System on hypothetical trial, we end by putting President Bush and his advisors in dock for their role in redefining torture as an acceptable, necessary tactic in their ubiquitous and nebulous war on terror.'

The investigations carried out by the army reveal a complex multiple causality for the events at Abu Ghraib. Zimbardo describes the structure that resulted:

> We can think of the torture dungeons at Abu Ghraib and similar facilities at Gitmo and other military prisons in Afghanistan and Iraq as having been designed by the senior 'architects' Bush, Cheney, Rumsfeld and Tenet. Next came the 'justifiers,' the lawyers who came up with the new language and concepts that legalized 'torture' in new ways and means – the president's legal counselors Alberto Gonzales, John Yoo, Jay Bybee, William Taft, and John Ashcroft. The 'foremen' on the torture construction job were the military leaders, such as Generals Miller, Sanchez, Karpinski and their underlings. Finally came the technicians, the grunts in charge of carrying out the daily labor of coercive interrogation, abuse, and torture – the soldiers in military intelligence, CIA operatives, civilian contract and military interrogators, translators, medics, and military police, including Chip Frederick and his night shift buddies.

Everyone who participated in this system should be accountable for it. Instead, only a few low-ranking soldiers were even brought to trial. The conscientious General Antonio Taguba, who directed a thorough investigation, was ridiculed by the Defense Department and forced to retire. And amazingly, the man sent to clean up operations after the scandal broke at Abu Ghraib had been in charge of Guantánamo. Clueless? One suspects this was less a lack of instinct for symbol than an unfailing instinct for choosing the wrong one. Zimbardo concludes, 'The seeds for the flowers of evil that blossomed in that dark dungeon of Abu Ghraib were planted by the Bush administration in its triangular framing of national security threats, citizen fear and vulnerability, and interrogation/torture to win the war on terror.'

Abu Ghraib was not unique. The same systems were put into place in military prisons that stretch from Cuba to Afghanistan, with similar if less public results. Nor were the techniques used in them brand new. According to military psychologist Dave Grossman, however, such techniques are fairly recent. His grimly fascinating book *On Killing* set out to explain a puzzle. The Second World War was as close to being a just war as wars ever get, and it was perceived as such by nearly every Allied civilian and soldier. Nevertheless, military studies showed that only 15 to 20 percent of soldiers actually fired their weapons in battle, even under conditions of great danger. Were they paralyzed by trauma and fear? Grossman compares the psychiatric casualties of soldiers and noncombatants under fire. A soldier in the First World War, for example, was more likely to become a psychiatric casualty than to die by enemy fire. The assumption that epidemic shell shock and other forms of trauma were reactions to fear caused by constant bombardment was key in both German and Allied decisions to subject civilians to heavy bombing in the Second World War. Despite the intensity of destruction, psychiatric casualties among the bombed populations were not much higher than those in peacetime. Grossman concluded that psychic damage in wartime is primarily caused not by the fear of being killed, but the fear of becoming a killer: 'The resistance to the close-range killing of one's own species is so great that it is often sufficient to overcome the cumulative influences of the instinct for self-protection, the coercive forces of leadership, the expectancy of peers, and the obligation to preserve the lives of comrades.'

That's the good news, and Grossman offers many kinds of data to support it. (Primatologists aren't the only sources of evidence that human nature is better than its reputation.) A lieutenant colonel who taught psychology at West Point, he argues that throughout history, the majority of men on the battlefield did not attempt to kill the enemy. His examples range from New Guinea tribesmen who exchange their excellent hunting arrows for featherless ones when they go to war, to Contra mercenaries who took pride in refusing to fire in Nicaragua. 'Note the nature of such a "conspiracy to resist." Without a word being spoken, every soldier who was obliged and trained to fire reverted to the simplest artifice of soldierly incompetence . . . These soldiers took a great and private pleasure in outmaneuvering those who would make them do what they would not.' Grossman concludes, 'Every soldier who refuses to kill in combat, secretly or openly, represents the latent potential for nobility in humankind.'

The bad news is that the military noticed. After General S. L. A. Marshall's study showed that 80 percent of the Second World War soldiers did not fire their weapons, the army set out to change that. Grossman describes the training that helped American soldiers overcome their resistance to killing. Starting with the Korean War, modern military officers introduced methods of desensitization, conditioning, and denial that increased the rate of firing to 55 percent; those methods were further developed to increase the rate to 95 percent in Vietnam. (Grossman's book was written before the war in Iraq, for which figures are unavailable.) 'In the second half of this century,' wrote Grossman, 'psychology has had an impact as great as that of technology on the modern battlefield.' To be sure, technology helps. Resistance to killing someone decreases in direct proportion to distance from them. Weapons of mass destruction are not only deadly because they kill more people at one time, but because it's easier to push a button than to pull a trigger or stab with a blade. The farther you are from the person you kill, the easier it is to forget you are killing him. Even killing from behind, apparently, is easier than killing someone whose face you can see. (Think about how hard it is to look a beggar in the eye when you walk by his outstretched hand, and multiply.) Prisoners about to be executed are not hooded and blindfolded for their own sakes, but to protect the mental health of their executioners.

But the physical distance produced by technology was less important, according to Grossman, than the psychological distance produced by various forms of conditioning. During his own basic training in 1974, Grossman's company was taught to sing chants. This one was sung running, with the emphasis shouted each time the foot hit the ground:

> I wanna
> RAPE
> KILL
> PILLAGE 'n'
> BURN annnn'
> EAT dead
> BAA-bies
> I wanna
> RAPE
> KILL . . .

That particular chant has been discontinued, but less extreme ones are still in use. Soldiers describe how being forced to shout KILL! KILL! KILL! till they were hoarse made shooting a human being come to seem as natural as squashing an ant. Assassins in training are put through more complex procedures devised by military psychologists who show them a series of progressively gruesome films, with the trainee's head held in a vise to prevent him from turning away and a special device used to keep his eyelids open. Such methods were so successful in conditioning men to ignore their natural reluctance to kill that the firing rate quadrupled in the unpopular war in Vietnam. Grossman argues that the extraordinary rate of posttraumatic stress disorders among Vietnam veterans was not only caused by the ambivalent nature of their homecoming, but by psychic conflicts stemming from the way they'd been forced to kill more men than any soldiers in history.

Grossman's study is not only relevant to conditions of war; he concludes it by warning that the same forms of desensitization deliberately used to make soldiers more lethal are now routinely part of American media. Through television and video games, FBI programs designed to enable officers to fire their weapons more readily encourage ordinary children to create a culture that, Grossman writes, increasingly resembles Hobbes's. 'To sponsors, media executives claim that just a few well-placed seconds can control how America will spend its hard-earned money. But to Congress and other watchdog agencies, they argue that they are not responsible for causing viewers to change the way they will respond.' Hundreds of studies confirm that it matters. We are malleable. Rather simple methods and rather common circumstances can turn most of us into creatures who will torture and kill. There's nothing more to the oft-criticized claim about the banality of evil than that. The evil isn't what's banal; we are.

Often enough. Yet we know we have other options. Mary McCarthy found *Eichmann in Jerusalem* 'morally exhilarating. I freely confess that it gave me joy and I too heard a paean in it – not a hate-paean to totalitarianism but a paean of transcendence, heavenly music, like that of the final chorus of *Figaro* or the *Messiah*. As in those choruses, a pardon or redemption of some sort was taking place.' What was redeemed, of course, was not Adolf Eichmann, but human possibility itself. For Arendt, and Zimbardo, and others who work in similar directions have drawn a model that avoids both cynicism and whitewash. Evil actions are easy, but they are not inevitable. Understanding how ordinary people undertake them can indeed be exhilarating, for it shows we have the power to do things differently. We are all partly responsible for the systems that make evils seem unavoidable, but systems can be changed. It's happened before.

What I've sketched is not a program of change but something that is prior to one. In addition to empirical understanding of the conditions under which most people will do evil, we need a conceptual understanding of how varied evil can be. There is no single feature of action that marks it. Intentions aren't necessary, but sometimes they're decisive, and the same is true for consequences. The repetition of the trifecta remark was less evil for what it did than for what it showed: a staggering lack of reverence for other people's heartbreak. Combined with a staggering excess of sanctimony – which is reverence as sham – when sanctimony looked expedient, the result was hypocrisy of historic proportions. In *On Revolution*, Arendt asks why hypocrisy, 'one of the minor vices, we are inclined to think – should have been hated more than all the other vices taken together.' It may be the vice that pays compliments to virtue by covering up other vices, but it is usually the one that proves to be the final, outrageous straw. Arendt explains that the hypocrite not only wants to appear virtuous before others, but also to convince himself. 'By the same token, he eliminates from the world, which he has populated with illusions and lying phantoms, the only core of integrity from which true appearances could arise again, his own incorruptible self.' Integrity, she thinks, can exist under the cover of all the other vices but this one. 'Only crime and the criminal, it is true, confront us with the perplexity of radical evil; but only the hypocrite is rotten to the core.'

Hypocrisy was also at issue in the second case I examined, but this wouldn't be enough to make it stand out. Not every lie is wrong, and very few are evil. What took place at Gorée was perverse. To produce an event celebrating the end of slavery and racism, whose staging entailed the reinstitution of temporary slavery and a degree of racism not met in similar security precautions, is to turn truth upside down. It was a perversion without immediate consequences, but future repercussions are easy to imagine. Not every Senegalese is as generous and forgiving as Bigné Ndoye. During the Bush administration, ever fewer people bothered to distinguish between the American government and the American people. (Understandably enough. As one African friend told me, 'I'm tired of hearing about the other America. If they can't even get rid of their own government, what good are they to the rest of us?') When Americans scrambled to answer the question *Why do they hate us?* Bush offered the answer: 'They hate us for our freedom.' For the Senegalese who were locked up while his entourage took over their island to talk about black liberation, it may have been true. In 2008, every opportunity for irony or bitterness notwithstanding, the world gave America another chance.

What makes the case of Abu Ghraib evil is not something intrinsic to it. Apologists are right to point out that there are worse forms of torture, and it's practiced today by some of the groups whose members were among the victims of U.S. military prisons. But if Caesar's wife has obligations, Caesar is doubly bound. Plato imagined a choice: Would you rather do evil and be regarded as good, or do good but be regarded as evil? It's a good puzzle for thinking about individual ethics, but good politics requires both appearance and reality. If the U.S. wants to maintain exceptional powers, it has to maintain exceptional standards. Abu Ghraib was evil because it occurred in a context whose ramifications are potentially infinite. The military has immediate worries. The Geneva Conventions are just that, conventions that only work as long as everyone honors them. When U.S. soldiers are known to violate them, they will likely suffer violations in return. Moreover, enemy soldiers who expect torture and humiliation will be inclined to fight more fiercely, and more lethally, rather than surrender. Those who have been tortured are likely to swell their ranks; as Lawrence Wright argues, the experience of torture in Egyptian prisons was a crucial element in radicalizing many of the first Al Qaeda members. For future U.S. soldiers, the impact of Abu Ghraib may be deadly.

But that's just the categorical imperative viewed as a bargain: I won't scratch your back if you refrain from scratching mine. John McCain has said that 'The mistreatment of prisoners harms us more than our enemies.' He argued that it undermines U.S. interests in a 'war of ideas' where moral standing matters – a reminder that the moral law has a majestic dimension. What are the consequences of Abu Ghraib for the world you would like to create in the future?

They are devastating. It could take decades for the nascent women's movements in Arab countries to recover from the photos of Lynndie England, which opened an abyss for men's worst night-mares of what unleashed female power can do. Struggles for human rights are likely to suffer even more than struggles for the rights of women. Anyone who proposes intervening in human rights will have to battle with the image of a wired-up hooded man teetering on that box. *That is not what I meant at all. That is not it at all.* The wasteland created in Baghdad in the name of human rights will be taken for the real thing – or used as excuse to deny human rights where they're needed most.

When criticized for his racist policies, Adolf Hitler liked to mention the number of lynchings that regularly occurred in America. In 1939, the SS journal put out a poster quoting FDR's reaction to Kristallnacht: 'I couldn't believe that this kind of thing could happen in twentieth century civilization.' But rather than showing the bloody Jewish bodies and smashed windows of the German pogrom, the poster depicted black men hanging from Southern trees. In the long run, of course, history rejected the equation. Carefully calibrated state-sponsored murder is not the same thing as mob murders occur-ring under the state's blind eye. (It's easier to be indignant about the comparison, however, if you don't know that Harry Truman refused to sign a bill outlawing lynching. The existing laws against murder were not enough to save scores of black veterans returning from the war. Though Albert Einstein and Paul Robeson headed a group of religious leaders who urged Truman to do something about it, he said the timing for a bill was politically inadvisable.) In the short run, however, Hitler's comparison worked, as similar comparisons do today. Already, repressive measures in China, Egypt, and Malaysia have been defended by local officials who point to the Patriot Act or Guantánamo. Evil? Everybody does it. Who can find their way through the moral morass?

The evil of Abu Ghraib lies in its consequences. They have the potential to undermine the struggle for human rights just as the Soviet Union undermined the struggle for socialism. When you torture and kill in the name of an ideal, it's the ideal that suffers most. Those who excuse the abuses at Abu Ghraib as better than other abuses, and necessary to win the war on terror, have forgotten an old refrain. Remember when the evils of socialism were better than the evils of capitalism, and in any case, necessary to the final struggle for liberation? If the ideal of human rights is destroyed by the violations that were said to be needed to realize it, our children will pay the price. Many of them are already paying, for they believe in next to nothing.

I've discussed three cases of evil. None of them is as evil as it could be, and all of them are evil in different ways. They do have one thing in common. What happened at Gorée was hidden because of geopolitical realities: The island is too far from centers of power to attract much international attention. It was an accident – though surely a calculated one – that this event remained unexposed. No one tried to cover up what was done there, or even suggested that doing so might be useful. This links it to the two other cases I examined, where what happened was in plain view. Bush's trifecta remark wasn't made in private, but repeated as a gag at a series of fundraising dinners. It was only suppressed after part of it was exposed as a lie; no one in the White House was concerned that it might be inadvisable language from a government busy trying to remake the world under the banner of 9/11. Not wrong, mind you; simply inadvisable – a concern equally missing in all the grinning soldiers who let their buddies record pictures of life on the night shift for the folks back home.

What links the three examples is shamelessness.

Guilt is the internal sense that you've done something wrong, even if no one ever discovers it. Shame records your consciousness of wrong before a community whose values you honor. Guilt is often thought to go deeper, but shame leaves marks that are public and private at once. This is one thing meant by Spanish philosopher Fernando Savater in calling ethics a matter of good taste. In *Amador*, his introduction to ethics, he characterizes conscience as 'continuing to develop good taste in the moral sense, to a point where some things repel us (so that, for example, lying becomes just as offensive as pissing in the soup before it is served).' Shame and guilt often stand and fall together, but they are quite distinct. The absence of shame in all these cases is critical, for *shameless* is not just a term of abuse. We have lost a sense of moral clarity that would give rise to the fear that certain actions – whether we privately feel guilty about them or not – could lead to disgrace. For they don't. If enough, and enough well-placed people do them, the only disgrace you need fear is the failure to get away with it.

The protests against the Vietnam War may not have contributed much to ending it, but they forced a president to resign; a few years later, the world admired a democracy strong enough to end another presidency after the revelations of Watergate. Though the crimes of the Bush administration were very much graver, impeachment was never a serious option. Such a climate allows writers like Gray to draw the conclusion that the law is whatever the government decides – rather than arousing outrage over massive legal violation. Enough shamelessness breeds the presumption: there are no moral rules. That's important enough to merit the word evil. Now shamelessness isn't new; more than one critic has compared the photos of torture at Abu Ghraib to the postcards of lynchings that were sold in the American South in the early twentieth century. As we saw, decline is no more inevitable than progress, and it's good to recall dimensions on which we've improved. Yet the openness with which all three examples were carried out points to a culture so debased it is speeding up its own ruin.

The only way to stop the further erosion of shame is to return to the language of good and evil. I've sketched ways to condemn acts of terrorism as evil without relying on a religious framework. But even if you grant that the idea of evil isn't theological, you may believe it is demonizing. The word *evil* was so often abused in recent years that many fear it's impossible to use responsibly. Often, as we've seen, it was no more than a way of disguising the distinction between friend and enemy to masquerade as a moral principle. For people do run on moral energy. Soldiers sign up to defend their clan or their country from evil; how many put their lives on the line for somebody's cronies? Conviction produces more bloodshed than expedience, and the invasion of Iraq, the deterioration of relations with Iran and North Korea, the rise in Muslim fear and rage were all foreseeable consequences of the rhetoric the White House began producing the day the towers fell. Many who want no truck with those consequences concluded that words like *evil* create more evil than anything else. American author Glenn Greenwald puts this view eloquently:

> The great and tragic irony of the Bush presidency is that its morally convicted foundations have yielded some of the most morally grotesque acts and radical departures from American values in our country's history. The president who insists that he is driven by a clear and compelling moral framework has done more than almost any American in history to make the world question on which side of that battle this country is fighting.

Greenwald is mistaken, however, to argue that 'what destroyed the Bush presidency' was 'a good versus evil mentality.' The idea of evil is neither demonizing nor Manichean, as many critics suggest. It becomes so if we fail to recognize that nearly anyone can come to participate in it, precisely because – as Arendt explained in calling it banal – it has lost that quality of temptation that once allowed us to recognize it immediately. *Evil*, I have argued, should be applied not to persons, but to actions, and the application should be a reason to start thinking, not to stop. Knowing how easily we can be drawn into evil must lead us to look for ways to understand it. There's no other way to get to work.

But if calling something evil should always be coupled with an attempt to understand it, we shouldn't let understanding deter us from calling things by their proper names. Actions may have multiple causes, circumstances may be murky, and responsibility diverse. It's important to untangle all of this in order to begin to attack it, but there comes a time to judge. Evil presents an unacceptable gap between ideals and reality; judging something to be evil is a way of setting limits on what we're willing to endure. The language of good and evil is vulnerable to exploitation because it's the most powerful language we have: Nothing moves men and women more deeply and surely, for better and worse. We must hone and refine and sharpen it, but we cripple ourselves when we try to do without it. The language of shame is the most effective moral weapon there is. To abandon talk of evil is to leave that weapon in the hands of those who are least equipped to use it.

CHAPTER TWELVE

ENLIGHTENMENT
HEROES

When we think about heroes, we think in outsize examples.
The Bible and the works of Homer have starkness and
grandeur no other texts share. They point to the strength of the
traditions that anchor so many of our beliefs. Our moral intuitions
may not come from above, but they didn't come easily, or yesterday.
Turning to Abraham and Odysseus and Job is a way of marking
that depth. Yet while none of these heroes is one-dimensional, all
of them are giants. How to move from them to the people you
might meet – or become – on an ordinary sidewalk?

Look for ordinary examples of evil and you'll find them everywhere; the three I discussed in the last chapter were not random,
but neither were they unique. Look for ordinary examples of goodness and you may well be stumped. Goodness is no less banal than
evil, but clear instances seem harder to find, which is why we turn
to literature and movies and myths. Given the years I'd spent thinking
about the fit between ideals and reality, I should have found cases
of goodness easy to name. But pressed for examples, my mind drew
a blank. Martin Luther King? I wasn't looking for martyrs. Mother
Theresa? Still less, saints. What I sought were examples of Enlightenment heroism – people whose minds were at least as engaged as
their hearts, whose moral clarity was won through reflection and

ongoing struggle. Einstein? He was not the loopy genius portrayed in caricatures, but his image is too intimidating to be useful. And none of the less familiar examples seemed, well, big enough.

And that was the point. I'd forgotten what I'd been preaching: Reality never looks like the ideals you have for it. Any time you move from ideal heroes to real ones you'll find buck teeth or hesitation or sleeping problems or awkward laughs. Once that became clearer, the heroes were not hard to find.

A person I'd known for decades quickly popped into mind, and then another. I thought of two I'd met in passing. If I reran the list of my friends and acquaintances I saw I would recognize several more. I settled on four people to illustrate Enlightenment values in action, and I'll wager you know others. However hard the times they experience in public and private, all of them are people who know about joy and how to express it. All of them have formidable powers of reason: Each is as ready to learn from the classics as from the market woman on the corner, one reason they all have first-rate minds. All of them have a powerful sense of limit and maintain a sense of wonder – in outrage as well as in the hope each maintains in himself and succeeds in creating for others.

Most important, I was looking for people whose moral courage could not only be honored but analyzed. Most heroes don't make that easy. We are moved by the shy dignity of Wesley Autrey, the construction worker who fascinated millions when he dived onto a New York subway track to save a stranger, but his refusal to say more than 'I did what I felt was right' leaves us with little to do but admire him.

As it happens, I chose to portray Americans. I might have chosen others, but having dwelled on some ways that Americans have acted to change the world for the worse, it felt right to offer examples of those who are working to change it for the better. The people I portray have also written books, all different in style, which probe and record their own searches for moral clarity and reasoned engagement. The portraits that follow, drawn from their own words, are no substitutes for reading the books themselves. My aim is to illustrate some of the different ways good people have used theoretical and practical reason to work out moral judgments of different sizes and to face the challenges they pose. Are they saintly? Not in the least, though you may find them extraordinary. I suspect each would say they are no more than what ordinary men and women can be – if they choose.

· · · · ·

David Shulman doesn't even like heroes, and when reluctantly agreeing to my request to portray him here, he asked me to record that. *Hero* is for him too macho, without nuance or complexity. Heroes, he feels, are relentlessly cheerful, never noticing the cold and the rain and the thirst and the boredom Shulman knows so well. We don't need any more heroes, he insists in his book *Dark Hope*; at best, they are a nuisance.

He doesn't look like one, either. He's a soft-spoken, gentle man with a faint resemblance to Groucho Marx – if Groucho Marx were balding and without a hint of barb. Shulman says he's not made to be an activist, and seems almost surprised by the force of his engagement in efforts toward Arab-Israeli peace. Decades back he came to Israel from Iowa because he fell in love with the Hebrew language and liked Mediterranean trees. By trade, he's a professor of Sanskrit, heaped with honors in the West as well in India, where he spends long stints; by avocation he's a poet in several languages. Like every Israeli, he served in the army, where he learned the medic's skills he now uses to treat those whose heads are bashed in by Israeli settlers' stones. When I first met him, however, he seemed the least politically conscious man in Jerusalem. At the height of one Middle East crisis or other he announced in disgust that he was going off with his son to hike the Himalayas, 'where there are no monotheists at all.' He doesn't think much of Abraham, whom he considers a destructive fanatic for smashing his father's idols.

But something exploded in him with the second intifada, as he wrote in *Dark Hope*:

Let no one say he did not know; let no one talk of vast historical forces, of wrongs piled on wrongs, of generalities and abstractions; let no one speak philosophy. What is real is this overriding anguish. It is in their faces; it is in my body; it is in these rocks and hills.

It was no longer particular acts or orders but the occupation itself, he came to feel, that was immoral. According to one friend, 'It is unreal to talk about this in academic terms. What is real must be known and experienced. Once you feel it, there is no longer reason to hesitate.'

Not that Shulman doubts the power of words. His book is the most passionate and articulate account that's been written of the Israeli peace movement. He knows how to mobilize words to stop the demolition of houses or the bisecting of a Palestinian university. When asked to step forward at rallies he quotes Gandhi and Rawls on civil disobedience. But the second intifada drove him to actions where words don't matter: picking olives, unclogging wells, harvesting wheat, facing down walls. Shulman joined Ta'ayush – Arabic for 'living together' – a mixed group of Israelis and Palestinians devoted to pursuing peace and ending the occupation. Convinced that unless both sides win this war, both sides will lose it, Ta'ayush uses the tactics of nonviolent resistance to support the two-state solution that recent Israeli governments have supported in principle. In practice, most of them have undermined it by supporting settlements that expropriate private land and settlers who make the Palestinians' lives wretched in the hope they will give up and leave. Between the limbo of the Green Line and the wall are Palestinian villages that have been cut off not only from nearby families, schools, and hospitals, but from any means of livelihood. The army can prevent the village from completing its olive harvest, all they have left to live on; it's a prelude, Shulman says, to annexing the land itself. This is the sort of outcome Ta'ayush works to prevent by bringing two hundred volunteers to help with the harvest.

Shulman has few illusions. 'This conflict is not a war of the sons of light with the sons of darkness; both sides are dark, both are given to organized violence and terror, and both resort constantly to self-righteous justification and a litany of victimization, the bread-and-butter of ethnic conflict. My concern is with the darkness on my side.' His activities, in part, reflect the principle we saw first in Kant: If everyone really cleaned up his own backyard, there wouldn't be much mess next door to worry about. But if Shulman's stance entails a commitment to the universal, it is also part of

a Jewish past with its dead voices whispering in my memory. 'Bind the wounds. Heal the sick. Don't forget you were slaves. To save one person is to save a world. Don't be afraid. All that lives is holy. Forgive. Wake up. Shake off the dust and stand up. Feed the hungry. Bring the poor into your home. Cover the naked. Break their chains.' Did I invent these voices? They seem to speak from some buried, dreamlike domain, as distant and insistent as childhood. It is nothing to be right, and a true disaster to be righteous, but it is everything to do what you can.

He finds the sentence *I'm only following orders* to be 'almost unbelievable from Jewish lips' and yet his view of human nature is such that when he hears it from an army captain it comes as no surprise.

If I look deeply into myself, I can identify – side by side with hope, faith, and a certain embryonic capacity for empathy – the same dark forces that are active among the most predatory of the settlers. I, too, am capable of hate and of polarizing the world. Perhaps the balance, individual or collective, is always precarious. Here is a reason to act.

Don't be naive. Be a man, and show them who's boss. Force is the only language they understand. Shulman hears the same message, in Hebrew and Arabic, in the space of a few minutes on each side of the border. In a world where each side has hung on to such claims for years, Ta'ayush works by the classic principles of nonviolent direct action. They hold teach-ins on war crimes and Gandhi's philosophy, learn how to refrain from hitting back when attacked, and how to go limp when arrested. Carrying blankets to refugees through the Hebron Hills they sometimes break into 'We Shall Overcome,' along with a psalm or two.

Peace work, says Shulman, is mostly boring, long waiting punctuated by occasional bouts of action or fear – much like war. Yet some of his descriptions are so lyrical you want to go off and join him just for the pleasure of it – like the Israeli novelist David Grossman who declared at a Ta'ayush olive harvest that he'd wasted his life writing books. In Shulman's words:

> Then to work: once again, the remembered eroticism of light and tree. From this moment on, and for the next few hours, there will be a constant pitter-patter of falling olives, the sweet percussion of an autumn day just before the rains. The olives sputter and spin; the sun beats down upon us through the silvery leaves; there is the good smell of earth and ripening fruit, of dry thorns and bleached rocks, of happiness.

Not every task feels so good. In 2005, for example, settlers poisoned the hills of Twaneh, where a group of Palestinians have lived for many generations in a series of caves. Tiny blue-green pellets of barley, dipped in rat poison, were found dropped behind rocks and thorns in an effort to kill the herds of goats and sheep that form the backbone of the cave dwellers' subsistence economy. When wild animals began to die, the Israeli newspaper *Ha'aretz* took note, but the nation soon lost interest. Ta'ayush volunteers spent their weekends working to clean the ground, bending over roots, clawing and sifting the dirt to pick out the elusive pellets decomposing in the soil and entering the food cycle. The work is hard, for the poisoners took pains to hide the deadly barley from everyone but the hapless animals. Shulman is enraged at the desecration of land itself, land the settlers call holy. What kind of man would deliberately poison a wild deer – or a herd of goats, and through them, a whole community?

The kind of man who does not stop at sheep, of course. The settlers don't shrink from violence against lone Palestinians, but though they usually win the cases that get to court, most of their tactics fall short of what can be prosecuted, and even their illegal activities are usually protected in practice by the army. A Palestinian mother and three children draw water from the well for their flock of sheep; just when they are finished, settlers descend to empty the buckets in the rocky soil. Palestinian farmers trying to plow their fields are driven off them at gunpoint. Ta'ayush sends volunteers to protect the Palestinians. The Jewish volunteers are particular targets for the fury of the settlers, who have no qualms about hurling rocks at those they consider traitors, or breaking clubs over their heads. At such moments, the volunteers shout reminders to one other not to respond to violence with violence, for one rock thrown from their side would be pretext for the other side to shoot.

Shulman has set limbs and cleaned wounds in these exchanges, and earned a few scars himself, but talking about that is not his style. He's committed to the ordinary: the dailiness of boredom, for example, that punctuates the peace movement. 'For once,' he records, 'the speech is short, lucid and focused.' But usually the long, flowery expressions of good will and solidarity go on and on. He finds himself hoping for rain so speeches will end sooner, then remembering he left his coat in the car miles away. He is always forgetting his coat when he needs it, and dragging it with him on the days it's too hot. On days when massive confrontations are expected, he takes a book to read in jail should he be arrested, then leaves the book in the wrong place, too. Shulman is suspicious of anything that sounds like fanfare. For

Living in Israel, on a certain level, is like living inside the *Iliad*. Israeli society feeds on notions of the heroic, of self-sacrifice in the name of the tribe. Anyone who has served in the Israeli army knows the rhetoric of selfless missions and glorious deaths.

But

> What if the *Iliad*, instead of telling the long story of Achilles'
> lunatic anger and destructive pride, had focused on some
> anonymous hero in the Greek camp who suddenly realized
> that he was to be killed for nothing, and that no measure of
> posthumous glory, the much-vaunted *kleos*, was worth his
> life?

For all his low-key manner, Shulman is not impervious to the
Iliad's appeal. Though he thought the 1982 war in Lebanon a terrible
mistake at the time, he was called to serve in it, and recalls

> a certain elation, the thrill shared by young men on the verge
> of the ultimate test, along with the intoxicating sense of merging
> into the collective mass of comrades-in-arms. The official
> ideology . . . was of no consequence compared to the 'high' we
> got from one another, from the wild, somewhat unnerving
> adventure of it all. There is also a certain uncharacteristic
> tenderness for one another of soldiers serving under fire –
> probably only under such conditions.

When he and his colleagues work to support soldiers who refuse
to serve in the occupied territories, he knows what their lives are
like. As he notes, 'Undoing evil, the evil that comes from within –
from yourself and your own people – is not simple.' It means
acknowledging that most moral realities are ambiguous and getting
at the truth is toil. It means accepting that the same settler who shot
a colleague during a harvest may tenderly care for the daughter of
another. It means resisting the pull of ethnic conflict, 'which
inevitably narrows collective vision and deadens the human heart.
The first thing to go is the ability to imagine the world through the
eyes of the other, the enemy, the victim-to-be.'

In the Middle East, retaining that ability to imagine through the
eyes of the other is a much harder task than picking olives from trees
or barley pellets from the earth, harder than facing rage-filled settlers

or lines of police. What sustains activists like Shulman is the almost painful gratitude of the villagers they help. The shepherds serve them tea and pita and thank them profusely for the hope that they bring. 'You cannot fully understand how much it means to us,' one tells him. Shulman cannot; he is wracked by how little he and his colleagues can actually do to make a difference. Yet harvesting olives is elemental, like baking bread; it's the sort of fulfillment political work seldom provides, and at the end of a long day he is pleased to have done something real. Sometimes he feels that every single patch of earth the villagers manage to plant or harvest is a near miracle, and a victory over the settlers, the army, the government. Sometimes he feels that every court order that delays an eviction for a month is an achievement, for nobody thinks the occupation can last forever. If Ta'ayush can draw out these struggles until peace comes, the families can remain on their land, and they will remember who helped them stay. The cave-dwellers tell and retell stories of the volunteers' visits the way they tell epics; 'for these people, Ta'ayush matters, like oxygen to the drowning.' Middle Eastern memories are as faulty as any others, but they are long. Even a few Israelis returning week after week undermines the anger that seems settled after decades of occupation; it may be enough to keep the promise of peace alive. It's always the few who set in motion the long business of change.

Or so Shulman thinks on good days; on others he's hit by despair. 'I don't want to act for the record!' he shouts at a colleague. 'I just want this misery to end.' It will not, not much of it, not soon; for the moment it's a matter of bringing food and blankets, helping to tend crops, stopping the demolition of one family's house there, the illegal encroachment of the security wall onto an orchard there. 'But then, as the Zen people say, you do not act in this mode, political action, with your eyes focused on results. You act because you must act, for the sake of what is right. The world takes care of the rest – or not.'

What keeps Shulman going? He insists that it's nothing special; that his motives, and those of his colleagues, are 'wildly obscure, oblique.' They have come out of loyalty to one another, to friends; nothing is worse than the shame of letting them down. Out of a certain insouciant taste for adventure, for something outside the usual routine. Out of anger – the rage at having been lied to by our government for years and years, at having been made silently complicit in *their* crimes. Out of the need to put oneself to the test. And then – last on the list – out of some inchoate, stubborn moral sense, after all, projected on to the shadow-play screen of politics.

I don't care about Shulman's motives any more than the cave-dwellers of the South Hebron hills do. He's the one who quotes the Greek poet Seferis: 'There are always but two parties – Socrates, and his accusers.' One most choose. 'A choice,' he writes, '– real, urgent, and agonizing – faces us. Each will have to answer. With the agony comes the gift – of looking deeply, of deciding, of becoming more fully human.' And because he has chosen I am not surprised when he describes 'a breathtaking experience of freedom, perhaps more complete and more satisfying than at any other point in my life . . . Perhaps it is a function of the play of shadows and light as evening falls in hills. Probably there is no point in analyzing it.' For

> action is not about results, not about 'having' or even 'winning.'
> It is, surprisingly, about 'being,' or about not deadening ourselves
> to the cruelty all around us. Thus, being alive, one takes a stand.
> It is not for us, now or ever, to complete the task, but, like the
> almond, we need to ripen, burst open, bloom.

· · · · ·

Change the clothing and she could pass for an unworldly, angular beauty about to enter the social whirl. As it is, my cousin Sarah Chayes dresses in the long tunic and flowing pants worn by men in Afghanistan – her home, more or less, since the Taliban fell. In a culture where women are invisible, it was the best solution for a reporter who wanted to stay as near as she could to her sources.

Her book *The Punishment of Virtue* explains, 'What were my choices? I could wear a *burqa*. Fat chance. I could give up the effort altogether and don Western garb. That would not solve the problem, since there were no more Westerners in Chaman than there were women. Cargo pants and a parka would draw gawkers to me just the same.' In the meantime, she has learned Pashtu, and keeps an AK-47 under her bed.

For years she'd been an NPR reporter with a flat in Paris and an eye for cutting edges that won prizes while getting her in fixes that, for example, made her throw her laptop out a window to keep it away from Serbian police. September 11, 2001, struck her as a crucial historical moment – like the assassination of Archduke Ferdinand that triggered the First World War. She asked her editor to send her to Afghanistan. Shortly thereafter she was waiting in Quetta with hundreds of other journalists eager to cross the Pakistani border. Chayes had studied Islamic culture in college when it seemed like a quirk – 'just a spirit of contradiction, I guess, when everybody else was doing Europe' – and knew some Arabic. During an early stint with the Peace Corps in Morocco she had kept the month-long dawn-to-dusk fast during Ramadan as a sign of respect for her host culture. As the only journalist in Quetta to do so, she so astonished the Taliban that they took her under their wing. On the eve of the fall of Afghanistan, they invited her to break the fast with them. It's the sort of instinct that led her to avoid the hotel designated for foreigners once she reached Kandahar to seek lodging with a family in a broken-down graveyard, and it's the sort of instinct that introduced her to so many Afghans that she found herself dining with President Karzai's uncle at the end of her NPR tour. 'The word *NGO* should be struck from the English language,' said Uncle Aziz of the opportunists he knew were ready to ride into the expected free-for-all. 'Wouldn't you come back and help us?'

Without pausing to consider, Chayes said yes. She had grown uncomfortable with the reporting she'd begun to consider highbrow entertainment: 'I could describe those dramas, with adrenaline-fired urgency, and then leave, go on to the next one. I was never held to account for how the stories ended.' She longed to do more than *talk* about crises, and she was falling in love with the wild complexity of Afghan culture. But more important than any of that was her sense that it was crucial for the U.S. to get Afghanistan right; its performance after defeating the Taliban would determine how many people will line up on what Chayes considers the most important issue of our time. The picture of the world as helplessly riven into two opposing blocks is one she rejects with all her being:

> I don't believe in the clash of civilizations. I believe that most human beings share some basic aspirations and some basic values: the right to participate in fashioning the rules that govern them, accountability, access to learning, and the reasonably equitable distribution of wealth, for example. The extent to which different peoples have been able to achieve these things depends a lot on what has befallen them over the course of time – not on some irrevocable cultural difference.

The former Taliban stronghold was a particularly symbolic place to put her convictions into practice.

> I sometimes feel I'm laying my body down as a bridge over the chasm that Bush and Bin Laden are trying to open. Not that I suppose my efforts are large enough to make a difference. Things are worse now than they were on September 12; what's pulling us apart has gained force. But if all you have to work with is one tiny hammer, you have to hit at a pressure point. Kandahar is a pressure point.

Chayes became field director for Afghans for Civil Society, a tiny organization another Karzai had founded earlier. It had no operations in Afghanistan, and she set about building some. In *The Punishment of Virtue* she describes her initial hopes:

With inspiring Karzai at the helm and Americans of good faith in the field, it actually seemed Afghanistan might be the place where some of the damage could be repaired – the damage caused by years of ignorance and neglect, arrogance and withdrawal; the damage caused by the surrender of the force of ideas, in much of the United States and the Muslim community, to those who would split the world into opposing civilizations, irrevocably hostile. Afghanistan might just prove them wrong. And how fitting: Afghanistan, which for seven years had symbolized the twisting of Islam into a glowering fascism, could regain its ancient role as a connector of empires, facilitating the exchange of riches, people, and ideas between them.

Among other things, her book is a chronicle of hopes disappointed. She supported the U.S. invasion, which was welcomed by Afghans – 'not quite with flowers, since Afghans are skeptical' – but they were sick of the Taliban and expected Americans to bring them peace and law. Instead, Chayes watched as the U.S. – through a mix of ignorance, distraction in Iraq, and sheer laziness – proceeded to reinstate just those warlords whose thuggery had driven Afghanistan into the Taliban's arms years before.

She did a great deal more than watch, however. Chayes raised money in the U.S. to rebuild houses bombed by U.S. forces, then returned to Kandahar to battle the local warlord over access to stone to do the job. She gathered the village children to help her clear piles of bricks and pushed authorities to build roads and drill wells. She read everything she could find about the history of the region, from Persian poetry to letters of nineteenth-century British soldiers stationed in Kabul, for she was committed to building an organization that offered both policy and practice. She organized groups of local elders, teaching them to state their cases effectively and bringing them to the capital to do it. She mobilized groups of women – some prominent, some illiterate – to debate women's priorities in her office before they flipped down their *burqas* to step outside. She agitated for the removal of corrupt warlords. She opened a dairy cooperative and sat on bureaucrats' tables till they gave her the permits required. Most recently, she founded a soap-making business, one way of encouraging local farmers to produce something other than opium.

And she learned, though not all the lessons were pleasant. Chayes's first project was to rebuild the village of Akokolacha, which had been close enough to the Kandahar airport – where the Taliban and Al Qaeda mounted their last stand – for the U.S. airforce to reduce to rubble. 'The bombing of Akokolacha was not a crime,' Chayes argues. 'The civilians had scattered, and Al Qaeda was there. But why should the villagers pay for what happened after they fled? If I scratch your car while backing mine out of a parking lot, I should make sure yours gets fixed.' Chayes thought it important for Afghans to see Americans fixing their village, and plenty of Americans agreed. The town of Concord, Massachusetts, still touched by the spirit of democracy that animated the American Revolution, was especially enchanted by the idea. Adults raised thousands of dollars, children made T-shirts for kids in the village. CONCORD AND AKOKOLACHA, they read, WE ARE THE BRIDGE TO PEACE. Chayes wrote the declaration in shaky Pashtu above an outline of the bridge at Concord and called Karzai's brother, who promised to tell the villagers about the importance of the place in America's own founding mythology. Chayes and her sister Eve, also coordinating the effort, were stunned and delighted by the outpouring of American energy.

Chayes returned to Afghanistan with the funds to rebuild the houses, never imagining that reconstructing the original layouts would present any problems – until she stood inspecting the mounds of wreckage with a group of village men. One insisted his pile of dirt had originally been nine rooms, each with a bathroom; the next backed him up and claimed he'd had seven. No villager would expose another's lie for fear of losing his chance at an American-bought mansion. Chayes wrote:

I was crushed and immediately faced with a moral dilemma. What to tell Concord? If I described the scene accurately, all those wonderful people would regret their contributions and good wishes, I was sure. But could I possibly lie, or gloss it over; tread on the slippery slope that led to such cynicisms as – in one example I had heard of – an aid agency photographing gifts unloaded in Somalia, for the donors' benefit, then carting them off to the beach for burning?

She worked to find terms that gave the disappointment the most sense. The country as a whole, she came to believe, is suffering from posttraumatic stress disorder, with tangible symptoms: the inability to bond, plan for the future, or think in collective terms. For decades the villagers' destinies were determined by outside forces beyond their control, and before that by age-old Afghan traditions of extracting and distributing subsidies. 'All of our lofty words to the Akokolacha *shura* about Concord, and democracy, and citizen participation, and cultural exchange were, in this context, meaningless. What we were doing fit too closely with the familiar pattern for the villagers to see anything distinctive in it.' In the end, the villagers got identical houses, which made some of them angry. Chayes was frustrated, but not bitter: 'There were too many other people to help. You get pretty utilitarian about things.'

About some things, perhaps, but it was only the first time Chayes weathered an apparent conflict between her own moral code and the one she had entered. Her decision to compromise concerning the status of women seems unavoidable; she could make sure women are treated differently within her own walls, but knows larger changes take more time. (Chayes herself seems to be regarded as a third gender in Kandahar, though locals have dubbed her the bravest man in Afghanistan.) On other matters she regrets the ways she initially wavered. 'I lost a lot of my moral compass when I got there,' she explains. 'I kept telling myself I didn't know enough about the culture to judge it.' So she turned a blind eye to one employee's

patterns of seducing local boys and petty thieving because he led
her to think it was accepted local practice instead of the misdeeds
of one corrupt, well-connected man. 'In fact,' she now says, 'every
moral compromise I made has been wrong.' Refusing to make moral
compromises is no contradiction with her painstaking work to make
local standpoints intelligible to the West. On the contrary, she holds
that the failure to understand the differences between its culture
and the one it has occupied led to the biggest American mistakes.

> Over the past three or four centuries, we in the West have designed
> and laboriously erected institutions as our bulwark against
> tyranny. And we have come to revere them, for they have indeed
> protected us. Westerners, to a degree unique in history, invest
> their loyalty in institutions, regardless of the individuals who
> happen to be staffing them at a particular time. The willingness,
> in 2000, of Americans to obey the ruling of a split Supreme Court
> in the most closely contested presidential election in their history
> is a striking example ... But Afghanistan is not there yet. In
> Afghanistan, loyalties and allegiances are to individuals.

The U.S. might combine both standpoints – for example, by holding
warlord governors to standards of accountability. Instead, American
officials made excuses for whichever ally told the most compelling
story, underpinned by their own uncertainty – just as Chayes herself,
she ruefully acknowledges, did with her own corrupt employee.

Chayes's readiness to work with the U.S. military brought accusations of compromise from some of the humanitarian organizations
in Kandahar, for whom she has, in turn, few warm words. Living
in guarded compounds, driven by chauffeurs, eating imported
Western food, and indulging in riotous drinking, they often succeed
in providing Afghans with little more than further arguments for
resisting Western influence. Unlike the military, humanitarian
organizations hide under the cloak of good intentions, using 'the
angelic nature of their self-sacrifice to cover everything from excessive salaries to utter lack of accountability, as they mount the steps,

measured off in one-year assignments, of their careers in the burgeoning aid industry.' Among the military, despite the constant rotation and the utter lack of training, she often met people who were eager to learn how to do it right. Whether or not it should be that way, she argues that the Defense Department is currently making foreign policy on the ground, and her efforts to influence that policy led her to offer briefings to hundreds of officers. Her book is now required reading at Canadian headquarters, and NATO forces regularly consult her. The U.S. military reception has been mixed. Some commanders have limited her access to the bases, while others have described her as changing their lives. Former Green Beret Lieutenant Colonel Tony Schwalm is one of the latter.

> Personally, I found Sarah challenging my sense of morality. What Sarah did is convince me by her conduct that I was not living the faith that I espoused. Most significantly she was risking life and limb to craft a better, freer, more secure way of life for a people that she did not know very long before she started her efforts. I could not say the same. Who do you want helping you? Somebody who helps or somebody who wants to help? No brainer. Sarah shamed me.

While Schwalm's correspondence with Chayes initially focused on security and politics in South Asia, it soon broadened out. He continues,

> I am a Calvinist. My hypothesis has always been that morality in the face of life or death crisis would only survive if the person so afflicted had a belief in God. Sarah's theology as she has explained it to me is of her own making. She knows that she isn't alive for any reason that is readily apparent. Boom. Target. How does this – what, deist? – survive the thought that at any minute her little red pickup truck can go straight into the air as she drives over a three hundred pound home-made bomb? My only answer is her clarity of purpose. I have likened her life to that of a free climber on a sheer rock face. You can tell people who climb with fear in

the eyes. They're worried about falling. The thought never occurs to the good climbers. To the observer, the act is super-human. To the climber, it's what he or she does. The thought of doing otherwise, of climbing with caution, never enters the mind. I can't explain the source of her morality if it isn't God. But that's my problem. She seems too busy climbing to consider such matters.

Chayes cherishes their theological exchanges, all conducted by e-mail, but is squeamish about initiating similar ones with her Afghan neighbors. 'Their experience of faith is extremely concrete and practical,' she notes. 'They can't imagine moral action that isn't directed by divine command.' Mujahadeen who died fighting the Soviets – or innocent civilians killed in today's suicide bombings – are considered martyrs rewarded with a trip straight to paradise, and a free pass for seventy of their closest friends. She sighs,

> To me, that seems like religion as bargaining. And very occasionally I try to suggest that. But it doesn't translate. Once I raised the issue of charity at Ramadan. Poor people are poor all year round, except for the superabundance they receive that month – because Afghans believe that distributing a sheep, say, at Ramadan, is worth more points in God's eyes than doing it the rest of the year. I asked, then, who they're really giving the sheep to – the poor, or their own accounts with God? I think I've convinced one man.

So is she a deist, as Schwalm says? Chayes answers,

> I don't even know what a deist is, but one thing I'm really afraid of is the sin of pride. The idea of a personal God always seemed like hubris; why should He pay so much attention to me? I believe He's sending us messages all the time, and He chooses human messengers to relay them. But He assumes we're adults. He refrains from controlling how we respond. That's as far as I go in that direction; sometimes I oscillate all the way to atheism.

'I wouldn't care if Sarah was Zoroastrian, I see more of the Jesus recorded in the Gospel of Matthew in Sarah of Kandahar than I do in most members of my church, but especially than I see in me,' muses Schwalm, until recently a lifelong Republican. But Chayes thinks less about religion than about geopolitics. She says the struggle to fight the assumption that our civilizations must clash is her generation's version of the fight against fascism. Like the Spanish Civil War in its day, Afghanistan represents the front line. Both her parents, distinguished lawyers with long records of public service, left her growing up with the view that devotion to the public good was something ordinary. 'It was never actually spoken, but that's what one did. And I never forgot what my father said after he was criticized by some Americans for representing Nicaragua at the International Court of Justice in The Hague when the Reagan administration mined the Managua harbor: "There's nothing wrong with holding the United States up to its own highest standards."' But she was also profoundly affected by a world her comfortable parents did not know, which she first encountered one summer while working on a study of Philadelphia's drug problems. Talking to prison inmates left her 'blown away by how much smarter and deeper and more beautiful they were than I was. I felt humbled and needed to get away from the hierarchies I'd been taught to believe were meritocracies. I wanted to get to know all that incredible richness that lay outside my lane.' Wanting to learn led her to drop out of graduate school and wait tables in backwater bars in the Deep South, collect folk tales in Morocco, and finally – for the moment – make soap in a collective in Kandahar.

It's work that involves everything from bargaining for pomegranate seeds and rose petals on the wholesale market to traveling through the U.S. to muster support that ranges from offers of supplies to services to customers. 'Not everybody can drop their life and move to Kandahar,' she grants readily, but Westerners want to help, if they have clear options to do so. 'I have come to feel that what we offer to people in the West – an opportunity to participate – may be just as meaningful as whatever benefits we bring to Kandahar,' wrote Chayes in a recent *Atlantic* article. There is, most centrally, the soap-making itself: pressing almond and apricot kernels to extract their sweet oil, letting soap set overnight and grating it down again, carefully dosing colors and fragrances before kneading the soap into irregular shapes that mirror the rocks of the Arghandab River. It takes days to make one batch of soap and a month to cure it in the cellar when all goes right. The proportions are a mixture of chemistry and art: The oil in one variety must be mixed in throughout the soap, while the dark color of the steeped walnut husks should run in irregular veins. Not everyone in the collective gets it right; she's often called in to save a batch of soap gone wrong.

Banal? On the contrary, Chayes answers that the mix of activity suits her precisely. Nothing about her life feels humdrum, though security concerns have constrained it; the increase in attacks has led her, like others in Afghanistan, to stay indoors when possible. Schwalm calls her a ballerina in a minefield, but Chayes demurs:

> I gained a reputation in Kandahar, but it is false. I am not so very brave. Only, I have not been through their trauma. I am not violated and indelibly damaged as Afghans are. Brutality and agonizing death have been visited on them in such unpredictable and unparriable ways that their ability to calculate risk is gone.

Before you meet Chayes, it's easy to dismiss her interest in soap, and her lack of interest in her own safety, as vaguely romantic and possibly unhealthy. After you've heard her, it's easy to agree with her own description of what moves her: 'This is not about selflessness. For the first time in my life I feel balanced. I don't feel well in my culture's model of success.'

What are the chances her own model will succeed?

> I don't use the word *hope*. I have determination; hope is almost irrelevant. What's important is to try – as hard as you can. That means you need to keep yourself open to astonishment and

wonder and outrage. Cynicism punctures the energy that leads you to try. It suggests that you know it all, so your reaction is always *Yeah? So what else is new?* Once you start saying that, you'll allow anything to happen.

· · · · ·

'We can't invite Ellsberg to any more of our meetings,' said the head of the Carnegie Endowment for International Peace. 'He's lost his objectivity.' It was 1969, and he was responding to a letter Daniel Ellsberg had written calling prolongation of the Vietnam War 'bloody, hopeless, uncompelled, hence surely immoral.' For the Endowment for International Peace, the last word was the last straw. For Ellsberg, it was part of a long process of development that tested the relative values of moral and political concerns. He would use politics to advance moral causes as long as it was possible, but morality had final say.

As he wrote in *Secrets*, a searing account of that development, he began by seeing the war as a problem and tried to help solve it; when he saw it as a stalemate, he tried to help extricate his country. When he saw it as a crime, he exposed and resisted it. As early as 1964 most advisors had grave doubts – not just about the feasibility of the war but about its justice. At a briefing on Viet Cong motivation, Ellsberg's own boss at the Department of Defense had exclaimed that if the reports about the Viet Cong's honesty, patriotism, and attitudes toward the peasantry were true, the U.S. was fighting on the wrong side. After reading the secret files that became known as the Pentagon Papers, Ellsberg 'saw that that way of putting it missed reality since 1954. We *were* the wrong side.' In hope of influencing policy he had worked on classified studies for Henry Kissinger, who had asked the Rand Corporation to prepare a study of strategic alternatives for Vietnam policy. Now he was addressing Kissinger at a public conference:

You have said that the White House is not a place for moral philosophizing. But in fact the White House does educate the people by everything that it does and everything it says and does not say. Specifically, tonight you *are* expressing moral values when you tell us the war is trending down, and then in that connection you mention only U.S. troop presence and U.S. casualties. By your omission, you are telling the American people that they need not and ought not to care about our impact on the Indochinese people. So I have one question for you. What is your best estimate of the number of Indochinese that we will kill, pursuing your policy, in the next twelve months?

It was an unlikely trajectory. Ellsberg had spent the first half of his life as a professional Cold Warrior. As a child he'd been profoundly shocked by newsreel images of the effects of Nazi bombings on civilians; nothing seemed so purely evil. 'It was uncanny to think of humans designing and dropping on other humans a flaming substance that couldn't be easily extinguished, a particle of which, we were told, would burn through the flesh and wouldn't stop burning even then. It was hard for me to understand people who were willing to burn children like that. It still is.' Raised a liberal Democrat who worked summers in an auto plant and dreamed of becoming a labor economist, Ellsberg's political commitments were formed in the shadow of two premises. One was the equation of Hitler with Stalin – an equation he now thinks might have been valid concerning their internal policies, but wrong about their respective threats to the rest of the world. The other premise was indubitable, the prospect of a nuclear war that could make the childhood newsreels look trivial. Ellsberg determined to do whatever he could to prevent it.

That determination led the unathletic intellectual to sign up for the officers' course in the Marine Corps. After studies at Harvard and Cambridge University he enjoyed the work of a rifle platoon leader. 'I was proud to read testimony by the Marine Corps commander before Congress that the Marines had three divisions to sacrifice to prevent having to go to nuclear war. That was my idea of a good reason to serve.' He was proud to be an American during the Suez crisis, when the U.S. opposed French and English attempts to reclaim the canal. 'Nothing could have confirmed for me more dramatically that my country was committed in principle to uphold international law against aggression, even against our closest allies.' Though he was pleased by Eisenhower's decision to oppose a colonialist policy, Ellsberg wrote that he would have carried out the opposite orders with full commitment. Even for people who cared enough to understand it, policy was the president's business. That attitude, a legacy of the Second World War and the Cold War, would be undermined by Ellsberg's own work.

Like the others portrayed in this chapter, Ellsberg could have walked through his choice of open doors. After his Marine service he returned to Harvard to do research at the Society of Fellows, one of the most prestigious of Ivy League appointments. He focused on decision theory and was recruited by the Rand Corporation to develop strategies of nuclear deterrence. His work there drew the attention of the assistant secretary of defense for international affairs, who offered Ellsberg a job as special assistant. It was 1964, and Ellsberg was interested in crisis research; 'Vietnam is one crisis after another, it's one long crisis,' the assistant secretary promised. Ellsberg took the job, with principal responsibility for understanding Vietnam and a very high security clearance. The rest is history.

Ellsberg's version of that history offers penetrating analysis of the way mechanisms of secrecy and contempt feed on each other and undermine democratic practice. A typical day found his boss shouting out an assignment: 'Bob [McNamara] is seeing the press at 8:30. We have ten minutes to write six alternative lies for him.' Ellsberg scribbled out yellow notepads for his boss to run down to the defense secretary. Minutes later the assistant secretary was back. 'Bob liked those. He wants four more. We have five minutes.' Very quickly, Ellsberg concluded,

It became clear to me that journalists had no idea, no clue, even the best of them, just how often and how egregiously they were lied to … Once I was inside the government, my awareness of how easily and pervasively Congress, the public, and journalists were fooled and misled contributed to a lack of respect for them and their potential contribution to policy. That in turn made it easier to accept practices of secrecy that fooled them further and kept them ignorant of the real issues that were occupying and dividing inside policy makers. Their resulting ignorance made it all the more obvious that they must leave these problems to us.

His years in the government led to other insights into how ordinary, hardworking people with decent intentions become accomplices to mass murder. For one thing, they work too hard. The norm was seventy-hour work weeks where everything was a crisis, and everything had a deadline; several participants in the Cuban Missile Crisis said it was almost relaxing to have a crisis so important you could concentrate on nothing but that one for thirteen whole days. 'All this was exciting. Both the incredible pace and the inside dope made you feel important, fully engaged, on an adrenaline high most of the time. Clearly it was addictive.' As an amateur magician and juggler, Ellsberg was impressed with the process as art form, 'but I asked myself more than once: Can they really get away with decision making like that?' It was an atmosphere that drew Ellsberg into gathering data to persuade the president to follow a course he considered disastrous – systematic bombing in retaliation for a North Vietnamese attack – but he had no time to reflect on the consequences. It was late at night, and the job had to be finished by eight in the morning. Gathering data in such circumstances led to gruesome forms of giddiness. 'The district chief had been disemboweled in front of the whole village, and his wife and four children had been killed too. "Great! That's what I want to know! That's what we need! More of that. Can you find other stories like that?"'

There was plenty of cognitive failure, too. Ellsberg describes what he calls institutional antilearning mechanisms that reinforced government ignorance: the rapid turnover, the lack of interest in history, the unwillingness to record mistakes that Sarah Chayes noted in Afghanistan forty years later. 'You Americans have not been fighting this war for seven years,' a Vietnamese friend told him. 'You have been fighting it for one year, seven times.' Few Americans with a hand in policy had experience on the ground. But the problem was conceptual as well: Ellsberg and his colleagues were working with a framework that prevented them from acknowledging the magnitude of what they were doing. He was struck by the observation of an Indian woman who worked for Gandhi's movement that she came from a culture without a concept of enemy. 'A strange statement,' recalls Ellsberg,

> Hardly comprehensible. No concept of enemy? How about concepts of sun and moon, friend, water? I came from a culture in which the concept of enemy was central, seemingly indispensable – the culture of Rand, the U.S. Marine Corps, the Defense and State departments, international and domestic politics, game theory and bargaining theory . . . To try to operate in the world of men and nations without the concept of enemy would have seemed as difficult, as nearly inconceivable as doing arithmetic, like the Romans, without a zero.

The other side of that equation was the importance of the concept of loyalty. Every government interaction was ruled by the attempt to do what was best for your boss, the man who hired you. Ellsberg watched his colleagues put that principle above every other, and for years he did the same. Embarrassing one's boss was the worst form of betrayal, and if avoiding that meant giving presidential advice you knew to be wrong, well, so much the worse for the country. In turn, presidents could rely on subordinates to cover for their lies, out of a mixture of loyalty and commitment to their own careers. Help your friends and hurt your enemies: No other moral code had force.

All these ways of thinking, or not thinking, contributed to

produce a situation that was grotesquely absurd: Virtually no one in the government supported the war, but no one was willing to take measures to stop it. By early 1968, one Pentagon official told Ellsberg, 'There are exactly three people in this government who believe in what we're doing: [national security advisor] Walt Rostow, [secretary of state] Dean Rusk, and the president.' What kept thousands of others silent? All the forces described above, but Ellsberg describes one more that was at least as crucial: the fear of embarrassment. The conflicts he felt over taking part in his first public demonstrations were conflicts about that. Tempted to join his new friends holding a vigil to support a war resister on his way to jail, Ellsberg was torn. He admired the resister, but knew that his colleagues would see his participation as a total sacrifice of dignity and insider status for an action of no consequence – surely explicable only as a fit of madness.

> You were making a spectacle of yourself, being a public nuisance, in front of people who didn't count for much themselves and felt free to ignore you. If you were going to confront the state with a public stand, it seemed hard to imagine a lower-status or less effective way to do it. The views of my fellow officials and consultants were mine as well. If you had nothing better to do with several hours of your time than to try to change the minds of a few dozen random pedestrians by handing them leaflets, you must be very powerless indeed. The thoughts 'Why are we doing this? What am I doing here?' seemed at first as visible on my forehead as the signboards my neighbors were carrying. I felt ridiculous.

The feeling passed as he stood on the sidewalk at the Philadelphia vigil, and Ellsberg felt suddenly lighthearted, exhilarated. It was a reaction he later came to see in others, and it felt like liberation.

> This simple vigil, my first public action, had freed me from a nearly universal fear whose inhibiting force, I think, is very widely underestimated. I had become free of the fear of appearing absurd, of looking foolish, for stepping out of line.

The road to Philadelphia had been anything but lighthearted, for Ellsberg had tried every way of working that an insider could. If he was disturbed by the degree of lying that took place in government service, he also had done his share of it. Some lies, he had decided, were clearly the right ones. At a time when U.S. military assumptions included planning for a nuclear first strike in Asia, Ellsberg learned that McNamara was completely opposed to it. As secretary of defense, however, McNamara felt bound to support U.S. policy by giving routine assurances to NATO about U.S. readiness to strike. Ellsberg viewed this as an instance of the secretary's wisdom and street savvy, his ability not just to have the right policies but to achieve them; had his secret opposition become public, McNamara could have been removed by Congress or the Joint Chiefs of Staff. Ellsberg himself worked the system for all it was worth. When Nixon was elected, he was willing not only to draft military strategies for Kissinger, but to provide political advice for how to realize them. It was crucial, he thought, that Nixon disavow the war as the Democrats' quagmire very early; otherwise Nixon would be identified with policies he could no longer retract. Unsurprisingly, the Democrats were appalled at Ellsberg's suggestion that stopping the killing was more important than political gain, and no Democratic senator was ready to help him.

One of Ellsberg's last attempts at inside influence was a remarkable speech he made in private to Kissinger in late December 1968, when Kissinger was about to take office as national security advisor. Ellsberg gave him the advice Ellsberg wished he'd been given before he received the security clearances that changed his way of thinking, for he understood their effects. First, you feel exhilarated by access to information you never even knew existed. Almost as quickly, you feel like a fool: for having analyzed these subjects for years without a clue about information this crucial, for having worked daily with people who did have access and kept the secrets so well. But once you get used to your new access to whole libraries of hidden information, you are aware of the fact that you have it and others don't – and view anyone else as a fool to whom you, in turn, are bound to lie.

In effect, you will have to manipulate him. You'll give up trying to assess what he has to say. The danger is, you'll become something like a moron. You'll become incapable of learning from most people in the world, no matter how much experience they may have in their particular areas that may be much greater than yours ... I ended by saying that I'd long thought of this kind of secret information as something like the potion Circe gave to the wanderers and shipwrecked men who happened on her island, which turned them into swine. They became incapable of human speech and couldn't help one another find their way home. Kissinger could be a good listener, and he listened soberly. But I knew it was too soon for him to appreciate fully what I was saying. He didn't have the clearances yet.

Less than a year later Ellsberg was opening the top-secret safe in the corner of his office in the Rand Corporation to take out the first of the forty-seven volumes he'd decided to copy. It was a violation of the code of honor he'd held all his life, and only the growing realization of how deeply the U.S. had violated a higher code led him to it. What had looked like a problem, and then a mistake, now looked like mass murder – yes, murder, for the evidence that it was long-standing, deliberate, and premeditated was there in the secret studies that even Ellsberg, as a high-security official at the Defense Department, had had no access to read. Now he hoped that the information, made public, would support the growing efforts of the antiwar movement to force the government to withdraw. The increasing resistance and the willingness of people to go to jail was influencing him profoundly; he also had begun to read Gandhi and King and Thoreau on the philosophy and practice of nonviolent direct action. Just as important, the lessons he had learned a few years earlier in Vietnam itself had gathered shape. Not wanting to confine his research to the Defense Department, Ellsberg spent two years in Vietnam as a foreign service officer. With the one U.S. official willing to leave the safety of helicopters and canned information, he had traveled the roads to every province in the country, accompanying troops through muddy rice paddies and jungle ambushes. It was after one of those expeditions that an analogy first occurred to him. 'By any chance,' he asked the young black radioman resting beside him, 'do you ever feel like the redcoats?' 'Without hesitating a beat the radioman said, in a drawl, "I been thinking that . . . all . . . day." You couldn't miss it if you'd gone to grade school in America.'

Before long Ellsberg was making other analogies. A meeting of the Vietnam establishment at the Council on Foreign Relations looked to him 'like the defense dock at Nuremberg. The difference was that none of us had yet been indicted.' Was the analogy appropriate? Ellsberg had encouraged a journalist to ask Kissinger if there were any circumstances that would lead him to leave the government and oppose its policy. Kissinger's first answer was no, but on being pressed he replied that he would leave if the government had plans for gas chambers. Ellsberg responded: 'For Henry Kissinger there is exactly one crime against humanity that he can recognize as such, and it's happened already, it's in the past. It was done by Germans, against Jews. That's the only political act he can conceive as being unquestionably immoral.' At the time Ellsberg knew nothing of conversations being taped in the White House that were finally released in 2002; they contain samples like this one:

President: How many did we kill in Laos?

Ziegler: Maybe ten thousand – fifteen?

Kissinger: In the Laotian thing, we killed about ten, fifteen . . .

President: See, the attack on the North that we have in mind . . .
power plants, whatever's left – petroleum, the docks . . . And, I still think we ought to take the dikes out now. Will that drown people?

Kissinger: About two hundred thousand people.

President: No, no, no . . . I'd rather use the nuclear bomb. Have you got that, Henry?

Kissinger: That, I think that would just be too much.

President: The nuclear bomb, does that bother you? ... I just
want you to think big, Henry, for Christsakes ... For once,
we've got to use the maximum power of this country ...
against this *shit-ass* little country: to win the war.

Secretly copying seven thousand pages in the days when photo-
copiers were slow was drudgery, but Ellsberg had knottier problems to consider as he worked through the night. He no longer
cared about losing the access and status he had worked to achieve;
it had all become the mark of a war criminal. But releasing the
documents would compromise friends he had worked with for
many years, who would pay a steep professional price for their past
associations with him. For himself, he was reckoning on prison for
the rest of his life, and he worried most about his children. He could
provide them with the sort of moral example he had found in the
war resisters as an adult, but he might not be in a position to do
anything else for them as long as he lived. All that for a revelation
that might make no difference to anything at all.

Is this a story with a happy ending? Partly because of the illegal
lengths the Nixon administration was willing to go to in order to ruin
him, Ellsberg's case was dismissed by the court. Years later, the children
whose future had so worried him helped edit the book that analyzed
what had happened. But Nixon went on to launch 1.5 million tons of
bombs on Indochina – the total tonnage of U.S. bombs dropped on
Europe in the Second World War – *after* the Pentagon Papers were
published, a fact Ellsberg noted with considerable depression. Yet the
publication of the papers, and the peace movement in general, played
a role in stopping the war. Perhaps most important, they changed the
way the American public viewed the presidency. They led journalists
to go 'through the same process I had, learning the need to think for
themselves, to use their own judgments about what was right to do in a
crisis.' As Nixon's chief of staff put it the morning the papers were released:

To the ordinary guy, all this is a bunch of gobbledygook. But out
of the gobbledygook comes a very clear thing: you can't trust the

government; you can't believe what they say; and you can't rely on their judgment. And the implicit infallibility of presidents, which has been an accepted thing in America, is badly hurt by this, because it shows that people do things the president wants to do even though it's wrong, and the president can be wrong.

It's an attitude that has stayed with us. What else do we need?

Ellsberg's father often quoted a line from the Bible: 'The truth will make you free.' That line sustained Ellsberg, not just through the publication of the papers, but in the years he has spent writing and speaking against war since then. In the fall of 2004 he published a particularly poignant op-ed essay in the *New York Times*, which reminded readers that the most damning photos from Abu Ghraib were still classified. He wrote of a senator who assured him that if the Pentagon Papers had been leaked earlier, Congress would never have authorized the Tonkin Gulf Resolution that committed the U.S. to war. He ended by begging someone – someone with access – to step forward with comparable documents *before* the impending November election.

> Surely there are officials in the present administration who recognize that the United States has been misled into a war in Iraq, but who have so far kept their silence – as I long did about the war in Vietnam. To them I have a personal message: Don't repeat my mistakes. Don't wait until more troops are sent, and thousands more have died, before telling truths that could end a war and save lives. Do what I wish I had done in 1964: Go to the press, to Congress, and document your claims. The personal risks of making disclosures embarrassing to your superiors are real . . . But some 140,000 Americans are risking their lives every day in Iraq. Our nation is in urgent need of comparable moral courage from its officials.

As I write these pages, Daniel Ellsberg is publishing similar appeals about Iran.

· · · · ·

Like Daniel Ellsberg, Bob Moses earned his place in the history books. Like Ellsberg, instead of settling down to rest on well-deserved laurels, he has continued to work in a way that challenges one assumption about what it means to grow up: The older you get, the more dreams you abandon. Moses, who lived for years in Tanzania, uses the Swahili word *fundi* to describe the skilled craftsmen and instructors who do just the opposite, passing on wisdom and encouragement that help build communities. As he records his debt to his own *fundis* in community organizing, the quiet, unknown motors of the civil rights movement, it's clear he sees his own place in structures that bind generations. He is careful to warn against romanticizing; the culture of change he helped build in the 1960s won't be reconstructed. 'For one thing, our kids are more aware of the obstacles.' Still, he thinks that 'one of the best things about [the U.S.] is that there's a tradition, you can actually live a life of struggle. You can have a really deep purpose in your life.'

"'Poor Bob," I thought, disheartened. "He's lost his mind."' That was the initial opinion of his colleague David Dennis when Moses began comparing algebra to the civil rights movement, and it was close to what most people thought when the celebrated organizer returned to the Harvard philosophy department to work on a Ph.D. thesis on W. V. O. Quine's philosophy of mathematics. As a student there myself at the time, I knew how remote it was from the real world Moses had succeeded in changing, and Quine was a conservative, at that. I would nod my head in deferential greeting when he left the professor's office I stood waiting to enter, but shake it right thereafter. Moses's story seemed another example of decisions that make no sense – as the professor, always happy for data to prove his thesis about the general irrationality of human nature, was first to agree. We were both completely wrong.

For lives take time to unfold. Moses's began in Harlem, where his parents encouraged him to get the education they could not. Excelling at Stuyvesant, New York's public high school for gifted students, Moses became one of the few blacks to enter the educational establishment of the fifties. His graduate study in philosophy was interrupted by his father's illness, and he returned to New York to care for his family, whom he supported by teaching at an elite private school. In 1960, pictures of the Southern sit-ins woke him up. Soon thereafter he gave up the hard-won, precarious rewards of an educated Northern black man to work in what he called the middle of the iceberg. Mississippi was the poorest and most dangerous place in America. But Moses believes that 'if you can really bring about any kind of change at the bottom it is going to change everything.'

That's what he wrote decades later about teaching algebra. To understand it is to know how he understood the civil rights movement, which is too often

> discussed as a series of protest marches. The people who really made change and the ways they effected change are not recorded in the official canon of 'civil rights history.' As a consequence, it is difficult for ordinary people to see themselves as being central to making change.

Arguing in 1964 to fellow SNCC staff members that the student-led civil rights organization should 'be above the race issue,' he maintained that it shouldn't be 'Negro fighting white, it's a question of rational people against irrational people.' During a meeting at Stanford he told students that the civil rights question was a spear-head for much deeper national questions. Those sorts of ideas might be one reason that a fellow SNCC organizer characterized him as, historian Taylor Branch reports, 'far too meekly intellectual to have the slightest chance against Mississippi segregationists.'

Moses proved them wrong with an organizing style very different from the visibly dramatic one of Martin Luther King. Moses's own kind of charisma was immense, and in a movement laced with biblical images his last name didn't hurt. (For a while he stopped using it in an effort to resist the mantle of authoritarian leadership he thought the movement should avoid.) But though his reputation for physical courage became legendary – a major head wound from white thugs did not deter him from a planned walk to register voters; he could fall asleep in an office other thugs had just ransacked – his appeal was that of the quiet in the eye of the storm. 'The thing is not how you're going to die,' he said, 'but how you're going to live.'

Working from the bottom reflects a commitment to ideals of liberation the Enlightenment itself did not achieve. But if you're determined to encourage people to take their lives in their own hands, it's the only way to go. For Moses, real progress could only come if leaders were less important than the ideas they advocated. His first mentor, Ella Baker, had taught him that people 'cannot look for salvation anywhere but to themselves.' This was literally true of voter registration. When Moses came to Mississippi, only a handful of black adults had dared register to vote. He could encourage them to do so, teach them how to navigate the bureaucratic tangle created to prevent them, and accompany them to the courthouse, but they were the ones who had to do it – take on the risks of harassment, economic ruin, and sometimes murder that registering entailed. For Moses, the process represented what all real change requires, and it was far from a one-way street. His vision of the possibilities that the barely literate sharecroppers might have was neither clouded nor posed. 'If we have any anchor at all,' he said, 'if there's any reason why we can skip around from the bottom of Mississippi to the top of the skyscrapers in Manhattan and still maintain some kind of internal sense of balance, I think a lot of it has to do with those people, and the fact that they have their own sense of balance.'

Sometimes Moses was as willing to work with cabinet officials as with sharecroppers. In 1963 he filed suit against Attorney General Robert F. Kennedy and FBI head J. Edgar Hoover in an effort to push them to enforce the federal law that makes it a crime to harass people trying to vote. Despite that law, FBI agents in Mississippi stood by idly while would-be voters were beaten and murdered. Rather than expressing rage at federal inaction, Moses called the suit a friendly attempt to prove to its targets that 'their powers are immeasurably greater than they possibly realize.' The Justice Department was not amused. Though his statement may have been wry, it was true to the organizer's lifelong goals.

Convinced that racism would not be overcome by desegregating lunch counters, where poor people could not afford to eat anyway, Moses persuaded the movement to focus on long-term political changes, which must begin by registering voters. Black people who were brutalized in the Deep South had disappeared nameless. Moses argued that white volunteers could help protect black ones and focus the nation on the struggle. Hundreds of young white students were eager for action; before going South they underwent a training program to make sure they knew what they were about to risk their lives for. Moses told them:

> Don't come to Mississippi this summer to save the Mississippi Negro. Only come if you understand, really understand, that his freedom and yours are one . . . In our country we have some real evil, and the attempt to do something about it involves enormous effort . . . and therefore tremendous risks. You have to break off a little chunk of a problem and work on it, and try to see where it leads, and concentrate on it.

And he warned

> You are not going down there to try to be heroes. You are heroes enough just going into the state . . . You have a job to do. If each of you can leave behind three people who are stronger than before, this will be 3,000 more people we will have to work with next year. This is your job.

Moses was deeply influenced by the French philosopher Albert Camus. For the organizer, racism was America's version of Camus' plague. 'The country isn't willing yet to admit it has the plague,' he told the volunteer students, 'but it pervades the whole society. Everyone must come to grips with this, because it affects us all. We must discuss it openly and honestly, even with the danger that we get too analytic and tangled up. If we ignore it, it's going to blow up in our faces.' Camus' idea that every victim is a potential executioner also struck deep chords – which led him to work to understand the source of the pestilence even in men who had beaten and tried to kill him many times.

> We are asking all white people in the Delta to do something which they don't ask of any white people any place . . . And that is to allow Negroes to vote in an area where they are educationally inferior but yet outnumber the white people and hence constitute a serious political threat. Because in every other area of the country, the Negro votes are ghettoized – the Negroes elect their leaders, but they don't elect leaders to preside over what we could call a numerically inferior but educationally superior white elite.

'It's important to struggle,' he told the poet Robert Penn Warren. 'And at the same time if it's possible, you try to eke out some corner of love or some glimpse of happiness within. And that's what I think more than anything else conquers the bitterness.'

Sally Belfrage's wonderful memoir *Freedom Summer* describes Moses as being 'like someone you only read about in novels. He has great currents of moral perplexity running through him.' Many moral judgments Moses had to make were the usual ones that confront any activist: How much compromise can you make before you lose your way entirely, how much purity can you keep before you no longer live in the world? Some of those decisions would have far-reaching consequences, like the refusal to accept a compromise the Democratic National Committee tried to force at the 1964 party convention. Moses had helped thousands of Mississippi's poorest citizens to organize an alternative delegation to the official, white supremacist one – an exercise in grassroots democracy for which they had risked their lives. The Democratic Party's refusal to seat them was the one occasion when Moses abandoned his usual reserve. As one Mississippi activist recalls,

Moses got up and spoke. It was really like listening to the Lord, I tell you it was! [Martin Luther] King had just finished some wishy-washy speech, you know. Moses could have been Socrates or Aristotle, somebody like that. I mean he tore King up. He said, 'This reasoning that you've been giving here is inaccurate. We're not here to bring politics into our morality but to bring morality into our politics.' And as Moses was finishing, King and everybody else knew the jig was up.

Some decisions were even harder to make. 'You killed my husband!' the widow of Herbert Lee, a farmer murdered for going to voter registration classes, accused Moses at the funeral, and he could not disagree; her husband 'was killed just as surely because we went in there to organize as rain comes from clouds.' Staying with the work was the only way to make any sense out of that death, he wrote later. Abandoning it would mean accepting Mississippi reality – that black people could be shot for trying to become citizens. Knowing this might ease Moses's pain, but it could not disperse it, for most days contained such decisions. Who do you urge to speak out? When does silence mean wisdom, and when does it mean complicity? Small judgments of character could affect other lives forever. Branch describes one:

A few of the boldest Amite County Negroes appeared at the nightly meetings to hear Moses talk about registration. He refrained from pressuring them, to the point of never asking whether anyone wanted to try to register. The unspoken question was left hanging. Finally, nearly two weeks after the first attempt, a farmer named Curtis Dawson volunteered to go down, and an old man known only as Preacher Knox jumped up to join him. Though their offer was applauded heartily in the meeting, Moses and Steptoe discussed it long into the night. Dawson was solid, they agreed, but Preacher Knox was flighty, voluble, and sometimes daft – given to random enthusiasms and endorsements of all opinions. Moses worried about whether it would be correct to refuse Knox's offer, and if he did, whether it would be fair to let Dawson go alone. Moses decided to take the chance on Knox.

Life and death hung on these chances, day after Delta day.

Although – or because – he had to make them daily, Moses had no more of a recipe for making the series of small judgments that add up to moral decisions than anyone else. In *God's Long Summer*, Charles Marsh writes that a paper, 'attributed to Bob Moses,' likened such situations to being in 'a boat in the middle of the ocean that has to be rebuilt in order to stay afloat. It also has to stay afloat in order to be rebuilt. Our problem is like that. Since we are out on the ocean we have to do it ourselves.' The metaphor is a good one for most difficult judgments, and anyone familiar with analytic philosophy will know where Moses found it. Quine had used it to describe the nature of knowledge, although the image was first suggested by Otto Neurath, a central figure in the Vienna Circle, which promoted logical positivism in the 1920s. Neurath would have been pleased to have his boat turn up in Mississippi, for unlike most of his colleagues, who thought sheer formal reasoning might be enough to combat the Nazis, the politically engaged Neurath spent considerable time explaining social and economic issues to uneducated Viennese. In today's Vienna, he is best known for the graphics and symbols he developed to aid in innovative forms of visual education.

Moses could scarcely have known at the time how well this string of connections foreshadowed his own future directions. The Democratic Party's response to his efforts was a terrible blow. His work in the civil rights movement was widely acknowledged as crucial, but it often put him at odds with every mainstream. He preferred local organizing to dramatic demonstrations; his focus on long-range political work like voter registration was sometimes attacked as too cerebral. His vision of the movement as a force for liberation was as universal as it was concrete. On one of the few occasions when he joined a picket line his sign read: WHEN THERE IS NO JUSTICE, WHAT IS THE STATE BUT A ROBBER BAND ENLARGED? Moses was concerned about the Vietnam War very early, despite warnings that black people should not jeopardize what had just been gained by taking on a new struggle. Moses, by contrast, saw Vietnam and segregation as aspects of the same problem. At the first organized antiwar protest in 1965 he told a crowd at the Washington monument, 'Use Mississippi not as a moral lightning rod. If you use it at all, use it as a looking glass.' The SNCC, along with much of the rest of the civil rights movement, was headed in other directions.

Partly to avoid the draft board, which was eager to punish his antiwar stance, Moses moved to Tanzania, where he and his wife taught school and began to raise four children. When he returned to Cambridge to work on his Ph.D. a decade later, his next engagement was almost an accident. His oldest child was ready to do algebra, which wasn't offered in her eighth grade class, but she rebelled against his efforts to work with her at home. So Moses went to her school and offered to teach her, along with a few other students, and developed methods to help children think mathematically in terms drawn from their lives. Concern for his daughter's education extended, in the first instance, to concern about the systematic lag in mathematical literacy between children of color and others, at a time when such a handicap would block them from better jobs down the road. Moses equates today's mathematically illiterate children to yesterday's sharecroppers. This led him to found the Algebra Project, which now has programs across the country using novel methods that have proved phenomenally successful in teaching mathematics.

But these concerns, though important, were far from the end of Moses's efforts. They were less about algebra than about empowerment – creating a culture of learning, collaborative thinking, and change. As he puts it in his book *Radical Equations*, core issues are

Who's going to gain access to the new technology? Who's going to control it? What do we have to demand of the educational system to prepare for the new technological era? What opportunities will be available for our children? These are questions that ultimately challenge power as the civil rights movement did, for that earlier movement was about more than lunch counters and ballots.

The work involved in creating the Algebra Project had none of the dangers of voter registration, but it was just as slow, quiet, and deliberate. Moses took children on tram trips to understand the concept of distance in algebra and created models based on Quine's philosophy of mathematics that children could represent. He insisted that parents, teachers, and, above all, the children themselves work together to construct the project, convinced that only by creating their own demands could the project's broadest goals succeed. He found the endless small steps it took to build the program neither boring nor banal but exhilarating.

What I was learning in my teaching was something I could not have learned in all my philosophy of math courses at Harvard, because I was learning from my students . . . We do not have enough people with a solid enough mastery of math who are so guided by their insights into the students' ways of thinking they can reconceptualize the math in terms that allow their students to connect. In fact, the culture moves people in the opposite direction. As you become more and more accomplished in the math, you become more and more distant from the students.

It's a process that echoes Ellsberg's description of the insulated thinking of national security experts. At bottom, both rest on a false conception of Enlightenment as confined to knowledge, and as a top-down procedure. That conception easily leads to the undermining of democracy – as Ellsberg analyzed or as Moses described some young people in 'a situation where they are just posturing, believing that what is important is holding office, or just being in an office, as opposed to really doing work.'

Jean-Jacques Rousseau sent his own five babies to an orphanage, while authoring the most important book ever written about raising children who will grow up to be free and independent citizens. Bob Moses and his wife raised four children, and he used the gritty business of teaching them to start a movement that went beyond anything he had planned. (The daughter whose refusal to do extra homework spawned the program decided, after graduating from Harvard, to work as a director of the Algebra Project.) Its goals are not to help black children enter the bourgeoisie – a charge Moses faced down in his earlier work on voter registration – but rather, as he puts it, to radicalize radicalism itself. It is work done to realize the vision Rousseau imagined – a vision of which, in Moses's words, even the civil rights movement itself is only an example.

> One of the valuable lessons to be drawn from the southern civil rights movement is that you have to shake free of other people's definitions of who you are and what you are able and willing to do.

And those who shake free will meet what Moses, in a letter from a county jail, called

> the deep hates and deep loves which America and the world reserve for those who dare to stand in a strong sun and cast a sharp shadow.

Cast a sharp shadow. I wrote this portrait before Barack Obama gave a 2008 interview to a journalist interested in his work as an organizer. 'What really inspired me,' said the Presidential candidate, 'was the civil rights movement. And if you asked me who my role model was at the time, it would probably be Bob Moses.'

CHAPTER THIRTEEN

MORAL CLARITY

Did Walt Disney write the ending to the Book of Job? Give or take a minor anachronism, it's hard to tell the difference. After all Job said and suffered, this is how his story ends:

> Then the Lord returned all Job's possessions, and gave him twice as much as he had before. All his relations and everyone who had known him came to his house to celebrate. They commiserated with him over all the suffering that the Lord had inflicted upon him. As they left, each one gave him a coin or a gold ring.

There follows an inventory of Job's rewards: Instead of the 7,000 sheep he began with, he now has 14,000, his 3,000 camels become 6,000, his oxen and donkeys are doubled as well. He is blessed with another batch of children, identical in number and gender to those he had before. His daughters, whose names translate as Dove, Cinnamon, and Eyeshadow, are the most beautiful women in the world and are given a share of their father's possessions, an unusual amount of privilege for the ancient world. Job lives to see his grand- and great-grandchildren and dies at a ripe old age. The message? Suffering pays. There is no injustice in the world, or anyway not for long. God is always right, and ultimately intelligible. The ending, in short, seems to ignore all the questions the rest of the book posed. That and its very conventional prose — which contrasts so starkly with the incomparable poetry of the rest of the book — led most scholars to conclude it was written by another author, probably long before the part of the book that holds readers' attention. The two parts, it is thought, were stitched together after heated debates over whether to include the book in the Bible at all. But the addition that was needed to satisfy earlier readers can leave modern ones feeling cheated: How can the author raise the deepest questions just to leave us hanging on such a wisp of an answer?

For without the happy ending the story is terrifying. A man of perfect integrity is put through torture after torture, and when he finally breaks down to ask why, he gets no answer. Because of Job's service, or perhaps his persistence, God deigns to put in an appearance, but it's only to let out a blast. *Why? You little bit of fribble, you want to know why? Because that's the way the world is!* Of the thousands of attempts over centuries to make Job's torment seem intelligible, one Jewish legend is particularly striking: It compares Job's reaction on the ash-heap to Abraham's at Sodom: 'Addressing God, Abraham said, "That be far from Thee to do after this manner, to slay the righteous with the wicked." Job exclaimed against God, "It is all one, therefore I say, He destroys the innocent and the wicked." Abraham was rewarded for this and Job was punished for it, for Abraham said it with due deliberation; Job spoke intemperately.'

Good grief. Job's sin was rhetorical tactlessness? True, Abraham's tactics were more effective: Holding someone to high expectations is more persuasive than expressing your disappointment. But it's easier to weigh all your words when your body isn't pain-racked, and you haven't just lived through the death of your children. This reading reveals little more than the lengths some will go to evade the truth that Job tells us: The world is not the way it ought to be.

When we look for moral clarity, what we often get is kitsch. Unable to bear the alternatives, earlier eras read Job's story as one or another of his friends do. There is sense in Job's suffering, and the suffering will bear fruit so sweet as to make it worth all the pain. The sense comes in two forms: Either Job has sinned in some way – a view held by authors as late as William Blake, who found Job's piety too mechanical – or Job is being tested. Either way, the friends promise, he'll be redeemed in the end:

> You will see your children flourish like grass
> You will die at the height of your powers
> And be gathered like ripe grain.

The ending seems crafted to show this. Who cares if we don't understand? Sheer and willful ignorance is better than what we're given at the start of the story. Surely God couldn't have punished Job just to win a bet with Satan?

Kitsch, wrote Milan Kundera, is the absolute denial of shit. In his novel *The Unbearable Lightness of Being*, the Czech author goes on to define kitsch more exactly as a categorical agreement with being as such: Whatever is, is right. The discussion occurs during a scathing description of a Prague May Day parade:

> As a group approached the reviewing stand, even the most blasé faces would beam with dazzling smiles, as if trying to prove they were properly joyful, or to be more precise, in proper agreement. Theirs was an agreement with being as such . . . The unwritten, unsung motto of the parade was not *Long live Communism!* but *Long live life!*

Kitsch portrays a world where providence always works: Evil is always punished and good is always rewarded, death is never tragic and life is always fair. There is no problem of evil; the *is* and the *ought* may tremble momentarily, but they always embrace in the end. Is this what we should glean from the story of Job?

Yet God Himself proclaims that Job spoke the truth about Him. In fact, He is angry with Job's friends because they did not. This is the only question left in an ending that looks tacky without it. The fairytale conclusion is denied by none other than the One who should know. What could it mean to say that Job spoke the truth – or as God's Voice from the Whirlwind puts it even more perplexingly, 'Am I wrong because you are right?'

I want to untangle something about moral clarity by sketching a reading that gives both God and Job their due. My thoughts here, as often, were prompted by Kant's – in this case Kant's description of Job's friends as a priori theologians, even inquisitors. Their claims are as dogmatic as those of Dr. Pangloss: The universe is ordered, its Creator is just. Claims like that are fine as expressions of reason's demands on the world, but the friends confuse them with statements, and make them without a bit of attention to experience. That attention is provided by the Voice from the Whirlwind, whose speech is sheer description – glorious description of the way the world is. Job looks at the world and asks where justice is. The Voice tells him the place of everything else. Has God missed the point, or is something even more sinister going on? Does the Voice have more to offer than a particularly poetic version of the idea that might makes right, or if you're the one who made the world you can run it however you please?

That's the way Hobbes read it, and it's worth thinking about why he named his two major works, *Leviathan* and *Behemoth*, after the monsters mentioned in the Book of Job. Though the last few decades have produced a rich body of scholarship intent on showing that his work was more complex than both critics and defenders assume, readers have showed remarkably little curiosity about why Hobbes did so. Some scholars believe Hobbes identified the friends of Job with his own opponents, the scholastic theologians who sought religious justification for political authority; God's rebuke of them is a way of saying, *He is too vast and mysterious to be bothered with political philosophy.* Thus Hobbes's use of Job is part of his argument for the separation of church and state. But the way Hobbes read *Job* sheds even more light on his moral and political philosophy, so his biblical references deserve further attention. For Hobbes, *Job* is a defense of the standpoint that God is beyond ethical reasoning; that's just what it means to be God. For when Job asks God to explain His justice, God responds by describing His power. Was Job present at the Creation? Could he make a beast like Behemoth, or catch the Leviathan like a fish? As *Leviathan* states: 'And Job, how earnestly does he expostulate with God for the many afflictions he suffered, notwithstanding his righteousness? This question in the case of Job is decided by God Himself, not by arguments derived from Job's sin, but His own power.'

Like his contemporaries, Hobbes refused to contemplate the possibility that Job's suffering was unjustified. His focus is not really Job but God; more particularly, the justification of sovereign power. Human sin and other doctrinal complexities are here irrelevant; events like Job's tragedy need no other justification than a reference to God's might. But God, for Hobbes, was mostly metaphor. Here's his own explanation for the strange title *Leviathan*:

> Hitherto I have set forth the nature of man, whose pride and other passions have compelled him to submit himself to government; together with the great power of his governor, whom I compared to leviathan, taking that comparison out of the two last verses of the one-and-fortieth of Job; where God, having set forth the great power of Leviathan, calleth him king of the proud. 'There is nothing,' saith he, 'on earth to be compared with him. He is made so as not to be afraid. He seeth every high thing below him; and is king of all the children of pride.'

This authority is amoral, based on sheer might: Only an absolute sovereign has power enough to ignore the monster's flaming breath, his spiked belly, his teeth cracking iron the way you crack straw.

Once again, I think Hobbes was wrong, and the reasons take us back to the differences between Hobbesian and Kantian worldviews with which we began. To see this, we must read the Book of Job as dialectic: God's statement as a reiteration of realism, the friends representing idealism in all its callow forms. If the Voice from the Whirlwind is the sheer assertion of reality, while the friends put forth the simple claims of reason, what does Job represent? I believe he's the claim that the two should come together. Confusing *ought* with *is*, the friends refuse to see that the world does not exhibit the moral categories we demand. Job *is* truly innocent, his suffering truly unjust. The Voice from the Whirlwind doesn't even address these questions; His focus is on Being or Creation as such. It is whole, it is awesome, it is riven through and through with order. Job's voice is needed to remind us that the moral order that comes from reason needs to be in the world as well.

Does this mean that the world is flawed? At the least, it's incomplete. Many traditions hold that God created us to make it whole. The Jewish theologian Joseph Soloveitchik believed God deliberately made the world imperfect to leave room for human creativity. The Persian poet Hafiz wrote: 'The burden is too heavy for heaven / And I, the fool, was chosen to carry it.' We might prefer an omnipotent Creator, but truth is not about what we prefer. If Job's claim is the claim that reality should become reasonable, both God and Job can speak truth: One tells it like it is, one tells it like it should be.

Both seek truth in details. The friends' dogma commits them to general claims – 'Your crimes must be inconceivable' – that would fit the truth of Job's pain to their theories. Job, by contrast, points out exactly how he understands goodness, and what he's done to show it. Just a bit of his final speech:

> If I ever neglected the poor
> Or made the innocent suffer
> If I ever abused the helpless
> Knowing that I could not be punished
> Let my arm fall from my shoulder
> And my elbow be ripped from my socket!
> If I ever trusted in silver
> Or pledged allegiance to gold
> If I ever boasted of my riches
> Or took any credit for my worship
> If I laughed when my enemy fell
> Or rejoiced when suffering found him
> If I ever covered my crimes
> Or buried my sins in my heart
> Afraid of what people thought
> Shivering behind my doors

If there's a better description of righteous living I'd like to see it.

Humility is one of Job's virtues. He isn't looking to understand the whole world, just one crucial bit of it. For though he begins, like most of us, with his own case, Job's indictment is universal. Perhaps it took his own suffering to make him notice the world's injustice, but now his outrage is general. What a world we inhabit! The poor wander like herds of cattle, picking up scraps for their children. The wicked, by contrast, prosper; not even their cows miscarry, and they lie back in comfort, watching their grandchildren skip like lambs. We are born with a sense of justice the world does not meet. Those who tell us not to see the world in human terms ignore the fact that that's just what we're made to do. At his most provocative, Job lashes out at God:

> Man who is born of woman
> How few and harsh are his days!
> And must *You* take notice of *him*?
> Must *You* call *him* to account?
> Look away; leave him alone
> Grant him peace, for one moment

I take Job to be saying that God can't have it both ways. If God has a plan for a universe of which we're an insignificant part, then why not just leave us alone? Leaving us alone would mean leaving us without moral categories. *Let us be part of nature and be torn apart like the prey the vulture feeds its children, but do not tear us apart with the particularly human pain of guilt, and outrage, and all they imply. On the other hand, if You're going to give us those categories and demand we maintain them, You have to be fair: Reflect them, somehow, in the structure of the universe.* This could be called a covenant.

When God finally appears to Job, His first line – 'Where were you when I planned the earth?' – seems like mere one-upmanship. But read on:

Who laid down its cornerstone
While the morning stars burst out singing
And the angels shouted for joy!
Were you there when I stopped the waters,
As they issued gushing from the womb?
When I wrapped the ocean in clouds
And swaddled the sea in shadows?
When I closed it in with barriers
And set its boundaries, saying
'Here you may come, but no farther
Here shall your proud waves break.'
Have you ever commanded morning
Or guided dawn to its place
To hold the corners of the sky
And shake off the last few stars?

In words of more wonder than any in the Bible, the Voice from the Whirlwind gives voice to Creation. Genesis merely tells us it was good; here it is great, and teeming. There are stars and thunder, mud and ice; lionesses feeding cubs aching with hunger and horses quivering before battle. There are extraordinary images of birth: antelopes panting and kneeling to bear little ones who never return, dumb careless ostriches laying eggs in the dirt. There are wildernesses blooming after rainfall and baby vultures drinking blood. Creation is full of force we cannot tame.

The speech reveals the Creator's pride, to be sure, but with language that justifies it. Life itself is a gift, when this is what it looks like, and each of us is in debt to the world for the gift of having lived in it. If Job speaks truth, as God admits, the truth may be this one: There is no moral order in the world as it is, and there ought to be some. If God speaks truth, as Job admits, it may be to say that creating moral order in the world is just what we're meant to give back to it. If there's going to be reason in the world, it is we who have to put it there.

This conclusion can be so alarming that most of us scramble to avoid it. Like the Voice from the Whirlwind, Hobbes stayed focused on the *is*: the world is structured in relations of power, so why look for anything else? Those unwilling to accept the thought of nature's stout indifference to the gulf between justice and its opposite tried one way or another to deduce some *ought* from our *is*. If God isn't going to tell us how to live right, isn't there something – perhaps biology – that will do so instead? In the reading I've sketched here, the answer is no. The book of Job's most important message is that morality is neither a divine category nor one reflected in nature; morality is – ought to be – human. Human attempts to construct moral order are always precarious: If righteousness too often leads to self-righteousness, the demand for justice can lead to one guillotine or another. Job's final humility reminds us of our fragility, as his last words are a dark reminder of the dust and ashes to which we go.

In this reading God is angry at the friends for offering false coin, moral simplicity where moral clarity is what's needed instead. Whatever else you may need to get clarity, you must start with open eyes. Without truth there can be piety, but no reverence; blind faith in Creation is not what this Creator wants. The friends remember the sparrow whose fall is gently guided, but not the foolish ostrich and the craggy vulture. The friends keep their eyes on softly rolling meadows, but Creation contains an abyss. Unlike kitsch, moral clarity is hard to come by. It means working to make sense of things you do not even want to acknowledge. It often means not knowing if you ever get it right.

Long live life makes no sense as it stands – which is why Kundera calls it an idiotic tautology. Perhaps this is what Job means when he rejects his friends' words as 'dusty answers.' If there is an answer to the problem of evil, it cannot be offered in prose: Something about prose is inadequate, even blasphemous, because it is insufficiently awed by the task. *Long live life* makes sense as music, which can render expressions that words cannot reach. (Was this why medieval Europe made Job the patron saint of musicians?) Very great poetry may do it as well – for example, that of the Voice from the Whirlwind.

If life is a gift, then the more you partake in it, the more you show thanks. If the alternative is inertia, outrage against injustice may keep you alive. Through grace or through struggle, some people resist inertia better than others. Odysseus, we saw, is one of them; Job is another. Where his words catch fire, his friends' are merely dusty, rote babble about experience they've never taken up and lived. Dogma – ideas uninformed by experience – is a form of ingratitude.

No reading of a classic text is ever decisive. But the fact that this reading is possible is one Enlightenment achievement. Frederick the Great thought *Candide* was Job in modern dress. As we saw in chapter 6, readers before the Enlightenment could not take Job's part. Taking his part means accepting the split of the modern: between *ought* and *is*, between justice and power. Where happiness and virtue are out of joint they need to be repaired – not by working on your own demands for reparation, but by going to work on the world. Our first impulse is not to condemn Job but to hear him. This is moral progress.

Naturally there were those who recognized injustice, or took up the cause of the underdog, before the Enlightenment, and plenty who failed to do so long after. But there's a difference between a world that produces libraries full of books to prove that Job was really guilty, or at the very least impatient, and a world that's ready to listen. The first is a world that accepts injustice as given, and probably deserved, and the second is one that is able to work to stop it. Neither Genghis Khan nor Hernándo Cortez nor King Leopold of Belgium nor Harry Truman lost sleep over the civilians their troops butchered. Even Voltaire took his time to condemn torture. Of course, acknowledging the reality of injustice is never enough. The death of innocent bystanders has been seen as a crime since Sodom, but Afghan children will be buried beneath some bombed-out ruin between the time I write these words and the time you read them. There is something appalling about the way we both accept it.

Biblical texts are ideal for learning about moral clarity – not because they make it easy but precisely because they don't. Examining them shows that clarity, like other virtues, is never a given, but something to be achieved – although, like other virtues, seldom for very long. The tension between complexity and clarity is what gives the Book of Job, in particular, its unmatched power. Job is shot through with clarity like flashes of lightning that leave you fumbling in the darkness when they're gone. Making sense of it takes work, and time, to undo the knots of happy endings that pack things up neater than life ever comes. His friends were lacking in patience, not Job: the patience to grapple with real questions before running for the cover of simple solutions.

Indeed, in some stories God Himself looks confused. At Sodom and Gomorrah, He seems loath to accept a general principle of justice, making Abraham propose number after number before inexplicably stopping at nine. Are they portable or disposable? In the Book of Job God seems positively muddled. Even if we ignore the bet with Satan, He appears as evasive or unable to distinguish between moral and nonmoral discourse. Job asked about the *ought*; God told him about the *is*. If not even God is always able to reach clarity, who are we to try?

We are finite and fallible and struggling, and we are nonetheless the source of moral reasoning. That lesson is one thing the two biblical tales have in common. Although (or because) they are the most memorable passages where God and men speak together, God's message is largely that we are on our own. We are the ones who give moral guidelines body and life. You can take, if you will, your solace in heaven, but you must work out your ethics on earth. Working them out will involve the complex and prosaic distinctions we saw demonstrated. God might have answered Abraham differently: *Save Sodom for the sake of fifty? Next you'll be letting the whole town go scot-free!* Instead He leads us through a series of tedious steps that show the need for judgment. Negotiating small differences is part of being grown up; no one can tell you in advance where to put your foot down.

Moments of moral clarity are rare in life, and they are exceed-
ingly precious. They usually follow upon hours – years – of
moral confusion; they seldom arrive all at once or definitively;
and they are never accompanied by a lifetime guarantee.

Those words were written by conservative moralist and former
Secretary of Education William Bennett in a little book called *Why
We Fight: Moral Clarity and the War on Terrorism*. He is right on every
count here, though the conclusions he went on to draw were muddy
enough to prove his point more ironically than he could have intended.
Still Bennett's general point is valid: Moments of moral clarity *are*
rare, and precious, and never guaranteed. They are also very short.
They serve as touchstones for something, but not daily policy.
Inspiration is not the same as clarity, which is rarely so bright.

As the world struggles to regain its composure in the wake of
the Bush administration, the revulsion toward striving for clarity is
likely to grow. This might be that administration's very worst legacy:
As the Soviets made the world lose its taste for anything that sounds
like socialism, Bush left it suspicious of anything that sounds like
moralism. Disgust with recent abuse of the longing for moral clarity
leads many to argue we should give up the notion entirely. Life is
cloudy, equivocal, and seldom transparent, and the longing for clarity
can lead to dangerous sentimental delusions. Every attempt at moral
clarity, they claim, is an attempt to impose order on a reality that
will always elude it. The pragmatic cynicism of Nixon and Kissinger
were easier to oppose.

Job stands as a reminder that life does not inevitably reward the
just. Because the left has always acknowledged the reality of injustice, it is wary of worldviews that offer false hope. In the hands of
the young this wariness looks like reaction to anything resembling
hope at all. For many, denying a world packed with happy endings
means that only tragedy is honest; disdaining a world of infinite
harmony requires a permanent diet of dissonance.

But we cannot allow those who have perverted moral language

to dictate its terms. You may think you're rejecting their clarity, but it's just a rejection of kitsch. Kitsch is much more than a question of style; it's a preference for consolation over truth. Disney's version of reality is not just cleaned up, it's pernicious. Unlike the best forms of art and philosophy, it undercuts the possibility of transformation because it portrays a world that's just fine as it is – or as it will be by the time the credits come up.

Enlightenment heroes know that it's harder to live for – and with – ideas than to die for them, but they're prepared in the end to do both. Just like doing evil, doing good involves occasional heart-stopping opportunities. You might, like Abraham, challenge power for the sake of justice; you might, like Kant's hero, even be asked to die for it. Mostly you'll be asked to do something more challenging and less dramatic: to live for it, making small decisions every day about what that comes to. We may need great deeds for inspiration, but they shouldn't distract us from good ones. Most of these are banal – acts that can be broken down into steps that are so easy to carry out that they're hard to recognize for what they are.

What good are small steps when my life is entangled in large evils? My taxes support unjust wars, my clothes support sweatshops, my life depends on machines that produce carbon. And if I really face the fact that thousands of children die every day for lack of $2, giving less than all I have seems churlish. These doubts may be honest, but they're more likely to put you to sleep than to put you in action; often arguments that insist on immediate radical action turn into excuses for doing nothing at all. The best lives combine both the great and the good. You can work for global responses to economic inequality while also giving something of your own to make up for what your government does not. You can work to force your government to act on the environment while turning down heaters and leaving your car at home. Those are steps that reveal something about character: You are able to challenge authority *and* willing to dirty your hands with details. Signing papers in triplicate and attending dull meetings doesn't look evil either, and as Eichmann repeatedly protested, it didn't feel that way at all. But one message of his story is: *It's not about your soul.*

Recall that Eichmann's motives were as unimpressive as his actions were appalling; whether he organized mass murder out of hatred or careerism simply doesn't matter. Sometimes motives are worse than indifferent: distractions from the content, and consequence, of the actions themselves. The rush to describe the war in Iraq as the result of misplaced idealism is such a distraction – even were it true. The belief that intention is the core of moral action leads many to confuse moral clarity with purity. But if intentions are secondary in deciding whether actions are evil, they are even less important in deciding if they're good.

There is more than one danger in focusing on the character of the actor rather than the action. It can lead us to think we need not scrutinize our own actions if we are confident our intentions are good. This is a road to lethal self-righteousness, as recent American foreign policy has shown. But another danger may be even more insidious; believing that intention is the heart of an action often inclines us to discount good deeds. *Did she do it to further her career? Her fortune? To appease her fans? Confuse her parents? Expiate her guilt over earlier misdeeds?* It's another way of undermining that ends in inertia, for knowing that your own motives are less than saintly gives you no reason to suppose hers are different. How can either of you do good if your motives for doing it are a stewed-up mix of desire? The allure of purity is a threat to the possibility of genuinely good action. Kant was right to say that you know some things for certain only if you're willing to stake your life on them. What Kant makes clear, however, is that the price of this much purity is death.

Heroism that stays alive is harder to notice, precisely because it is impure, hazy, and jumbled. Ordinary goodness is fraught with veins of vanity and self-interest and above all with pleasure – because goodness makes you feel more alive. To accept that good and evil actions come from a mixture of motive and desire is not to throw up your hands, still less to hold that the bottom line is the bottom line. The desire to do good for its own sake is one of the things that keeps us going, but going in the right direction will often be banal. If the good can be banal, the banal can be good – and full of the dignity human activity can unfold. This is not a matter of modern, much less postmodern virtue. Or if it is, then the modern began long ago – when Achilles and Odysseus met in hell.

Plato's *Republic* ends with a myth in which the souls of the dead are allowed to choose new lives. Patterns of lives of every kind of animal and every kind of man and woman are spread on the ground; once chosen, lives cannot be exchanged. Thus Socrates says that the most crucial thing to learn is the difference between good and bad lives,

> to know how beauty commingled with poverty or wealth and combined with what habit of soul operates for good or for evil, and what are effects of high and low birth and private station and office and strength and weakness and quickness of apprehension and dullness and all similar natural and acquired habits of the soul, when blended and combined with each other, so that with consideration of all these things he will still be able to make a reasoned choice between the better and the worse life.

He goes on to describe the souls of great heroes: Ajax chooses to become a lion, Agamemnon an eagle. Odysseus is the last to choose and finds a pattern lying in a corner disregarded by the others – the life of a common citizen. Though Plato didn't like *The Odyssey*'s disdain for glorious deaths, he has its hero declare that he'd gladly choose a life of ordinary human possibility over any other.

If being a hero is a matter of small steps and everyday distinctions, it's hardly what it's cracked up to be.

You know what? Neither is being a grown-up.

To say this is not to suggest you should narrow your vision of either, but to view both as within your reach. Our ambivalence about the idea of the hero is mirrored by our ambivalence about the idea of growing up. Real heroes rarely see themselves as such

– and as long as you live, grown-ups remain what the other folks are. As we saw in the beginning, realism and maturity are thought to go together, combining to convince you that the more you know of life, the less you should expect of it. To grow up, some say, is to listen to doors of possibility closing behind you. That view is not just a poignant expression of failure but a skewed product of hindsight; children's possibilities are in fact quite constrained. Adolescent options are expanding, but rarely enough for them to know it. Few things are more insidious than Western culture's blasted message that the cusp between childhood and maturity is the best time of your life. In suggesting that everything afterward will be a disappointment, it prepares you to demand nothing.

But to accept boredom in exchange for security is to let yourself be cheated. Here what passes for maturity is not only resignation, but regression as well – back to the schoolchild's rote copying of the lessons her teachers deliver. Real grown-ups, like Abraham, stand ready to call any teacher into question.

But however many limits we allow ourselves to question, one limit is final: All of us are mortal.

Vitality is not the denial of mortality, but the grown-up way of facing it. The only lesson Odysseus learned in the land of the dead was the value of life itself.

ACKNOWLEDGMENTS

· · · · · · ·

This book began at the suggestion of my brother, Adam Neiman, as we sat bewildered in Boston on the morning of November 3, 2004, trying to understand what had happened to the world. He urged me to write something. Something became a book proposal in the hands of Sarah Chalfant, under whose warm, wise, and tough guidance this book took shape. Without her, it wouldn't exist – only one of many reasons I'm so grateful to have her as my literary agent. Dominic Bonfiglio was a superb research assistant, knowing which references I needed and how to find the perfect example to support a point, as well as pushing me to strengthen arguments at several junctures. In addition to her day job as publisher, Becky Saletan made time to be a wonderful editor, who left alone the things that were finished and forced me to rework the things that were not. Later, Dan Hind's careful reading as well as his own writing helped me think through several important points, which led to real improvement in the second edition.

Versions of several chapters were read as the Thomas More Lecture in Amsterdam, the Simone Weil Lectures in Sydney and Melbourne, and talks at the Collège International de Philosophie, Dartmouth, The New School for Social Research, the Salk Institute, Yale, and the Einstein Forum. I am grateful to audiences at all these places for making me think harder. The Institute for Advanced Study at Princeton was an ideal refuge in which to wander between old commentaries on *The Odyssey* and the latest Republican scandals; this book could not have been written without a year of the institute's support. In addition, many people offered comments on different parts of the book: Doron Ben-Atar, Dan Brudney, Antonia Handler Chayes, Lorraine Daston, Eva Illouz, Tony Judt, Jeremy Bendik Keymer, Robert Pippin, James Ponet, Martin Schaad, Michael Walzer, and Shira Wolosky. I am blessed to have such thoughtful and generous friends. Still my greatest debt is to Felix de Mendelssohn, who was the first to read every chapter, often in several drafts. While I have succeeded only in answering some of his criticisms, I have profited from all of them – as from his steadfast enthusiasm and encouragement.

My first lessons in moral clarity came from my mother, Judith Chayes Neiman, who helped desegregate the public school system of Atlanta, Georgia, where I was a child. She taught me that ordinary people with good will and guts can change the world. This book is dedicated to her.

BIBLIOGRAPHICAL NOTES

. . . .

In the interests of reaching the broadest possible audience I have dispensed with most scholarly apparatus, including footnotes. Instead, for readers interested in tracing sources cited or following arguments further, I offer those references not given directly in the text here. The bibliography that follows lists, in addition to sources quoted directly, books from which I learned, often through profound disagreement, while working on this one.

. . . . .

Introduction. For most of the biblical discussions I have followed the translation of Robert Alter, *The Five Books of Moses*. I have also used the Jewish Publication Society's translation of the *Tanakh*, and the Union of American Hebrew Congregations' *The Torah: A Modern Commentary*. For the Book of Job I have largely relied on Stephen J. Mitchell's translation. For extra-biblical glosses on the story of Sodom and Gomorrah I relied on Bialik and Ravnitzky's *The Book of Legends* as well as Louis Ginzberg's *Legends of the Jews*. The Brecht quote comes from his *Die Dreigröschen Oper*; the Yeats quote from his equally famous 'The Second Coming.' Kierkegaard's reading of Abraham at Mount Moriah can be found in his *Fear and Trembling*. Plato's most sustained discussion of piety can be found in his *Euthyphro*. Kant's most famous discussion of lying is found in his *Groundwork of the Metaphysics of Morals*, which should be tempered by his different discussion of the same subject in his *Metaphysics of Morals*. Richard Dawkins's central statement of his view of altruism can be read in his *The Selfish Gene*; the concession mentioned was made to me in discussion at the conference Beyond Belief at the Salk Institute in La Jolla, California, in November 2006. Michael Walzer's description of the left's failure to offer a general picture was quoted from his essay 'All God's Children Got Values' in the spring 2005 issue of *Dissent*.

Chapter 1. Quotations from Hobbes are taken from his treatise *Leviathan*. Despite great recent interest in Hobbes's work, few scholars discuss his use of the Book of Job or the reason for the titles of his major works. Noel Malcolm's 'The Name and Nature of *Leviathan*' (*Intellectual History Review* 17, 2007) was the notable exception, but it did not, unfortunately, treat the issues here in any detail. Robert Kagan's much-discussed 2003 *Of Paradise and Power* was used for quotation in the first half of this chapter; his 2006 *Dangerous Nation* is the source of the Kagan quotes in the latter half. Kagan's changing views – unremarked by himself or major reviewers – nicely reflect the changing views of the White House, which E. J. Dionne called 'the freedom shuffle' in his *Washington Post* column of January 25, 2005. Tony Judt's remarks were taken from his essay 'America and the World' in the *New York Review of Books*, April 10, 2003. For a detailed account of the U.S. treatment of the International Criminal Court see, for example, David J. Scheffer's 'Staying the Course with the International Criminal Court' (*Cornell International Law Journal*, 2002). The enthusiastic European references to America as the realization of the Enlightenment are only a few of those which can be found in Commager, *The Empire of Reason*. Grover Cleveland's remarks on the takeover of Hawaii were made in a speech to Congress on December 18, 1893. The remark about reality-based communities was originally quoted in the *New York Times Magazine* of October 17, 2004; the *NYTM* of June 26, 2006, was the source of the essay 'Who Are Americans to Think That Freedom Is Theirs to Spread?' by Michael Ignatieff that is quoted here.

Chapter 2. William Safire's December 24, 2006, column in the *New York Times Magazine* was devoted to the question of realism, as was George Packer's November 27, 2006, column in the *New Yorker*. I used Paul Shorey's translation of Plato's *Republic*, supplemented by a helpful explanation from Heinrich von Staaden. Carl Schmitt's views on the relationship between politics and morality are summarized in his book *The Concept of the Political*. See Jan Werner Mueller's *A Dangerous Mind: Carl Schmitt in Postwar European Thought* for an English discussion of his work, but also Raphael Gross's *Carl Schmitt and the Jews*. I quoted from the first chapter of Bernard Williams' *Truth and Truthfulness* on the tediousness of deflationary rhetoric. Alan Wolfe's *Moral Freedom* offers a useful exploration of contemporary American moral attitudes; in a very different vein, I have also made use of William Bennett's *Book of Virtues* as well as his *Why We Fight: Moral Clarity and the War on Terrorism*, along with his books for children on heroism and virtue. Trotsky's *Their Morals and Ours* is a good statement of reductionist views of morality common to many Marxists. For an excellent account of Kantian voices in socialist thought see Harry van der Linden, *Kantian Ethics and Socialism*, where this and other of Edouard Bernstein's quotes can be found. All quotations from Foucault were taken from the collection *Power/Knowledge*, except for the televised debate with Chomsky, available on YouTube. Of the many discussions of Foucault I particularly profited from James Miller's *The Passion of Michael Foucault*. See also Michael Walzer's critique in his *Company of Critics*, and Alexander Nehamas's discussion in his *The Art of Living*. Richard Rorty's remarks about the Foucauldian left were taken from his *Achieving Our Country*. Martha Nussbaum's 'The Professor of

Parody' was published in the February 22, 1999, issue of *The New Republic* and deserves rereading. Anthony Grafton's remarks were made to me in conversation. Joseph Nye's book *Soft Power* was the source of all Nye quotes. For Cornel West's views of racial versus moral reasoning see his *Race Matters*; for Stephen Carter's critique of the assumption that racial identity determines political identity see his *Reflections of an Affirmative Action Baby*. Todd Gitlin's *Letters to a Young Activist* were quoted in this chapter; see also his *Intellectuals and the Flag*. Ian Buruma's book *Murder in Amsterdam* was quoted on the shift in European political discussion; see also, for example, Frits Bolkestein, 'Building a Liberal Europe in the 21st Century' (Walter Eucken Institut, 2000). A good, nonideological definition of ideology can be found in David Gauthier's paper 'The Social Contract as Ideology' (*Philosophy and Public Affairs*, 1977). Richard Rorty's essay 'The Continuity Between the Enlightenment and "Postmodernism"' in Baker and Reill, *What's Left of Enlightenment?* is the source of the quote about Derrida.

Chapter 3. Kant's gallows (or brothel) example is found in his *Critique of Practical Reason*, whose final chapter also contains a related discussion of heroism. Arendt's remark was quoted from her essay 'Organized Guilt and Universal Responsibility' in the collection *Essays in Understanding*, edited by Jerome Kohn. Cornel West's remark was made at A Conference on Evil: Dialogue Among Psychoanalysts, Philosophers and Theologians, sponsored by the Metropolitan Center for Mental Health in New York, April 2005. Scott Atran's views are quoted from his papers 'The Moral Logic and Growth of Suicide Terrorism' (*Washington Quarterly*, volume 29, spring 2006), 'Global Network Terrorism' (briefing to National Security Council, White House, 2006) and 'Sacred Bounds on Rational Resolution of Violent Political Conflict' (*Proceedings of the National Academy of Sciences*, 2007). Barbara Ehrenreich's quote appeared in her article 'The Faith Factor,' which appeared in the November 29, 2004, issue of *The Nation*. Marx's opium analogy originally appeared in his 'Critique of Hegel's *Philosophy of Right*,' as did the claim about religion that follows it here.

Chapter 4. J. G. Ballard's belief that Hurricane Katrina revealed the collapse of the Enlightenment was expressed to an interviewer for *Die Zeit* and published September 8, 2005. For a thorough historical account of the Lisbon earthquake and its aftermath see T. D. Kendrick's *The Lisbon Earthquake*. Wendy Doniger's discussion of witches was taken from her article 'Agony and Apostasy,' from the *New York Times* of April 19, 1987. For Heinrich Heine's views of Kant and Robespierre see Part Three of his wonderful, and wonderfully flawed, *History of Religion and Philosophy in Germany*. Carlyle's discussion of heroes was taken from his *On Heroes, Hero-Worship and the Heroic in History*.

Chapter 5. I quoted Edmund Burke's *Reflections on the Revolution in France*; the Goethe citation was taken from Ernst Cassirer's *Kant*. On the relation between philosophy and revolution see Jonathan Israel's *Radical Enlightenment: Philosophy and the Making of Modernity*. Walter Benjamin's short and trenchant Kant commentary can be found in his essay '*Dialoge über die Religiosität der Gegenwart*,' published in volume two of his *Gesammelte Werke*. My reading of Kant is based on his three *Critiques* as well as the fifteen popular essays he wrote for the *New York Review of Books* of his day, the *Berlinische Monatsschrift*. Good studies of Kant fill libraries, and lives, and there are many from which to choose. Those interested in further explanation of the interpretation offered here should see my *Evil in Modern Thought* or, for even more detail, my *The Unity of Reason*.

Chapter 6. Steven Vicchio's three-volume history of the reception of the Book of Job is a rich guide to 2,000 years of Job interpretation. Voltaire's noxious but interesting reading of Job can be found in his *Philosophical Dictionary*, as can a variety of his remarks about happiness. For a discussion of what Saint-Juste might have meant by his claim see Raymond Geuss, 'Happiness and Politics.' Rousseau's comments on Voltaire's views of happiness occur in a never-answered letter to the older philosopher dated August 18, 1756. Leibniz's thoughts on repeating one's life can be found in his *Theodicy*. For Herder's description of Kant I used the translation provided by Lewis White Beck in his introduction to Kant's *Critique of Practical Reason*. The song 'Satisfied Mind' was written by Jack Rhodes and Red Hayes, and recorded by, among others, Johnny Cash and Bob Dylan. Kant's important analysis of the difference between his views and Stoicism is located in the *Critique of Practical Reason*. All of the quotes concerning Rousseau's conception of happiness were taken from Book IV of *Emile*. Adam Smith's remark comes from *The Theory of Moral Sentiments*. Captain James Cook's *Journals* are a great source of information on eighteenth-century attitudes about universalism as well as about happiness. The quote from Lessing comes from his *Die Erziehung des Menschengeschlechts*.

Chapter 7. For Isaiah Berlin's summary of the views he attributes to the Enlightenment see, for example, 'The First Attack on Enlightenment' in his *The Roots of Romanticism*. Rorty's views of what he calls the philosophical as opposed to the political Enlightenment are summarized in his 'The Continuity Between the Enlightenment and "Postmodernism"'. The quote from Peter Gay was taken from his two-volume history of the Enlightenment, still a great source for further study. Lorraine Daston's *The Claims of Order* is a superb discussion of the history of Western inclinations to draw moral conclusions from nature. Spinoza's classic critique of religion is found in his *Theologico-Political Tractatus*. For Donald Brown's studies see his *Human Universals*. Rousseau's discussion of fear was taken from *Emile*; Al Gore's from *The Assault on Reason*. Gilbert Ryle's critique of the picture of human beings as ghosts in machines can be found in his *The Concept of Mind*. The quote from Sharon Begley was taken from 'How the Brain Revises Itself' in *Time* magazine, January 19, 2007. Daniel Gilbert was quoted from his *Stumbling on Happiness*. For Kant's discussion of reason and the garden of Eden see his essay 'On the Conjectural Beginning of Human History.' Trotsky's optimism about human capabilities was expressed in his *Literature and Revolution*. D'Holbach's views are quoted in Gay's *Enlightenment*, volume one, chapter one. Rousseau's attack on Eurocentrism can be found in his notes to the second *Discourse*. Sade's gruesome parodies of eighteenth-century anthropology occur, at more length than most will stomach, in his novel *Juliette*. For Kant's discussion of the Categorical Imperative see his *Groundwork of the Metaphysics of Morals*. His problematic final essay is 'On the Supposed Right to Lie from Altruistic Motives.' For more on fuzzy concepts see Stephen Pinker's *How the Mind Works*. John Dewey's related discussion was taken from his *Human Nature and Conduct*, Cardozo's from his *The Nature of the Judicial Process*. Stephen Toulmin's exploration of Montaigne, Descartes, and much else can be found in his *Cosmopolis*.

Chapter 8. Hume's famous treatment of miracles can be found in section ten of his *Enquiry Concerning Human Understanding*. Voltaire's dialogue between the Jesuit and the Chinese emperor was taken from Peter Gay's *Voltaire's Politics*, which was also the source for the otherwise unidentified Voltaire quotes in this chapter. The full text of Pope's reference comes from his *Essay on Man*: 'All this dread ORDER break – for whom? For thee? Vile worm! Oh madness! Pride! Impiety!' Kant's discussion of the purity of Jewish monotheism occurs in his *Critique of Judgment*. Voltaire's brief discussion of Sodom occurs in the *Philosophical Dictionary* under the entry 'Jews.' Hume's deathbed thoughts on religion were described in a moving account by James Boswell. Kant's account of rational faith is best stated at the end of the *Critique of Practical Reason*, but see also the essay 'What Is Orientation in Thinking?' Hume's brilliant attack on the argument from design, and the notion of providence, can be found in his *Dialogues Concerning Natural Religion*; see also his *Natural History of Religion*. Kant's remark about King David occurs in his *Religion Within the Limits of Reason Alone*. For more on the Pantheism Controversy, see my *The Unity of Reason*; the original documents were collected by Henrich Scholz as *Die Hauptschriften zum Pantheismusstreit zwischen Jacobi und Mendelssohn*. Stephen Jay Gould's *Rocks of Ages* was the source for his statement on the independence of science and religion. The suggestion to send Bach into space was made by Lewis Thomas in his *Lives of a Cell*. I took Rush Limbaugh's statement about the environment from his *The Way Things Ought to Be*. On gratitude, I quoted Hume, *A Treatise of Human Nature*. Kant's discussion of the subject is found in his *Metaphysics of Morals*; Georg Simmel's remark was made in his 'Faithfulness and Gratitude,' which can be found in *The Sociology of Georg Simmel*. Nietzsche introduces the madman, with his account of the death of God, in his early work *The Gay Science*, for which I quoted Walter Kaufmann's translation.

Chapter 9. Pierre Bayle's view of the essence of human history is repeated throughout his *Historical and Critical Dictionary*. Rousseau's description of the arts and sciences as garlands of chains occurs in his *Discourse Concerning the Sciences and the Arts*; his *Discourse on the Origins of Inequality* records his determination to set aside the facts. For Lévi-Strauss on Rousseau see the former's *Tristes Tropiques*. Rousseau's replies to the readers of his *Discourses* are published in the fine edition prepared by Victor Gourevitch, the source of Rousseau's remark about doctors and patients. Jane Starobinski's excellent study of Rousseau, *Transparency and Obstruction*, provides more enlightenment than reasons for disagreement. *Good Natured* is the source of the quotes about Frans de Waal's work. The quote from V. S. Ramachandran was found in Gore's *The Assault on Reason;* the one from Mencius is in de Waal's *Good Natured*. All quotes from Alexander Pope are from his *Essay on Man*. David Brooks's conclusions about Rousseau and Hobbes were taken from his *New York Times* column of February 18, 2007. For Engels on Darwin see Lewontin's *Biology as Ideology*. Illouz's arguments can be found in her *Saving the*

Modern Soul. Clifford Geertz's remarks on sociobiology were quoted from his November 30, 1995, *New York Review of Books* article 'Culture War.' I took the N. T. Wright quote from his *Evil and the Justice of God.* Vivian Gussin Paley's story was taken from her book *The Kindness of Children.* Moreno-Ocampo's remarks were found in an article by Elizabeth Rubin in the *New York Times Magazine* of May 4, 2006. All quotes by Lynn Hunt are taken from her *Inventing Human Rights.* I quoted Alexander Nehamas' *The Art of Living* on Foucault, and Jean Améry's essay 'Michel Foucaults Vision des Kerker-Universums' in the collection *Der integrale Humanismus.*

Chapter 10. In reading *The Odyssey* I relied on the translations by Robert Fagles and Robert Fitzgerald; since I don't read Greek, I've tried to triangulate between them for poetic sense rather than linguistic faithfulness. Occasionally I consulted older translations, particularly that of Alexander Pope, in search of understanding the ways in which Odysseus was viewed by the Enlightenment. My understanding of the history of readings of *The Odyssey* was greatly furthered by William G. Thalmann's *The Odyssey: An Epic of Return.* See also Seth L. Schein's *Reading the Odyssey: Selected Interpretive Essays*; Martha Nussbaum's 'Transcending Humanity' in her *Love's Knowledge*; and Laura M. Slatkin's 'Homer's Odyssey' in Foley's *A Companion to Ancient Epic.* Apart from the *Dialectic of Enlightenment,* Thalmann's book was the source of the quotes that attack Odysseus. Hegel's discussion of heroes and their valets occurred in his *Phenomenology of Spirit,* but the original quote is attributed to the seventeenth-century Parisian *salonière* Madame Bigot de Cornuel. The miniature scandal at the Leibniz Book Fair took place in February 2004. Jan Philipp Reemtsma's remarks on Benjamin Wilkomirski were made in a lecture held at the Einstein Forum's conference on victims in June 2006; for more information on this case see David Ganzfried, ed., . . . *alias Wilkomirski: Die Holocaust-Travestie.* For Améry's remark see his 'Resentments,' published in English in the book *At the Mind's Limits.* Rousseau's *Emile* is the source of the claim that we do not know what our nature permits us to be. For the story of the nonviolent resistance in the Rosenstrasse see Nathan Stolzfus's *Resistance of the Heart.*

Chapter 11. Harald Welzer's studies of ordinary Nazi brutality were published in his *Täter: Wie aus ganz normalen Menschen Massenmörder Werden.* Quotes from Hannah Arendt are taken from her *Eichmann in Jerusalem*; those of Philip Zimbardo, from his *The Lucifer Effect,* which is also the source of the citations of Stanley Milgram. For further discussion by Todorov see his *Facing the Extreme.* Paul Krugman's *New York Times* column from August 29, 2003, was the source of this quote. The record of Bush's attempted jokes about the trifecta is available in the records of the office of the White House press secretary. They were also the subject of articles by Paul Krugman and Jonathan Chait. John McCain's take on the Beach Boys is available on YouTube. Richard Rorty compared the effect of 9/11 on the United States to the effect of the Reichstag burning on Germany at an Einstein Forum conference on terror and justice in March 2003. Diane McWhorter's 'The N Word' is a bold and careful argument for the legitimacy of such comparisons. The description of Bush's 2003 visit to Gorée Island is based on interviews I made on a visit to the island a year later; outside of Senegal, only *L'Humanité* recorded the incarceration of local residents during the presidential visit. Jean Améry's analysis of torture can be found in his essay 'On Torture' in *At the Mind's Limits*. For Margalit's discussion of humiliation see his *The Decent Society*. Seymour Hersh's reports on Abu Ghraib were published in the *New Yorker*. The Human Rights Watch report is quoted by Zimbardo, as is the report from the journal *Torture*. Lawrence Wright's argument on the role of torture in radicalizing Islamicists is taken from his *The Looming Tower*. On the Nazis' use of American racism to excuse their own crimes see Koonz, *The Nazi Conscience*. For more on Einstein's political engagement see my 'Subversive Einstein' in Galison, Holton, and Schweber, *Einstein for the 21st Century*. Glenn Greenwald's views can be found in his book *A Tragic Legacy*.

Chapter 12. David Shulman's book *Dark Hope* is the source of all citations about him and Ta'ayush. Sarah Chayes's book *The Punishment of Virtue* was used for most of the quotations concerning her; I also relied on interviews with her and with Tony Schwalm. On Daniel Ellsberg, see his book *Secrets*, as well as his op-ed article in the *New York Times* of September 28, 2004. Robert Moses's book *Radical Equations* was the main source of material about him. In addition, I also drew on Taylor Branch's *Parting the Waters* and *Pillar of Fire*, and especially Sally Belfrage's *Freedom Summer*.

BIBLIOGRAPHY

· · · · · · ·

Alter, Robert. *The Five Books of Moses: A Translation With Commentary*. New York and London: W.W. Norton and Co., 2004.

Améry, Jean. *Der integrale Humanismus*. Stuttgart: Klett-Cotta, 1985.

Améry, Jean. *Jenseits von Schuld und Sühne*. Stuttgart: Klett-Cotta, 1966.

Améry, Jean. *Weiterleben – aber wie?* Stuttgart: Klett-Cotta, 1982.

Anders, Gunther and Claude Eatherly. *Burning Conscience: The Guilt of Hiroshima*. New York: Paragon House, 1989.

Anderson, Perry. *The Origins of Postmodernity*. London, New York: Verso, 1998.

Arendt, Hannah. *Eichmann in Jerusalem: A Report on the Banality of Evil*. New York: The Viking Press, 1964.

Arendt, Hannah. *Essays in Understanding*. New York: Schocken Books, 2003.

Arendt, Hannah. *On Revolution*. London: Penguin Classics, 2006.

Atran, Scott. 'The Moral Logic and Growth of Suicide Terrorism,' *Washington Quarterly*, volume 29, spring 2006.

Atran, Scott. 'Global Network Terrorism,' briefing to National Security Council, White House, 2006.

Atran, Scott, Jeremy Ginges, Douglas Medin, and Khalil Shikaka. 'Sacred Bounds on Rational Resolution of Violent Political Conflict,' *Proceedings of the National Academy of Sciences*, volume 104, 2007.

Baker, Keith Michael and Peter Hanns Reill (eds.). *What's Left of Enlightenment? A Postmodern Question*. Stanford, California: Stanford University Press, 2001.

Bayle, Pierre. *Historical and Critical Dictionary: Selections* (introduction, translation and notes by Richard H. Popkin). Indianapolis: The Bobbs-Merrill Company, 1965.

Belfrage, Sally. *Freedom Summer*. Charlottesville: The University Press of Virginia, 1965.

Bellah, Robert. *Beyond Belief: Essays on Religion in a Post-Traditional World*. Berkeley, Los Angeles, and London: University of California Press, 1970/1991.

Bellah, Robert N. and Richard Madsen, William M. Sullivan, Ann Swidler, Steven M. Tipton. *Habit of the Heart: Individualism and Commitment in American Life*. Berkeley, CA, London: University of California Press, 1985/1996.

Bennett, William J. (ed.). *The Book of Virtues: A Treasury of Great Moral Stories*. New York: Simon and Schuster, 1997.

Bennett, William J. *Why We Fight: Moral Clarity and the War on Terrorism*. Washington, DC: Regnery Publishing, 2002.

Berlin, Isaiah. *The Roots of Romanticism*. Hardy, Henry (ed.). Princeton, NJ: Princeton University Press, 1999.

Berlin, Isaiah. *The Sense of Reality: Studies in Ideas and Their History*. New York: Farrar, Strauss and Giroux, 1996.

Bernstein, Richard J. *The Abuse of Evil: The Corruption of Politics and Religion since 9/11*. Cambridge, UK: Polity Press, 2005.

Bialik, Hayim Nahman and Yehoshua Hanna Ravnitzky. *The Book of Legends*. New York: Schocken Books, 1992.

Bork, Robert H. *Slouching Towards Gomorrah: Modern Liberalism and American Decline*. New York: HarperCollins, 1996/2003.

Boyers, Robert et al. (eds.). 'Kitsch,' *Salmagundi: A Quarterly of the Humanities and Social Sciences*, Winter/Spring 1990. Saratoga Springs, NY: Skidmore College.

Branch, Taylor. *Parting the Waters*. New York: Simon and Schuster, 1988.

Branch, Taylor. *Pillar of Fire*. New York: Simon and Schuster, 1998.

Bromwich, David. *Politics by Other Means: Higher Education and Group Thinking*. New Haven and London: Yale University Press, 1992.

Bronner, Steven Eric. *Reclaiming the Enlightenment: Toward a Politics of Radical Engagement*. New York: Columbia University Press, 2004.

Brown, Donald. *Human Universals*. New York: McGraw-Hill, 1991.

Burke, Edmund. *Reflections on the Revolution in France*. London: Penguin Classics, 1976.

Burner, Eric R. *And Gently He Shall Lead Them: Robert Parris Moses and Civil Rights in Mississippi*. New York: New York University Press, 1994.

Buruma, Ian. *Murder in Amsterdam: The Death of Theo van Gogh and the Limits of Tolerance*. London: The Penguin Press, 2006.

Carlyle, Thomas. *On Heroes, Hero-Worship and the Heroic in History*. UK: Kessinger – reprint des Originals: Chicago: A.C. McClurg and Co., 1897.

Carter, Jimmy. *Our Endangered Values: America's Moral Crisis*. New York: Simon and Schuster, 2005.

Carter, Stephen L. *Civility: Manners, Morals, and the Etiquette of Democracy*. New York: HarperCollins, 1998.

Carter, Stephen L. *Reflections of an Affirmative Action Baby*. New York: Basic Books, 1991.

Chayes, Sarah. *The Punishment of Virtue: Inside Afghanistan After the Taliban*. New York: The Penguin Press, 2006.

Commager, Henry Steele. *The Empire of Reason: How Europe Imagined and America Realized the Enlightenment*. London: Phoenix Press, 1977/1978.

Cook, James. *The Journals*. London: Penguin Books, 1999/2003.

Damasio, Antonio. *Descartes' Error: Emotion, Reason, and the Human Brain*. London: Penguin Books, 1994.

Darnton, Robert. *George Washington's False Teeth: An Unconventional Guide to the Eighteenth Century*. New York and London: W. W. Norton and Co., 2003.

Daston, Lorraine. *The Claims of Order*. Cambridge, MA: Harvard University Press, 2008.

Dawkins, Richard. *The Selfish Gene*. Oxford, Oxford University Press, 1989.

Dean, John W. *Conservatives Without Conscience*. New York: Viking, 2006.

De Waal, Frans. *Good Natured: The Origins of Right and Wrong in Humans and Other Animals*. Cambridge, MA, and London, England: Harvard University Press, 1996.

De Waal, Frans. *Primates and Philosophers: How Morality Evolved*. Princeton and Oxford: Princeton University Press, 2006.

Diderot, Denis. *Political Writings*. Mason, John Hope and Robert Wokler (eds.). Cambridge, UK: Cambridge University Press, 1992.

Easterbrook, Greg. *The Progress Paradox: How Life Gets Better While People Feel Worse*. New York: Random House, 2004.

Ellsberg, Daniel. *Secrets*. New York: Viking, 2002.

Emmons, Robert A. and Michael E. McCullough. *The Psychology of Gratitude*. Oxford: Oxford University Press, 2004.

Etzioni, Amitai. *From Empire to Community*. New York: Palgrave Macmillan, 2004.

Etzioni, Amitai. *The New Golden Rule: Community and Morality in a Democratic Society*. New York: Basic Books, 1996.

Etzioni, Amitai. *Security First: For a Muscular, Moral Foreign Policy*. New Haven and London: Yale University Press, 2007.

Fish, Stanley. *Is There a Text in This Class? The Authority of Interpretive Communities*. Cambridge, MA, and London: Harvard University Press, 1980.

Foley, J. M. (ed.). *A Companion to Ancient Epic*. Oxford: Blackwell, 2003.

Foucault, Michel. *Politics, Philosophy, Culture: Interviews and Other Writings, 1977–1984*. Kritzman, Lawrence D. (ed.). New York and London: Routledge, 1988.

Foucault, Michel. *Power/Knowledge: Selected Interviews and Other Writings, 1972–1977*. Gordon, Colin (ed.). New York: Pantheon, 1980.

Ganzfried, David, ed. . . . *alias Wilkomirski: Die Holocaust-Travestie*. Berlin: Jüdische Verlagsanstalt, 2002.

Gauthier, David. 'The Social Contract as Ideology.' *Philosophy and Public Affairs*, 1977.

Gay, Peter. *The Enlightenment: The Rise of Modern Paganism*. New York and London: W. W. Norton and Co., 1966.

Gay, Peter. *The Enlightenment: The Science of Freedom*. New York and London: W. W. Norton and Co., 1969.

Gay, Peter. *Voltaire's Politics: The Poet as Realist*. 2nd ed. New Haven and London: Yale University Press, 1988.

Geuss, Raymond. 'Happiness and Politics.' *Arion: A Journal of Humanities and the Classics*, 2002.

Gilbert, Daniel. *Stumbling on Happiness*. New York: Vintage, 2005.

Ginzberg, Louis. *The Legends of the Jews, Volume I*. BiblioBazaar, 2007.

Ginzberg, Louis. *The Legends of the Jews, Volume II*. BiblioBazaar, 2007.

Gitlin, Todd. *The Intellectuals and the Flag*. New York: Columbia University Press, 2006.

Gitlin, Todd. *Letters to a Young Activist*. New York: Basic Books, 2003.

Gordon, Daniel (ed.). *Postmodernism and the Enlightenment: New Perspectives in Eighteenth-Century French Intellectual History*. New York and London: Routledge, 2001.

Gore, Al. *The Assault on Reason*. New York: Penguin Books, 2007.

Gould, Stephen Jay. *Rocks of Ages: Science and Religion in the Fullness of Life*. New York: Ballantine Books, 1999.

Gray, John. *Al Qaeda and What It Means to Be Modern*. Kent: Faber and Faber, 2003.

Gray, John. *Enlightenment's Wake: Politics and Culture at the Close of the Modern Age*. New York: Routledge, 1997.

Gray, John. *Heresies: Against Progress and Other Illusions*. London: Granta, 2004.

Gray, John. *Straw Dogs: Thoughts on Humans and Other Animals*. London: Granta, 2002.

Greenwald, Glenn. *A Tragic Legacy: How a Good vs. Evil Mentality Destroyed the Bush Presidency*. New York: Crown Publishers, 2007.

Gross, Raphael. *Carl Schmitt and the Jews: The 'Jewish Question,' the Holocaust, and German Legal Theory*. Madison: University of Wisconsin Press, 2007.

Grossman, Lt. Col. Dave. *On Killing*. New York and Boston: Back Bay Books, 1995.

Hacking, Ian. *The Social Construction of What?* Cambridge, MA, and London: Harvard University Press, 1999.

Hannity, Sean. *Deliver Us from Evil: Defeating Terrorism, Despotism, and Liberalism*. New York: HarperCollins, 2004.

Harrison, Lawrence E. and Samuel P. Huntington (eds.). *Culture Matters: How Values Shape Human Progress*. New York: Basic Books, 2000.

Hartman, David. *A Living Covenant: The Innovative Spirit in Traditional Judaism*. Woodstock, VT: Jewish Lights Publishing, 1997.

Heine, Heinrich. *Sämtliche Schriften: Schriften 1831–1837*. Pörnbacher, Karl (ed.). Frankfurt/Main: Ullstein, 1981.

Himmelfarb, Gertrude. *One Nation, Two Cultures: A Searching Examination of American Society in the Aftermath of Our Cultural Revolution*. New York: Vintage, 1999/2001.

Himmelfarb, Gertrude. *On Looking into the Abyss: Untimely Thoughts on Culture and Society*. New York: Vintage Books, 1994.

Himmelfarb, Gertrude. *The Roads to Modernity: The British, French, and American Enlightenments*. New York: Alfred A. Knopf, 2004.

Hobbes, Thomas. *Human Nature and De Corpore Politico*. Oxford and New York: Oxford University Press, 1994.

Hobbes, Thomas. *Leviathan*. London: Penguin Classics, 1968 (1651).

Horkheimer, Max and Theodor W. Adorno. *Dialektik der Aufklärung*. Frankfurt/Main: Fischer, 1969.

Hume, David. *Dialogues and Natural History of Religion*. J. C. A. Gaskin, ed. Oxford: Oxford University Press, 1998.

Hume, David. *Enquiries Concerning Human Understanding and Concerning the Principles of Morals*. L. A. Selby-Bigge and P. H. Nidditch, eds. Oxford: Oxford University Press, 1975.

Hume, David. *A Treatise of Human Nature*. L. A. Selby-Bigge, ed. Oxford: Oxford University Press, 1967.

Hunt, Lynn. *Inventing Human Rights: A History*. New York and London: W. W. Norton and Co., 2007.

Huntington, Samuel. *The Clash of Civilizations and the Remaking of World Order*. New York: Simon and Schuster, 1996.

Illouz, Eva. *Saving the Modern Soul: Therapy, Emotions, and the Culture of Self-Help*. Berkeley, Los Angeles, and London: University of California Press, 2008.

Israel, Jonathan I. *Enlightenment Contested: Philosophy, Modernity, and the Emancipation of Man 1670–1752*. Oxford: Oxford University Press, 2006.

Israel, Jonathan I. *Radical Enlightenment: Philosophy and the Making of Modernity 1650–1750*. Oxford: Oxford University Press, 2001.

Jewish Publication Society. *Tanakh*. Philadelphia and New York, 1985.

Juergensmeyer, Mark. *Terror in the Mind of God: The Global Rise of Religious Violence*. Berkeley, Los Angeles, and London: University of California Press, 2003.

Kagan, Robert. *Dangerous Nation: America's Place in the World from Its Earliest Days to the Dawn of the Twentieth Century*. New York: Alfred A. Knopf, 2006.

Kagan, Robert. *Of Paradise and Power: America and Europe in the New World Order*. New York: Vintage Books, 2003/2004.

Kahneman, Daniel, Ed Diener, and Norbert Schwarz (eds.). *Well-Being: The Foundations of Hedonic Psychology*. New York: Russell Sage Foundation, 1999.

Kant, Immanuel. *Kritik der praktischen Vernunft*.

Kant, Immanuel. *Kritik der reinen Vernunft*.

Kant, Immanuel. 'Über die Unmöglichkeit jeder zukünftige Form der Theodizee.'

Kant, Immanuel. 'Was heisst Aufklärung?'

Katznelson, Ira. *Desolation and Enlightenment: Political Knowledge After Total War, Totalitarianism, and the Holocaust*. New York: Columbia University Press, 2003.

Kendrick, T. D. *The Lisbon Earthquake*. London: Methuen, 1956.

Kierkegaard, Søren. *Fear and Trembling*. New York: Penguin Books, 2005.

Kimball, Roger. *The Long March: How the Cultural Revolution of the 1960s Changed America*. San Francisco: Encounter Books, 2000.

Konner, Melvin. *The Tangled Wing: Biological Constraints on the Human Spirit*. New York: Henry Holt and Co., 2002.

Koonz, Claudia. *The Nazi Conscience*. Cambridge, MA: Harvard University Press, 2004.

LaHaye, Tim and Jerry B. Jenkins. *Glorious Appearing: The End of Days*. Wheaton, Illinois: Tyndale House Publishers, 2004.

Lewis, C. S. *The Complete C. S. Lewis*. San Francisco: HarperCollins, 2002.

Lewontin, R. C. *Biology as Ideology: The Doctrine of DNA*. New York: Harper-Collins, 1992.

Lewontin, R. C., Steven Rose and Leon J. Kamin. *Not in Our Genes*. New York: Pantheon Books, 1984.

Limbaugh, Rush. *The Way Things Ought to Be*. Thorndike, ME: G. K. Hall and Co., 1992.

Lindberg, Todd (ed.). *Beyond Paradise and Power: Europe, America and the Future of a Troubled Partnership*. New York and London: Routledge, 2005.

Locke, John. *A Letter Concerning Toleration*. Tully, James H. (ed.). Indianapolis: Hackett Publishing Company, 1983.

Lorenz, Konrad. *Das sogenannte Böse. Zur Naturgeschichte der Aggression*. München: dtv, 1983, 2004 (original 1963).

Malcolm, Noel. 'The Name and Nature of *Leviathan*.' *Intellectual History Review* 17, 2007.

Margalit, Avishai. *The Decent Society*. Cambridge, MA, and London: Harvard University Press, 1996.

Margalit, Avishai. *The Ethics of Memory*. Cambridge, MA, and London: Harvard University Press, 2002.

Marsh, Charles. *God's Long Summer: Stories of Faith and Civil Rights*. Princeton: Princeton University Press, 1997.

Marx, Karl. 'Critique of Hegel's *Philosophy of Right*,' in Kamenka and Marx, *The Portable Marx*. New York: Viking Penguin, 1983.

McCarthy, John C. (ed.). *Modern Enlightenment and the Rule of Reason*. Washington, DC: The Catholic University of America Press, 1998.

McWhorter, Diane. 'The N Word.' *Slate*, November 28, 2006.

Miller, James. *The Passion of Michel Foucault*. New York: Simon and Schuster, 1993.

Miller, William Ian. *The Mystery of Courage*. Cambridge, MA, and London: Harvard University Press, 2000.

Mitchell, Stephen. *The Book of Job*. New York: Harper, 1987.

Moses, Robert M. and Charles E. Cobb, Jr. *Radical Equations: Civil Rights from Mississippi to the Algebra Project*. Boston: Beacon Press, 2001.

Mueller, Jan Werner. *A Dangerous Mind: Carl Schmitt in Postwar European Thought*. New Haven: Yale University Press, 2003.

Murdoch, Iris. *Metaphysics as a Guide to Morals*. London: Penguin Books, 1992.

Nehamas, Alexander. *The Art of Living: Socratic Reflections from Plato to*

Foucault. Berkeley and Los Angeles: University of California Press, 1998, 2000.

Neiman, Susan. 'Subversive Einstein,' in Galison, Holton, and Schweber, eds., *Einstein for the 21st Century*. Princeton: Princeton University Press, 2008.

Neiman, Susan. *Evil in Modern Thought: An Alternative History of Philosophy*. Princeton: Princeton University Press, 2002.

Neiman, Susan. *The Unity of Reason: Rereading Kant*. New York: Oxford University Press, 1994.

Nussbaum, Martha. *Love's Knowledge*. New York: Oxford University Press, 1992.

Nussbaum, Martha C., ed. *For Love of Country: Debating the Limits of Patriotism*. Boston: Beacon Press, 1996.

O'Reilly, Bill. *Culture Warrior*. New York: Broadway Books, 2006.

Paine, Thomas. *Collected Writings: Common Sense, The Crisis, Rights of Man, The Age of Reason, Pamphlets, Articles, and Letters*. New York: The Library of America, 1995.

Palast, Greg. *The Best Democracy Money Can Buy*. New York: Plume, 2003.

Paley, Vivian Gussin. *The Kindness of Children*. Cambridge, MA, and London: Harvard University Press, 1999.

Pinker, Steven. *The Blank Slate: The Modern Denial of Human Nature*. New York: Penguin Books, 2002.

Pinker, Steven. *How the Mind Works*. New York and London: W. W. Norton and Co., 1997.

Plato. *The Collected Dialogues*. Hamilton, Edith and Huntington Cairns, eds. Princeton: Princeton University Press, 1961.

Plaut, Gunther, ed. *The Torah: A Modern Commentary*. New York: Union of American Hebrew Congregations, 1981.

Quartz, Steven R. and Terrence J. Sejnowski, *Liars, Lovers, and Heroes: What the New Brain Science Reveals About How We Become Who We Are*. New York: Quill, 2002.

Rorty, Richard. *Achieving Our Country*. Cambridge: Harvard University Press, 1997.

Rorty, Richard and Gianni Vattimo. *The Future of Religion*. Zabala, Santiago (ed.). New York: Columbia University Press, 2005.

Rousseau, Jean-Jacques. *The Discourses and Other Early Political Writings*. Victor Gourevitch (ed.). Cambridge, England: Cambridge University Press, 1997.

Rousseau, Jean-Jacques. *Emile or On Education* (introduction, translation and notes by Alan Bloom). New York: HarperCollins, 1979.

Sagan, Carl. *Cosmos*. New York: Random House, 1980.

Saul, John Ralston. *Voltaire's Bastards. The Dictatorship of Reason in the West*. New York: Vintage Books, 1992.

Savater, Fernando. *Amador*. New York: Henry Holt and Company, 1994.

Scheffer, David. J. 'Staying the Course with the International Criminal Court.' *Cornell International Law Journal*, 2002.

Schein, Seth L. *Reading the Odyssey: Selected Interpretive Essays*. Princeton, NJ: Princeton University Press, 1996.

Shklar, Judith N. *Ordinary Vices*. Cambridge and London: The Belknap Press of Harvard University, 1984.

Shulman, David. *Dark Hope: Working for Peace in Israel and Palestine*. Chicago: University of Chicago Press, 2007.

Simmel, Georg. *The Sociology of George Simmel*. Glencoe, IL: Free Press, 1951.

Singer, Peter. *Writings on an Ethical Life*. New York: HarperCollins, 2000.

Spiegel, Shalom. *The Last Trial: On the Legends and Lore of the Command to Abraham to Offer Isaac as a Sacrifice*. Woodstock, VT: Jewish Lights Publishing, 2007.

Stern, Jessica. *Terror in the Name of God: Why Religious Militants Kill*. New York: Harper Perennial, 2004.

Stolzfus, Nathan. *Resistance of the Heart: Intermarriage and the Rosenstrasse Protest in Nazi Germany*. New Brunswick, NJ: Rutgers University Press, 1996/2001.

Talking About Genesis: A Resource Guide. New York: Doubleday, Public Affairs Television, 1996.

Taylor, Charles. *The Ethics of Authenticity*. Cambridge, MA, and London: Harvard University Press, 1991.

Taylor, Charles. *Varieties of Religion Today: William James Revisited*. Cambridge, MA, and London: Harvard University Press, 2002.

Thalmann, William G. *The Odyssey: An Epic of Return*. Twayne Publishers, 1992.

Thomas, Lewis. *Lives of a Cell: Notes of a Biology Watcher*. New York: Penguin, 1978.

Todorov, Tzvetan. *Facing the Extreme*. New York: Henry Holt and Company, 1996.

Toulmin, Stephen, *Cosmopolis: The Hidden Agenda of Modernity*. Chicago: The University of Chicago Press, 1990.

Trotsky, Leon. *Literature and Revolution*. Russell and Russell, 1977.

Trotsky, Leon. *Their Morals and Ours: The Class Foundations of Moral Practice*. New York: Pathfinder, 1973.

Van der Linden, Harry. *Kantian Ethics and Socialism*. Indianapolis: Hackett Publishing Company, 1988.

Vicchio, Steven. *The Image of the Biblical Job: A History*. Eugene, OR: Wipf and Stock Publishers, 2006.

Voltaire. *Candide*. Daniel Gordon (ed.). Boston and New York: Bedford and St Martin's, 1999.

Voltaire. *Philosophical Dictionary: A-I* (translation, introduction and notes by Peter Gay). New York: Basic Books, 1962.

Wallis, Jim. *God's Politics: Why the Right Gets It Wrong and the Left Doesn't Get It: A New Vision for Faith and Politics in America*. New York: HarperCollins, 2005.

Walzer, Michael. 'All God's Children Got Values.' *Dissent*, spring 2005.

Walzer, Michael. *The Company of Critics: Social Criticism and Political Commitment in the Twentieth Century*. New York: Basic Books, 2002.

Walzer, Michael. *What It Means to Be an American: Essays on the American Experience*. New York: Marsilio, 1996.

Weaver, Richard M. *The Ethics of Rhetoric*. Davis, CA: Hermagoras Press, 1985.

Weaver, Richard M. *Ideas Have Consequences*. Chicago and London: The University of Chicago Press, 1948.

Welzer, Harald. *Täter: Wie aus ganz normalen Menschen Massenmörder Werden*. Frankfurt am Main: Fischer Verlag, 2005.

West, Cornel. *Democracy Matters: Winning the Fight Against Imperialism*. New York: The Penguin Press, 2004.

West, Cornel. *Prophesy Deliverance! An Afro-American Revolutionary Christianity*. Louisville, KY: Westminster John Knox Press, 1982/2002.

Williams, Bernard. *In the Beginning Was the Deed: Realism and Moralism in Political Argument*. Hawthorn, Geoffrey (ed.). Princeton and Oxford: Princeton University Press, 2005.

Williams, Bernard. *Truth and Truthfulness: An Essay in Genealogy*. Princeton and Oxford: Princeton University Press, 2002.

Wolfe, Alan. *Moral Freedom: The Search for Virtue in a World of Choice*. New York and London: W. W. Norton and Co., 2001.

Wolfe, Alan. *Return to Greatness: How America Lost Its Sense of Purpose and What It Needs to Do to Recover It*. Princeton and Oxford: Princeton University Press, 2005.

Wolfe, Alan. *The Transformation of American Religion: How We Actually Live Our Faith*. Chicago: The University of Chicago Press, 2003/2005.

Wolin, Richard. *The Seduction of Unreason*. Princeton: Princeton University Press, 2004.

Woodruff, Paul. *Reverence: Renewing a Forgotten Virtue*. Oxford: Oxford University Press, 2001.

Wright, Lawrence. *The Looming Tower: Al-Qaeda and the Road to 9/11*. New York: Alfred A. Knopf, 2007.

Wright, N. T. *Evil and the Justice of God*. Downers Grove, IL: IVP Books, 2006.

Wright, Robert. *The Moral Animal: Why We Are the Way We Are*. New York: Vintage, 1994.

Zimbardo, Philip. *The Lucifer Effect*. New York: Random House, 2007.

PERMISSIONS ACKNOWLEDGMENTS

· · · · · · ·

INDEX

· · · · · · ·

Abraham
    obedience at Mount Moriah, 13–14,
        16, 35, 105, 134, 141
    questioning of God at Sodom, 2–4,
        16–17, 18, 24, 90, 96, 134, 232,
        287, 334–5, 336, 337, 340–1, 423,
        432
    brief references, 381, 383
Abraham Lincoln Brigade, 60
Absolute Idealism, 57, 162
Abu Ghraib prison, 291, 349, 364–70,
    375–6, 377, 378, 411
Achilles, 23, 300, 303, 308–9, 312,
    328–9, 330, 333
Adam and Eve story, 167
Adorno, Theodor W., 72, 124, 290
    & Max Horkheimer: *Dialectic of
        Enlightenment*, 318–19, 329
Afghanistan, 100, 128–9, 366, 370,
    390–401
Africa, 138–9 *see also* Gorée, Senegal
Agamben, Giorgio, 67
Agamemnon, 303, 307–8, 312
Agnew, Spiro, 9
Akil, Bakari, 359
Akokolacha, 394–5
Al Qaeda, 55, 100, 199, 264, 296, 335,
    338, 357, 375, 394
Algebra Project, 419, 420, 421
Alinsky, Saul, 91

altruism, 19, 269, 270, 274, 275–6
American Philosophical Association, 5
Améry, Jean, 295, 325, 362–3, 364
Amis, Martin, 102
animals, 258, 259, 267, 268–70, 272–3
anti-semitism, 168, 232, 263
Arendt, Hannah, 97, 316, 342, 346–7,
    354, 368, 379
    Eichmann in Jerusalem, 343–4, 373
    On Revolution, 374
    Thinking, 340
Aristotle, 10, 246, 294
Ashcroft, John, 369
atheism, 17–18, 127, 227, 233, 238, 240,
    284, 285
Athena, 311
Atlantic, 399
Atran, Scott, 99–100, 101, 115
Atta, Mohammed, 229
authority, 14–15, 89–90, 110, 194–6,
    206, 335, 426
Autrey, Wesley, 382

Badiou, Alain, 70
Baghdad, 55, 376
Baker, Ella, 414
Ballard, J.G., 121, 123
Bayle, Pierre, 190–1, 209, 210, 227–8,
    233, 240, 250, 254
    Historical and Critical Dictionary, 190

Beavis and Butt-head (TV series), 251
Begley, Sharon, 201
Belfrage, Sally: *Freedom Summer*, 416
Belgrade, 139
Bellah, Robert: *Habits of the Heart*, 69
Benjamin, Walter, 158
Bennett, William, 12, 69
  *Why We Fight: Moral Clarity and
    the War on Terrorism*, 433
Berkeley, Bishop George, 151
Berlin, Isaiah, 125, 189, 190, 205
Berman, Paul, 56
Bernstein, Edouard, 72
Bernstein, Richard, 336
Bible, criticism of, 194–5, 226–7, 227–8
Bill of Rights, 40
bin Laden, Osama, 264, 335, 338, 362
Black Book of Communism, The, 343
Blackburn, Simon, 280–1
Blair, Tony, 56
Blake, William, 424
Bork, Robert, 281
  Slouching Towards Gomorrah, 279
Bougainville, Louis-Antoine de, 184
Branch, Taylor, 413, 417–18
Brecht, Bertolt, 5, 116–17
Brewster, Kingman, 25
Breytenbach, Breyten, 359
Britain, 48, 56, 127
Brooks, David, 149, 278
Brown, Donald, 198–9
Brzezinski, Zbigniew, 85, 347
Burger, Jerry, 346
Burke, Edmund, 123, 140, 152, 193
  *Reflections on the Revolution in
    France*, 146–8
Buruma, Ian, 43
Bush, George W.
  addresses and speeches, 37, 58, 86,
    106, 335–6, 355; Axis of Evil
    speech, 85, 335
  and Bin Laden, 335
  election victory of 2004, 4–5, 199
  and foreign policy statements, 37
  Greenwald on, 379

  and terrorism, 338
  trifecta remark in response to 9/11,
    353–7, 377
  and torture, 367, 369
  and unilateralism, 80
  visits Gorée, 359–62
  brief references, 30, 56, 375
  see also Bush administration
Bush administration, 21, 52, 54, 55, 57,
  80, 86, 291, 336, 338, 347, 352, 353,
  354, 357, 370, 375, 378, 433
Butler, Bishop Joseph, 20
Bybee, Jay, 369

Calas, Jean, 228–9, 291
Calypso, 300, 314–15, 317
Camus, Albert, 415, 416
capitalism, 109, 110–11
Card, Andrew, 358
Cardozo, Judge Benjamin, 217
Carlyle, Thomas, 135, 321
Carnegie Endowment for Inter-
  national Peace, 401
Carter, Jimmy, 60
Carter, Stephen, 83
categorical imperative, 157–8, 183,
  212–13
  objections to and discussion about,
    213–25
Catherine the Great, 40
Center for Cultural Decontamination,
  Belgrade, 139
Chait, Jonathan, 356
Charybdis, 309, 315
Châtelet, Madame de, 293
Chayes, Sarah, 390–401, 405
  The Punishment of Virtue, 391,
    392–3
Cheney, Dick, 30, 367, 369
children/childhood, 150, 161, 218, 258,
  259, 260, 270–1, 287–8
China, 58, 115, 209, 210–11, 274, 351,
  377
Chomsky, Noam, 74
Christian Democrats, 43

Christian fundamentalism, 103–4, 336
Christianity, 174, 210, 228–30, 231, 232, 233–4, 242, 284–5
church authority, 195, 227
CIA, 357
Circe, 306–7, 309, 315, 317
civil rights movement, 6, 68, 83, 291, 295, 413–19, 421
Civil Society, 392
Cleveland, Grover, 50
Clinton, Bill, 54, 359, 360, 361
CNN, 87, 122
Cohen, Nick, 56
Cold War, 5, 10, 24, 110–11
colonialism, 139, 209–10, 281
Commager, Henry Steele, 39–40
Communist Party, 69–70
Concord, Massachusetts, 394, 395
Condorcet, Marquis de, 41
conservatives/the right, 106, 147–8, 159
    and human nature, 279–80
    and human rights, 84
    and intellectual ideas, 9–10
    and Islamic fundamentalists, 101–2, 105
    metaphysical strands underpinning position of, 30–59, 140
    and terminology, 24
    willing to speak in moral terms, 21–2
consumerism, 114–15
Contra mercenaries, 371
Cook, Capt. James, 185–6, 187, 210, 256
    Journal of a Voyage Round the World, 185
Cortez, Hernándo, 431
Council on Foreign Relations, 409
Counterenlightenment, 78, 128, 194
Crespin, Marie-José, 360
Cuba, 42, 370
Cuban Missile Crisis, 404
cultural studies, 68
custom and habit, 143–4, 146, 149

Cyclops, 304, 305, 314, 318
cynicism, 26, 30, 101, 159, 277–8, 401

Dakar, 362
Daniels, Mitchell, 354
Danner, Mark, 55–6
    Torture and Truth, 366
Darfur, 58, 110, 351
Darnton, Robert: 'George Washington's False Teeth', 127–8
Darwin, Charles, 198, 270, 276, 281, 282, 285–6
    The Origin of Species, 266, 285–6
Darwinism/evolutionary theory, 266–7, 270, 276–8, 280, 281–2, 285–6, 288
Daston, Lorraine, 193
Dawkins, Richard, 19–20
Dawson, Curtis, 417–18
De Waal, Frans, 267–8, 269, 270, 272, 274
    Good Natured, 270
Dean, John: Conservatives Without Conscience, 5
Declaration of Independence, 51, 54
Declaration of the Rights of Man, 40
Defense Department, 37, 369, 370, 397, 401, 408
Deism see natural religion
Democratic Party/Democrats, 5, 407, 416, 418
Dennis, David, 412
Derrida, Jacques, 88, 89
Descartes, René, 145, 155, 200–1, 207, 219–20
    Principles of Philosophy, 219
    Rules for the Direction of the Mind, 219
Dewey, John, 216–17
Dickens, Charles, 321
Dickerson, John, 359
Diderot, Denis, 40, 44, 127, 192, 208, 291
    Encyclopedia, 199, 208, 233, 240

Rameau's Nephew, 192
Supplement to Bougainville's Voyage,
    184–5
dignity, 4, 98, 111, 112, 113, 117, 128,
    159, 160, 293
Dionne, E.J., 58
Doi, Takeo, 114
Doniger, Wendy, 130
Dostoevsky, Fyodor: *Notes from the
    Underground*, 222
doubt, 143
Dovlatov, Sergei, 70
D'Souza, Dinesh: *The Enemy at Home*,
    104–5

Easterbrook, Gregg, 278–9
Eastern Europe, 70, 85, 324
economic independence, 117
Egypt, 87, 377
Ehrenreich, Barbara, 103–4
Eichmann, Adolf, 94, 343, 344, 347,
    351, 434–5
Einstein, Albert, 198, 376, 382
Eisenhower, Dwight, 85, 86, 403
elections
    2004, 4–5, 53, 199
    2008, 6–9, 84
Ellsberg, Daniel, 401–11, 420
    Secrets, 401
emotions/passions, 192–3, 196, 200,
    206, 221
empiricism, 151, 152–3, 160
Encyclopedia, 199, 208, 233, 240
Engels, Friedrich, 280
England, Lynndie, 376
Enlightenment, 25, 68, 70–1, 72, 78,
    88, 102, 106, 111
    attacks on, 121–6
    and Europe, 39, 40, 43, 47–8, 49
    and fundamentalism, 128–9, 131–3,
        135–6, 137
    issues opposed by, 129–30
    problems in defining, 126–8
    and U.S., 39–40, 41, 43, 44–5, 49
    see also Enlightenment values;

    names of Enlightenment
        philosophers
Enlightenment heroes *see* heroes
Enlightenment values, 25, 119–96
    embodied in heroes *see* heroes
    happiness, 133, 163–88
    hope, 134, 252–96
    metaphysics, 131, 138–62
    reason, 133, 189–225
    reverence, 133–4, 226–51
environmentalism, 245
Enzensberger, Hans Magnus, 102
Epicureans, 174–5
Epicurus, 19
epistemology, 142, 220
ethics *see* morality
Euripides, 296, 303, 320
Europe, 23–4, 31–2, 37, 40, 42, 43, 45,
    46, 47–8, 49–50, 70, 289–90, 294
European Union, 43
evil, 150, 167, 168, 203–4, 334–80
evolutionary psychology/sociobiology,
    266–7, 273–4, 276–8, 281, 285, 286
evolutionary theory/Darwinism, 266–7,
    270, 276–8, 280, 281–2, 285–6, 288

false consciousness, 103, 116
Falwell, Jerry, 168
Farrakhan, Louis, 350
FBI, 60, 373, 414
fear, 38–9, 53, 199, 337–8
Feyerabend, Paul, 198
financial crisis, 6–7
Fischer, Joschka, 36
Fleischer, Ari, 358
Foucault, Michel, 72–4, 76, 77, 81,
    156–7, 295
    Discipline and Punish, 73–4, 290,
        295
Fragonard, Jean-Honoré, 41
France, 56, 58, 127, 290, 292
Franco, Francisco, 60
Frank, Robert, 275–6
Frank, Thomas: *What's the Matter with
    Kansas?*, 115–16

Franklin, Benjamin, 40, 41
Frederick, Chip, 369
Frederick the Great, 40, 122, 431
  Anti-Machiavel, 66
French Revolution, 9, 24, 40, 43, 78, 123, 141, 289, 293
  Burke's critique of, 146–8
Freud, Sigmund, 72, 192
Frum, David, 335
Fukuyama, Francis, 43, 52
fundamentalism see religious fundamentalism

Galileo, 198
Gandhi, Mahatma, 332, 384, 386, 405, 408
Garaudy, Roger, 359
Gauthier, David, 87
Gay, Peter, 124, 125, 191
Geertz, Clifford, 106, 282–3
Geneva Conventions, 375
Genghis Khan, 431
Germany, 8, 56, 58, 66, 97, 127, 332, 352–3
Gilbert, Daniel, 202
  Stumbling on Happiness, 174
Gilmour, Emma and Andrew, 360
Gitlin, Todd: Letters to a Young Activist, 82–3
Gitmo, 369
Global Black News, 359
globalization, 110, 115
Glucksmann, Andre, 56
Goethe, Johann Wolfgang von, 122, 142
Gonzales, Alberto, 369
good and evil, 297–437
  Enlightenment heroes, 381–421
  evil, 334–80
  moral clarity, 422–37
  The Odyssey, 299–333
Gopnik, Adam, 342
Gore, Al, 199
Gorée, Senegal, 358–62, 374–5, 377
  Institute, 138, 359

Gould, Stephen Jay, 241
Grafton, Anthony, 78
Grameen Bank, 117
Graner, Charles, 368
gratitude, 246–7, 248
Gray, John, 88, 125, 197–8, 296, 378
  Al Qaeda and What It Means to Be Modern, 264, 296
  'Back to Hobbes', 33
  Black Mass, 57
  Straw Dogs, 198
Greenwald, Glenn, 379
Grossman, David, 386
  On Killing, 370–3
Guantánamo, 365, 370, 377

Ha'aretz, 8, 386
Habermas, Jürgen, 88
Hades, Odysseus in, 307–9
Hafiz (poet), 427
Hamas, 103
happiness, 133, 163–88
Hart, H.L.A., 216
Hawaii, 50, 131–2
Hegel, Georg W.F., 57, 59, 61, 162, 296, 323
Heidegger, Martin, 80, 124, 190, 262–3
Heine, Heinrich, 135, 140, 141–2, 150
Herder, Johann Gottfried, 173
heroes, 95–6, 97–8, 135, 222, 225, 300, 318, 321–3, 325, 326–7, 328–33, 381–421, 434, 436 see also Odyssey, The
Hersh, Seymour, 365, 366
Himmelfarb, Gertrude, 41
  The Roads to Modernity, 41
Hind, Dan, 43–4, 45
  The Threat to Reason, 44
Hiroshima, 11, 342
Hitchens, Christopher, 56
Hitler, Adolph, 357, 376, 377, 402
Hobbes, Thomas
  background, 32
  and book of Job, 35–6, 425–6, 430

and evolutionary theory, 280, 281
ideas of, 32–6, 284
and progress, 289–90
and Rousseau, 257, 258, 265
U.S. politics in relation to ideas
of, 30, 31, 37, 38, 39, 44, 45,
48, 49, 53, 54, 55, 56, 57, 58,
80, 81, 281–2
brief references, 42, 61, 65, 73,
149, 191, 257, 270, 285, 373
Writings:
Behemoth, 425
Leviathan, 32, 34–6, 425–6
Holbach, Baron d', 189, 208
Holland, 127, 129
Holocaust, 11, 169, 262–4, 324, 340,
343, 350–1
Homeland Security Council, 358
Homer, 23, 64, 381
The Iliad, 300, 328, 330, 387, 388
The Odyssey, 299–321, 328–30, 436
Hoover, J. Edgar, 414
hope, 134, 252–96
Horkheimer, Max, 190
& Adorno, Theodor: Dialectic of
Enlightenment, 318–19, 329
House Armed Services Committee, 366
Hulsman, John & Lieven, Anatol:
Ethical Realism, 84–6
human nature, 147, 148, 160, 210,
252–61, 265–86
human rights, 60, 68, 84, 147, 159, 293,
376, 377
Human Rights Watch, 365, 366–7
Hume, David
as atheist, 127, 227
and attitudes to life, 171
Burke and, 146–7
and custom and tradition, 143–4,
146–7
Kant and, 142, 152, 192
and laziness, 186
and Newton, 145, 152
political conservatism, 127, 162,
227, 240

and reality, 142–3, 145, 162
and reason, 196, 200, 221, 227
and religion, 132, 226, 227, 230–1,
234, 240, 246, 250
brief references, 148, 151, 158
Writing: Of Miracles, 226
humiliation, 113, 363–4
Hunt, Lynn: Inventing Human Rights,
291, 292, 293
Hurricane Katrina (2005), 37–8, 121,
122, 123
Hussein, Saddam, 60, 199
Huxley, Thomas H., 282
hypocrisy, 67, 104, 136, 293, 374

Ibrahim, Saad Eddin, 100
ideals/idealism, 30, 117, 128, 137, 140,
203, 205, 243
discussed as one of the metaphysical strains underpinning
conservative position in U.S.,
38–57, 58–9
in relation to ideology, 60–92
and Kant, 153, 154, 156–7, 158–9,
160–2
ideas, 64, 71, 76, 77–8, 79, 91, 116,
142–3, 151, 152, 153, 154
identity politics, 82–3, 90
ideology: discussed in relation to
ideals, 60–92
idleness, 183–4, 186–7
Ignatieff, Michael, 53
Iliad, The, 300, 328, 330, 387, 388
Illouz, Eva, 279
individualism, 82
intention, 55, 341–4, 352, 435
International Court of Justice, 399
International Criminal Court, 38, 54,
290, 294
Iran, 87, 355, 379, 411
Iraq/Iraq War, 31, 42, 43–4, 52, 55–7,
85, 88, 149, 199, 351–2, 364, 371,
379, 411, 435
and torture, 364–70
see also Abu Ghraib

Islam, 210, 362
Islamic fundamentalism/Islamists,
    99–105, 113, 168, 327, 335
Israel, 8, 289, 384, 387
    peace activism in, 384–90
Israel, Jonathan, 127, 147, 208, 239–40
    Enlightenment Contested, 78–9

Jacobi, F.H., 240
Japan, 209, 342
Jefferson, Thomas, 40
Jenkins, Brian M., 102–3
Job, Book of, 35–6, 163–6, 168–9, 176,
    236, 381, 422–31, 432, 433
Johnson, Dawn, 353
Joyce, James, 329
Judt, Tony, 36
Juergensmayer, Hans, 103
justice, 62–4, 65, 67–8, 70, 73, 74, 130,
    140, 142, 153, 223–4

Ka'ahumanu, Queen, 131
Kagan, Robert, 30–2, 36, 37, 41–2,
        57–8, 85, 296
    Dangerous Nation, 41–2
    Of Paradise and Power, 31
    *The Return of History and the End
        of Dreams*, 57–8
Kandahar, 391, 393, 394, 395, 396, 399
Kant, Immanuel
        and Abraham, 14, 35, 96, 141
        and book of Job, 168–9, 425
        and categorical imperative,
            157–8, 183, 212–13, 214–15
        character and personality, 135,
            173–4
        and democratic powers, 48
        desire to learn about, 139
        and epistemology, 142
        Europeans as Kantians, 31–2,
            47, 49
        as focus in study of Enlighten-
            ment, 131
        gallows example, 93–5, 101, 243
        and happiness, 170, 171–2, 174,

        176, 177, 178, 179, 183–4,
            187, 188
        Heine's view of, 135, 140,
            141–2
        Herder's tribute to, 173–4
        on heroes, 95–6
        and Hume, 142, 145–6, 192
        and ideas and idealism, 151–4,
            156–7, 158–9, 160–2
        and ingratitude, 246
        and intention, 341
        and judgment, 217
        and keeping promises, 19
        and law, 35, 215
        life and achievement, 140–2
        and Lisbon earthquake, 122
        and lying, 214
        and mathematical model, 220
        and maturity, 218
        metaphysics, 118, 131, 142,
            151–4, 156–8, 160–2
        and morality and ethics, 23,
            93–6, 97, 98, 111–12, 157–8,
            212–25
        and progress, 9, 252–3, 288–9
        and reason, 141, 146, 151, 152,
            153, 154, 161, 162, 189, 191–2,
            193, 195, 201, 202–3, 205, 206,
            212–15, 218, 220
        response to Burke's book on
            revolution, 148, 152–3
        and religion, 111–12, 231, 234–5,
            238, 239, 240
        and reverence, 243, 245
        and Rousseau, 141, 149–50, 179
        and similarities between science
            and morality, 156–7
        and socialism, 72
        and Stoics, 175–6
        and torture, 364
        and ways of looking at the
            Holocaust, 351
        brief references, 42, 57, 76,
            127, 137, 257, 272, 299, 385,
            435

Writings:
    The Critique of Practical Reason,
      95, 169
    The Critique of Pure Reason, 22,
      154, 189, 190
    "The End of All Things", 171–2
    The Metaphysics of Morals (*The
      Foundations of the Metaphysics
      of Morals*), 169–70, 178,
      183–4, 214
    'On the Impossibility of Every
      Future Attempt at Theodicy',
      168–9
    'On the Old Saw: That May Be
      Right in Theory, But It
      Won't Work in Practice',
      148–9
    *Religion within the Limits of
      Reason Alone*, 252–3
    'What Is Enlightenment?', 218
Karpinski, General, 369
Kennedy, John F., 54
Kennedy Robert F., 414
Kenya, 8
Kierkegaard, Soren, 14
killing, 370–3
King, Martin Luther, 332, 381, 408,
    413, 417
Kirk, Russell: *The Conservative Mind*,
    124
Kissinger, Henry, 38, 58, 85, 401–2,
    407, 408, 409, 433
kitsch, 424, 434
Klein, Joe, 43
knowledge, 131, 132, 142, 143, 144,
    156, 157, 160, 198–9, 202, 220
Knox, Preacher, 417–18
Konner, Melvin: *The Tangled Wing*,
    273
Korean War, 371
Kristol, William, 52
Krugman, Paul, 352, 358
Kundera, Milan: *The Unbearable
    Lightness of Being*, 424, 430

Land of the Lotus Eaters, 304
language, 22, 69–70, 380
Last King of Scotland, The, 340
law, 35, 215–16, 217
Lebanon, 388
Lee, Herbert, 417
left, the, 10–11, 21–2, 24, 43, 59, 60–1,
    67–8, 75–6, 77, 90, 102, 104–5, 106,
    140, 159
Leibniz, Gottfried Wilhelm, 107, 141,
    172, 197, 201, 211
Leopold, King of Belgium, 431
Lessing, Gotthold Ephraim, 186–7,
    189, 190, 195, 240
Levi, Primo, 340
Lévi-Strauss, Claude, 257
Levy, Bernard-Henri, 46, 67
Lewontin, Richard C., 281, 286
liberals/liberalism, 24, 66, 67, 80, 88,
    101
Liberty Fund, 10
Lieberman, Joe, 335
Lieven, Anatol & John Hulsman:
    Ethical Realism, 84–6
Lifuka, 185
Limbaugh, Rush, 53, 244–5
    The Way Things Ought To Be, 76
Lincoln, Abraham, 41, 58, 192
Lisbon earthquake (1755), 121–3, 167
Locke, John, 38, 155, 191, 208
lying, 214, 403–4, 407
lynching, 376

McCain, John, 58, 355, 376
McCarthy, Mary, 373
    "The Hue and the Cry", 344
Machiavelli, Niccolo, 58, 65, 66
MacIntyre, Alasdair: *After Virtue*, 322
McKinley, William, 42
McNamara, Robert, 403, 407
McWhorter, Diane, 352
Malagrida, Father, 123
Malaysia, 377
Managua, 399
Mandela, Nelson, 322, 359

Marcuse, Herbert, 72
Margalit, Avishai, 363–4
Marsh, Charles: *God's Long Summer*, 418
Marshall, General S.L.A., 371
Marx, Karl, 70–1, 82, 91, 108–9, 123, 162, 296
Marxism, 70–2, 73, 74, 75, 76, 77, 78, 82, 86, 102, 105, 111, 140, 249
materialism, 105, 111, 127, 137
mathematics, 144, 145, 219, 220, 412, 419, 420
maturity, 161, 218, 225, 260, 437
Mayer, Jane, 38
Melville, Herman: *Moby Dick*, 321
Mencius, 274
Mendelssohn, Moses, 240
Merleau-Ponty, Maurice, 75
metaphysics, 20–1, 29–30, 88–9, 90, 131, 138–62
    two strands underpinning conservative position in U.S., 30–59
Michnik, Adam, 56
Midrash, 166
Milgram, Stanley, 335, 346
militarism, 281
Miller, General, 369
Milosevic regime, 139
Mississippi, civil rights movement in, 413–19
Mitchell, Stephen, 164
Mitterand, François, 359
modernity, 125–6
Montaigne, Michel de, 191, 219–20
Montesquieu, Baron de, 39, 208
moral needs, 3–4, 6
moral reasoning, 211–25
morality, 93–9, 156, 157–8, 160, 268–9, 270–1
    and religion, 13–19, 89–90, 106–7, 110, 111–12, 232–3, 234–5, 241, 334–5
    see also categorical imperative; moral reasoning
Moreno-Ocampo, Luis, 290

Morocco, 391
Moses, Bob, 412–21
    Radical Equations, 419–20
Mount Moriah, Abraham at, 13–14, 16, 35, 105, 134, 141
Mujahadeen, 398
Musharraf, President, 101
music, 241–2
Mussolini, Benito, 326

Nagasaki, 342
National Defense Strategy 2005, 36
National Security Council, 115
NATO, 407
natural religion/Deism, 127, 236–43, 247–50, 397–8
nature, 144, 147, 160, 162, 181, 193–4
    see also human nature
Nausicaa, 315
Nazism, 65–6, 97, 124, 263, 264, 324, 326, 331–2, 342–3, 344, 347, 351, 353, 357, 368, 402, 418
Ndoye, Bigné, 360–1, 362, 375
Nehamas, Alexander, 295
Neiman, Susan: *Evil in Modern Thought*, 4, 167
Neurath, Otto, 418
neuroscience/neurology, 190, 201, 221, 271–2
New Guinea, 371
New Labour, 56
New Orleans, 121, 357
New Republic, 356
New York Times, 61, 110, 149, 352, 411
New York Times Magazine, 51, 53
New Yorker, 61, 342
Newton, Isaac, 144–5, 150, 152, 198, 208, 237, 239, 271
Nicaragua, 371, 399
Nietzsche, Friedrich, 79, 107, 250–1
Niger, 38
nihilism, 107–8, 132, 222, 240, 251, 263
9/11 *see* September 11, 2001 terrorist attacks
Nixon, Richard, 407, 409–10, 433

North Korea, 379
Northern Ireland, 289
Nussbaum, Martha, 77
  'Transcending Humanity', 317
Nye, Joseph, 80–1, 84, 86

Obama, Barack, 6–9, 54, 83–4, 90–2,
  353, 421
objectivity, 151, 152
Observer, The, 58
Odysseus, 23, 299–321, 327–30, 332,
  333, 381
Odyssey, The, 135, 299–321, 328–30, 436
Oedipus, 167
Olin Foundation, 10
Onion, The, 37
O'Reilly, Bill, 12
original sin, 258, 284–5, 286
Orwell, George, 55, 60, 79
  1984, 52, 202
  The Road to Wigan Pier, 105
Oslo Accords, 115, 289

Packer, George, 61
Paine, Tom, 40
Pakistan, 87, 99, 101
Palestinians, 103, 384, 386, 387
Paley, Vivian Gussin, 287
Parris, Matthew, 54
passions/emotions, 192–3, 196, 200,
  206, 221
Patriot Act, 377
Penelope, 310, 312, 313, 314, 315–16,
  317, 328
Pentagon, 338
Pentagon Papers, 401, 410, 411
Peres, Shimon, 115
Pindar, 320, 321
Pinker, Steven, 201, 215–16, 276, 278
  How the Mind Works, 200
Plato, 10, 17, 20–1, 22, 39–40, 77, 89,
  130, 219, 220, 328, 375
  The Republic, 61–5, 151, 219, 333,
  436
PLO, 289

Plutarch: Lives, 96
politics, 65, 82–3, 136 see also conser-
  vatives/the right; left, the
Pombal, Marquis de, 122
Pope, Alexander, 144, 177, 230, 274,
  275
  Essay on Man, 175
postmodernism, 88, 284
post-traumatic stress disorder, 373, 395
Powell, Colin, 361
power, 33, 34, 63, 65, 66, 72–4, 76
  soft, 80–1, 86
Power, Samantha: A Problem from
  Hell, 351
pragmatism, 61
primates, 267, 268–70, 272–3
principle of sufficient reason, 4, 133,
  145, 151–2, 162, 167, 198, 201–2, 203
privilege, inherited, 130
progress, 9, 265, 279–80, 288–96
progressivism, 24–5, 88, 146, 153
psychopaths, 339–40

Quetta, 391
Quine, W.V.O., 412, 418, 420

racism, 291–2, 359, 361, 374, 415–16
Ramachandran, V.S., 271
Rand, Ayn, 10
Rand Corporation, 401, 403, 408
rationalism, 191, 192
Rawls, John, 11–12, 117, 223–4, 384
Raynal, Guillaume, 40
Reagan, Ronald, 10, 294, 327, 399
realism, 25, 29, 61, 84–6, 140, 149, 158,
  159, 161
  discussed as one of the metaphysical strands underpinning
  conservative position in U.S.,
  30–8, 39, 48, 57, 58–9
  and Hobbes, 30–6
reality, 154, 162
  and Hume, 142–3
  and Kant, 148–9, 151, 153, 156–7,
  160–1, 162

realpolitik, 47, 49, 53
reason, 15–16, 17, 123, 124, 133, 134,
    137, 141, 145, 146, 149, 151–4, 161,
    162, 189–225, 263–4, 287 *see also*
    principle of sufficient reason
Reemtsma, Jan Philipp, 324
    Trust and Violence, 340
Rehov, Pierre, 101
religion, natural (Deism), 127, 236–43,
    247–50, 397–8
religion, traditional
    and Chayes, 397–9
    Enlightenment attitudes to, 133–4,
        194–6, 226–36
    and Hobbes, 35–6
    and idea of evil, 336, 339
    and Marx, 108–9
    and morality, 13–19, 89–90, 110,
        111–12, 232–3, 234–5, 241, 334–5
    and need for transcendence, 111–12
    reasons for turning to, 106–8
    see also religious fundamentalism
religious fundamentalism, 1, 14–15,
    16, 17, 18, 99–114, 117, 118, 128–9,
    131, 132–3, 135–6, 137
Republicans, 5, 6, 7, 31, 43, 53, 87, 115,
    116, 357
reverence, 133–4, 226–51
Rice, Condoleeza, 361, 367
Rich, Frank, 352, 353
Richardson, Louise: *What Terrorists
    Want*, 103
right, the *see* conservatives/the right
rights, 147, 148, 194, 292–3 *see also* civil
    rights movement; human rights
Robertson, Pat, 335
Robeson, Paul, 376
Robespierre, Maximilien, 135, 142
Rockefeller, John D., 281
Romantics, 192, 193
Rome Statute (1998), 54
Rorty, Richard, 76–7, 88–9, 190, 357
    Achieving Our Country, 88–9
Rostow, Walt, 406
Rousseau, Jean-Jacques

background, 260–1
and childhood and children,
    150, 218, 259, 260, 271, 287–
    8, 421
and colonialism, 209–10
compared to Newton, 150
and draft constitutions, 40
and fear, 199, 337–8
and happines, 170, 171, 178–9,
    180–2, 183
and human nature, 255–61, 270,
    330
and inequality, 91
and Kant, 141, 149–50, 179
and reason, 195
and religion, 239, 240, 283–4
on Socrates, 331
and Voltaire, 171, 178–9, 183
brief references, 46, 56, 127, 158,
    192, 262, 265, 286, 292, 316
Writings:
    Le devin du village, 261
    *Discourse Concerning the Origins of
        Inequality* (Second Discourse),
        179, 257–8
    Emile, 169, 171, 180–1, 259–60,
        284
Rumsfeld, Donald, 349, 365, 366–7, 369
Rusk, Dean, 406
Russia, 58
Ryle, Gilbert, 200

Sabbath, 243–4
sacrifice, 13, 101, 103, 112, 113–14
Sade, Marquis de, 1, 211, 222
    Justine, 276
Safire, William, 5
Saint-Juste, 169
Sanchez, General, 369
Sarajevo, 139
Saudi Arabia, 87, 351
Saul, John Ralston: *Voltaire's Bastards*,
    263
Savater, Fernando: *Amador*, 378
Schama, Simon, 40

Schlesinger Commission, 367
Schliemann, Heinrich, 301
Schmidt, Anton, 347
Schmitt, Carl, 65–7, 73, 87–8
Scholl, Hans and Sophie, 331–2
Schwalm, Col Tony, 397–8, 399, 400
science, 142, 144–5, 152, 156, 196,
    197–8, 237, 265
scientific revolution, 144–5
Scotsman, The, 8
Scowcroft, Brent, 87
Scylla, 309, 315
secularists, 102
Seferis, 390
self-criticism, 136, 140
self-deprecation, 140
self-interest, 19–20, 80–1, 95, 96–7,
    174–5, 271, 273–4, 279
self-respect, 160, 222
Senate Armed Services Committee, 367
Senegal see Gorée, Senegal
Senghor, Léopold, 359
September 11, 2001 attacks (9/11), 37,
    84, 168, 264, 335–8, 354–8, 391
sex, 135, 172, 283
Shakespeare, William, 342
shame/shamelessness, 377–9, 380
Shulman, David, 383–90
    Dark Hope, 383–4
Silence of the Lambs, The, 339
Simmel, Georg, 247
sin, 1–2, 167
    and book of Job, 164, 165–6
    see also original sin
Singer, Peter: The President of Good
    and Evil, 335
Sirens, the, 309–11, 314, 318, 319, 329,
    330
slavery, 149, 160, 208–9, 291, 292, 293,
    294, 359, 361, 374
Smith, Adam, 182
    The Theory of Moral Sentiments,
    246–7
SNCC, 413, 419
social Darwinism, 281, 282

socialism, 105
sociobiology see evolutionary
    psychology
Socrates, 17, 18, 61–4, 66, 69, 70,
    89–90, 222, 331
Socratic ideas, 67, 68
Sodom, 1–3, 13, 16–17, 18, 24, 35, 90,
    96, 134, 213, 232, 287, 334, 337, 423,
    432
soft power, 80–1, 86
Soloveitchik, Joseph, 427
South Sea islands, 183–8
Soviet Union, 10–11, 377
Soweto, 99
Spain, 69–70
Spanish Civil War, 60, 69–70
Spinoza, Baruch, 127, 191, 194–5, 227,
    240
Stalin, Joseph, 82, 324, 402
Stalinism, 11, 30, 324, 326
Stanford University, experiment at,
    345–6, 367, 368
Starobinsky, Jean, 261
state power, 34–5
Stendhal, 114
Stern, Jessica, 103
    Terror in the Name of God, 113
Stoics, 96, 174, 175, 176–7, 321
Strauss, Leo, 10, 55, 57
Suez crisis, 403
Suicide Killers, 101
superstition, 122, 129, 131, 132, 196
Suriname, 208–9
Sweden, 136

Ta'ayush, 384, 385–6, 387, 389
Taft, William, 369
Taguba, General Antonio, 370
Tahiti, 184
Taliban, 128–9, 390, 391, 392, 393, 394
Tamil Tigers, 114
technology, 125, 153, 262–3, 263–4,
    371–2, 420
Telemachus, 314, 315
Tenet, George, 369

terrorism/terrorists, 44, 99–101, 102,
    103, 112–14, 336–8 *see also*
    September 11, 2001 terrorist attacks
Thatcher, Margaret, 48
Thebes, 167
Thoreau, Henry David, 408
Thrasymachus, 62–3, 64, 66, 67, 70, 71,
    72, 73, 77, 86, 222, 281–2
Times, The, 54
Tiresias, 307
Todorov, Tzvetan, 351
tolerance, 132, 134
Tonga, 185
Tonkin Gulf Resolution, 411
torture, 129–30, 290–1, 293, 294, 295,
    349, 362–70, 375, 377
Toulmin, Stephen, 219–20
transcendence, 108, 111, 112, 113, 114,
    117, 118
Trojan War, 1, 300, 301–3
Trotsky, Leon, 67, 206
    Their Morals and Ours, 71–2
Truman, Harry S., 86, 376, 431
truth, 95, 156–7, 187, 199
Tucholsky, Kurt, 352
Tucker, Karla Faye, 356
Turgot, Anne-Robert-Jacques, 40–1, 186
Turkey, 43
Twaneh, 386

Ukraine, 99
UNESCO, 359
United Nations (UN), 36
    General Assembly, 37
United States, 11, 24, 60–1, 80–6, 90–2,
    104–5, 199, 291, 292, 294, 393,
    394, 396
    civil rights movement, 6, 68, 83,
        291, 295, 413–19, 421
    evil considered in relation to,
        351–62, 364–77
    and Iraq *see* Iraq/Iraq War
    metaphysical strands underpinning
        conservative position in, 30–59
    and Vietnam, 401–2, 404–11

universal suffrage, 153–4
universalism, 3, 42, 67–8, 82, 123, 136,
    206, 207–8, 214–15, 221, 222–3

victims, 323–6
Viet Cong, 401
Vietnam War, 371, 373, 378, 401–2,
    404–11, 419
Voltaire
    and atheism, 233
    and Bayle, 191, 233
    and book of Job, 168
    and Calas case, 228–9, 291
    and children, 287
    and Frederick the Great, 40, 66
    and happiness, 170, 172, 179–80,
        183
    and human nature, 255, 287
    and Islam, 210
    and Leibniz, 107
    and Lisbon earthquake, 122
    and *The Odyssey*, 320
    and passions, 192
    and reason, 191, 195
    and religion, 210, 228–9, 231,
        232, 235–6, 238–9, 246, 247–8
    and Rousseau, 171, 178–9, 183
    and slavery, 208–9
    and torture, 291, 431
    brief references, 44, 127, 141
    Writings:
        Candide, 122, 125, 179–80, 191,
            208–9, 247–8, 254–5, 431
        'Le Mondain', 179
        Philosophical Dictionary, 168, 172,
            180, 191, 229, 236, 255, 287
        Treatise on Metaphysics, 192
voting registration (in Mississippi),
    414–18

Walcot, Derek, 306
Wall Street, 6, 34, 338
Wall Street Journal, 201
Walzer, Michael, 21–2, 74
Warren, Robert Penn, 416

Washington, George, 335
Washington Post, 31, 58
Watergate, 378
Weaver, Richard M.: *Ideas Have Consequences*, 53, 279–80
Welzer, Harald, 343
West, Cornel, 83, 98
White Rose resistance group, 332
Wiesel, Elie, 165
Wilkomirsky, Benjamin, 324, 325
Williams, Bernard, 65
Wilson, Edmund O., 266
Wittgenstein, Ludwig, 12, 241, 348
Wolfe, Alan, 69
women, 129, 135, 136, 149, 154–6, 292, 332, 395
women's movement, 68, 376

Woodruff, Paul, 241, 242, 243
World War I, 322, 342, 370, 391
World War II, 370, 371
Wright, N.T., 284
Wright, Lawrence, 375
    The Looming Tower, 100
Wright, Robert, 273, 274, 284, 286
    The Moral Animal, 277–8

Yeats, W.B., 12
Yoo, John, 369

Zimbardo, Philip, 340, 347, 367, 368–9, 370, 373
    The Lucifer Effect, 344–6
Zeit, Die, 54, 121
Žižek, Slavoj, 88

Made in the USA
Monee, IL
20 October 2020